ReMembering Cuba

Andrea O'Reilly Herrera, Editor

ReMembering

Cuba

Legacy of a Diaspora

UNIVERSITY OF TEXAS PRESS, AUSTIN

Publication of this book has been assisted by a challenge grant from the National Endowment for the Humanities.

FRONTISPIECE: *Ella me prefiere* by Ana Albertina Delgado, 1999. Oil on canvas, 49" x 43". Courtesy of the artist.

Requests for permission to reproduce material from this work should be sent to Permissions, University of Texas Press, P.O. Box 7819, Austin, TX 78713-7819.

(∞) The paper used in this book meets the minimum requirements of ANSI/NISO Z39.48–1992 (R1997) (Permanence of Paper).

LIBRARY OF CONGRESS CATALOGING-IN-PUBLICATION DATA

ReMembering Cuba : legacy of a diaspora / Andrea O'Reilly Herrera,
    editor.—1st ed.
     p.   cm.
    Includes bibliographical references (p.   ).
    ISBN 0-292-73146-9 (alk. paper) — ISBN 0-292-73147-7 (pbk. : alk. paper)
     1. Cuban Americans—Ethnic identity—Miscellanea. 2. Cuban Americans
—Social conditions—Miscellanea. 3. Exiles—United States—Social
conditions—Miscellanea. 4. Cubans—Migrations—Miscellanea. 5. United
States—Emigration and immigration—Miscellanea. 6. Cuba—Emigration
and immigration—Miscellanea. 7. Cuban Americans—Biography. 8. Exiles—
United States—Biography. 9. American literature—Cuban American authors.
10. Reportage literature.   1. Herrera, Andrea O'Reilly.

E184.C97 R39   2001
305.868'7291073—dc21   00-061606

In memory of Heberto Padilla,

and

all of those who have died,

in exile,

with the unfulfilled hope

of returning to a free Cuba.

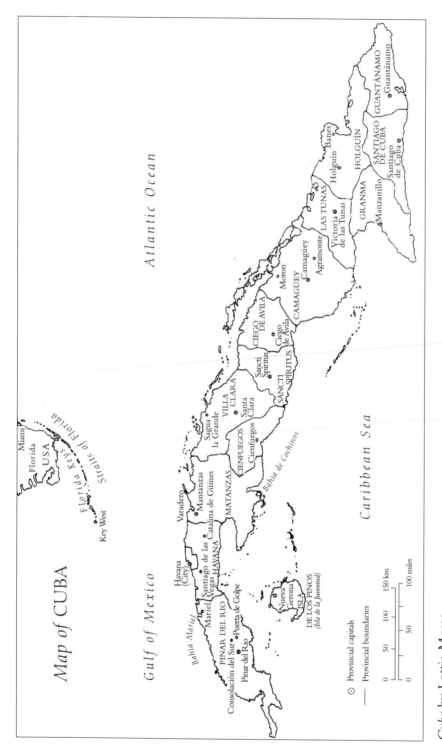

Map of CUBA

Cuba by Lottie Morse

CONTENTS

PREFACE

> To think of exile as beneficial, as a spur to humanism or to creativity, is to belittle its mutilations. . . . For exile is fundamentally a discontinuous state of being. Exiles are cut off from their roots, their land, their past.
>
> —*Edward Said, "The Mind of Winter: Reflections on Life in Exile"*

In truth, this project was first conceived when I was about seven years old. Driven by what I have come to believe is an ancestral yearning for all things Cuban, I used to beg to hear my grandparents repeat their stories about their lives on the Island—stories that fed my imagination and have since become the wellspring of my scholarly work and much of my fiction. At one point, I even followed my grandfather, Pipa, around the borders of his beloved garden with a tape recorder, watching him pull the stubborn weeds from among the lavender and blue hydrangeas. We all knew that he had been involved in some type of clandestine activity in Cuba following the revolution, but he persistently refused to talk about it. Unable to overcome my gnawing curiosity, I pleaded with him, convinced that my dogged persistence (a universal family trait) would eventually wear his resistance down and convince him to record these stories. I can still remember the way he mopped his brow with the handkerchief that perpetually hung from his back trouser pocket like a panting dog's tongue. His agitation was visible to me in the impatient movement of his hands; his resignation, in the long sigh that he gave out. "In the first place," he told me in his booming voice (which usually sent his grandchildren scattering in all directions), "I cannot tell you those stories—mostly because I am afraid." "For whom?" I asked. "For those who are left behind," he answered, lowering his voice. "In the second place," he added, "no one would ever believe me if I told them what I knew."

Over the years, I have never forgotten his response—little did he know that his words had only sharpened my desire to act as the guardian of our stories, our history.

The actual catalyst that prompted me to begin the arduous task of gathering together the works in this collection occurred many years later in the wake of my grandfather's death. It was during a trip to south Florida, where I attended the Caribbean Writers Summer Institute at the University of Miami (1996). During the course of that trip, I had the opportunity to reunite—after many years—with family members and close friends who had all left Cuba under duress during the various waves of immigration following the 1959 revolution. Although they all shared the same urgency to relate their experiences and to talk about their lives in exile, perhaps the most emotional reunion was with two of my grandfather's sisters, both of whom had never learned to speak English and both of whom still considered themselves to be in a state of exile after nearly forty years.

The eldest sibling, Tía Asela, was 101 years old at the time. When I asked her to tell me stories, she began by recalling the changed atmosphere in Cuba following the Spanish-American War. Gently stroking my hand as she spoke, she then told me about the volunteer work she'd been involved in following her husband's premature death. "Tell me stories about Cuba after the revolution," I finally asked. At my words, Tía grew silent, her mouth drawn into a thin curve of pain and sorrow. After a few moments, she signaled to Tía Yoyín, the youngest of her siblings. "Tell her about when the soldiers took the house," she said, leaning forward in her chair and gesturing at her sister. "We had only a half an hour to pack our bags," Tía Yoyín began, taking up the cue. "A lifetime of memories," she added, with lowered eyes, "in only one bag."

For the remainder of the afternoon I, along with my husband and three children, listened to Tía Yoyín as she recited a series of stories at her sister's prompting—stories, she told me, that were too painful for Asela to relay herself, but that she nevertheless wanted me to know. Just as my grandparents had, she wanted me to know what they had witnessed—what we had lost. At the time, I could not help but recall my first visit to Miami, not long after Tía Asela had arrived from Cuba. I will never forget the tone of their voices as she and her sisters described the conditions under which they had lived. In vain, I attempted to record their stories and capture with words the emotion that thickened their voices and galvanized their slight frames. It wasn't until I saw for the first time the "Dark Paintings" of Goya that I found images that came close to representing the nightmarish vision that the old aunts described.

Tía Asela died shortly after celebrating her 102nd birthday. Though I choose to believe that chance had nothing to do with it, I was in Miami at the time of her death and was able to hold vigil (with a room full of women who recited a litany of prayers together in one voice) and wish Asela safe passage to the other side. After the funeral mass, we buried Tía in a mausoleum beside her sister, Teté. (Long before, the three sisters had arranged to be laid to rest side by side.) As I watched her coffin slide into the slot beside Tía Teté's and my gaze fell upon the empty crypt where Tía Yoyín would eventually lie, I could not help but think that we were laying Asela, the matriarch of our family, to rest in what was to her a foreign land. She had left us with the unfulfilled hope of seeing her beloved motherland again. Exile, for her, was a permanent mutilation, a wound that would not heal. Never before had the proportions of this loss, this tragedy, seemed so immediate and so great to me.

In the short amount of time that has passed since I first began writing this preface, we have now lost Tía Yoyín, the last of my grandfather's siblings. As I sit in my home in Colorado, revising this passage to register the loss, I can almost feel the weight of time pressing down upon me, for I write with the knowledge that at this very moment Yoyín is surrounded by a dwindling group of old women holding vigil at her side. I write with the knowledge that the next time I return to Miami, my remaining tía-abuela (my grandfather's sister-in-law, Ada) might be gone, taking with her the stories—the memories—of this world that I have never seen, but to which I somehow belong. Frustrated at the ground that seems to be slipping away at my feet and the immense distance that separates me from my family; filled with regret at the thought that I can no longer sit on the arm of my grandmother's recliner at her shore house, listening to her and my grandfather recite stories (as she rubbed circles into my back and he rocked back and forth in his brown leather chair, twirling his thumbs together); I realize, as my dear *compañera* Lourdes Gil has reminded me, that I number among those who are "burdened" and "blessed" by this history that resides in my name and sits upon my shoulders. And so it occurs to me that this most sacred task of delivering over these testimonials is finally at hand. (February 9, 1998; September 15, 1999)

ACKNOWLEDGMENTS

This collection was made possible, in part, through the support of the Scholarly Incentive Award, the Amy Everett Memorial Award, and the Dr. Nuala McGann Drescher Affirmative Action Leave.

I would also like to acknowledge the many people who have assisted me, in one way or another, along the way—and so my deepest thanks go to Richard Reddy, Sandra Lewis, and Cathy Kilpatrick, for their guidance and assistance; to my dear friends Jan McVicker, Candice Brown, Bill Spanos, Jan Fairbairn, Carl Smith, Vivian García-Conover, Steve Warner, Julius Adams, Peter Schoenbach and Anne Tobey, Marcia and Ray Belliotti, Bob Schweik, Jim and Ruth Shokoff, Chris Davis-Mantai, Pat and Dan Astry, Patty and Bill Dionne, Linda Dorsten, Dirk and Jerry Raat, Adrienne McCormick, Bruce Simon, Robert Jorden, Thelma and Bill Proweller, Bob Marzec, Paul Schwartz, Dennis Hefner, Angela Herrera, and Angela Martín for their encouragement and support; to Jan Stryz, who convinced me to put aside my other work and go on with this collection; to my dear friend Maggie Bryan-Peterson, for her endless energy and her invaluable advice and assistance at every turn; to Jerry Hoeg, Martín Herrera, and Jorge Guitart, for their excellent translations; to my cover artist Ana Albertina Delgado and my photographer Tony Reus, for their amazing talents, and to Lottie Morse for the beautiful maps; to Ellen Litwiki, Juan Clark, Frances Aparicio, Ricardo Viera, Lizabeth Paravisini-Gebert, Dennis Maloney and Elaine LaMattina, Ampy Arechabala, and Ricky and Vivian Sanchez, and most especially to my *queridos amigos* Vivian de la Incera and Efrain Ferrer, for guiding me in the right directions; to my roomie, Jeannette Reus, for the mattress and the conversation, *mi amiga* Vivian López-Mendoza, for her dining-room table, and my dearest *primi,* Paul Vandevere, for allowing me to disrupt his life for eighteen hours; and to Virgil Suárez, Delia Poey, María Cristina García, Ileana Fuentes, and Jorge Santis, for all of their generous advice and assistance.

I feel especially indebted to Lourdes Gil (*mi querida* Condesa), Pablo Medina, Marjorie Agosín, Antonio Benítez-Rojo, Heberto Padilla, Gustavo Pérez Firmat, Ricardo Pau-Llosa, Isabel Alvarez-Borland, Robert Deming, and Paul Harvey for their precious time, their wisdom, their intelligent editorial assistance, and their friendship; and I am most grateful to Catherine de la Garza Millard, Leslie Doyle Tingle and Jenevieve Maerker, for their careful attention to detail, and to my editor, Theresa May, for her unwavering enthusiasm, trust, and patience.

Most of all, thanks to my beloved Mima, Pipa, and Tracy, and to Avi and Adele, for watching over me; to my dearest parents, Terry and Hugh; to my brothers, Barry, Philip, and Rob, and my sister Chris; to my beautiful children, Alex, Niki, and Marty, for their inexhaustible patience and love; and to my *querido compañero*, Martín, for giving me strength and inspiration.

¡Te amo!

FIGURE 1. *Dead Rafter II* by Luis Cruz Azaceta, 1994. Mixed media on canvas, 70 ½" x 60 ½". Courtesy of Museum of Art, Contemporary Cuban Collection, Ft. Lauderdale, Florida.

FIGURE 2. *The Garden and the Fruit* by María Brito, 1987. Acrylic on wood/mixed media, 70" x 61 ¾" x 64 ¾". Courtesy of the artist.

FIGURE 3. *Merely a Player* (inside labyrinth, detail) by María Brito, 1993–1994.
Multimedia installation, 8 ½' x 15' x 17'. Courtesy of the artist.

FIGURE 4. *Our Lady of Fashion* by Juan Manuel Alonso, 1994. Magic marker on paper, 18" x 24". Courtesy of the artist.

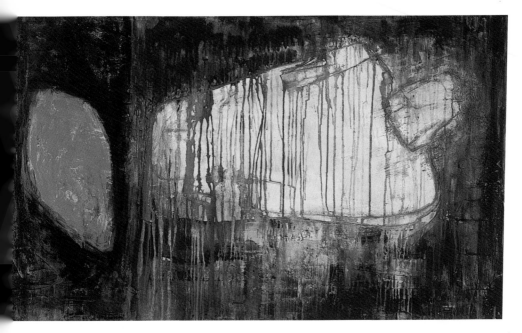

FIGURE 5. *In Silence* by Connie Lloveras, 1998. Mixed media on canvas, 60" x 36". Courtesy of the artist.

FIGURE 6. *Cabello Plantation House, "Luisa y Antonia"* by Carlos J. Alvaré, 1985. Watercolor, 18" x 12". Courtesy of the artist.

FIGURE 7. *Ochun* (video installation, detail) by Leandro Soto, 1998. Courtesy of the artist.

FIGURE 8. *Yemayá* (video installation, detail) by Leandro Soto, 1998. Courtesy of the artist.

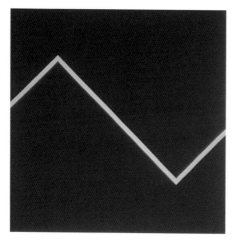

FIGURE 9. *Yesterday/Ayer* by Carmen Herrera, 1987. Acrylic on canvas, 45" x 60". Courtesy of the artist. [Reproduced from *Outside Cuba/Fuera de Cuba: Contemporary Cuban Visual Artists,* with permission from Ileana Fuentes, co-author and editor.]

FIGURE 10. *El descanso de héroe* by Rafael Soriano, 1992. Oil on canvas, 50" x 60". Copyright © Rafael Soriano. Courtesy of Lowe Art Museum, University of Miami, Coral Gables, Florida.

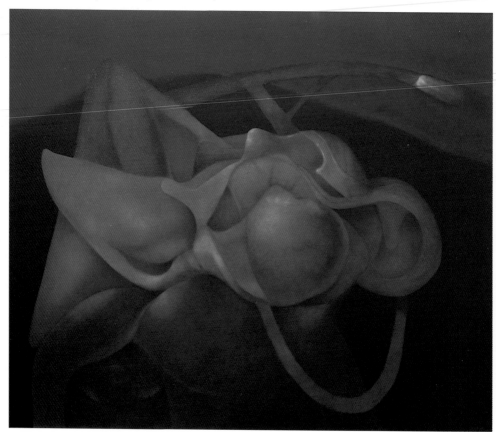

FIGURE 11. *Head and Vessel* by Rocío Rodríguez, 1991. Oil on canvas, 84" x 70".
Courtesy of Museum of Art, Contemporary Cuban Collection, Ft. Lauderdale,
Florida.

FIGURE 12. *La tierra no pudo tanto* (The Land Could Not Hold It Anymore) by María Martínez–Cañas, 1993. Gelatin silver print, 25" x 25". Courtesy of Museum of Art, Contemporary Cuban Collection, Ft. Lauderdale, Florida.

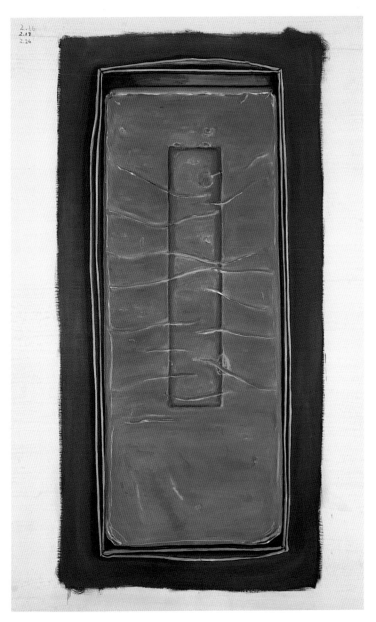

FIGURE 13. *Ansel Guava Paste* by Alberto Rey, 1995. Oil on plaster, 91" x 60" x 4". Courtesy of Museum of Art, Contemporary Cuban Collection, Ft. Lauderdale, Florida.

FIGURE 14. *Niagara Falls/Isla de Pinos* by Alberto Rey, 1996. Oil on plaster, 36"x 48"x 4".

Royal Palms in Granma Province by Tony Mendoza. Courtesy of the photographer.

Peso store in Havana with nothing to sell by Tony Mendoza. Courtesy of the photographer.

Havana portrait studio by Tony Mendoza. Courtesy of the photographer.

Two uses of iron at Morro Castle, Havana by Tony Mendoza. Courtesy of the photographer.

Esto sí es vida, calle ocho by Anthony Reus, 1998. Courtesy of the photographer.

Flores, calle ocho by Anthony Reus, 1998. Courtesy of the photographer.

La milagrosa, calle ocho by Anthony Reus, 1998. Courtesy of the photographer.

Our Wedding: Yara and Matías, December 6, 1953, Corpus Christi Church, Havana, Cuba by International Photo, Havana, Cuba, 1953. Courtesy of Yara González-Montes.

INTRODUCTION

I

Le pays même émigre et transporte ses frontières.

The country, though it has emigrated, transports its borders.
—*Jacques Derrida, "Shibboleth, por Paul Celan"*

Since the very outset of the diaspora, scholars from a wide range of disciplines have explored the complex relationships and differences among Cuban political refugees and their offspring and considered the manner in which the various generations of refugees have adapted to and transformed their receiving cultures as they continue to make their transition into exile.[1] As many have observed, the realities of exile have informed the Cuban consciousness and imagination for over two centuries; however, the exodus prompted by the 1959 revolution is distinguished not only by its proportions and longevity, but by the fact that what Carolina Hospital calls a "consciousness of exile" traverses several generations of "exiles," including those born or raised outside the Island.

The richly textured voices that together constitute the body of this collection—coupled with the many conversations I've had with people who are only indirectly represented—not only illustrate the heterogeneity of the Cuban exile community, but put into relief the need to formulate a more inclusive thematic for what I call the Cub*and* 'presences' in the United States and to rework some of the existing paradigms regarding cultural identity and exile.

Indeed, the pressing need to reinvent the way we define and speak about Cuban exiles and their children was brought home to me when I first began circulating my call for testimonials. Defying my expectation that I would receive a series of straightforward narratives generated mostly by political refugees, the project soon took on a shape of its own—for among the most enthusiastic respondents were an Anglo American woman who lived on the Island prior to 1959 for significant portions of time and whose creative work primarily focused on Cuba; a third-generation *tampeña* who identified herself as "a born-again Cuban"; and several others who referred to themselves as "ABCs" (American-Born Cubans), the acronym Gustavo Pérez Firmat devised for the children of Cuban exiles born in the United States but raised with a Cuban sensibility.[2] In the case of the Anglo American and the *tampeña*, birthright or heritage had little to do with their deep-felt sensibilities; on the other hand, not one of the ABCs had ever been to Cuba, and only one was raised or resided in Miami. All of them, however, claimed that their cultural identities and consciousness were as deeply informed and shaped by Cuba and/or Cuban culture as those of people born and raised on the Island. In short, the first responses I received profoundly destabilized and confounded my previously held, perhaps naïve, notions regarding what constitutes or gives one claim to cultural identity.

As the word spread about my call, potential contributors from all over the country—representing an increasingly complex array of responses and an even wider range of perceived cultural identities in relation to Cuba and the U.S.—began to contact me. Regrettably, a number of those who initially expressed interest in the project eventually declined my invitation to participate for a variety of reasons. Several, for example, insisted that they did not perceive themselves as being in a state of exile, for they had "segregated" or (as one contributor put it) "individuated" their Cuban and American identities. (Quite a few told me that they did not realize how American they actually were until they traveled outside the States.) Others who confided in me said that their experiences in Cuba and/or the United States were too painful to record; some feared retribution, either for themselves or for their friends or relatives who remained on the Island; and quite a few suggested that they were saturated with the subject.[3]

I was also disappointed that I did not receive a more racially diverse response to my call. Despite my active solicitation of testimonials from a wider group, first-generation Cubans who left the Island in the late

'50s and early '60s (most of whom are White, middle- to upper-class professionals), and/or their offspring, ultimately claim the greatest representation in the collection. Though several discuss the differences among the generations and focus upon gender, few address the interrelated themes of race, racism, class, and discrimination in their testimonials. By way of explanation, one contributor has suggested that this silence is symptomatic of a larger cultural silence regarding race and, consequently, class that can be applied as readily to the Cuba of today as it could to the prerevolutionary Island. A second person, who wished to remain anonymous, posed the possibility that middle age might play a role in explaining the preponderance of responses from members of the first wave of immigration. "In the first place," she argued, "this first wave of exiles was overwhelmingly White and relatively well off. In addition, many are now reaching middle age; and middle age is a time when most people begin to review their lives—something which prompts many to trace their roots and construct family trees. Enough time has passed for this generation to be able to speak about their losses not only with some perspective, but without the pain. You have to realize that the world these exiles left behind—a world which they were certain they would return to—has essentially disappeared. This fact alone may explain their willingness—even eagerness—to record their experiences."

Despite these obstacles and limitations, I continued to actively seek contributors. Although the peripheral boundaries of the collection were clearly defined from the outset—in that it would primarily feature the voices of Cuban exiles and their offspring residing in the United States— the submissions that I consequently began to receive confirmed my impulse to abandon my original concepts regarding who should or should not be included. As might be expected, several people objected to my decision to include ABCs. One such person insisted that the second generation's *cubanidad* was merely symbolic and, therefore, inauthentic; whereas another maintained that by including ABCs and "ARCs" (American-Raised Cubans, who left the Island as infants or toddlers) in a collection that also gives voice to those who were persecuted in Cuba, I was diminishing the latter group's suffering and leveling all of the contributors' experiences. Taking the same tack, a handful of others went a step further by encouraging me to omit the contributions of White Cubans who left the Island in the late '50s and early '60s. In essence, they argued that there existed a kind of "hierarchy of suffering" to which those who abandoned the Island (many with their possessions) before Fidel had consolidated his power and publicly allied himself with the Soviet Union had no claim.

In spite of these objections, I invited everyone who expressed interest in the project to consider and freely respond to a set of general "guide" questions, which primarily focused upon the intertwined themes of exile and loss, identity formation, and the preservation or perpetuation of Cuban culture. I assured several anxious callers, who were convinced that I had some predetermined or hidden left-wing agenda, that they need not feel as though they were required to respond in any prescribed manner. In addition, I made it clear that they were free to negotiate the discursive or artistic conditions of their submissions. In other words, they could respond in any way, shape, or form they desired, for my perceived role as editor was to act as a kind of *partera* (midwife)—as opposed to a curator, prompter, or censor—standing ready to assist them with what many have since described to me as a laborious task, as therapeutic as it was painful.

Although a number of the testimonials in the collection are based on interviews that I conducted at the request of the contributors, I soon began to receive a wide generic range of submissions. Many adopt the more traditional testimonial form in that they feature first-person narratives that either attempt to reconstruct the pre-1959 Cuba I had grown up hearing about or describe the conditions under which their authors fled the Island. Others, such as a number of the works that appear in Section IV (Snapshots), take the form of personal memoirs or reflections upon close relatives. I also received a rather eclectic array of artwork, poetry, fiction, recipes, photographs, letters, journal entries, newspaper articles, and essays that freely blur the lines between fiction and "reality" to the point that at least one contributor continues to refer to himself in our correspondence as a character in his testimonial. In effect these meditations, with their total disregard for the boundaries that traditionally separate generic forms, challenged my safe academic assumptions regarding testimonial practice and agency and began to erode the thick stone walls that appear to separate language and history; history and imagination; imagination and memory; memory and art.

II

The exile knows his place, and that place is the imagination. . . . Exile finds its reflection in the dream that memory has transformed into concept and universal. Exile's time and place is made of numbers; exile measures everything, even the space between the numbers. Exile dwells in the theatre of memory.

—*Ricardo Pau-Llosa, "Identity and Variations:*
Cuban Visual Thinking in Exile Since 1959"

In addition to suggesting the inadequacy of the available generic forms to articulate personal experience and thought regarding the relationships among exile, culture, and identity formation, the testimonials in this collection suggest that no single or fixed response to, or definition of, these terms exists. Clearly, the Cuban exodus or diaspora and the consequent condition of physical exile are painful realities that are often obscured, minimized, fetishized, and even effaced by the thickly layered cloud bank of theoretical jargon that claims to describe and analyze the relationships between culture and identity, the post-colonial condition, and the diasporic or nomadic consciousness. Yet in weaving together this collection, I soon came to realize that the term "exile" occupies many alternative places and meanings. Not only was I forced, as a result, to reconceptualize my entire approach to the relationships between exile, history, nostalgia, and the imagination, but I had to rethink my former, empirical notion that the term could only be conceptualized in physical, spatial, or geographical terms. Indeed, the very terminology I was employing came under scrutiny, for as one person pointed out early in the process, the term "exile"—as opposed to "émigré"—resonates in a variety of ways. For some, he pointed out, it is a politically charged term, in that it implies a very specific legislative status in the eyes of the government. For others, the term's conditional nature simultaneously implies the hope of returning to Cuba and a certain resistance to, or refusal to acknowledge, the Castro regime.

In approaching the central theme of exile, a number of contributors featured in Section VII ("Grace under Pressure") emphasize the fact that for them, exile is a spur to creativity. Through art they simultaneously transform the losses of exile and channel their pain and yearning. Conversely, many of the contributors featured in Sections v (The Culture Wars) and vi ("The Bite of Exile") express the difficulty of coming to terms with their cultural ambiguity and their bitterness over the losses they have sustained.

Taking a slightly different tack, the contributors in Section i (The Interior Exile), who suffered both physically and emotionally under Castro's repressive regime, speak of the "inner" or "internal" exile ("*insilio*") they underwent while still residing on the Island—a direct consequence of the fact that either they refused to become ideologically integrated into what several refer to as the "cult of Fidel," or they had gradually become disillusioned with the government.[4] In other words, they claim to have experienced a kind of exile of the inner imagination or spirit—a mental exodus, as it were—long before they left Cuba; in consequence, their initial exile experience was psychological as opposed to physical.

In contrast, an equally large group of my contributors characterize themselves as being in a state of exile despite the fact that they have little or no first-hand experience of Cuba. Many, for example, left Cuba as toddlers and therefore have only fleeting, dream-like impressions of their lives on the Island. Others, such as those featured in Sections iii (Crossing the Generational Divide), v (The Culture Wars), and viii ("Inheriting Exile"), number among the second generation, born to Cuban exiles in the United States, and, for the most part, have never set foot on Cuban soil.

Despite the fact that this latter group's bond to the Island and notions about Cuba are products of what I call the "vicarious imagination"—for, as Gustavo Pérez Firmat claims, their concept of Cuba is "forged by their parents' experiences rather than their own"—they all insist that their consciousness of exile is genuine or "authentic" and that it manifests itself in their everyday lives.[5] What is particularly noteworthy about several of the members of this collective group is the fact that many were raised outside of the Miami enclave.

Although some of my contributors would argue that Miami is a pale mirage or "imitation" of Havana and that its Calle Ocho *cubanía* is "hybridized" and "false,"[6] most of those who did grow up in south Florida account for their consciousness of exile and their strong sense of ethnic identity by pointing out that the Miami enclave has recaptured, and thereby preserved in their original forms, "authentic" Cuban traditions, recipes, and cultural mores (some of which have actually ceased to exist on the Island).[7] Their exile consciousness, therefore, can be attributed both to the physical proximity of Miami to the Island, and to the fact that they were socialized in a socioeconomic environment that reinforces a particularly strong sense of Cuban cultural identity. As a result, quite a few pointed out that when they are in Miami, they never have to think about their identities. (In fact, several *cubanas* who were in their mid- to late forties insisted that they would never consider marrying a Cuban as long as they remained in south Florida. "They expect us to behave like our mothers," one woman told me. "Who needs that? Anyway, we are so surrounded by Cuban culture that there's no need to reinforce our sense of ethnic identity in this way.")

Though one cannot rule out the ancestral call that pulses within some of us like some ancient drum, it is more difficult to account for the nomadic self-conception, the longing for Cuba, and the attraction to what Fernando Ortiz called *cubanía* expressed by those who grew up and reside outside of the Miami enclave. Though most were raised in what María Cristina García refers to as "cultural isolation" and were not insulated by an extended community that consciously and publicly preserved and perpetuated Cuban cultural values and practices, these contributors share a longing for the Island and tenaciously lay claim to a strong Cuban cultural identity and exile consciousness. Yet unlike those born and raised in Miami, most (with the exception of a few who grew up in New York City) claim to be in a state of perpetual cultural dislocation.

Not identifying entirely with either Cuba or the United States, these contributors share a sense of "unbelonging" and perceive themselves to be "spiritual exiles."[8] In effect, they suffer from a kind of vicarious Odyssean complex, caught in the double bind of the person who returns home only to find himself a stranger in his own land. At home (wherever that may be), they are insiders who always feel like outsiders; yet in Cuba or Miami, they are outsiders who feel as though they ought to be let into the circle.

Although one cannot deny that ABCs and ARCs have the choice, if they so desire, to identify themselves as Cuban Americans, or simply as Americans, these contributors tell me that they feel compelled, rather than choose, to identify themselves in relation to their Cuban origins or heritage, regardless of where or when they were born or raised. Though this phenomenon is not exclusive to these two groups, many, as a result, have made *cubanas* and Cuban cultural identity the focus of their research or art.[9] In effect, their work has become part of a process of self-identification and, for many, self-realization. Unlike some of their counterparts in Miami or their siblings (many of whom do not share their longing for Cuba or their sense of cultural isolation or dislocation), a significant number have chosen Latino/Hispanic partners. Quite a few have also expressed to me their resentment over the fact that they took no part in their parents' decision to leave Cuba. As a result, they were "merely players" caught in the midst of historical events that "robbed" them of or "denied" them the opportunity to "know" Cuba—a place where their roots lie dormant, despite the passage of time and political upheaval (see especially Sections II, "Merely a Player," and VIII, "Inheriting Exile").

Most ABCs and ARCs, such as those featured in Sections V (The Culture Wars) and VIII ("Inheriting Exile"), also characterize themselves as being caught in a kind of culture war that requires them to mediate between an old-world ideology (with its attendant set of mores, which dictate accepted modes of social and sexual behavior) and a post-1960s American value system (which defies the traditional paradigm of the neolocal family and blurs the lines between male and female gender roles in the private and public spheres). Others claim that being suspended in the limbo of the hyphen not only creates havoc on their pantry shelves, but it also determines what one contributor calls his "language identity," a phenomenon that manifests itself in everyday life and prompts some to draw distinctions between Castilian and the Spanish spoken on the Island; others to make a bid for standardizing what I call *cubano* Spanglish; and another to naturalize code-switching and refuse to italicize Spanish words.

III

The exile is a person who, having lost a loved one, keeps searching for the face he loves in every new face and, forever deceiving himself, thinks he has found it.   —*Reinaldo Arenas,* Before Night Falls

As one may gather, the "multi-tongued" voices (to borrow Mikhail Bakhtin's term) represented in this collection clearly demonstrate that rather than being a fixed concept or signifier, the Cuban 'presences' residing in the United States, and consequently Cuban exile identity itself, are complex and protean—for what it is to be Cuban or Cuban American, to be an exile or an exile artist, is constantly being displaced and renegotiated. Although all of my contributors claim to possess an exile consciousness, each, like a spider spinning its web, is engaged in mediating his or her unique subject position in regard to Cuba and the United States. More simply put, though the various testimonials in this collection share some common thread and therefore resonate in surprising ways, they also stand in striking counterpoint to one another, for each has its own individual "points of connection" and its own peculiar set of subjective and unstable references and identifications.

For some, exile can only be approached in personal terms; for others, it represents what one contributor has described as the "catastrophic" loss of an entire civilization. Although the thematic—as opposed to chronological—framework of this collection makes the generational distinctions among the contributors less apparent, the responses to exile and the descriptions of the Island and its culture shift and change from wave to diasporic wave. For example, those who left Cuba as adolescents in the late '50s or early '60s have vastly different memories from those who left during the '70s, for many of those contributors representing the first wave of exiles (*gusanos*, "worms")[10] were raised in a world that was virtually swept away by the violent red winds of the revolution and scattered to the four ends of the earth. In the same vein, those who fled Cuba during the Mariel Boatlift did not suffer the same conditions as those who experienced the Special Period; nevertheless, many of these contributors were raised under the communist regime and are therefore collectively termed *rosaditos* (pinkos). To further complicate the mix, factors such as race, class, gender, age, and sexual orientation serve to distinguish the experiences, remembrances, and constructions of cultural identity even of contributors within single generations or between generations (see especially Section III, Crossing the Generational Divide).

The consequent task of finding a way to speak about the Cuban exile experience and Cuban cultural identity in such a way that it simultaneously acknowledges both the deeply rooted forms of cultural life and practice that bind the various Cuban 'presences' together and the complex differences among them is formidable. In his essay "Cultural Identity and Diaspora," Stuart Hall proposes a bifocal approach to diasporic identity that broaches this cultural conundrum. "There are at least two different ways of thinking about 'cultural identity,'" Hall writes,

> the first position defines 'cultural identity' in terms of one, shared culture, a sort of collective 'one true self,' hiding inside the many other, more superficial or artificially imposed 'selves,' which people with a shared history or ancestry hold in common.[11]

When applied to the question of Cuban American diasporic identity, this first position acknowledges the common historical experiences or events—such as Fulgencio Batista's overturning of the Cuban Constitution in 1952 and the relinquishment of power to the 26 of July Movement in 1959—and the actual geographical places—one of which happens to be shaped like a crocodile and the other like a house with only two walls—that irrevocably link all Cuban American exiles and their offspring together. At the same time, however, it implicates the very deepest and most fundamental structures and practices that underpin and constitute shared cultural codes (language, food, music); cultural practices and characteristic attitudes (strong family ties, the importance of socializing, and what one contributor calls "the Cuban work ethic"); and the modes of interacting (such as *choteo* and the ability to carry on five conversations simultaneously) to which contributors allude throughout this collection. As a result, it bolsters the notion of a seemingly stable, collective cultural identity (*cubanidad*) and allows for the possibility of transcending the process of refashioning and transcoding that is a necessary aspect of diasporic and exilic cultural transmission.

Approaching the Cuban diaspora from this first position confirms the belief that continuity exists both inside and outside of history, politics, space, and time, despite the ideological and generational differences and the watery passage that separates Cuban exiles and their children living in the United States, not only from one another, but from Cubans residing on the Island. In other words, it provides a unified concept of cultural identity that somehow diminishes the sense of fragmentation and dislocation that is inherent to all diasporic and exilic experiences. In its total effect, adopting this first position allows the reader to join together the dismembered parts of the collection in order to create the illusion of wholeness.

The obvious problem with this collective "all Cubans are united, all Cubans are family in exile" approach, however, is that at the same time that it acknowledges the dense kinship networks and strong cultural, social, and economic ties that characterize the various exile enclaves in the United States and establishes their opposition to Fidel, it subordinates or downplays previously mentioned categories of distinction such as class, race, gender, sexual orientation, and age. As Antonio Benítez-Rojo once noted in our personal correspondence, for example, a Black Cuban necessarily formulates a distinct Cuban cultural identity from that of a White Cuban. "The Black Cuban's *ajiaco* [the Cuban stew that takes all and accepts everything]," he observed, "has more *plátano* and *ñame*, whereas the White Cuban's *ajiaco* tends to have more *carne y res*."

The second view of cultural identity that Hall posits overcomes this omission and thickens the stew by acknowledging that the "points of similarity" affirmed by the first view coexist with the "points of deep and significant difference" alluded to above. According to Hall, these points of difference constitute what the exiled "really are" or—since "history has intervened"—what they "have become."[12] Cultural identity in this second sense traverses time and remains fluid, for it

> is a matter of 'becoming' as well as of 'being.' It belongs to the future as much as to the past. It is not something which already exists, transcending place, time, history and culture.
>
> Cultural identities come from somewhere, have histories. But, like everything which is historical, they undergo constant transformation.[13]

Although I would tend to agree that history has indeed intervened and, as a result, identity is subject, as Hall contends, to the "continuous play" of "history, culture and power" (as opposed to being eternally fixed in some essentialized past), one cannot ignore the role that desire plays in the conscious construction or acquisition of cultural identity. Nevertheless, this second way of approaching diasporic cultural identity puts into relief the "sliding differences" that separate not only the various waves of refugees represented in this collection, but the various generations either born or raised in exile. Rather than denying or excluding difference, this second position engages it.

IV

> Identities are the names we give to the different ways we are positioned by, and position ourselves within, the narratives of the past . . .
> —*Stuart Hall, "Cultural Identity and Diaspora"*

Finally, in addition to pointing to the need to formulate a more inclusive thematic regarding exile in general, and Cuban cultural identity in particular, the variety of responses to the condition of exile outlined in the second and third parts of this essay, coupled with the sometimes contradictory images or remembrances of life on the Island described above, also draws attention to the need to devise a more inclusive tag or moniker that acknowledges and validates the points of similarity and difference that tether and separate those who claim to possess a Cuban exile consciousness.

To date, scholars have yet to devise the elastic terminology that allows ample space for the subtle nuances that characterize the multifarious responses to Cuban cultural identity and exile formulated by my contributors. The war that is waged over labeling, coupled with this pressing need to develop more inclusive, yet complex, terminology, also became present to me at the very outset of this project, for I unwittingly adopted the terms of identification "ABC" and "1.5" or "one and a half" generation in my questionnaire.[14] I soon heard from a number of my contributors, who took umbrage at my decision to employ what several described as "meaningless," "reductive," and "simplistic" labels.[15] In their views, these tags veiled or even effaced the categorical differences (such as gender, race, age, class, geographical location, sexual and religious orientation, education, and occupation, as well as place of birth and/or the time period in which they or their family members left Cuba, etc.) that distinguished them from one another.

In addition, many expressed their objection to the practice by which persons of Cuban origin or heritage residing in the U.S. are classified under the monolithic rubrics "Hispanics" and/or "Latinos." Arguing along the same lines, several contributors pointed out that the moniker "Cuban American" has been applied as a kind of broad brush stroke to include all naturalized Cuban exiles and their offspring residing in the United States. As a result, I soon began to realize that all of these tags treat Cuban exile identity as though it were some one-dimensional category of essence. Just as the word "hybrid" carries with it its own death sentence[16] and its own "checkered" past,[17] ultimately the tag "Cuban American" consumes itself—like Saturn eating his own children— for it is an inherently fixed signifier, embedded with its own internal contradictions and limitations, not to mention its own shortcomings and dislocations. In its failure to take into account the complexity of the Cuban exile consciousness and to embrace the various Cuban 'presences' in the United States, it simply functions as a way of imposing order and coherence on the experience of fragmentation, loss, and transformation that is not only the legacy of the various waves of the Cuban diaspora, but the legacy of all diasporic experiences.

If pressed to use a tag at all, an open-ended and more inclusive phrase such as "the Cuband 'presences'" better functions (if only symbolically as opposed to practically) as a kind of lightning rod that grounds Cuban exile identity to an actual place and an idealized, rather than imagined, geography and history, which are at once both present and absent. As many critics have observed, Cuba has become a kind of "real-and-imagined" place or space. It is an absent "notion" (as opposed to "nation"), as José Martí observed, which has partly become the object of imagination or desire. In other words, the idea of Cuba that most Cuban exiles nurture and seek to preserve gives itself out as a refracted, shadowy image of a lost world, a fragmented void, an appropriated recollection partially "re-membered" (as the title of this collection suggests) through the blue cloud of nostalgia or reconstructed through the vicarious imagination of those who either have never been to the Island, or were not old enough to remember when they left. On the other hand, it is an actual place, a physical space whose waxy green shrubbery and red earth and tourmaline sea function for many as an atemporal and ahistorical synecdoche, representing a spirit, a sensibility, a worldview that unites all Cubans and, therefore, transcends the ravages of time and human endeavor. For others, as Narciso G. Menocal observes, Cuba's lush vegetation has become a kind of nationalistic metaphor, as seen in the image of the tropical landscape that political exile José María Heredia "fixed" in his 1824 ode "*Niágara*" and Esteban Chartrand captured in his painting *Paisaje*.[18]

Adding a "d" to "Cuban" also allows for the infinite number of "couplings" and identifications that together constitute the Cub*and* 'presences' in the United States. "By allowing the infinite possibility of an 'and' when discussing ethnic or racial identity," Stuart Hall observes, the "logic of coupling," as opposed to the "logic of binary opposition," avoids the "essentializing of difference into ... mutually opposed either/ors" ("What is this 'black' in black popular culture?").[19] By extension, employing the moniker "Cub*and*" acknowledges the oftentimes subtle nuances that separate the multigenerational exile identities represented in this collection. By yoking this term to the word 'presences,' we allow for the fact that all of these identities are aspects of a kind of palimpsest of visible/invisible "inheritances," which together constitute an identity that bears the scars of colonialism, revolution, diaspora, and exile.[20] Because its meaning resides in the nostalgic desire for a fixed and stable location—albeit in the zone of memory or imagination—the phrase "the Cub*and* 'presences'" functions as a kind of harmonious dislocation (reclining somewhere in between Antonio Benítez-Rojo's notion of "free orbit" and Jacques Derrida's concept of "*différance*"), for it acknowledges that identity is in a state of constant flux and motion and allows for the "slippages" that are occurring even as I sit here writing and a new set of Cuban refugees are washing up on the shores of south Florida.[21]

V

The Occasion for Speaking
Lo único vivo es la mano. . . . Tal vez sea la mano de un testigo y la mancha en el muro es su sombra y otras sombras más.
The only thing alive is the hand. . . . Perhaps it's the hand of a witness and the mark on the wall is its shadow and other shadows.
    —*Gabriel Cabrera Infante,* Vista del amanecer en el trópico

In its total effect, *ReMembering Cuba* is not a single *ajiaco cubano,* the metaphor employed by both Fernando Ortiz and Gustavo Pérez Firmat, but, as Antonio Benítez-Rojo suggests, it is many *ajiacos cubanos* with variations. Nevertheless, this collection neither pretends to be comprehensive or all-inclusive, nor does it purport or claim to be either a sociological or psychoanalytical analysis of the Cub*and* 'presences' in the United States, or a definitive historical interpretation of the exile experience. In some sense, rather, the voices, the visions, the nightmares, and the dreams that are represented in this collection are more like photographs that have slipped from some collective album. Though each seeks to represent or capture some unique "reality," and thereby endow the life and experience of each author with some sense of historical significance or meaning, I feel compelled once again to acknowledge the unspoken and the unseen; the gaps and the spaces; the information and the stories consciously withheld or altered; the shadows that gather just beyond the serrated borders of these snapshots.[22] Although some may regard this collection as remiss, while others may view it as being radically inclusive, it partly seeks to "de-territorialize" (to borrow Ray Chow's term) the fenced-off terrain of testimonial practice. It also partly aims to complicate the monolithic stereotype that all Cuban American exiles reside in Miami and are overwrought, fanatical nationalists—a stereotype that is persistently portrayed in the national and international media (as witnessed in the recent coverage of the Elián González case) and is consequently widely accepted both here and abroad. Moreover, in its attempt to acknowledge and, to some extent, redress the need for a more representative concept of exile identity, it points to the correlative need to explode the myth of authenticity that purportedly determines not only who can and cannot speak about exile and loss and convey personal experience, but how they can do so. In short, among its aims this collection simultaneously seeks to give voice or narrative/ artistic status to those whom the dominant discourse in academia and in the media—the self-appointed center, as it were—has suppressed or silenced and to acknowledge and validate the existence and the ongoing struggle and suffering of those who remain exiled on Cuban soil.

Author's Note: All translations are mine, except where noted.

NOTES

1. See the select bibliography.
2. Pérez Firmat, *Life on the Hyphen*, 5.

3. One such person insisted that Cuban exiles' "solipsistic obsession" with loss has prevented them from developing the capacity to situate the diaspora in the context of larger historical events. "Cuban exiles," she observed, "cannot get out of their own shadow; as a result, virtually everything that has happened in the United States (or in the world for that matter) over the past forty years has been subordinated in their minds to the exodus that came in the wake of the 1959 revolution."

4. Several members of the latter group claim that the revolution never actually triumphed, for the ideals that the 26 of July Movement purportedly represented and aspired toward were never actually realized; as a result, these contributors either avoid using the term "revolution" altogether and refer to the events surrounding January 1, 1959, as before and after Castro; or they refuse to capitalize the term. Others, such as Carmen Herrera, have observed that their experience of exile spanned several regimes: Machado, Batista, and Castro.

5. Pérez Firmat, *Life on the Hyphen*, 5.

6. Several insist that they have undergone a kind of double exile—one from the Island and a second from Miami.

7. One such person (who was raised in Miami) objected to my use of the term "diaspora" in the title. Despite the fact that the exile is now over forty years old (a kind of archetypal number in the history of diasporas, I might add), in his view the term implies a state of impermanency or perpetual wandering. Moreover, he argued, it suggests that the Cuban exile has no center. In response, I noted that Cuban exiles not only were spread throughout the United States, but could be found in nearly every corner of the world; nevertheless he remained unconvinced. When I asked where this center to which he was referring was located, he quickly responded, "Miami."

8. The experience of those who spent significant portions of their childhoods in Puerto Rico, such as María Cristina García, María Martínez-Cañas, and María de los Angeles Lemus, adds another dimension to the collection. One such contributor identifies herself as a CubaRican, a label that expresses her divided allegiance to both islands.

9. For more on this subject, see Gustavo Pérez Firmat's discussion in *Life on the Hyphen* of the "beneficial consequences" of the "biculturation" or cultural blending that is "specific to" or "characteristic of" the ABC and ARC generations.

10. "*Gusano*" is a pejorative term that Castro devised.

11. Hall, "Cultural Identity and Diaspora," 393.

12. Ibid., 394.

13. Ibid.

14. Gustavo Pérez Firmat transcoded the latter tag from the work of sociologist Rubén G. Rumbaut. When applied to Cuban American refugees, the moniker "1.5 generation" refers to those who were born on the Island but were educated and came of age in the United States. See "The Agony of Exile: A Study of the Migration and Adaptation of Indochinese Refugee Adults and Children" in *Refugee Children: Theory, Research, and Services*. Ed. Frederick L. Ahern, Jr. and Jean L. Athey (Baltimore: Johns Hopkins University Press, 1991), 61.

15. One contributor commented that, in some sense, being categorized numeri-

cally (1.5), and "fractionally" at that, "dehumanizes" her personal experience and fails to represent the complexity of her cultural identity.

16. A colleague and fellow gardener once informed me, upon hearing me use the term at a postcolonial studies conference, that in the natural world, "hybrid" offspring are always sterile.

17. See Bruce Simon's discussion of the etymological evolution of the term "hybrid" in his essay "Hybridity in the Americas: Reading Condé, Mukherjee, and Hawthorne" in *Postcolonial Theory and the United States*. Ed. Amritjit Singh and Peter Schmidt (Jackson, Miss.: University Press of Mississippi, 1999).

18. Narisco G. Menocal, "An Overriding Passion," 187–219.

19. Hall, "Cultural Identity and Diaspora," 472.

20. Although most critics position Cuban cultural identity in relation to four 'presences' (Spain, Africa, the United States, and the Soviet Union), there are many additional constitutive cultural identities or 'presences' that are, at first glance, less visible (such as those drawn from China and Ireland, as well as the Taino and Ciboney heritage, etc.).

21. See Benítez-Rojo's *The Repeating Island* (Durham: Duke University Press, 1992).

22. As I write these words, it occurs to me that perhaps my insistence that the poems that were submitted to me in Spanish appear both in their original language and in translation registers an awareness of the sometimes impassable chasms that invariably exist between the reader and those who attempt to describe the experience of living in exile or to recreate the world they left behind.

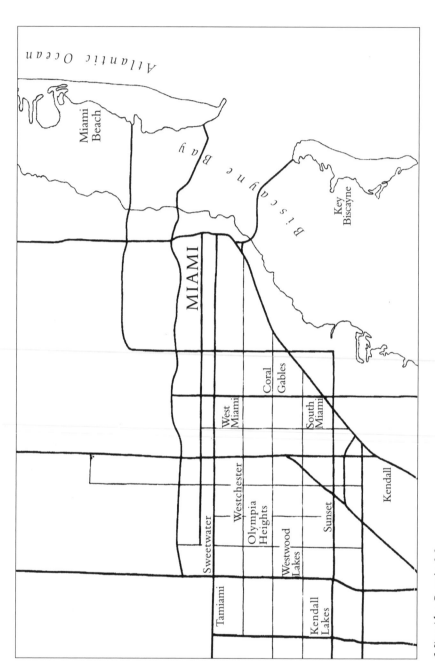

Miami by Lottie Morse

The Interior Exile ("*insilio*")

Testimonio de un artista

Leandro Soto

Born in Cienfuegos in 1956, Leandro Soto left the Island in 1988. After spending five years in Mexico, he arrived in the United States in 1994. He and his wife, Grisel Pujalá, reside in South Hadley, Massachusetts.

To be in exile is an interior feeling that you experience for the first time living inside Cuba, something which Lezama Lima, in a 1960 letter to Orbon, refers to as "*insilio*" or interior exile. You begin by wishing that you were born in another place, that you spoke another language other than your native tongue, that you dressed differently, had other distant tastes which are, perhaps, better, etc.; these feelings are bound together by the sensation of not belonging. There is, inside your being, a nostalgia for the continent, a desire to learn about distant ancestors from a family that originated in Spain and France on one side, and Africa and perhaps China on the other. One imagines, visualizes, and acknowledges in the face of the sea (to "Yemayá Asesu") that life has to be something more than the limitations that the conditions on the Island place upon the personal and the political, the social and the economic. The sea—boundary, altar, natural frontier, and at the same time, the place of liberty and escape.

Outside of Cuba, exile becomes the history of survival, ingenuity, abandonment, and infinite "I will get up agains," of pretending ignorance, voluntary forgetfulness, intense dreams of returns with impossible departures, and yet above all, a poetic condition, artistic and cultural, which one discovers without even knowing it, little by little. In Mexico, Spain, and other countries with Spanish heritage, you easily fall into the trap of their respective idioms, a verbal mirage that appears to be similar. But speaking the same language guarantees nothing; "you have to annul the differences"—your *cubanidad* (now you know all at once that you are Cuban), your sonorous accent, and the manner in which you organize or view the world according to a certain definition. (October 15, 1998)

Oh, La Habana
Rafael E. Saumell

Rafael Saumell was born in Havana in 1951; he left Cuba with his family in 1988. Although he lived in St. Louis, Missouri, for many years, he now resides in Conroe, Texas.

Before leaving Cuba with my wife and two sons on May 9, 1988, I had already had numerous experiences of internal exile. I was in Cuba, but I didn't belong there; I lived as if bound to the Island and felt condemned living there.

Before the Revolution, my mother worked as a servant for various families. When I was born in Havana, she earned a living as a domestic servant to her cousins, who were wealthy and were also attending college. My father had no profession and little schooling. After my mother died in 1956, my father took me with him to Guantánamo in search of a better life.

From Guantánamo, I went to Santiago de Cuba to live with my maternal aunt in January of 1959. In truth, I don't remember the Revolution as being a happy matter for the better part of my family on my mother's side. Although they were all poor, that one reason did not convert them to the new regime. In other words, they were anti-Batista but not procommunist. They liked the promise of stable employment, public health care, and a lower cost of living; but they disliked the official atheism, the closing of private schools and businesses, the closing of independent newspapers, the indoctrination of youths, the massive incarcerations, the speedy trials, the executions, the increasing exodus of relatives and friends, the material and spiritual scarcity, and the demonization of Americans. The more the government attacked the Yankees, the more they listened to the short-wave broadcasts, such as the Voice of America (or, in official terminology, the "BOA"—the snake that exuded the venom of capitalism), coming from the Keys or the islands near Cuba.

With the passing years, the "BOA" became more than just a radio station, for it introduced the Cuban public to another world, another point of view in the shape of a book, a foreign publication, an exiled singer, a film, commercial propaganda, a brand of chewing gum, clothing designed abroad, a Canadian or European tourist, a relative abroad, or a visitor from the Cuban community residing on the other side of the "pond" (either Miami or Madrid). The ideas of *Glásnot* and *Perestroika*, coupled with Gorbachev's speeches, were also snakes, as was anything that Castro prohibited, from an idea to a brand of soap wrapped in paper, rather than Nácar, the dry and odorless Cuban soap produced by the Ministry of the so-called "Light" Industry, which was distributed through ration cards.

As a result, my first experience of exile began when I was only a child, for most Cubans, including my mother's family, didn't see Cuba the way Fidel Castro claimed to see it, with his visions of milk farms, rich plantain plantations, infinite sugar cane fields, and distilling volcanic sugar. Perhaps we Cubans were blind and deaf and dumb, for we were surrounded by buildings collapsing around us from old age and lack of care and dairies falling to pieces. And each time milk was watered down and production was less, the official vision claimed that the factories were up and running. In effect, communism is like *meringue*: the red roses grown by the working class are sold to foreign tourists, who pay with dollars; the athletes abandon the competitions; the few vaccines invented end up being exported or used in hospitals that offer health benefits for those who have strong foreign currency. (The vaccines given to ordinary Cubans are acquired through international charities.) In Cuba, human rights do not exist for all; world leaders arrive on the Island and leave promptly, their arms full of tobacco, rum, sunshine, beaches, and mulatto men and women. The vast majority of Cubans live on an island very different from the one described by the commander. This is the craziest form of exile that one could ever imagine. As a result, Cubans emigrate, looking for lands where they can use their own eyes to see.

In 1968, when I was seventeen years old, I began my second exile after participating in a student meeting sponsored by the Communist Youth Organization at Máximo Gorki, where I was studying French. The purpose of this meeting was to discuss the content of an official document in which that organization condemned the music and "alienated lifestyle" of local and foreign rock groups, alcohol consumption, and the nightlife in clubs. Among the denounced vices were the "bad habits" adopted by young Cubans of growing their hair long and dressing "extravagantly." I was the only one who openly opposed this document.

My father did not take the news well. As a result, I had to leave Havana and go to live in Santiago de Cuba in my aunt and uncle's house, where I had spent a large part of my childhood. There, I began what I refer to as my internal exile. During the day, I worked hard as maintenance help and a prep cook in the Pedagogical Institute of the University of Oriente; in the evenings, I revived from the exhaustion and solitude by participating in the intellectual groups of the Café Isabelica and the less formal gatherings at Céspedes Park. Even though I adored my family, I was ultimately unable to adapt to living in Santiago de Cuba; so at the end of 1971, I returned to Havana—a city equally ruined, with few remaining signs of its original splendor.

After the storming of the Peruvian Embassy and the Mariel exodus of 1980, Havana seemed to me to be even more empty and desolate, for most of my dearest friends left the Island at that time: Ricardo Oteiza, Jorge Posada, Roberto Madrigal. Only a few of us remained; and we were profoundly saddened. For us, Havana was destroyed; it was like the cratered surface of the moon. Nothing made sense, for the places and sites of Havana had lost their significance. The only thing that stayed intact was the sentiment we felt for the people we loved.

The various exiles that I suffered in Cuba culminated in a surprising and violent manner the morning of October 14, 1981, when I was arrested and charged with "crimes" that would have made Franz Kafka and Orson Wells blush: possession of enemy propaganda and pornographic materials. At first I didn't understand the legal significance of either of these charges. In effect, I was being accused of dissidence—a result of a series of stories I had written, whose main theme was how different people succeeded or failed to leave Cuba. The charge of pornography was made by an informant, who visited my house from time to time and posed as a fan of literature. This person told the police that I showed old, pornographic films in my home and that he had attended one of these sessions. Although the police were unable to find anything among my property that would support his accusation, they nevertheless claimed that my short stories demonstrated my "rebellion" against the revolutionary state. This is what the two "experts" from the Union of Cuban Artists and Writers (whose names I will not reveal at this moment) argued.

During the interrogations at the Department of State Security headquarters, the official in charge of my case showed me a form with the Union (UNEAC) letterhead, read the political charges aloud, and even let me know the names of my accusers. My personal profile, which I was allowed to read, portrayed me as a vulgar political imposter who had written counterrevolutionary literature. This was enough to put me behind bars. The "legal process" carried out by the Department of State Security and its socialist laws eventually led to a prison sentence of five years, of which I served four and a half. The classified crime was Enemy Propaganda; with this charge on my back, I went through three different prisons: La Cabaña, Combinado del Este, and Guanajay.

I was released from Combinado del Este on April 11, 1986, around two in the afternoon (note that I avoid using the word "freedom" here, given that this concept does not exist in Cuba, inside or outside of prison). I had waited for this moment for years with never-ending anxiety and variable optimism. My time in the "tank" made me an expert on unspeakable horrors and a cautious thinker regarding any kind of positive future. It was Jorge Valls, a poet and former political prisoner, who coined a sad but true phrase regarding the destiny of Cubans behind bars. It is stated, I believe, in the documentary *Nobody Listened* (1987) that "It is easy to die in prison." During my time in prison, I saw many people die in different ways: by execution, by suicide, by acquired illness and despair.

After crossing the last gate at Combinado del Este upon my release, I found my father waiting for me, seated on a bench. Once we had greeted each other, he told me that he would call someone who could take us to Havana by car—we were in Guanabacoa—but I declined his offer, telling him that I preferred to take a bus in order to feel people pushing against me. I wanted to smell their smells, observe the color in clothing, and later, go to the Malecón to see and touch the sea, which is the border and beginning of freedom on the island of Cuba. I wanted to yell in front of the waves "Fuck it!" and to release my sorrows, to cry, to shake my arms, my whole body, and then, in that moment, to look behind me toward Havana and repeat the old saying that I had heard on the television program where I was a script-writer, "Everybody Is Singing" (*Todo el mundo canta*), whose refrain reads, "Oh Havana, Oh Havana, he who doesn't see you doesn't love you!" (*¡Oh, La Habana, Oh La Habana, quien no la ve no la ama!*).

I also wanted to see the sites that I remembered so fondly while in prison: the streets, corners, certain shadows, lights, silhouettes of houses and of buildings. I wanted to hear the sounds that do not exist in the cells: that of strolling people, running cars, functioning machinery. I wanted to sense the smell of certain things—some of them repulsive—like the liquid gas that filtered through the pipes of Old Havana, the rotten and oily water from Havana's port, the perfumes and body odors of the passersby, the aroma emanating from the bakery ovens, the caramel and chocolate factories, the restaurants, the pizzerias. I wanted to walk to the ice cream parlor Coppelia, to feel the air conditioning in the Habana Libre and Capri hotels, to smell the stench of the Almendares and Kibuz Rivers.

The Havana of my memories, however, was both ugly and beautiful. It had been the city I most hated and most loved—the first capital of my repeated exiles. Nevertheless, I had to return to see her because she was the most important witness of my life, though she represented both the good and the bad; for Havana was the place where my wife and children were, where three faithful friends (whom I still can't even mention today) survived underground, and where my formerly esteemed classmates (who had repudiated me in order to save their jobs) and my accusers still remained.

When I arrived in Havana, however, I wanted to die, for the city of my dreams had been replaced by another Havana epitomized by what I saw on San Lázaro Street: propped up, dirty, dusty, untidy, chaotic. The lost city was held together by the wooden beams supporting cracked roofs at the point of falling down. It was a city lost in time, a beautiful place that resided in my memory.

When my family and I boarded an Eastern Airlines plane on May 9, 1988, at three or four in the morning, we began a journey that all Cuban refugees experience: in a craft we crossed airy pathways, over water and land, which took us to the destiny that we had dreamt of throughout long years of spiritual, political, and economic misery. The present would quickly become the past; the island of Cuba, which we carried with us in body and soul, would take off with us upon leaving the airport runway of Rancho Boyeros. The lights of Havana, in the obscured background and denseness of the tropical night, were left behind.

Miami is both near and far from Cuba. In forty-five minutes all ends so that it can begin again. How long, we often wondered, does one have to wait for those damn forty-five minutes to pass? It seemed like an eternity. I measure the time by intervals of anxiety. They can also be counted by the number of lines in which every Cuban has to wait: in front of the grocery stores, in the bus and rail stations, airports, taxi depots, lines to take ferries to Regla and Casablanca, to make reservations in hotels and motels, to eat in the cafes, restaurants, and pizzerias, to eat ice cream in Coppelia, to buy clothing in the empty bargain stores, to shop in the fish markets, meat markets, produce stands, bakeries, *cafeterías*, to face the paperwork in the offices of Public Safety, to buy medications in the weary pharmacies or additional food in the free farmer markets, to buy milk, to wait at the dry cleaner's, in bookstores and newsstands, at repair shops for shoes, watches, eyeglasses, for radios and televisions, posts to refill gas lighters, gas company tanks, the water pipes always short in supply, the breweries.

When my feet finally touched ground in the Miami airport, I remembered what Jerry Scott, an official of the U.S. Interest Section in Havana, had said to me days before leaving: "You are going to arrive in the twentieth century." We did not stay in Miami, however; rather, we went to St. Louis, Missouri, where the International Institute had promised to give us shelter. (Even though we had family and friends in Miami, of whom we knew little since their departure, we didn't think it correct for us to just show up and give them the responsibility of feeding four more mouths without knowing of their financial situation.)

Although the apartment that was assigned to us was located in the most poverty-ridden zone of south St. Louis, to us it seemed like a postcard of the USA in the fifties and sixties. The street's name was Iowa, which intersected with Miami Avenue. We lived on the second floor with two rooms, a bathroom, a living room, a den, and a kitchen. The only furniture was a table, which held packages of rice, beans, canned goods, cooking oil, and other tidbits, and we found three bare mattresses on the floor. A large suitcase and a small handbag were all that we had brought from Cuba. We didn't speak English, didn't have any job, and we didn't know if there were any Latin Americans living in the city. In other words, we were in the "Yuma" (USA) with a million questions running through our heads.

To learn to live as an exile is a daily job. In our case, there were many lessons to learn: some through the children, and some by ourselves as adults. There is, however, an important point in common: how to struggle with the new language. The boys learned English in the twinkle of an eye because of the intensive courses they received in school and the relationships they had with their peers. It was another thing for adults. After a long day at work, we would go to night school, where they taught English. Eventually, our persistence was rewarded through our efforts; nevertheless, attending those night classes required much patience and a tremendous desire to be successful.

My wife, Manena (María M. Bastón-Chils), and I also demanded that our sons study hard. Given our experience, we insisted they positively value that which many Americans do not: study, textbooks, free transportation, excellent meals at cheap prices, school supplies, and above all, an insured future thanks to educational preparation. This is the best legacy that we can leave Abdel and Michael because exiles like ourselves don't bring fortune with us and have given up on our plans to go back to our motherland anytime soon. In Cuba, there is no war that will end sooner rather than later.

After learning the English language, the next challenge Manena and I faced was to know what kind of legacy about our homeland we should pass on to our sons. We decided the first thing to do was to preserve our native language. There are ethical and practical reasons for this. In the first place, the language helps to maintain one's identity, the kind of identity that serves to remind us of where we came from. In the second place, it is important to speak more than one language (here or in any part of the world, for that matter) in order to have access to more information (culturally speaking) and to be more competitive in the labor market.

The rest of Cuban life (*lo cubano*) our sons would learn in their daily home life, from history to customs to attitude to the music of Cuba. Given that we lived in exile, we made sure that the homeland and its traditions were present in breakfast, lunch, and dinner. There was always a different flavor on each plate that sent us back: rice, beans, shredded meat, fried steak, ground beef, roast pork, meat and baked potatoes, plantains, *ajiaco* (Cuban stew), chicken soup, Galician soup, beef soup, and the wonderful papaya! We believed the presence of this food forms the personality of a child or adolescent in exile. In their own time, our children have brought the outside world into our home through their American friends and the children of other immigrants or exiles, television programs, new dietary habits, ways of dressing, games, and textbooks. Their new personality has been developed somewhere in between the consumption of black beans and the newcomer macaroni and cheese. They live halfway between the soap operas and the news on Univisión and Telemundo of the adult world, and the Disney channel, MTV and ESPN. It's a practice of mutual learning.

Some of the habits of many American adolescents, however, clash with those of our children's Hispanic origin. Sometimes we think that they listen to a sort of noisy music. Too often, they are exposed to lyrics that glamorize illegal drugs, alcohol, and suicide. To this one might add the irreverent behavior with which many American youths treat adults. We tried to discourage these attitudes in our children, although we tried to avoid taking an intolerant stance, which would generate serious conflict. We did not promote self-imposed segregation in our relations with co-workers, nor in the friendships our sons chose. I think that we have been successful because today, after ten years of exile, people's comments about Abdel or Michael are favorable; we often hear them say that our boys are "educated like in the old time," they have good manners, they are respectful.

I have not spoken much about Manena, as she has her own ideas and points of view. But I think I should say something anyway: it is she who has worked the hardest both inside and outside the home. She has preserved the Cuban culture in all corners of family life. In the kitchen, she has preserved our land without shutting out the new world. Her dishes are like a bridge between the memory of Cuba and the reality in the United States. Although her "Havana accent" (from Marianao, to be specific) has changed little, in her speech one can nevertheless detect inflexions typical of Cuban exiles. From her cooking to her speech, all of these things tell me that she is becoming more Cuban American every day. As a result, she seems to be the one who is suffering less by being outside of Cuba.

Manena's nostalgia is in music. Although she doesn't miss the Cuba we left behind, with all its painful memories, her nostalgia for the Island lies in her hope for a better future. When that time comes, she wants to return to visit, perhaps as a tourist, when there is no longer a system or a ruler like Castro. To Manena, Cuba is lost as a territorial nation; the place that she misses is more like a way of being. Manena is a kind of new Cuba—the new homeland emerging in exile—exiled in her language, in her walk, in her recipes, in her resistance to tyranny, in the care of her sons, in her work ethic and sacrifices, in her love for a country where there are no longer fear, suspicious motives, or separated families.

In my case, I have rediscovered a sacred Cuba in the music, the best contribution Cubans have made to humanity. In the Republic's fifty-seven years and Castro's forty, that which has endured and united us as a nation is the sound. When I hear a septet, for example, I rediscover the Cuban rhythm in thought, speech, walk, and all that is me. I rediscover the lost speech—that which I no longer hear on a daily basis—for it remains alive in the recordings I collect. When I hear Havana's orchestra Los Van Van performing "*Soy Todo*" or "*La Shopimaniaca*," I don't think of them as being on Castro's payroll. When I listen to the music of my generation, I feel as though I have never left the Island. I see myself in the reflection of these great Cubans, for they (unlike Silvio Rodríguez and Pablo Milanés) don't live in the actual territory of the country but, rather, in the Cuban musical key. In some sense, moreover, the true Cuban democratic revolution occurred in music. One might compare it to the freedom African American musicians enjoyed in creating the jazz tradition, as opposed to the freedom they lacked at a time when civil rights were nonexistent for them.

Cuban music is my motherland. It is politically inclusive and diverse; it doesn't require proof of physical residence: it is here, it is there, it is everywhere. Anyone can enjoy Cuban music—in tropical regions, in temperate climates, even as far as planet Mars; there, neither Batista nor Castro has control. (Remember the cha cha cha "*Los Marcianos llegaron ya*": Martians have arrived . . . and they came dancing cha cha cha!) If not for Cuban music, I would be an exile without a home, without a motherland to live in for the rest of my life, inside and out of this place—this word—we call Cuba.   (*Translated by Kristen Evans*)

Manena's Cuban American Recipes

POLLO COCA-COLA

Ingredients: one small chicken (cut up), $^1/_4$ cup Coca-Cola, $^1/_4$ tsp. salt, ketchup to taste, $^1/_4$ tsp. black pepper, 1 small onion, 3–4 garlic cloves, 2 carrots, 2 stalks celery (do *not* add water).

Put all of these ingredients in a pressure cooker; set on high heat until the top is dancing; turn down heat to medium-low and cook for 10-12 minutes. Serve with rice or potatoes.

CUBAN CHICKEN BARBECUE

Ingredients: No salt! No water! One small chicken (cut up), 2 Tbs. butter, soy sauce to taste, 3–4 cloves garlic, 1 onion.

Put all of these ingredients in a pressure cooker; set on high heat until the top is dancing; turn down heat to medium-low and cook for 10-12 minutes. Serve with rice or potatoes.

Both recipes serve approximately four people.

Life in Exile
MY PERSPECTIVE

Hector R. Romero

Hector R. Romero was born in Santa Clara, Cuba, in 1942; he escaped from the Island at the age of nineteen in 1961. He now resides in Edinburg, Texas.

I am an exile; there is no doubt in my mind about this fact. At nineteen, I was forced to make a decision that would drastically alter my life for years to come. I chose to leave Cuba, my homeland, because it was clear to me that I could no longer endure, or even survive, in that type of repressive regime. After two unsuccessful attempts, I finally managed to escape in a small boat in the middle of the night, sneaking out and looking over my shoulder, just like a thief who is trying to get away with something that is not his. In my case, I was indeed trying to get away with something, but it was all mine: my freedom, my dignity, my beliefs, my individuality, my rights, and my culture. Let me summarize the events that led to that decision and to my subsequent exile.

On December 31, 1958, the rebel forces of Che Guevara entered Santa Clara, my hometown, where the most violent battle of the Revolution was fought. I was sixteen years old. Caught in the romantic idealism of the moment, I joined the rebel forces as a scout, or *práctico*, as we were called—local residents who could guide the rebel forces throughout the city. My stint as a *rebelde* lasted only for a few days, but the events I witnessed in that short time impacted me forever. In 1960, disappointed by what I had seen and by the direction in which the Revolution was turning, I joined the MRR (Movement for the Recovery of the Revolution). As a result of my clandestine activities against Castro's communist regime, I was incarcerated three times: twice at the G-2 headquarters in Santa Clara, and once at the San Severino Castle in the Matanzas province. In addition, I was expelled from the University of Havana in 1961, and my picture was prominently displayed, along with many others, on a bulletin board referred to as the "Gallery of Maggots." We had been found to be traitors to "the magnanimity of the Revolution."

I guess my exile really began on April 15, 1961. That was the day when the preliminary aerial attacks were made on Castro's air force as preparation for the Bay of Pigs invasion a couple of days later. In a matter of hours, Castro's repressive police launched a massive raid throughout the Island. Five percent of the population was incarcerated. When jails became full, theaters, sports arenas, schools, and even fenced fields were used to hold all the prisoners. I escaped the raid because I was in transit between Santa Clara and Havana. When the militia came to my home to arrest me, I wasn't there. But they didn't leave empty-handed; they took my mother and my brother instead.

With the defeat of the Bay of Pigs operation, all hopes for a free and sovereign Cuba collapsed like a house of cards. Many more were arrested, tried, and sentenced to long prison terms or executed. Others made desperate plans to escape the Island. I was one of those people. After two failed attempts, a friend and I, with several other men, women, and children (twelve in total), arrived at Marathon Key on November 3, 1961. We had made it across the Gulf Stream in just over two days on a seventeen-footer with an unreliable inboard motor. I had just turned nineteen, and that was one of the best birthday presents I had ever received.

The INS authorities took us to an old military base in Opa Locka, where we spent a few days under fairly constant interrogation. We were finally given parolee status and taken to a hotel in downtown Miami to spend the night. The following day we were directed to go to the Cuban Refugee Center. There, I received sixty dollars and some second-hand clothes. Up to that point, I possessed nothing more than the clothes on my back and about fifteen dollars, which I had brought from Cuba. After leaving the refugee center, I was free and on my own. Now the big question was, "What am I going to do?" I did not know a soul in Miami. I had escaped from Cuba for two reasons. First, I could no longer live there; and second, I was driven by the desire to enroll in one of the training camps and return with the next invasion. Little did I know what I was about to encounter in the exile community.

I had the names and telephone numbers of several representatives of the major anti-Castro groups in Miami and immediately established contact with them. I soon realized that chaos and confusion reigned over the exile community. All the training camps had been dismantled. Each group wanted to gain preponderance over the others. As time passed, I was becoming more and more saddened and disillusioned, for it was becoming clear to me that the Cuban situation would not have a quick solution. I had to survive, to open some doors that would lead me to a less confusing and more stable situation.

In Miami, I had a number of menial jobs, from strawberry picker to sugar cane cutter, from dishwasher to floor sweeper, from factory worker to a short stint as a stevedore. All of those jobs helped me pull from one week to the next, or from a couple of days to the next couple of days. During the periods in which I was unemployed, I had seriously considered a couple of alternatives. One was to enroll in the armed forces and go to Vietnam. I still felt anger within me, and going to Vietnam did not appear to be a far-fetched idea. I had also toyed with the idea of moving to Australia. The Australian government was granting homesteads and paying all transportation costs to immigrants who were willing to move there as settlers. After thinking all this through, I decided to write to the University of Illinois, upon the recommendation of a friend, and request admission. (My mother had taken the precaution of preparing a sealed plastic bag that contained my Cuban passport, my high school baccalaureate degree, about fifteen dollars, and some miscellaneous papers. It proved to be a great idea because when I applied for admission at the University of Illinois, I made copies of the pertinent documents and sent them with my application.)

My experiences at the University of Illinois were very positive at the personal as well as the intellectual level. Because of my experiences in Cuba and later as an exile in Miami, I had a sixth sense that had helped me adapt and roll with the punches in unfamiliar surroundings. At the Illinois campus, on the other hand, I felt I had entered a marvelous new world full of young people, wide and open spaces, and new things to learn. From time to time, though, I remember having awful nightmares about Cuba and the difficult times I had endured there. The nightmares lasted for years. I had some academic problems during my first semester, but by the second term my English had improved considerably, and I was doing fine.

The mid-sixties were incredibly rich in terms of experiences for young people. Because of my extroverted personality, I had made many friends from different nationalities and cultures. Those years were also dominated by the "hippie" culture and a sense of freedom and experimentation. I shared my free time with two totally different groups. I spent much of my time with Cubans and other Latinos, but I also shared many experiences with my "hippie" friends. It was fun to be around them, but we did not really have a philosophical or cultural affinity and started to drift apart. Within the Cuban group, I found my real friends. We were almost like a large family. Several had left Cuba at a relatively young age (some without their parents) as part of Operation Peter Pan. I think that was the primary reason why we were so close and had an implicit support group. We really needed each other, more than we believed. Those who had families invariably offered the support of their families to the others. I remember spending precious holidays, such as Thanksgiving and Christmas, at the home of one of my best friends. It was always a bit sad to stay behind when the campus was empty and everyone had gone home. Some of us didn't have a home to go to. Later on, I tried to help others who were a bit disoriented (like I had been) and did not know about the opportunities we could avail ourselves of to get an education and succeed.

Looking back (from 1962, when I arrived in Urbana, to 1970, when I finished my doctorate), I can see that my passion for the Cuban cause, if we can call it that, diminished considerably. This doesn't mean that Cuba was no longer important to me, for it was. I carried Cuba within my heart and often got into arguments with some of the "intellectuals" who plagued college campuses during those years and regarded Castro as some sort of a mythical hero. I think the reason why I felt less passionately toward Cuba was that I had intuitively come to the realization that my future was being forged here in a new land and environment that were both very attractive to me, and to which I was very grateful. In essence, I was adapting to a new way of life. Notice that I use the term "adapting," because I believe that I was becoming part of that culture, but the culture was not becoming a part of me. I have always had some reservations about the term "melting pot" in reference to the coalescence of the many cultures that form part of our country here in the United States. I do not believe that cultures have really melted in that cauldron, nor that it would be a good thing if they had. At any rate, inside that melting pot I was an ingredient that absorbed the broth but did not melt. As for my diminishing passion for the Island, I think that I still felt that my Cuba, the Cuba of my memories, was within reach. Cuba had not changed, as it now has, and I could still "return" to her through my vivid memories, in conversations with friends, in a Proustian remembrance of faces, songs, smells, words, and landscapes. Also, and perhaps more importantly, I still had the hope of a physical return to Cuba, a return that could validate those remembrances and confirm that Cuba was not lost. I guess that one can only become impassioned when the object of one's affection is lost forever; and later, hopefully, acceptance painfully sets in. I strongly believe that if a political change had occurred in Cuba during the years prior to my marriage, I would have returned without a doubt. The possibility of going back, of returning to a time and a place that could be validated by my memories, and vice versa, was important to me then. Now I understand why. When the social and political reality in the evolution of a country no longer conforms with the memories of an exile, there is no longer hope, for there is no possibility of returning. If one does return under those conditions, it is to continue being an exile, a wanderer in the land where one saw the light for the first time. In this sense, an exile is truly a *desterrado*, a person whose roots have been forcefully pulled from the ground and for whom, at least in my case, there is no returning. What makes the life of an exile tragic is the yearning to fill the void of an absence with hope and nostalgia. The first one to disappear is hope. Nostalgia never leaves us; it just fades away with us. This, I believe, is our tragedy—or perhaps I should say, my tragedy.

I cannot tell exactly when or how the passion that I now feel for Cuba and Cuban things started to regenerate. It was, I believe, a long and complex process of maturation and reflection, of self-discovery, of cultural reidentification, of search and recovery, and lastly, of close examination of the roots that we all carry within ourselves. There is usually something that serves as a trigger for the chain reaction of this complex process. In my case, as I reflect upon the possible causes, I identify two key factors.

First, aging always brings a sense of nostalgia for times and places gone by. An exile is considerably more vulnerable to nostalgia because it is a mechanism that enables him/her to fill that void, that absence, that I mentioned before. Nostalgia also allows the exile, in another way, to assume an objective view of his/her cultural heritage, to separate myth from reality, to dive into his/her own soul in search of his/her cultural identity, while at the same time validating his/her findings in the history of his/her country. Once this has been accomplished, the exile is in a better position to examine his/her "exilic" experience.

After analyzing my experience retrospectively, I have come to the realization that I have never been truly integrated into this culture. At times, and perhaps as a necessary defense mechanism, I have led myself to believe that my level of integration was more solid or stronger than it really was. This mechanism of self-deceit was necessary to compensate for my daily existence in a world that, albeit attractive and generous, was still foreign. A world where I had to adopt a language and a culture that were not my own—a difference that many members of that world respected, others tolerated, and some flatly rejected. I would like to end this thought on a positive note. In spite of its shortcomings, this is a great country, a generous country. I have learned many things here, things that I am sure I could not have learned if I had never been an exile. As painful as those experiences have been at times, I believe that I am a better human being because of them. I have incorporated many elements of this culture into those that I was fed through my mother's milk. As a result, my cultural horizons are now considerably wider.

If nostalgia has been one of the factors in my evolution, the other factor is the thirty-two years I have been married to my beloved wife. She has brought to our marriage a very strong cultural heritage. Her personality and character reflect the cultural mores of the Cuban women of her generation. Her loyalty, kindness, maternal and caring instinct, her support, and above all, her unwavering Cubanness have been important factors in the evolutionary process that I have outlined above. It was at her insistence, while living in cultural isolation in Nebraska, that we made our first trip together to Miami in 1973, when she was pregnant with our first child. I had not returned to Miami since 1962, when I left for the University of Illinois. That visit was an extraordinary experience that can only be compared to a return to Cuba. We met with relatives who had left Cuba during the interim and rediscovered many friends, and through them made many more friends. Cuban culture was in the air, in the music, in the words of the people in the streets, in their mannerisms, in the recreations that Cubans had made in their little enclaves. That first visit awoke in me an insatiable appetite for Cuban culture, which was whetted more and more by every visit.

Although the Miami of today can hardly be compared with any city in the Cuba we remember, it is a place where Cubans do not have to assume an identity or a language foreign to their culture. There, an exile has a choice to be one, the other, or both, and to communicate using English, Spanish, or both languages—this is a key point. For my wife and me, Miami has been a cultural haven where we have been able to resort to nostalgia in order to fill our void, that absence to which I referred earlier. On the other hand, it has provided us with invaluable social, intellectual, and cultural experiences that have enabled us to contrast myth with reality and arrive at a clearer understanding of who and what we are. Our marriage and the experiences that we have had together have undoubtedly nourished our roots, thus making them and us stronger. We now have two adult children who speak Spanish and are proud of their Cuban roots. They believe that their upbringing, speaking both languages and moving in two cultures, has widened their horizons and given them richer experiences.

I would not like to end these thoughts without addressing my feelings for that Island that is still called Cuba. To simplify my feelings as much as possible, I would have to compare them with those of a husband whose wife has been unfaithful. Divorced and living apart, he thinks of her every day, hating her new lover and asking himself if a reconciliation is possible. Is it possible to forgive, forget, and rekindle the passion that was there before? How much is he, through his own nostalgia, idealizing the past? Today, I am convinced that the Cuba I remember no longer exists. Cuba is decaying both morally and physically. There, the structures are crumbling down; while here, my memories are beginning to fade, just as old pictures do in family albums. There is no return either to a time or to a place. If there is any hope for the future, it is to be found in our own history—the history that has been erased from the memory of Cubans still living on the Island. The new foundation, if one can be built, must be erected on our common past, on the basis of our history, of our roots, and of our culture. Adjustments will have to be made in the nation and in the diaspora, but these will only be successful if the voices of our history can rescue from oblivion the common past that will open into the future and, hopefully, into a new space wide enough for all of us to fit.

Milan Kundera, in his extraordinary novel *The Book of Laughter and Forgetting*, summarizes a conversation with his friend Milan Hubl. Those words pertain as much to Cuba today as they did to Czechoslovakia after the Russian invasion. Hubl, a historian, said, "The first step in liquidating a people … is to erase its memory. Destroy its books, its culture, its history. Then have somebody write new books, manufacture a new culture, invent a new history. Before long the nation will begin to forget what it is and what it was. The world around it will forget even faster."

The "Sandwich" Generation

Sara Rosell

Born in Banes in 1957, Sara Rosell moved to Havana with her family at ten years of age. She left Cuba at twenty-two in May 1980 as part of the Mariel Boatlift. She lives in Cedar Falls, Iowa.

For me, exile is a constant sailing, physical and emotional, between both sides. Before living through geographical exile, for many years I was in exile while still living on the Island. In fact, I believe that ostracism is almost a precondition to geographical exile. During those years, I lived the departure through every friend that left, the same way that I now live the return, because for the exile leaving or returning becomes, to some extent, a collective act.

The Revolution triumphed when I was two years old. I belong to what I call the "sandwich" generation—the generation that grew up between the Catholic bourgeois and the generation that hoped for a different future (although the latter generation is not exempt from the characteristics of the former, as time has shown). We were affected, therefore, by both fronts. My generation is that of the experiment—the first pioneers, the first farming schoolchildren, the first militants of the Communist Youth Organization, the first to learn Russian, the first to leave after the *gusanos*. The frustrated generation; the one out of step. Many of us could never comprehend how one could think of a different Cuba when everyone, from our families up to the highest leaders, refused to change. Our generation was denied the opportunity to really grow within the new system. The Revolution never put its trust in us, despite the slogans that proclaimed that it did. In a matter of days, we were regarded as the "scum," though months before we were applauded in the Square of the Revolution and were portrayed on newscasts all over the world as the example of the new Cuban youth.

I could have been just one more number in the statistics of prisoners and insane people who arrived in the States from the port of Mariel. If I wasn't, it's because I didn't tell the entire truth about my homosexuality. And I didn't tell the truth not because I suspected that there would be a surge of negative propaganda following our arrival, but because I was afraid that my declaration could be taken out of context and I might be forced to go back to Cuba. For although it is true that a percentage of the *Marielitos* came directly from prisons and hospitals, it is no less true that an even larger percent had, at some point, been in both places during their lifetimes. What homosexual in Cuba during the '70s wasn't the victim of a police raid or didn't end up in a psychiatrist's office? The police raided us, and our families sent us to the psychiatrist.

Homosexuality in Cuba is a sin, an insult, a provocation, a threat, and an impediment. At the age of fifteen, I already knew that I could never be part of the Communist Youth Organization; that I probably would not be allowed to go to college; and that almost all of my family would reject me. When I first had a sexual relationship with a woman at sixteen, I knew that in the future I would have to leave Cuba. Out of those six years of waiting, I spent the first three trying to "change." I call it the "psychiatric phase." The last three years were spent in the street, and many times in the *calabozos* or police stations, because I had given up trying, and now it was only a matter of surviving and waiting.

In 1975, the psychiatrist at the hospital on Santa Catalina Street in La Víbora told me he had a "cure" for me. He explained that what I needed was a man like him, who could make me feel that my life from then on would be different. I told him to go to hell; and he sent me to Gali García Psychiatric Hospital. I was in the hospital for a month; then one day the assistant to the psychiatrist, surprised to see me there, released me as an outpatient. For almost a year, I was on a daily experimental treatment of insulin. The treatment consisted of injecting the patient with insulin until a low level of blood sugar provoked some sort of shock to the nervous system. Once the patient was on the verge of collapsing, she was injected with glucose in order to regain her balance. With this treatment, it was expected that the patient would have a good night, eat well, not think, and sleep. Apart from having a medical record at the psychiatric hospital, the actual long-term result of these treatments is living for the rest of my life with weight and blood sugar problems.

The year of the World Youth Festival (1978) was the year of the police raids. We were caught in the street, at the bus stop, in a coffee shop, coming out of the movies, or at the carnival. In short, you could be caught anywhere and for no reason, just because you "looked" like a homosexual—something that was worse in Cuba than actually being homosexual. The only way to avoid being raided by the police was to stay home and not participate in the Festival—one of the few events in the '70s that gave one the opportunity to find out what was happening in the arts around the world. That year my friends and I spent many nights sleeping in the *calabozos* of Havana. The conditions of the stations depended on where you had been caught. For me, the worst was the one in Guanabo; the best, relatively speaking, was the one in El Cerro.

A few months before the Mariel Boatlift, I was detained for three days in El Cerro. Out of all my experiences, those were the most difficult days of all because the lieutenant insisted on taking disciplinary action against me, which meant that I could face two to four years in prison. There, I met Margarita. She was anxiously waiting to be taken to Nuevo Amanecer, the women's prison. She had just been released from prison only two weeks before; a few days after her release, she went to a restaurant, didn't pay her bill, broke a table, and hit a policeman. She did all that just to be at her lover's side in prison—the only place, ironically, where she could attain greater sexual liberty. Today, Margarita might also be included in the list of criminal *Marielitos*. Somehow disciplinary action was never brought against me; the opening of the port of Mariel took me by surprise while I was in the street, the place where I had spent the last two or three years.

In April, after the storming of the Peruvian Embassy, my lover and I reported to the police station in La Víbora. There, we told them all the incriminating details about ourselves that we could think of—we told them everything they wanted to hear. As a result, they gave us a permit to leave the country that same day.

I waited for my departure at my lover's house. On the 16th of May, a policeman came with a summons at two o'clock in the morning, thus sparing me from becoming the target of the acts of repudiation I had witnessed so many times during those days. I took a taxi to Cuatro Ruedas; and as we drove past the corner of Diez de Octubre and Coco, I waved and sent a telepathic good-bye to my mother, who at that moment was working the night shift at Acción Médica Hospital. It was the most painful moment of my departure.

The night of May 17, 1980, I slept on a ship anchored at the Port of Mariel. To spend the night there was like being in limbo, like having one foot here and one foot there. I was afraid both to leave and to stay; afraid that something unplanned would happen and force me to walk the dock back to the place I had not yet left; afraid that nothing would happen and the ship would start moving in search of something that only existed in my dreams. I was twenty-two and was leaving my entire family behind. Only my lover was going to be on one of the other ships—or perhaps she wasn't on any one of them. I sat on the floor, leaning against a wall in the bow with my head between my knees, and cried until I fell asleep. That night, I could not imagine that for years I would feel the same feeling, the same anxiety of that moment; I could not imagine that somehow that night would mark my experience of exile.

The night of the 18th of May, our boat arrived at the coast of Florida. There is no need to talk about the trip. Suffice it to say that ever since that trip, I try to avoid getting on a boat. Two days later, I found my lover in a refugee camp, and that same day we were taken to Indiantown, Pennsylvania, where I spent three months waiting to be sponsored. In Miami, my lover and I reunited again, only to break up a few months later. I have not seen her since, in spite of all the years we were together.

The saddest thing about exile is, precisely, its ability to destroy what one regards as being everlasting. In Cuba, the hope that one day we could live together, work and live without fear, kept us together. In 1980 we achieved almost everything we wanted (I say almost everything because it has taken me years to lose my fear), and we couldn't take the reality of so much change.

I bought a plane ticket to Iowa City, Iowa, where some friends were arranging for me to go to college. Then I began my studies and didn't stop until I graduated with a doctoral degree in 1995. I lived in Iowa City longer than I had in any other place during my whole life. (Of the twenty-two years I lived in Cuba, I spent half of my time in Oriente and the other half in Havana.) I think of Iowa City as my hometown. The years that I spent teaching at a university in upstate New York following my graduation were like living a second exile. Once more I had to leave behind friends, familiar streets, my environment. Once again, I was over-taken with a sense of nostalgia; I experienced the mingled yearning to walk down Clinton Avenue or Prado to Coppelia or the Great Midwestern. Moreover, I missed my friends from Iowa and from Cuba. In spite of these feelings, exile always gives way to continuity—to the feeling that things don't have an end, a complete and final closure. For the exile, feelings, relationships, and events never end completely because they are always determined by the knowledge of what loss means.

In over eighteen years, I have never gone back to Cuba. The first time that I saw a relative since my departure was twelve years after my arrival, even though both my cousin and I came to the U.S. at the same time. During the three days of our visit, we did nothing but talk. Now, after the arrival of the *balseros* [rafters] and the events at Guantánamo, many of my friends and half of my family on my mother's side are in the United States. However, so much time has gone by that things are no longer the same. Once again, I feel as though I belong to yet another "sandwich" generation in yet another exile. For years, I heard many Cubans who had arrived in the '60s say that we didn't know what exile really was; that we had come to a ready-made community; that we didn't have to start from scratch and go through what they had gone through. The *balseros*, on the other hand, resent our opinion because, they argue, we didn't live through the Special Period and left when "things were still good."

This situation has made my communication with both groups of exiles rather difficult. I live constantly seeking the middle ground where I can negotiate cultural, racial, and sexual issues, notwithstanding the future of the Island. These multiple mediations, which are sometimes intergenerational and at other times within my own generation, are, however, as vital to me as Cuban food. In some respects they are what makes me feel part of the exile community. The Mariel generation— the "sandwich" generation—is located between the euphoria of the triumph and the disillusionment, between the *gusanos*, the *maceítos,* and the *merenguitos*; we cannot maintain anything other than a critical position or attitude toward both the Cuban and the American governments and the Cuban community in exile. Many of us never wanted to be like El Che, the only role model offered to the Pioneers, but neither do we remember the "good times," the invasion of Bahía de Cochinos, or what Brigada Antonio Maceo represented for the second generation of Cubans in exile. Likewise, we never saw the "dollar stores," where very few are allowed in, nor did we witness Spain's incursion into the new economic scene. In spite of all the differences there might be among the various groups, we are all bonded by the nostalgia for what we left behind because, upon leaving, one way or the other, we all took the Island away "on our backs."

The inescapable reality is the fact that every exile guards an imaginary idea of Cuba, which is a product of his or her own experience. In fact, I have always believed that my yearning for the Island goes beyond my own experience and finds a place among the experiences of others; it is this that to some extent defines my condition as an exile. Many times it is difficult for me to talk about my own memories without the risk that they might be closely interwoven with the memories of others. In fact, this is the first time that I have reflected in writing on what it has meant to me to leave Cuba and live in exile. For years, I resorted to creative writing in an attempt to rearticulate the cultural repertoire of the Cuba that I have imagined in exile. Fiction has allowed me to express that feeling of both belonging and loss so common among the majority of those who have been forced to emigrate. Being in contact with other Latin communities in the United States, crossing the geographical, cultural, national, and linguistic border, has created for me a new space of negotiation between the past and the present, between the "here" and "there," and, ultimately, between fiction and reality.

(Translated by Francisco Kuhn-Bolaños)

POSTSCRIPT: Two important changes occurred in my life during the time in which I was revising this essay. Both, in certain ways, affected my thoughts regarding what constitutes exile. On the one hand, I have made a kind of return—if not to Cuba, to Iowa, a place that I regard as my second home. On the other hand, my mother died after eighteen years of waiting and exhausting every available avenue to join me in the United States. Without a doubt, this work has turned into a tribute to her memory.

The Thirteenth Suitcase

An Interview with Efraín J. Ferrer and Vivian de la Incera

Efraín J. Ferrer was born in Consolación del Sur, Pinar del Río, in 1951, and his wife, Vivian de la Incera, born in 1954, was raised in Matanzas. They defected from Moscow, Russia, in August 1990, resided for a brief period in Madrid, Spain, and finally arrived in the United States in February 1991. They currently live in Dunkirk, New York.

In some sense I have been preparing for exile my whole life. I was seven years old when the revolution started; Vivian was four. From the very beginning, my family and I witnessed the horrors of Castro's regime. My cousin, who was openly against the government while at the University of Havana, was arrested and sent to a prison on Isla de Pinos at the age of twenty-two; he was murdered in cold blood when they caught him trying to escape eight years later. He had just turned thirty.

During the early years of the revolution, most of my family left the Island. Some of my relatives wanted to take me with them to the States, but my parents wouldn't allow them to do so; they didn't want us to be separated. They had decided to stay behind mostly because my father was already in his sixties when the revolution started; he knew that it would be impossible to start over again in the United States with two small children. In addition he, like so many others, was certain that Fidel would be toppled within a year or so.

In Cuba at that time, there were only two options for males when they reached the age of fifteen or sixteen: either you were sent to the military, or you became an intern at one of the schools in Havana, where you were simultaneously educated in the sciences and humanities and indoctrinated in the new Marxist-Leninist ideology. As a result, in 1964 I entered Raúl Cepero Bonilla, a special high school located on the grounds of a former Marist private school in La Víbora, Havana. I, along with two hundred of the brightest students from all over the Island, was selected to study there as a result of my academic grades. In that school I, along with my classmates, was being molded to become one of the country's future leaders; in theory, we were the future elite, the "new men and women" of whom Che Guevara dreamed.

Although we were cloistered like priests in the school, we were allowed to go out on Saturdays and Sundays. I remember going home one weekend only to find out that my cousin had been shot. When I returned to school that following Sunday evening, I had to conceal my suffering and my sadness. I wasn't allowed to attend his funeral because my parents would have had to take me out of school, and this would have marked me as being sympathetic to a political dissident, which means that I would not have been able to continue my studies. Having witnessed so much hate and horror, I was filled with terror at the thought that my peers, many of whom were the children of the "new class" (which was composed of the new political leaders), would find me out. Of course, there were people who felt like I did; in time, I learned to read between the lines and figure out who was really against the government, but I never dared to speak openly with them about it. What I remember most about my childhood was fear and the lack of freedom. My only sanctuary from fear was my parents' home, with its walled garden. For me, those walls shut out the world of politics and repression.

In Cuba, you have to learn to live with a mask on; over the years, the mask grows thicker and thicker. Even as a child, I began to feel somewhat schizophrenic—it was as though there was one person inside me and an entirely different person outside. For example, when I would return home for winter break from school, we would set up a crèche and an artificial Christmas tree, which my mother kept hidden away in a closet, out of view in a back room (as you know, we were forbidden to celebrate Christmas after 1969). The memory of me in my school uniform, which resembled a military outfit, hanging ornaments on the tree is still a painful reminder of my inner turmoil. At school, I was even more tormented by the fact that I was miserable and all of my class-mates, who seemed to accept everything without question, were happy.

During my years at the University of Havana, my terror increased after I witnessed *las depuraciones*—the mandatory gatherings at which students who had been selected ahead of time were singled out and denounced for their presumably dissident views or "antisocial" behavior. It was like the Inquisition. One of Vivian's classmates, for example, was thrown out of school because he wore blue jeans—a symbol of Ameri-can capitalism, he was told—and because he listened to The Beatles; others were denounced because they had long hair (like the hippies in the States) or simply because they were openly Christian. We were also made to fill out forms that required that we reply to questions such as whether or not we believed in God; did we have family in exile; if so, did we communicate with them, etc. I was always filled with fear at the thought that they would find out about my family in exile and my political position—day and night, I lived in terror. Those who were in-tegrated into the *Juventud Comunista* [the Young Communists] lorded over the rest of us; they were always trying to bully and intimidate us. From early childhood, you were made to feel as though you were living in a country divided into two classes, and that you belonged to the lower class. In such a system, hatred and intimidation are the engines that move society. As a result, you feel unprotected and very vulnerable.

Though I did go to meetings, I was in the *guardia* [guard], and I cut cane, I was never a Pioneer or a Young Communist. Even though I was once told while riding a bus that I had been selected for denounce-ment at the *depuración*, no one ever bothered me, probably because I took a vow of silence and never spoke about my true feelings. I was completely apathetic, without illusions or hope; I knew that change was impossible in Cuba.

There is one particular event, which I witnessed as a kid, that encapsulates for me just how primitive the ideology that my classmates supported with unquestioning obedience was. A *juicio popular* [a popular court] was set up in the middle of my town to try a group of political dissidents who were hiding a counterrevolutionary in the surrounding hills. I can still hear them screaming, "*al paredón*" [to the wall]. They killed every one of them. I'm telling you, the Cuba that I left was a hell; as they say on the Island, *Cuba es una gran cárcel y su última gálera es la calle* [Cuba is a big jail, and its last cell is the street].

In self-defense, I threw myself into my studies and dedicated myself to math and physics. The pursuit of my studies—which was officially condoned by the government—became my refuge and my escape, for the sciences represented for me the only thing that remained apart from politics and ideology.

Vivian and I met in one of the old halls of the central library at Havana University; we got married in 1976. Although the material conditions in Russia were horrendous, when we were sent to the Soviet Union in 1984, we experienced more freedom than we had ever had in our lives together. Arriving just a year before Gorbachev introduced the concept of *Perestroika*, we not only benefited from the gradual changes in Russia but, among other things, we were alone together for the first time since we had been married (in Cuba, both personal and public spaces are always shared and surveyed). In addition, the Cuban government had considerably less control over us, primarily because there was no CDR [Committee for the Defense of the Revolution] in Moscow. Also, at the Lebedev Institute we were surrounded by first-rank scientists; many, such as Sakharov (who was working at the Institute after Gorbachev released him from Gorki), were openly opposed to communism. More fundamentally, however, the Institute was like an intellectual monastery—a space where our cultural differences could co-exist and a space that promoted unfettered collaboration and a sense of intellectual community. In addition to experiencing the freedom of being geographically dislocated from Cuba in that privileged, isolated space, we felt as though we were immune to dominance and authority.

Nevertheless, Vivian and I continued to dream about escaping to the United States, a place that had special meaning for me because my father had attended a preparatory school in Pennsylvania and then went on to study at Cornell University. His stories, coupled with the fact that we grew up being taught that America was the land of freedom, made me long for this country. The opportunity to escape presented itself thanks to *Perestroika*. Taking a huge risk, Vivian confided in an American physicist and his wife, whom I had met some days before in Helsinki, by asking them what was the safest route to take if we were to defect. A year later, at a conference, we saw this man again; he suggested that the best plan of escape was through Hungary because Austro-Hungarian relations were very good at the time and, as a result, the borders were virtually open. In preparation for our escape, we traveled to Helsinki University (where we had been invited to work) in June 1990. We filled our suitcases with cheese and sausage and Russian black bread in an attempt to save the money we were receiving from the university. On the 8th of August, 1990, we bought three train tickets to Hungary. Thinking that we would be detained indefinitely in an Austrian refugee camp, we packed thirteen suitcases with clothes, assorted toiletries such as soap and toothpaste, which we had stock-piled, a samovar, the Bible, and some of our physics books and our more important calculations—can you imagine: we defected from Moscow with thirteen suitcases! Because we had no visa, we were taken off the train (along with our thirteen suitcases) at the Austro-Hungarian border and had to travel back to Budapest, where we asked for help at the American Embassy. (We had so many suitcases that the guard at the gate mistook us for ambassadors!) We remained for a week in Budapest, waiting for the visa, which eventually would send us to Madrid. We were absolutely terrified at the thought that we would be caught; as a result, we spoke nothing but Russian. This was, perhaps, the longest and most stressful week of our lives. After spending six months in Madrid, we finally got permission to come to the United States in February 1991.

I have few regrets about anything in my life. All of life's experiences, including the most adverse, eventually enrich you and make you more human. As a result of my experiences, I have developed a kind of transcultural perspective, which allows me to appreciate and be receptive to all cultures. I am a little of everywhere I have been. I feel that I am part of all the world.

Unlike Efrain, I was raised in a family that supported the revolution. Though my grandfather was imprisoned during the invasion of Playa Girón and my aunt, who was a high school teacher, decided to defect in 1965 when government officials replaced the textbooks in her classroom and insisted that she teach what she refers to as "the official version of history according to Marx and Lenin," this part of my family history was never discussed at home. It was erased in my early childhood, probably because my aunts and grandfather were afraid to express their discontent in front of the children, and later because my mother married a high-ranking government official. I was also influenced by one of her maternal aunts, who still remains passionately devoted to the revolution. The revolution was, and still is, her religion.

As a direct result of my upbringing, coupled with the fact that the overtly repressive measures that characterized the '60s in Cuba were largely conducted behind closed doors by the time I reached early adulthood, I grew up largely unaware of the horrors that my husband witnessed firsthand. I was completely naïve as a student at the University of Havana. Unlike Efrain, I believed in the ideals of the revolution and, moreover, was convinced that change was possible. However, even as a child I was aware that something was not right. It wasn't that I thought that Fidel was bad; we were led to believe that the problems in Cuba were the fault of his officials. In truth, the machinery of repression was manifest everywhere you looked. For example, when I was in grammar school it became apparent to me that mediocre students could succeed by demonstrating their fanatical devotion to the regime. *Ganabas méritos a través de la política* [you gained merit through your politics]. Even though I had been promoted and was two years younger than my classmates, the *militante* [political peer and mentor] who was assigned to look after me and see to my "political growth" accused me of being "politically immature" simply because I was openly critical of those around me. She said I wasn't militant enough and that even though I was just a child, I had not demonstrated that I could be "vigilant" over others.

Despite my discontent, I succeeded as a result of my high grades. In my third year at the University of Havana, I was accused once again of political immaturity, due to the fact that I openly challenged the system and associated with a group of "apathetic" peers who were not "militant enough" or visibly supportive of the regime. If not for my stepfather's intervention, I would have been thrown out of the university after openly defending a friend during a *depuración*. (Though they blamed my friend's expulsion on the fact that she was regularly late for her obligatory work at the factory—due to her long commute to the city from her home in Bauta—the real reason she was thrown out was because she was a silent *gusana*, who also happened to be religious.)

Despite all that I had witnessed, I remained skeptical and unconvinced when Efrain told me about the atrocities he had witnessed. I could not believe that people had been murdered and tortured in the ways that he described. I did not realize the magnitude of corruption and the absolute lack of freedom until I was forced, along with other non-militant students, to enter the *militancia* [the Union of Young Communists]. This was the outcome of a new government policy, which slowed down the purging and, instead, pressured all the nonconformists (those who were "noisy" as opposed to openly dissident) to enter into the *militancia*. In the *militancia*, we were led to believe that we could openly complain all we wanted; in reality, however, we were tightly controlled from the inside, and our opinions and views were squelched. Ultimately, we were silenced.

Though we had virtually given up on the idea of escaping, our hope was briefly rekindled in 1980 by the prospect of being able to leave Cuba as part of the Mariel Boatlift. Although Efrain's uncle was told that he could take only one family member, we still remained hopeful when we saw that people were actually leaving the Island. Before Mariel there were no options, no doors. When we realized that we would not be leaving, that the curtain had fallen back down again, we lost all hope. We felt desperate with disappointment. It was as though we were suffocating.

For me, the absolute turning point was when we were in Moscow. Although I, too, enjoyed the relative degree of freedom that we experienced there and regarded the Institute as a kind of intellectual sanctuary, the realization that we were nothing more than slaves to the communist regime hit me when our son, Efraincito, became ill. The doctor who took care of him insisted that he attend a nearby Russian public school, rather than the Cuban Embassy school, which was quite a long distance from home. In response, the Cuban ambassador stepped in and indirectly made it clear to us that he alone had the right to decide where Efraincito would go to school. Then he turned around and publicly insinuated that we were more devoted to our work than to our family and suggested that we were negligent parents who didn't know how to properly care for our child. Though we had long since given up the dream that most married couples have of owning a home, in that moment I realized that as a Cuban citizen I did not have the right to fulfill my role as a mother. In other words, I could neither protect nor freely care for my child. For me, this epitomized the degree of oppression and the lack of freedom that Castro's regime represented. Though I did not dare to say this aloud, I began to ask myself, "Am I going to raise my child to be a hypocrite; to teach him to be a liar and force him to wear a mask?"

We didn't realize the degree of terror and repression we had experienced until we arrived in the United States. We all underwent very severe culture shock, and it took us quite a while to recuperate from the trauma we had experienced. For example, it took us a long time to get used to even the most basic freedoms that every American takes for granted, such as the idea that we could travel wherever we wanted without asking for permission, or that we could actually make decisions for ourselves. To give you an example, while sitting at the bar at the Fountainbleau Hotel in Miami, Efrain was expecting to be asked to leave because in Cuba, entrance to hotels and certain beaches was—and still is—reserved for foreign tourists.

Though we stayed with relatives in Miami until 1993, we were very anxious to move. We couldn't bear to even talk about Cuba; as you know, in Miami that is the only topic of conversation among Cuban exiles. In addition, we realized that the Island we had left behind was not the idealized place that our relatives abandoned in the early '60s. The differences among us were marked. In their view, we were "*rosaditos*" (pinkos), while they had left Cuba before communism had fully taken hold. In effect, we had come from two completely different worlds.

Although we realize that it's not perfect here in the United States (we have witnessed racism and sexism firsthand and have repeatedly experienced what we call intellectual discrimination or jealousy in the workplace), we love the United States and have made it our home because above anything else, it is a country where in theory everyone has equal rights; and when this does not happen in practice, there are always conscious people who have the right to protest. For us, perhaps the most painful thing about exile is being separated from our aging parents and our extended families; the worst experience was when Efrain's brother grew ill with cancer and he could not return to Cuba, for fear of being captured, and be at his side when he died. Though we carry the pain of Cuba on our backs like a cross, time and distance have enabled us to appreciate our culture and our roots—our *patria* [country], as opposed to Castro's *gobierno* [government]. Though we have become American citizens and have benefited from the opportunities here and the various cultural experiences, we will always be Cuban more than anything else. We have learned that you don't have to live in Cuba to be Cuban. Rather, being Cuban is a state of mind—a very particular way of seeing the world, with humor and *alegría* [joy]. Nevertheless, we love both Cuba and the United States; when you have two children (even though one is adopted), how can you love one child more than the other? (February 9, 1999)

(Interview conducted and translated by Andrea O'Reilly Herrera)

Sin calcetines

An Interview with Enrique Patterson

Born in 1950 in San Andrés, Enrique Patterson left the Island in 1992. He currently resides in North Miami with his family.

My father was quite a personality in San Andrés—the town where I was born in 1950—in part because he was an outsider who had established a factory, which supplied shoes not only to the community but to the stores in the city. My mother gave classes in our home to children; she taught them to read and write. What was most extraordinary—considering the time period—was the fact that my parents were Black. Because of their many sacrifices, my family lived well. It was expected, however, that Blacks should be on a lower economic level than Whites. Because my father was an exception, the people of the town began to "whiten" him a little, something like the *limpiezas de sangre* in colonial Spain. The townspeople would tell us that we really weren't all that Black, and they took to calling me mulatto. One day, as we were walking in the park, my father heard someone call me mulatto. It was one of the only times that I saw him lose his temper—I'll never forget it. He turned to me and said, "You're Black; don't let anyone call you anything else." My father, who was associated with (though did not fully embrace) the Communist Party, was really the one who taught me to be conscious of race and class; he was the one who encouraged me to stand up for myself. He helped me shape my identity.

My father lost everything after his shoe factory burned to the ground in 1953; the cause of the fire is still a mystery. Soon after, we moved to Camagüey. I remember the war against Batista very well because in the little town where we lived with my grandmother in San Andrés, the rural guard had an unspoken agreement with the rebel soldiers. The guard patrolled the streets during the day and allowed the rebels in at night; they would come into the houses around eleven o'clock to have coffee and eat. I remember this well. I also remember when Batista's army sent an armed column of men to sack the town. They raided all the goods and murdered many of those who stayed behind attending the stores in cold blood. I spent three days hidden away with my family. Since I was only eight years old at the time, it was like a big adventure for me, even though everyone around me was crying and filled with fear.

I was nine years old when the revolution triumphed. Although there were no laws that segregated Blacks and Whites in Cuba before the revolution, everyone was conscious of the color line. There were many places we could not go—though nothing was ever said, this was something everyone understood. To give you an example, my grandmother lived in the country, and every now and then there would be parties. The Whites in the neighborhood would put up a rope [*una soga*]. They would dance on one side, and the Blacks would dance on the other; the rope was meant to keep us from crossing over. Whites, however, could cross to our side. In some sense, the rope was a symbol of the racist ideology that had become embedded in Cuban society since the conquest.

Although many people do not know this, very few Blacks fought in the rebel army; race was not part of the agenda for the 26 of July Movement. Like most Blacks, however, my family supported Fidel at the outset of the revolution; we believed that he would fulfill the promise he made before the revolution to restore democracy and, following the triumph, improve conditions for Blacks in Cuba. At first, things seemed to get better; Fidel eliminated the segregation that existed in many public places, and Blacks were mixed into the *masa* [dough]. Yet we soon began to realize things were not as good as they seemed. For example, before the revolution Blacks had their own societies where they could gather together to talk about their problems. After the revolution, Black organizations were formally disbanded. Although Fidel had theoretically dissolved all organizations, groups such as the Gallegos, the Cataláns, and the Jews continued to meet, and the Chinese still had their newspapers. No one interfered with them. The official version or rationale was that since the regime had "eliminated" discrimination, there was no reason for anyone to have a separate organization. By breaking up these gatherings, including those attended by the Black communists (many of whom were middle class), Fidel (who had allied with the Russian communists, as opposed to the Cubans) later prevented Blacks from assuming leadership roles in the revolutionary party. This was a very subtle form of discrimination to which no one could object because if you protested, you were regarded as a counterrevolutionary. In truth, Fidel was afraid of the Blacks who had begun to gain a voice before the revolution.

To give you another example, before the revolution there were no Blacks working in the banks or the department stores or any public offices in Havana. In the early years of the revolution, Fidel saw to it that a number of Blacks were strategically placed in jobs that had previously been reserved for Whites. However, they were not in high-power positions. Blacks were also given academic scholarships; even though they could study with fewer sacrifices, once the regime had solidified its power, it gradually became apparent that Blacks did not advance at the same pace or to the same levels as Whites. I know this for a fact because when I was a professor of the history of philosophy at the University of Havana, I was the only Black person in my department— the only Black person! So although it appeared as though conditions were changing for Black Cubans, in reality, Fidel maintained the same balance or distribution of power along class and race lines that had been in place before the revolution. Today, White Cubans who are receiving dollars from exiled relatives living in the States make up the middle class; the only Blacks in Cuba who are making it into the middle class are the musicians and the athletes. Cuba has come full circle, and history has repeated itself, for a classist, racist system is firmly in place once again. In my view, Fidel has set up the next conflict in Cuba, but this time race and class will be the central issues.

Although my mother continued to be a Fidelista, my father began to lose faith in the revolution early. My disillusionment and the beginning of my psychological or interior exile began when I was only sixteen years old; it was a process that began when I started to get tired of the racist treatment to which I had been exposed since my early childhood. I had gone to Havana alone at the age of fifteen as part of my training at the military high school Héroes de Yaguajay. Finding that the environment was too rigid and controlled, I accepted a scholarship to Alfredo López, a graphic arts technical school. Because I had no home in Havana, I lived at the school seven days a week. During my tenure there (from 1966–'68), I refused to take part in many of the activities in which other boys participated. I preferred to read and to be alone. They began referring to me as the Black boy who spent the entire day reading. My behavior prompted the teachers to treat me differently. I also refused to ingratiate myself with the White principal by cleaning his car (he always used Black students to do this) or playing dominoes or laughing at his jokes. In other words, I refused to be subservient or submissive or to behave the way Blacks were expected to behave. As a result, the principal did everything in his power to keep me from graduating. Do you know what it is to have aspirations, to be independent and believe in your own capabilities, and to find that you are faced with all kinds of limitations?

The real blow to my faith in the revolution came in 1968, the year that witnessed the implementation of the *ofensiva revolucionaria* (which terminated all private activity in the city and, therefore, marked the moment when socialism established its stronghold in Cuba and, as a result, prompted the beginning of the great hunger) and the Czechoslovakian crisis. At the outset of the crisis, Fidel did not take a position; eventually, however, he supported the Russians. I happened to be in favor of the Czechs. Once Fidel made his stance clear, we were assembled at the graphic arts technical school to publicly condemn the Czechs. (By that time I was a member of the Young Communists.) When my turn came to speak, I criticized the Russian invasion of Czechoslovakia and said that the Russians were imbeciles. Then I went on to say that Fidel was wrong and had made a mistake.

As you can imagine, I was immediately expulsed from the Young Communists, and from that time forward I was labeled as having "ideological problems" and was punished for my disobedience. Not only was I let go from every position I had, but I was eliminated as a possible candidate to receive a scholarship to study in Germany and banned from traveling anywhere outside of Cuba. At one point, when I worked at a print shop, I was reprimanded for not wearing socks to work. (Although I was wearing shoes, I had chosen not to wear socks because of the heat.) My supervisor and the secretary of the party called me in to the office to tell me that coming to work without socks (*sin calcetines*) was tantamount to saying that there are no socks in Cuba. I politely thanked him for his guidance. The next day, I came to work without shoes. Everyone just stared at me. When my supervisor confronted me, I told him that I had come to work without shoes because there were no shoes to be had in Cuba. Needless to say, I was literally put out on the street that same day (because I had no home, I used to sleep at a shelter provided for the workers who did not have relatives in Havana). Luckily, my teachers at the high school where I was studying at the time did not communicate with my supervisor at work and, therefore, were unaware of what had happened. So I was able to continue my studies during the day, and I spent the nights sleeping on the benches in the Parque Central.

The turning point came when I was teaching at Escuela de Cuadros de Mandos Agrícolas del Partido in 1971, a secondary school in Havana that supposedly trained all of the future leaders of Cuba's agriculture. The school happened to have a very good library, so once again I spent my time reading, among other things, all of the classic philosophical texts, rather than partaking in the military activities in which my colleagues engaged. Soon I began to hear horror stories about me. I was accused of reading counterrevolutionary texts, such as Heberto Padilla's *Fuera del juego*, and of publicly defending dissidents. (To tell you the truth, I think that the real reason they were angry was that I was dating one of my colleagues and hadn't told the director of the school about our relationship—something we were expected to report. In my mind, I had a right to keep my personal affairs private.) Up to that point, I had never spoken a word against the regime in public at the school, so they really had no proof against me. Fed up with the constant persecution and the trumped-up charges that they kept inventing, I finally snapped and spoke my mind. I told them that when I came to work at ECMA, I thought it was a communist school; I soon discovered, however, that it was a monastery filled with cynical nuns and Jesuits. I went on to say that everything I had seen at the school was a lie. Even the cane (which I was sent to cut during the *zafra*, the harvesting of the cane) was dry and rotten and filled with water. In response, they called together a meeting of the *repudio*, and I was relieved of my duties at the school.

During the years that I taught at the University of Havana (1973–1981) the police kept raiding my house. Finally, I decided that since I was going to be persecuted no matter what I did, I might as well become a real counterrevolutionary. As a result, I decided to move to the country in 1981, where I joined two human rights groups: La Comisión Nacional de Derechos Humanos y Reconciliación Nacional and El Comité Cubano Pro Derechos Humanos. Soon after, I joined a group of eight young intellectuals (including Che Guevara's and Blas Roca's sons); together we formed La Corriente Socialista Democrática, an organization that promoted democracy and human rights. Among the eight, I was the only Negro; I am certain that because of my race, I was the first member of the group that the political police went after. As a result, I was hauled away to the station about every fifteen days. To tell the truth, I don't think they knew what to do with me—I was literally the only Black intellectual who had joined the opposition.* Rather than calling for a meeting of the *repudio*, they started a file on me (*un expediente de peligrosidad*). They accused me of being a delinquent who had a predilection for dangerous behavior. The police warned me that the next time I committed a "crime" against the government, I would be sent to jail. Knowing that I was asthmatic and that on two different occasions I had stopped breathing, they told me, "Since your North American friends are still imposing their embargo, medicine is very scarce. If you end up in jail, we won't have any to give you. Besides, medicine is for revolutionaries! We won't even have to kill you; you'll die on your own." At that point I really became scared, not because I was afraid of going to prison, but because if I was convicted as a delinquent, as opposed to a political prisoner, no one would be able to trace me.

Facing the possibility of being disappeared and forgotten, I decided to leave Cuba. In my view, dying in prison for the cause was pointless;

unlike my ancestors, I refused to be just another Black martyr. I decided to make an appointment with the American consul at the Oficina de Intereses. After looking at my record, the consul asked me why I hadn't left the Island earlier. I told him that I had always preserved the hope that if we kept fighting, change would eventually come about. "If people like me leave," I told him, "nothing will ever change at all." It will come as no surprise to hear that I had no trouble whatsoever getting permission from the U.S. office to leave the Island; in June 1992, within forty-five days of my visit to the consul, I arrived in San Francisco. I'm certain that the authorities in Cuba were convinced that I would disappear in exile. Indeed, I spent the first years here in the States trying to learn English and struggling to survive. Once I arrived in Miami, however, I began writing for *El Nuevo Herald*. At this point, I am a real thorn in the side of the regime.

In regard to life in exile, I must say that I had never felt like a minority until I arrived in the States. Here, your identity completely changes. If you can believe it, one day somebody actually asked me if I was Black, despite the fact that I am as dark as coal. I'm still not sure what they meant. In general, either people here group me with African Americans, simply because my skin is black, or I am labeled as an Hispanic, a tag that completely negates my past and the history of slavery in Cuba, the history of the war for independence against Spain, the racism during the Republic, the discrimination Blacks continue to suffer under the revolution. It's not that I have anything against Spain; on the contrary, I feel very much at home there because we share a language and have many customs in common. Nevertheless, I belong to the Blacks as a social group. But who, for that matter, can claim the patrimony of Blackness or Negritude? If I had to single out a group, I would say the Africans; but the truth of the matter is that it's a patrimony that belongs to people scattered all over the world.

Calling me Hispanic also invalidates my reasons for leaving Cuba; it negates my right to reclaim and defend my African roots. In reality, I am neither wholly Hispanic, nor am I wholly Afro-Cuban. Rather, I identify myself as a Black Cuban, a moniker that simultaneously acknowledges my African ancestry and my ties to Spain. If I am Afro-Cuban, then White Cubans should be called Hispanic Cubans, right? Of course, if Blacks had a separate language and distinct cultural practices that were set apart from White Cubans, then I could understand the label. But the reality is that both Black and White Cubans share a culture that is a syncretic blend of elements drawn from Africa and from Europe; so calling me Afro-Cuban is nothing more than a trap.

In February 1993 I relocated to Miami, where I still reside. Although I feel less like a minority here, partly because on some level all Cuban exiles share a sense of unity—not only because of a common culture but because of their opposition to Fidel—the ideological identity of Cuban exiles is characterized by certain aspects of the "American way," with its mores and work ethic. Nevertheless, the White Cuban exile community in south Florida continues to perpetuate the codes and ways of thinking about race relations that were already present on the Island before the revolution. In a word, White Cuban exiles have constructed a racial myth that virtually erases all traces of the racial discrimination that I mentioned early on. As a result, prerevolutionary Cuba is often depicted as a lost paradise characterized by prosperity and racial harmony, a notion that is frequently evidenced in the Miami press. According to this myth, Castro invented racism (of course Fidel blames the exile community for racism in Cuba). This idealized vision of Cuba before Castro exempts the Cuban exile community from taking any responsibility for the current racial tensions present in south Florida.

White upper-class Cubans' paradoxical and delusive denial that racial discrimination and classism existed on the Island, despite slavery, can only be explained by the fact that they, as a result of their heritage and consequent social status, had never experienced (or perhaps they just don't recognize) discrimination firsthand. The very concepts of racism and subordination had been naturalized from the time of the Conquest, to the point at which they became unaware that their views were racist. What I call the Spanish model of racial relations, which included the interaction among people of different races, further serves to shore up this position, for many Cubans of Hispanic origin interacted in prerevolutionary Cuba on a daily basis with people of other races. As a result, it is not unusual to hear many White Cuban exiles claim that the fact that they went to integrated public schools and that there was no legislation that discriminated against Blacks was proof that racism did not exist on the Island. In short, they don't really know what racism is.[†]

Without a doubt, White upper-class Cuban exiles suffered a shock when they arrived in south Florida and discovered signs in store windows and on buildings that read, "No Cubans. No Blacks. No Jews. No Dogs." For the first time in their experience, they became "the other" and were forced to share the same space with Blacks and Jews. The Anglo-Saxon model of race relations, which was in place in the United States until the mid-1960s, seemed brutal to them. As a result, they began to identify racism and discrimination with that model. That identification, in turn, confirmed their notion that racism or racial discrimination did not exist in Cuba but did exist in the U.S.

Clearly, racism does exist in the U.S., a fact attested to by those who could not rent in the southern regions of Miami where their White compatriots resided. However, one cannot lose sight of the fact that the Cuba of today is worse than the Cuba before the revolution in terms of the standard of living, the economy, and human rights. So anything that I say about my life in exile as a Black Cuban is relative to my experience of racism and inner exile in Cuba. Although the identities of social groups in the United States are still defined according to race and, consequently, class, in Cuba you have to fight to make race an issue; whereas here it is an acknowledged fact. Here, we have more means to improve our lot and defend ourselves; and believe me, I learned to fight for my rights in Cuba. Here, we are allowed to speak openly about our condition. (October 9, 1999)

(Interview conducted and translated by Andrea O'Reilly Herrera)

* Few Blacks had joined the opposition because, many argued, the Whites had put Fidel in power, so it was up to them to get him out.

† The success of White Cuban exiles can be attributed to many factors; among them was the fact that although Castro was able to expropriate the possessions of most of the wealthy upper class and a large portion of the middle class, he could not rob them of their skills. These skills, combined with the support of the American government and the help of the Civil Rights Movement and Affirmative Action policies, helped to elevate the White Cuban community. The fact that they were white also facilitated their assimilation into American society. These factors, combined with the consequent formation of predominantly White Cuban enclaves across the United States, also served to widen the gap between Black and White Cubans. Moreover, they allowed this first wave of exiles to re-create, with stronger ties than those they had established on the Island, the Spanish model of race relations.

Beyond Fear

An Interview with Julio J. Guerra Molina

Born in 1968 in Camagüey, in la ciudad de las tinajones, Julio J. Guerra Molina fled Cuba along with thousands of balseros (rafters). Though he left the Island in August 1994, he did not actually emigrate to the United States until April 20, 1995. He and his wife reside in Buffalo, New York.

I never dreamed of leaving Cuba the way I did. Although I was raised within the revolution and my father was in Fidel's army, by the time I was born my parents (and most of their friends) realized what was happening in Cuba. My sister and I grew up hearing my parents criticize the regime; in addition, we continued to practice Catholicism, even though it was banned. Then in 1980, my grandparents unsuccessfully tried to get into the Peruvian Embassy.

Like many young people of my generation, I was influenced by Radio Martí. Not only did they play rock 'n' roll, but they brought us news and ideas that contradicted the official version of history that we were taught. In some sense, Radio Martí made the cauldron boil for my generation.

By the time I was about thirteen years old, I already wanted to leave Cuba. When I was sixteen, I was drafted to go to Angola on a special mission. Most of my friends did not believe in the war; it was something like Vietnam for young Americans growing up in the sixties. (The truth of the matter is, Fidel kept us in the war because he needed the money— very few people know that he received from three to five dollars a day per soldier from the Soviets and the Angolans.) By that time I was working as a correspondent in the Press Department for Radio Rebelde. I had many good friends there, two of whom were killed in Angola. Somehow I was able to avoid being drafted; and at eighteen, I became the director of radio programming at Radio Nacional in Camagüey.

Aside from the fact that most people I knew were starving and Cubans were banned from having all of the things that were available to tourists, two occurrences marked the breaking point for many of us. First of all, Fidel had General Arnaldo Ochoa, who was in charge of the Angola mission, shot; then he brought home all of these empty coffins, which were supposedly filled with the remains of the soldiers who had died in battle, and made a big show out of it, claiming that he was burying them with honor. When people found out that they were empty, they went crazy. The second event that incited people's anger was when Fidel's coast guard sunk the tugboat *13 de Marzo*, which was carrying men and women fleeing the country and many children. When people heard the news, the cauldron boiled over!

By 1994, the situation in Cuba had gotten so tense that I began openly speaking to some of my friends against the government at the radio station. Regardless of the consequences, I was also very candid when visiting ballerinas and actors, who were attending local festivals, asked about what was really happening on the Island. My boss in the Press Department, who was very fond of me, warned me that if I didn't leave the Island, I would be imprisoned. He told me that he was certain that the coasts would be open soon—that something big was going to happen. The truth of the matter is, people were demonstrating all over the Island—we were sure there was going to be another revolution. In response, Fidel opened the doors and let his opponents leave, just like when he opened the port of Mariel. I can still remember when he appeared live on the television and announced that the coasts were open to anyone who wanted to leave—the coast guard would not bother them. People began making rafts out of anything they could find—*¡nos tiramos al mar!* [we threw ourselves into the sea].

On the 28th of August, 1994, at four in the afternoon, my father and I, along with eleven other acquaintances (including a three-year-old girl and several women), found a small boat with a two-cylinder engine and headed out to sea with two days' worth of water. (We had decided to leave my mother and my sister behind with the idea that we would establish ourselves in the States and then bring them over. I can still remember my mother's face when she said goodbye to us; she was almost afraid to hug us, for fear that this would be the last time.) As luck would have it, on the 29th we got caught in a storm that sent us back to Cuban shores. We were investigated for three days and then let go. (We had to hide the little girl, otherwise they wouldn't have let us go.) About the 1st of September we were intercepted by the coast guard a second time. They were verbally abusive and told us we couldn't leave. For some reason, they decided to let us go on the 7th of September; the people in the town of Baracoa, where we were detained, smuggled us sugar and fuel for our trip. Of course, they waited until a terrific storm came up to put us out to sea. The storm was so bad that we headed toward the south coast of the Island, away from Florida and toward Guantánamo. It's hard to describe what it's like to be out in the middle of the ocean in such a small boat. In addition to fighting against the rain and the wind, we were facing waves that we calculated were about five meters high. It was something fearful; I can honestly say that I have never felt death so close to me.

On the 8th of September, the feast day of la Caridad del Cobre, we prayed to the Virgin to give us safe passage; all the while, I held the two stamps my mother had given me before my departure—of the Virgin of Regla and Caridad del Cobre—in my fist. With the combined help of God and the Virgin, and the expertise of Jesús Diegues (a passenger who had been a fisherman for over thirty years), we arrived safely in Guantánamo Bay on the afternoon of the 9th of September. By that time we were exhausted, both physically and mentally, for not only had we struggled to keep afloat during the storm, but our flimsy little boat was surrounded by sharks during most of our trip. Over the course of nine days, the men had virtually gone without eating or drinking. We gave the little food we had to the women and the little girl (each man had about a mouthful of SPAM a day), and we all shared the little bit of water that was on board. Although we were all very weak, we had to row to shore because one of the lines on the motor had split; we had to strip pieces of wood from the false floor of the boat and use them as oars. Nevertheless, we were grateful to reach shore, for Fidel closed the coasts on the 12th of September.

My father and I spent about a month at Guantánamo Base; then we were sent to Base Howard in Panama, where I worked as a radio programmer for the U.S. government. After four months, we were returned to Guantánamo.

Guantánamo was filled with hard-core criminals and communist infiltrates. Many were people who had been returned to Cuba after Mariel because they committed crimes in the U.S.; they were sent back out with the *balseros* [rafters]. During our stay, we witnessed assassinations and incredible violence. In response, the intellectuals and the artists tried to separate and distinguish themselves from the criminals. Though we were surrounded by marines, we formed a literary group, which met at least once a week to put on shows and poetry readings to entertain ourselves and pass the time, and published a periodical (*El periódico de los balseros*). The *santeros* also formed their own circles, too. Nevertheless, many people tried to kill themselves, thinking that they would be sent back to their homes; others just gave up and went back on their own, though they were not welcomed and were tagged as *vende patrias*. There was also a great deal of anxiety in Guantánamo because those of us who weren't criminals were afraid that we would be rejected both by Americans and by Cuban exiles in Miami because of the negative repercussions from Mariel. The whole time that I was at Guantánamo, I couldn't help but think how ironic it was that we were exiles, despite the fact that we were still on Cuban soil. Even though I was still able to communicate with my family through a mail service that went through Miami, it was like I was a million miles away from them.

After almost nine months, I was sent to a *tránsito* (transition) house in Miami. Through the auspices of the World Church Services (Servicio Mundial de Iglesias), my father and I were then sent to Buffalo, New York, with four hundred dollars between us (they gave us each two hundred dollars). Refusing to take welfare, we rented an apartment and found a job washing dishes at a local restaurant, the Anchor Bar (the home of buffalo wings).

Upon our arrival in the States we were struck by how much food there was and how many choices we had; in fact, we still feel guilty when we sit down at the table because we know that our family in Cuba is without food. Here, you can go where you want and say what you are thinking. What impressed me most, however, was the idea of controlling my own American dollars. To me, two hundred dollars was a fortune.

Although my father and I had no one to meet us or help us, unlike many Cuban exiles who had networks of family and friends, I was always confident and never afraid. After growing up in Castro's Cuba—a place where you live in constant fear and can't believe in, or count on, even the simplest things (not even in *la luz eléctrica!*)—and then spending twelve days at sea surrounded by sharks, you get beyond fear, if you know what I mean. In fact, I don't know what the word "fear" means, something that I proved when I learned to drive on the Skyway in Buffalo—a day my wife, Marilyn, will never forget as long as she lives.

Perhaps the most painful thing about my exile is the fact that I haven't seen my mother or my son, Adrian, in four years. It still gives me pain when I think that my mother went four months without hearing about our whereabouts after our departure in that boat. Even though we write to one another and call, many times our phone conversations are cut off. I have great faith, however, that one day soon I will be able to hold my mother in my arms and hug her once again with the certainty that we will never be separated.

Even though I miss my family and am always conscious of the fact that I am an exile, I have worked hard ever since I first arrived in this country and, as a result, have had much success as an Amway businessman. From the outset, I separated myself from Cubans who have taken the easy route and accepted handouts, even though I make a point of identifying myself as Cuban mostly because many people believe the myth that all Cubans are hard working! Since our arrival, my father and I have experienced discrimination because of our Spanish accents (in this country, all Spanish-speaking people are lumped together), and we have been stereotyped simply because we are *balseros*. I always overcome this, however, by proving that I am hard working and reliable.

Despite all of this, I believe that in this country, nothing is impossible. The success of a person depends on whom he or she associates with and how hard he or she works. Any foreigner has more rights and access to things here in the United States than Cuban citizens have in their own native land. Compared to Cuba, this is the land of opportunity; whether you have success or not depends on you. (February 21, 1998)
(Interview conducted and translated by Andrea O'Reilly Herrera)

Dead Rafter II
FROM *Breaking Barriers*

Luis Cruz Azaceta

Luis Cruz Azaceta was born in Havana in 1942. He left Cuba in 1960 and now resides in New Orleans, Louisiana.

I have been doing works dealing with the journey since the late '60s. American viewers have associated the work with mythology and as a

universal symbol for reaching unknown shores (the dream utopia)....
We all have a yearning for a journey of action....We feel anchored and
feel the need to escape the existing condition . . . whether it be social,
psychological, cultural or political.

But I should say that not until recently, when we were bombarded
with TV images of stranded *balseros* reaching the coast of Florida, did the
Cuban experience become a universal reality (FIGURE 1).

Balsero Singing
FROM *The Secret History of Water*

Silvia Curbelo

*Silvia Curbelo was born in Matanzas, Cuba. She left the Island for Mexico in 1966
and emigrated to the U.S. in 1967 at the age of eleven. After living in Miami for a
year, her family settled in Carroll, a small town in Iowa. She now lives in Tampa,
Florida.*

When he opens his mouth
he is drifting, he is
in the air, and the child

he's remembering leans out
of some dark window
in his head. The sunlight

is incidental, falling
all around him like a word
or a wing. In another dream

he is dancing in a cottage by the sea
and music is a language he has just
learned to speak, the cool *yes*

of her throat. The sky goes on
for days with its one cloud waving,
the song lifting him like a sail.

The real boat is lost
at sea, one voice nailed
to the planks of history, salt

on the tongue of 30 years.
A window empties
its small cargo—

an eyelash, grief. Each new breath
is a harbor, then a wave
closes over it

like a book.

The Secret History of Water *was published by*
Anhinga Press, Tallahassee, Florida in 1997.

SECTION II

"Merely a Player"

Los que se alejan siempre son los niños
FROM *El hombre junto al mar*

Heberto Padilla

Heberto Padilla was born in Puerta de Golpe, Pinar del Rio, in 1932; he arrived in the
United States in 1980. At the time of his death, he lived in Auburn, Alabama.

Los que se alejan siempre son los niños,
sus manos aferradas a las grandes maletas
donde guardan las madres los sueños y el horror.

En los andenes y los aeropuertos
lo observan todo
y es como dijeran: "¿A dónde iremos hoy?"

Los que se alejan siempre son los niños.
Nos dejan cuerdecillas nerviosas, invisibles.
Por las noches, tenaces, nos tiran de la piel,
pero siempre se alejan, dando saltos, cantando
en ruedas—algunas van llorando—
hasta que ni siquiera un padre los puede oir.

IT IS ALWAYS THE CHILDREN WHO DISTANCE THEMSELVES

It is always the children who distance themselves,
their fingers grasping on to huge suitcases
where their mothers have saved both dreams and horrors.

On platforms and in airports
they take note of everything
as if they were saying, "Where will we go today?"

It is always the children who distance themselves.
They leave their nervous, invisible strings.
At night they cling persistently to our bodies,
but they always distance themselves, jumping about, singing
in circles—some leave in tears—
until not even a father can hear them.

(Translated by Alistair Reid and John A. Coleman)

Merely a Player

María Brito

Born in Havana, Cuba, in 1947, María Brito left the Island at the age of thirteen in 1960. She lives in Miami, Florida.

I daydream about my return to Cuba. It happens whenever someone or something triggers memories that, in turn, bring about what of late has become an ongoing yearning.

When I see myself there, I am invisible. And in that improbable state, I just *am*. I *feel* places that I used to occupy. Reminiscing. Reliving. Especially important to me would be the house where I was born and where I spent the first years of my life, near where my grandmother lived. And the last house in which I lived, my most recent memories—those of a thirteen-year-old—before coming to Miami in 1961.

I don't know if I'll ever go back. The memories, although almost a blur, bring with them a magical comfort. They are usually linked to a physical space and to objects. I think I am afraid that magic will just go away.

The Garden and the Fruit (see FIGURE 2)* deals specifically with an event related to exile. It was inspired by an informal meeting that I had with a man who had been a political prisoner in Cuba. I was teaching an art class at a local senior center in Miami when someone who I thought was a resident of the place approached me to ask a question. I addressed him with the formal *usted*, and at some point during our conversation he very graciously complained that my doing so made him feel like a "*viejo*." He pointed out to me that he was probably not much older than I was (I was in my late thirties at the time) and that if he looked older (which he did) it was due to the many years he spent in Cuban jails. He proceeded to tell me about some of the horrific experiences he had had and the torture he had endured as a political prisoner, such as being confined in a windowless room the size of a closet. The one feature about the man that stayed with me, aside from the fact that his wrinkled skin made him look so much older, was that he hardly had any teeth. This work was provoked by the memory of that encounter; I created it as an homage to that man (the spikes that surround the bed thus function, simultaneously, as symbols of Cuba's vegetation and as reminders of the cruel instruments of torture). As Lynette Bosch observes, "although the work may be construed as being political and reflective of realities in contemporary Cuba, it is also meant to be understood as an indictment of any regime that uses torture and constant vigilance" ("Maria Brito: Metonymy and Metaphor").

The second work included in this collection is a detail from the inner portion of a multimedia installation called *Merely a Player* (FIGURE 3). *Merely a Player* is a metaphor for the human psyche. It consists of the evocation of a living room, open like a stage set, which also serves as the entrance to the installation. Beyond this point, as the viewer physically enters the structure, the installation takes the shape of a labyrinth with corridors and rooms containing imagery related to the various stages of life, existential change, and transformation. (Visible through the circular cutouts on the six squares, which are seen in this figure, are images taken from old photographs of me and people I knew back in Cuba. I altered the images to create different kinds of interactions between me as a kid and somebody else. Inside the small lidded container is an image of me as a child.)

Included in this installation is a black-and-white 16-mm film that is seen through a peephole and relates to the other imagery in the piece dealing with childhood. The setting for the film is a long, narrow corridor with a series of closed doors on both sides. A little girl is seen crisscrossing the corridor as she knocks on doors that do not open. She continues to do this, all the while ignoring an open door at the end of the corridor that leads to a brightly lit place. The film is a loop, so there's no beginning or end. I shot the film in a building in Little Havana, where I lived for a short period of time with my grandmother, my aunt, her husband, my cousin, and my brother (all in a small apartment!). I exhibited this work at the Herbert F. Johnson Museum at Cornell University; it was presented by means of a poem, which appeared in the exhibition catalog, that deals with isolation, masking, and the quest for transcendence and peace symbolized by the ladder that reaches to the sky.

* This work was commissioned for the exhibition "Art is Politics: Sculptural Visions," InterAmerican Art Gallery, Miami-Dade Community College, June 9–July 29, 1988.

MERELY A PLAYER (1993)

Aunque sea por un rato
me quito mis máscaras
una por una
aunque duela
me despojo de todo
y todos
aunque sea por un rato
aunque duela.

Memorias de lo que fué encajonadas
en una pared
perduran
muñecas de adorno y nada más,
en su cama
una niña—
soledad que penetra la piel,
hasta las muñecas sonríen
y deja marcas que no se ven,
de puerta en puerta que no se abren.

A ladder to reach the sky.
The sky is now.
In it I am.
Y me hace sonreir
felicidad que perdura
aunque sea por un rato
aunque sea por un rato
ya dolerá.

Even if only for a while
I take off my masks
one by one
even if it hurts
I deprive myself of everything
and everyone
even if only for a while
even if it hurts.

Memories of what was boxed
in by a wall
remain
dolls on display and nothing more,
in her bed
one girl—
loneliness that pierces the skin,
even the dolls smile
leaving behind tracks that cannot be seen,
from door to door that do not open.

Una escalera para llegar al cielo,
el cielo es ahora.
En él soy.
And it makes me smile
happiness that endures
even if only for a while
even if only for a while
it will hurt.

(Translated by the staff at the Herbert F. Johnson Museum
at Cornell University)

This testimonial was edited by Andrea O'Reilly Herrera, with the author's permission, from a series of letters that they exchanged and articles that the author supplied.

Portrait of Wendy, At Fifty, With Bra
(RETRATO DE WENDY, A LOS CINCUENTA, CON AJUSTADOR)

Ileana Fuentes

> *Ileana Fuentes was born in Havana, Cuba. She left the Island as part of Operation Peter Pan on October 20, 1961, two days before turning thirteen, and was relocated to an orphanage in Denver, Colorado. She currently resides in Miami, Florida.*

"Here. Put this on."

I couldn't believe my eyes. A cup-B brassiere I really didn't need. At thirteen, I had no breasts to speak of, much less to fill a cup of any size. But there it was, my godmother's cotton-stitched, lace-trimmed bra, bleached, washed, starched, and ironed, ready to be passed down to me for the special journey.

"You are a young woman now. *Tienes que usar un ajustador...* and this, too. You can't go out there flaunting your body like a child anymore. You are thirteen."

As if the trauma of leaving friends behind and leaving home weren't bad enough, or the terror of being sent to a strange land, alone.... As if being unable to refuse a premature adulthood weren't frustrating enough, I now had to strap my body with contraptions more fit for cattle than for humans. "I want to call Martica and María Julia, go bike riding with them," I thought.

It was October 20 of that year 1961. Tragic for Cuba and for our family, for that was the year the political honeymoon ended; the year I had to quit eighth grade because the government nationalized foreign schools and was threatening to send students on "scholarships" to the Soviet Union; the year that all the Catholic nuns left the country, and previously holier-than-thou lay teachers took over the classrooms in the name of Karl Marx. Tragic, for it was the year of the Bay of Pigs Invasion and my uncle's twenty-day imprisonment, which forced the women of our family—including his pregnant wife, *mi tía* Carmita—to run from jail to jail, stadium to stadium, to locate his whereabouts. Tragic, for it was the year my grandmother Carmen died, the matriarch of the Ramos family, and my cousin Tutty—the spitting image of the deceased octogenarian—came into this world only to be surrounded by sorrow and separation. Tragic, because it was the year Cuba would become part of my past, exile my uncertain present, and "next-Christmas-in-Cuba" our obsession.

On that sunny day of October 1961, another Wendy-in-ten-thousand-Wendys left Cuba for Never Never Land, wearing a girdle, ridiculous *medias de nylon con costura*, and an itchy, oversized bra. It was nothing like the Peter Pan story I had read.

Not until decades later did I understand that the overdressing ordeal of that morning was a ritual among women: a female rite of passage. Mamá, Tía Carmita, and Madrina had actually enacted an obligatory ritual, whose fulfillment was as important at that moment as the visa waiver stamped on my passport. Sending me out of the country into safety, but devoid of their matriarchal protection, required extra insurance against potential transgressions against my female innocence.

Lest I or anyone else get indecent ideas, the bra hid my tender nipples. God forbid that they should become erect with excitement or with the cold air *del norte*. My ass could not be allowed to provoke the slightest desire in me or others; thus it was constrained under a weave of elasticized rubber. The tiny hairs on my legs needed camouflaging as well, for men, you know, often associate hairy legs with pubic frond-ness—*¡Virgen de Regla! Esta niña* cannot leave this house without the nylon hose *¡y la faja!*

[I shaved my legs with a brand new Gillette at some point during the months of separation. When I reunited with my mother a year later, the first thing she did was stroke my legs. She took the prickly hairlessness as the rebellious statement of an unruly and *americanizada* fourteen-year-old in need of revitalized discipline *a la cubana*. She was right about the statement. But her days of stern glances and Spanish rectitude were over. The female side of the family blamed my behavior on the "loose American morals" that were perverting my Cuban character. My wise father, may he rest in bliss, found it all very amusing. That would be one of the many painful contradictions Cuban parents of Pedro Pan children had to deal with, especially those who back in Havana had favored American schooling to enhance their daughters' future careers, but who now found themselves in "liberal" America longing for Cuban traditions and calling the host culture degenerate.

It took poor Mother a long time to recognize her disenfranchisement both as an authority figure in my eyes and as a respected professional in the eyes of others. My personal safety in the context of Cuba's upheaval soon took second place to my moral and sexual safety in the context of lax American mores . . . which leads me to think about the hidden motivations for taking me out of Cuba. I have come to think that perhaps it wasn't so much about political oppression as it was about premature personal freedom . . . mine! Perhaps it was more about being sent to the Cuban countryside on a literacy campaign, free from parental supervision, than it was about being sent to the communist Soviet Union on a scholarship. Perhaps it was more about Rosita, my puppy love Joe's mother, a young, lily white divorcée who walked out of her house one morning escorted by her new, militia-clad mulatto lover, than about the spinster Inés spying on our family. Perhaps it was more about lust taking over our pubescent bodies than about communism taking over our minds. It was too high a price for everyone to pay just to get us out of Fidel's way, especially since his days in power, everyone thought, were numbered.]

The phone rang while I sat in the living room waiting for everyone else to get ready. It was Martica. My mother stared at me with military sternness. "Not a word," she said. I turned down Martica's invitation. No bike riding for me today. "I'm sorry; I'm going out." I wanted to tell her that there was another ride in store for me that morning . . . the ride of my life, Martica, away from here, from you, from Mari and Lalita, away from Joe and Olguita and Hirian, from Maribel and Yoli, and Jesusito and Chemi, and old Inés with her *comité de defensa* . . . away from *la quincalla* downstairs, and the *frita* stand on the corner, and Aldito with his loud-mouthed parrot, and old man Elías, whose crippled mind we haunted so many times . . . away from everything familiar, Martica . . . your ride is coming, too, one of these days, really soon . . . will I ever see you again, *mi amiguita querida?*

[I did see Martica in Miami ten years later, a new mother of a baby boy, frustrated and unhappy. That was the first and last time I saw her after we left Cuba. She died of cancer a few years later, at age thirty-seven. I never told her how much I wanted to go bike riding with her that autumn morning. As for María Julia, I haven't seen her since 1961. She saw my photograph in a newspaper back in 1977 and tracked me down. I was living in New York; she was in California, divorced with two children, soon to be remarried and resettled in Seattle. I still picture her in her black-and-white uniform, hanging out of the school bus waving at the boys.]

As I boarded the plane that would take me to Miami, I looked back one last time. Unknowingly, I caught a final glimpse of my childhood. It stood there, inside the airport behind glass partitions, staring at me through the eyes of my mother, my aunt, and my godmother, kerchief in hand, like them . . . dressed in black from head to toe, like them . . . in mourning, not just for my grandmother, who had died a month before, but for its own death on that October morning.

Martica and María Julia traveled with me in a photo album all the way to the Kendall barracks-on-the-swamps, which Catholic Charities set up in Miami—with United States government money—to temporarily house the Cuban "orphans." They came with me a month later to Queen of Heaven, a majestic hospice in Denver, Colorado, like Wendy's travel-mates to *Nunca Jamás*. Queen of Heaven, run by the Sisters of Charity, was an earthly world of English only, frosty Rockies, weekly confession and daily communion, generous *gringos* turned weekend fosters, invisible Mexicans and even more invisible Indians not yet known as Chicanos and Native Americans, and bitter nuns all dressed in black from head to toe, as if in mourning for the death of life, or laughter, or pleasure, or all of the above . . . a familiar bleakness *vestida de negro* like an October portrait.

Nine months later, I boarded another flight—this one bound for New York. The end of orphanhood had come! Mom and Dad met me at Newark Airport; I hadn't seen them in almost a year. Head-to-toe black had been replaced with gray and purple, a color upgrade in Cuban mourning folklore.

I went to high school and college in the sixties, amid the rise of every anti-this and pro-that movement. The war in Vietnam affected us; we couldn't understand why Americans were fighting communism in

Asia when they had Castro next door. We suppressed the contradictions and cheered for the American side. Little did we know that in the eyes of other U.S. Latinos and hip Anglo Americans—even to Blacks—our anticommunism made us "imperialist lackeys." We became Spics and *gusanos*, political immigrants and Third World traitors, all at once. To an ignorant American Left and to *yanqui*-go-home Latin American millions, Cuban exiles were fleeing oppressors of poor Cuban folk, whom Castro's revolution had set free. We were *pitiyanquis,* as a Puerto Rican professor once called me; worms to a Jewish American princess from the Venceremos Brigade, who refused to believe that the term *gusano* had been coined by Hitler against her own people, the German Jews.

Thus apologizing for our existence, for a destiny forced upon us by a maniac in fatigues, most Cuban American women of my generation closed rank with our besieged community. We watched from the curb and the hand-me-down sofas as the Civil Rights Movement triumphed, cheering softly so as not to arouse familial suspicion.

The Women's Movement passed us by as "another liberal *commie* conspiracy," as the elders of the tribe would say, "another front in the Cold War." American women taking off their bras, proclaiming the end of marriage and motherhood, advocating for abortion on demand and other reproductive rights, and denouncing the oppression of their gender supposedly had nothing to do with us, surviving as we were on transplanted Cuban traditions like home, school, church, family, and that good old antidote for lust: morality.

For a young *exilada cubana* to have joined Waspy feminist ranks would have been treason, the ultimate subversion of the very delicate balance that kept our homes afloat. Little did we know that other ethnic women faced the same dilemma. Who knew back then about cross-cultural female bonding? At twenty-one I staged my own private revolt and left home. To the women in my family I had run away, unmarried, to live a life of anarchy and sin. In their eyes, American liberal values had won. So, indirectly, had Fidel: one more *gusano* family gone to hell!

Not until years later—after Daly and Griffin and DeBeauvoir and Dworkin—did I recognize two essential things: one, that gender blindness is rampant in Cuban culture; and two, that women are socialized to keep *machismo* alive. I was almost forty, unhappily married, raising a seven-year-old daughter ideology- and religion-free, still at odds with my stern mother, still looking for answers to being Cuban in Manhattan, when I stumbled upon Susan Sontag's analysis of masculinized culture and Robin Morgan's concept of terrorist patriarchy. It was a turning point.

As if someone had snapped her fingers and brought me out of a trance, the slogan of feminism revealed itself for the truth that it was: the personal was political. I understood for the first time the nature of my sin: the innocent revolt I had thought was private in fact had been a very public mutiny. From that moment on, the crisis of the Cuban nation took on another name—*caudillismo*—and it was decipherable. I now saw Fidel for what he really was: Morgan's demon lover, the latest in a long line of Cuban political studs, clad with all the macho trimmings—beard, army boots, fatigues, fame, absolute power, and a cigar. Now his political longevity was explainable; a feminist interpretation of Cuba, urgent; a different future, plausible; Wendy's return home, only a matter of time.

The women in the Ramos family still keep up with their rituals—the *quinces*, the bridal showers, the weddings, the christenings, the ballet recitals for the girls, the baseball games for the boys—all those scenarios that gild their respective cages and keep them in their assigned places. Theirs is a perpetual mourning. For the matrons of my family, especially my mellowed mother, mourning has returned with the return of death. This time grays are more in fashion. I think of my father, Juanito *el tremendo*, always yearning for Cuba, his beloved Cuba. Papá, who wished me female since I was in the womb, and who, since our exile in New York, taught me how to long. (I often wonder if my mother prayed for a boy, so she could deliver the kind of firstborn the culture expected.)

I never burned my bra, you know—not the starched and ironed chastity cups that Tía, Madrina, and Mamá wrapped me in before sending me to outer nation-space, nor any of the hundreds of styles and versions of the Sadeian breast harnesses I've worn over all these years. (The rubber girdle died a terrible death inside the clothes drier at the orphanage in Denver.) I regret not having kept the first *ajustador* in some drawer, like a relic or a fossil ... like an amulet guarding the return portion of a Cubana de Aviación round-trip ticket purchased many snows ago.

The Wooden Suitcase

An Interview with Luz Irene Diaz

Luz Irene Diaz was raised in Matanzas, Cuba; she left the Island as an adolescent in June 1962 as part of Operation Peter Pan and was relocated to Iowa, where she completed her education. She now lives in Rosemont, Pennsylvania.

There is a universality that informs all exile experiences. At the same time, however, the idea of Cuba that I have attempted to preserve is, perhaps, romanticized and idealized. For example, over the years I have imagined that if I ever return to the Island, the small wooden *nécessaire* suitcase that I left behind in my childhood home long ago will still be waiting there for me in the very spot where I left it, filled with paper and the short stories I used to write. In effect, I—like so many other Cuban exiles—have nourished the hope that certain things will have remained unchanged on the Island, regardless of the passage of so many years.

Although I am deeply nostalgic for the world that I realize no longer exists, and I was raised in a comfortable old family, even as a child I was conscious of the poverty in the Cuban countryside and the problems that existed before the 26 of July Movement began. During the summer of 1962 my father, who was a real estate proprietor and businessman in Matanzas, decided to send me to Miami to live with my older sister, who had recently married. I ended up coming to the States as part of Operation Peter Pan. Soon after my arrival, I was sent to a girls' camp in Florida City (part of the network of camps established by Catholic Charities) on my way to a foster home in the United States. Despite the fact that the separation from my parents was painful, my arrival in the United States was mollified by several factors. Unlike many children who were sent to live with complete strangers, I was greeted at the airport by my sister. Like many of my peers, I was already familiar with many aspects of American popular culture. As a group of teenagers who could afford it, my friends and I would pile into cars and go to the movies to see our favorite stars, like Cary Grant, Rock Hudson, Doris Day, Tab Hunter, and Grace Kelly; and we listened to American singers, such as Nat King Cole, Harry Bellafonte, Elvis Presley, and The Platters. We all wore American fashions too, such as bobby socks and saddle shoes—they were the rage among Cuban teenagers. My initial experience in the States was also eased by the fact that the camp offered both companionship and the opportunity to socialize with adolescents who not only were my own age but shared a common language and experience. I can still remember learning to do the Twist and eating at fast-food restaurants, where car-hops on roller skates served us shakes and burgers and fries. Nevertheless, like most of the children attending camp, I was certain that our stay in the United States was only temporary. The thought of the finality—that I would never go back—did not cross my mind.

My initial experience in the States was positive; however, unlike other Peter Pan children, over time I discovered that I was an outsider in a world that was vastly different from my native country. Until I came to this country, I never knew what it was to be a minority. I remember when someone (who obviously heard my name as "Luz Día") asked me if my parents named me Luz because together my first and last names mean "daylight." On the contrary, I told her, my name carries the weight of generations of family tradition. Not only did people fail to under-stand the meaning—the history and tradition—that stood behind my name, but they couldn't pronounce it, either. Finally, after a seemingly countless number of experiences in waiting rooms and doctors' offices where receptionists would call out something that vaguely resembled my name (Is there a Looz Daze here?), I took the course of least resis-tance and began to introduce myself as Lucy. Eventually I adopted the spelling "Luce" to avoid hearing my Spanish name mispronounced; and I considered the possibility of legally changing my name when I be-came an American citizen in the '70s to something that would be easier to pronounce. I discovered, however, that emotionally I couldn't go through with it. In some sense, renouncing my heritage and my family in this way was tantamount to renouncing an integral aspect of my self.

Regardless of the fact that I was a teenager at the time of my arrival in the States, emotionally I was much younger than my age as a result, perhaps, of my strict, conservative upbringing in Cuba. Even though I hold the degree of Doctor of Education (second language acquisition), I have chosen to teach thirteen- and fourteen-year-old adolescents, rather than college students, probably because I can relate to that part of my-self that marks my last emotional sequence in Cuba. In some sense, dealing with adolescents allows me to nurture that aspect of myself that was prematurely stunted as a result of my experience.

Part of me is definitely American; nevertheless, an older Cuban ancestral voice continues to influence aspects of my behavior. But rather than seeing my identity as being divided, I see myself as possessing what I call "a developing identity," an identity that is composed of both Cuban and American elements. Even after all these years, I can be driving along in a car and without explanation experience what I call a "simultaneous occurrence." It might be the way that the sun feels or the formation of the clouds, but in that moment I am reminded of an afternoon in Cuba.

Although I have an equally strong sense of the Cuban and the American aspects of my identity, as I grow older I have become more concerned about preserving my deepest Cuban roots. Perhaps age, accompanied by a new, multicultural awareness in the United States, has prompted me to explore that part of my identity and has allowed me to listen to and hear my Cuban self once again and to take pride in my heritage and my past. (July 9, 1998)

(Interview conducted by Andrea O'Reilly Herrera)

Once upon a Time in May of 1961 . . .
María Emilia Castagliola

María Emilia Castagliola was born in Havana in 1946 and moved to Los Palos at the age of nine. She immigrated to the United States in 1961 at the age of fourteen and is currently a practicing artist, who lives in St. Petersburg, Florida.

Once upon a time in May of 1961, I found myself dressed in my best clothes and separated from my parents by a glass wall. I was at the Havana airport traveling alone. When I arrived in Miami, my eyes were swollen by tears. Once I stepped off the plane, I never cried again. Not about the loss or the separation. But I never forgot the apparent abandonment, the feeling that had my parents loved me, they would not have sent me away. As a child, I did not understand the breadth of their sacrifice. As an adult, no rational defense has ever weakened the remaining trace of fear.

A few of my first impressions remain of interest to me after thirty-eight years. I remember Miami as a Technicolor city. There was a combination of neon and sparkle that made everything look brighter than anything I had ever seen. Those were the days of yellow Cadillacs and rhinestone glasses. Then, there were the old women—women past fifty and sixty—lounging on South Beach with paper-thin skins, wearing bikini bathing suits. My own mother, a beautiful woman in her early forties, had not been seen in a bathing suit for years. In fact, I had never seen an old woman wearing a bathing suit of any kind, much less a bikini. These women appeared to be happy and carefree. I also remember the switch that allowed me to get along before I understood the language. Within days of being the kid who *didn't* speak English, I had given full range to my intuition and become proficient in body language. I still rely on these skills; they serve me well. I can read a face faster than it can speak a phrase. I mostly remember the absence of smell, the surgical quality of air. Robbed of street vendors, wild flowers, and open windows, Miami was without scent.

I know myself as a Cuban. I read Latin American literature and engage in "*El Tema*" whenever the question comes up. I know that my life is profoundly colored by the exile experience, yet I seldom think of it. On a day-to-day basis, I tend to wield the American cultural vehicle with ease and comfort. It is within the context of my work that the bicultural dichotomy can best be understood. When I make art, I work within the Latin American traditions. My content is political, and my delivery is dense with references to the religious and Spanish icons that were prevalent in my childhood. When I write, I tend to decide in favor of extremes; I find the middle ground to be a dangerous and unstable place. When I teach, I focus on process. This is perhaps a remnant from having lived in a place where people often walked without a destination. When I curate an exhibition or organize an event, I am ever vigilant of diversity and inclusion. I work in the mainstream but understand myself to be an outsider. I express myself best in a foreign tongue but keep pace to the rhythmic measures of the old songs.

Crossing into the Mainstream

Juan Manuel Alonso

Born in Havana in 1952, Juan Manuel Alonso left the Island with his family in 1967 at the age of fourteen and settled in New York City. He now lives in Miami Beach, Florida.

I left Cuba with my family in 1967 at the age of fourteen. Because my parents were against the Castro government, our lives were made impossible. Since I didn't join any of the government organizations, I was harassed not only by officials but by my classmates as well. We arrived in the United States as part of the Freedom Flights with only a little clothing in a suitcase. The only monetary assistance we received was one hundred dollars from a Protestant organization, which my father obtained upon his conversion (the Catholic organizations didn't help anyone who stayed in Miami). Friends of our family picked us up at the airport. As a kid, it seemed to me that Miami was a big swamp filled with mosquitoes; among my first impressions were seeing segregated water fountains for Whites and Blacks and encountering rental signs that read "No Blacks, No Dogs, No Cubans."

Upon our arrival, I had to begin working in order to help my parents make ends meet. Up to that point in my life, I had had almost no responsibilities; my parents had always provided for me. In this strange new world, I had to learn to survive as an exile and face a reality that required that I leave not only my country, but my childhood, behind.

My first work experience was in a meat-packing factory. In order to obtain that job, I had to lie about my age and say that I was eighteen. My first day, I was given a meat cleaver and put to work on an assembly line. As the cows started rolling out of a truck on hooks, my job was to butcher them into different parts. After my second cow, they transferred me to the meat-stringing department—it was obvious that I had never butchered anything in my life. That same day, after stringing up my arm along with a rolled beef loin, I was transferred to the cleaning department. (While I was rolling loins, the woman next to me offered to help out; when I got home that night and told my mother her name, I discovered that unbeknownst to either of us, she was my godmother; she had gone into exile in the early '60s!)

Although my father wanted to stay in Miami, in 1968 we moved to New York City, where there would be more job opportunities for my parents. (Also, my parents wanted to be closer to my sister, who had relocated to New York with her husband and child when they first arrived.) There, I began taking art courses in high school; I quickly discovered that painting allowed me to escape the harsh realities of my life in exile. After paying my way through college, I attended the Fashion Institute of Technology. Upon my graduation in 1981, I began working as an international fashion designer.

In 1985, I discovered that I was HIV-positive. My deteriorating health, coupled with the pressures of the fashion industry, prompted me to relocate to Miami in 1992. My decision to move there had less to do with being near a Cuban or Spanish-speaking community and more with the fact that my entire family was living there by that time. (Quite frankly, it took me a while to readjust to the Cuban community, since I had already crossed into the mainstream as a result of my education and my work experience.)

Though my life has changed a great deal since I first arrived in the States, my art continues to function for me as a way to escape everyday reality. Although these escapist tendencies are clearly visible in my work, my religious heritage, which is a mixture of Afro-Cuban elements and Catholicism, manifests itself in my paintings. *Our Lady of Fashion*, for example, not only reflects my experience as a designer in the "unreal" world of fashion, but it is inspired by the collection of *santas* and *orishas* who were part of my everyday life in Cuba and who continue to watch down upon me and protect me from the top of the wardrobe in my bedroom (FIGURE 4).

Fragmented Memories
AN EXILE'S RETURN

Gabriella Ibieta

Gabriella Ibieta was born in Havana, Cuba, in 1953 and left for the United States in January 1966 through the Freedom Flights. She lives in Philadelphia, Pennsylvania, with her family.

I was sleeping in a strange bedroom. Trying to wake up within my dream, I realized that I was back in the small apartment where I had lived with my parents in the neighborhood of Vedado, La Habana, Cuba. In my nightmare, I couldn't scream or wake up or turn on the lights to prove that I wasn't really there, that this world was all gone; or rather, that it was I who was gone because I had left my birthplace, scratched out my history, abandoned my world; and it was terror that I felt.

When I left Cuba in January 1966 I thought it would be forever. For years after my arrival in the U.S., I avoided re-creating my memories, reliving my lost space, remembering the people and things I had left behind, or allowing the feelings aroused by such memories to flow freely. For years I systematically refused to put much value on objects and to define myself through possessions or even relationships; all, potentially and symbolically, might have to be abandoned at some point, and I didn't want to make any investments or take any risks. For years I avoided responding to the well-meaning questions of people at parties: "How did you leave Cuba? What was it like when you got to the States?" Unwillingly I would respond, "It was hard—it's a long story." But another part of me wanted to speak nonstop, to tell my story as vividly as possible, to reconstruct my elusive memories, to try to repossess my past.

The catalyst I needed to begin to tell my tale didn't come until 1988 when I accompanied my husband, on his teaching Fulbright Fellowship, to Copenhagen. I had taken an unpaid leave of absence from my university, and I was jobless, friendless, and unmoored. Living in a new place, deprived of a common language and away from my home in Philadelphia, the feelings of deracination and anguish that I had felt as an adolescent during my first few years in the U.S. came back to haunt me, crashing down on me with unexpected force and demanding to be acknowledged, accepted, and expressed. The sense of dislocation and anomie that I experienced as I walked the streets of Copenhagen that bleak, gray winter triggered a vast array of complex emotions and initiated yet another process of self-scrutiny. I realized that my Cuban American identity, taken for granted not only by me but by most people who knew me or would meet me in the U.S., was not immediately recognizable to the Danes. I found it increasingly difficult to explain my status and to define myself; thoughts of my childhood in Cuba and the experience of uprootedness and exile kept flooding into my brain. I wrote countless letters to my friends, trying to give shape and voice to my feelings; and I also started working on these memoirs.

As the Revolution moved inexorably on during the early sixties, the sheltered and privileged world of my childhood started crumbling. Everybody I knew started to leave: my father's parents; his brother, sister, and their families; my mother's oldest sister and her children; my parents, aunts, uncles, cousins, friends, acquaintances, colleagues, neighbors; my own friends. Even though my father left in 1963, it would take another three years before my mother and I could go (through the Freedom Flights sponsored by the U.S. government during Lyndon B. Johnson's term in office).

One day in January 1966, two members of the neighborhood's spy group, the CDR (Comité de Defensa de la Revolución/Committee for the Defense of the Revolution), knocked at our door. They informed us that we would be leaving the country in a few weeks and that in accordance with the established procedures, they had to check the inventory of all of our possessions in order to verify that nothing was missing. (Like everyone who intended to leave the country, we had had to file this document.) After this process was completed and we had packed, the "good" neighbors from the CDR informed us, we were to evacuate the premises; the apartment, with everything in it, would be closed and officially sealed.

When we walked out of our home, never to return, I knew how deep my loss was. All that I was and had been, as defined by my things—especially my books—would be no more. I was leaving my identity behind without having a new one to take its place. Part of me was dying, and that knowledge tore me to pieces.

Was it a sense of relief I felt when we boarded the plane? Fear? An overwhelming sense of sadness? What stands out most vividly in my memory of that short flight was looking down at the Island and crying at last, inconsolably, convinced that I would never see it again, not like that. I remember thinking, even as I cried, how different this island was from the one I had seen on maps—a long, monolithic, continuous curvy strip of land with little lines to mark its rivers. This place I was leaving behind was beautiful from above—waterways crisscrossed several large pieces of land, which fitted together in a loose arrangement of neatly delineated shapes. I could see the mountains. The sea was brilliant and tranquil, lighter in color as it approached the shore. It all looked so alive and distant, and I felt so much pain. The Island's shapes began to fade as we gained altitude, and after a while I could no longer see it.

Upon our arrival in Miami, we were taken to Opa Locka, a refugee camp in North Miami; from there we would fly to New York to meet my father, my mother's brother and sisters, and my cousins. The people at Opa Locka were very kind, and they spoke in Spanish. We were fed (Jell-O and Tang, perhaps) and given winter clothes for our flight to New York. My coat was a black, imitation-leather jacket, which I came to abhor over the following months since nobody at school wore anything even remotely like it. This jacket signaled my difference as a new arrival—especially among other Cuban children—and I soon got rid of it. I didn't want the image that it projected to be associated with the real me, whoever that was, or with the person I wanted to become. But I did wear it on the plane, self-consciously, and it was under this guise that I arrived in New York.

My first memories of New York City are jumbled and imprecise. I remember thinking how utterly different everything looked. The baroque colors of old Havana and the tropical shades of my Vedado neighborhood had given way to a city of dark colors, vast and crowded spaces, buildings of dark red brick and grayish concrete, old, dirty snow, people in coats, hats, and gloves; you could see your breath, and it was windy.

My father's building was at the southwest corner of 75th Street and Broadway. It was a plain brick building, five or six stories high, and its window frames and fire escape were painted a dark, ominous green. Upon entering the long, dimly lit hallway on the ground floor, I detected a then unfamiliar odor; it wasn't a bad smell, but a stuffy, windowless, steam-heat radiator smell that I had never experienced before. I was surprised, too, by the apartment's wooden floors, which were not polished or smooth but, rather, the nondescript color of age and neglect. We had had off-white, cold tile floors in Havana, smooth and clean-looking and new, but these old floors creaked when I walked, and bare feet could get splinters.

Food, too, would be different from what I had expected. That first night I wanted a ham sandwich. Ham had been a delicacy and a reward when I was little—we would go to a special store to buy the right brand—and we hadn't had any in Cuba for quite some time. But this American ham was disappointing; it didn't taste as good as the kind we used to eat back in Havana, at least as I remembered it. It took me years to discover that I didn't have to buy prewrapped cold cuts or single-slice cheese; but that was what we had that night at my father's New York City apartment: a modest ham sandwich on Wonderbread, with A & P marmalade as a spread. There was plenty of Coca-Cola, and I got to watch TV.

My first impressions of Manhattan were something of a letdown (nothing matched the images on the postcards that my father had sent me for almost three years), but I nonetheless felt challenged by its possibilities, which seemed to be endless. There were lots of people around, and cabs, and buses, and a noisy, bustling energy. My mother, who had been for me a kind of urban amazon (strong, enthusiastic, and courageous), would never be quite that way again. New York City scared her; she couldn't figure it out, and she didn't even want to try. Although New York was in code for me also, it was a code I was eager to decipher and interpret; I found the city exciting in its ugliness and its splendor. But my adolescent experience of New York would soon come to an end. Domesticity, at least with us, was not what my father had in mind that bleak and strange winter of 1966. My parents' marriage had not been a good one for several years before my father left Cuba, and it was evident that time and distance had made their differences even more marked. As a result, about six weeks after my arrival, I would undergo yet another displacement.

Across the Hudson River, my new home waited in obscurity: my mother and I left New York and crossed into *West* New York, which is, ironically, in New Jersey. While Manhattan had been a strange and hostile environment for my mother, *West* New York was a safe haven of close familial relationships, a place where Cubans had created a shelter from the big city across the river—an ugly paradise. It was here in this immigrant town that my mother's brother and sisters had settled during the 1950s and early 1960s, and this was where my grandmother would die years later. My uncle had found us a cheap, one-bedroom apartment; and even though it was small, once my mother started working she made the place cheerful and comfortable. (Over the next seven years we would move four times, always to bigger and better apartments.)

I had no idea what kind of place *West* New York was when we first arrived there; I only knew that it was in New Jersey. It's ironic to think that although they seemed to us to be a monolithic group of people, *los americanos* of the area were, instead, multiethnic and multicultural. When I started school a few weeks later, we practiced "When Irish Eyes Are Smiling" in music class several times a week. Although I knew that shamrocks were a symbol of good luck, I couldn't figure out why there were so many of them on the bulletin boards; and I found it totally baffling that many of the children wore big, round buttons with green letters saying "Kiss me, I'm Irish." I also didn't understand why my schoolmates defined themselves as Italian, German, Irish, or Polish when, in fact, they had all been born here and spoke English as their native language.

Through my high school graduation in 1971, my closest friends were Cuban, my lifestyle was Cuban, and my boyfriend was Cuban; I dressed Cuban, ate Cuban food, and went to Cuban parties. But every two weeks or so, we would escape our ethnic ghetto and cross over into Manhattan for movies, dinner, or sightseeing. Even though I was not aware of it, my Cuban-exile identity of those days was inauthentic, patterned as it was on family traditions and negotiated through an unconscious fear of assimilation. I didn't have to prove my mettle within that protective, albeit stifling, environment. But I realized that I couldn't do what was expected of me: to live at home with my mother and attend a local college such as St. Peter's or Jersey City State, for example; to become engaged; and to remain within the boundaries of that safe Cuban cocoon, dull and ugly as it was. Unsure of myself and my identity, awkward at self-definition, and tormented by guilt at wanting to "escape" from my family, I nonetheless decided to cross another frontier: I broke up with my Cuban boyfriend and went away to school.

During my college years, I found that acting Cuban was definitely not cool. How could I, a student at a large state school (Douglass College, Rutgers University), remain parochial, provincial, and tied to outdated cultural traditions? Even though I had hardly noticed the turmoil of the 1960s in my East Coast Cubatown, the tremendous changes that it brought about were palpable everywhere. And I adopted a new identity: I listened to Joan Baez, Dylan, and The Grateful Dead; wore ragged jeans; read Henry Miller, Virginia Woolf, and Jack Kerouac; and became an English major. Most of my friends were modified Americans—that is, Hungarian American, Jewish American, Italian American, but not Cuban American.

Although I wasn't aware of it at the time, that identity had also been negotiated: I had gained a lot, but I had also lost touch with parts of myself that I wouldn't recover (or re-create) until much later.

My bohemian years in New York City expanded my horizons once again; my old love affair with Manhattan resumed when I moved to a tiny studio apartment on the fringes of the West Village in the mid-1970s and started working on a degree in comparative literature at the Graduate Center of the City University of New York. I felt that I could explore several cultures at the same time without belonging to any, and that being Cuban was like being anything else: one could always dilute origin through culture, intellect, and career. Thus, when I moved to Philadelphia in 1984 to take a job at St. Joseph's University, I thought I had transcended my ethnicity and that I was, and forever would be, a citizen of the world. But sure enough, the older I got, the more Cuban I felt.

In retrospect, I think I was totally unprepared for the series of major life changes (stressful, wonderful, frightening) that happened to me in a relatively short period of time: in 1987 I got married for the first time, to Miles Orvell; newly pregnant upon our return from Copenhagen, I accepted a job at Drexel University; our daughter, Ariana, was born in March 1989, and we bought a house that summer; two years later I was tenured; and in May 1992 our son, Dylan, was born. Although I was beginning to feel comfortable crossing boundaries and going back and forth among my intersecting identities, I also experienced a "Now, what?" sort of feeling, becoming dispersed and unfocused in my activities and again struggling with new ways of defining myself in all of my various roles. I can't say that my trip to Cuba in 1995 resolved this conflict altogether, but going back after almost thirty years helped me to see it in a different light and to understand it better: exile and displacement became less opaque and, therefore, more tolerable.

Traveling to Cuba with a delegation of radical philosophers from the U.S. turned out to be one of the strangest things I have ever done. The fact that I was participating in the Seventh Conference of North American and Cuban Philosophers and Social Scientists at the University of Havana in June 1995 was incidental—almost comical, in fact—to me. Going with the group trip was simply an easy option, a legal and safe way for me—a Cuban American on a return mission—to explore what had become unknown territory: the place where I had been born.

I didn't want to talk with anyone during the short flight from Miami to Havana—my emotions were too intense. As we approached the Island, my face stuck to the window. I could see red earth, empty country roads, the brilliance of the sea all around. I remember crying. The moment I breathed in the air after we landed, I was overwhelmed by a flood of sensory impressions; the cells of my body remembered how the air felt inside the nostrils and how the heavy humidity of the atmosphere would be suddenly and pleasantly dispersed by cooling breezes from the sea. The evening sky was soft and beautiful. I felt a deep sense of happiness—an almost unconscious feeling of recognition and wholeness, something I had never experienced before upon arriving anywhere.

The day after my arrival in Havana, I escaped from the confines of the conference at the university (the brilliant sea beckoned through the high windows) and started walking toward my neighborhood in Vedado. I wanted to take in every sight, find the matching images inside my brain, and consciously experience going back to what had been for years a landscape of memory and the imagination. For almost thirty years I had felt that my life had been split in two when I left Cuba; once I became conscious of this doubleness, what pained me the most was the fact that I couldn't connect the two parts, that what I had left behind in Havana was completely separate from my life in the U.S., and that I might never be able to integrate the pieces or to write about my experiences. My journey to Cuba bridged the gap between these two separate spheres of my life; it was as healing as it was painful.

Beneath the squalor and dirt of the city and the smell of old garbage, everything was recognizable in its shocking decay. I walked and walked, the sun pounding on my head, sweat rolling down my torso, feeling that I was simultaneously in the present and in the past. Following Calle 23, one of the main streets, to its intersection with Calle 12, I turned right toward the corner of Calle 17 and reached my old school. It was like looking at a double exposure: the way I remembered it and the way it was now, in ruins but still functioning. That feeling hit me even harder when I walked a few blocks from the school to my home: Calle 16, #267, *entre* 17 y 19, Vedado, la Habana, Cuba.

The place where I had lived with my family was probably built in the early 1950s and could be loosely described as a four-dwelling gar-den-apartment building. Like many others in Havana, the garden was now totally overgrown with weeds; the bushes, tall and brownish, al-most covered the front windows. The building needed paint badly; the three marble steps leading to the open vestibule were gray with years of dirt and grime; and a rusty iron gate blocked the stairs to the second-floor apartments. In disbelief I stared at this, my home, from across the street, and eventually got closer. Later, as in a dream, I took some pic-tures. I had no desire to go inside the apartment; even though I knew it was not unusual for Cuban Americans to visit their former homes in Cuba, I wasn't the least bit curious. Emotionally, I wasn't able to un-dergo the experience; but I also think that I chose to keep the vision of my home's interior intact—to preserve it in my memory as it had been for the twelve-year-old who I once was—so that I could continue to see it, in my mind, as a permanent refuge. I knew then that I would never have my home back in any other way, but neither would I yearn for it. My loss was total, but it was no longer unknown. This place existed, but it wasn't mine; I felt profoundly sad.

It was painful to look at the faces of these *cubanos de Cuba* and to hear them talk about their endless needs, their hunger, not only for food, medicine, decent housing, and *fulas* (dollars), but for something to be-lieve in, given the failure of the Revolution and its broken promises of independence and self-sufficiency. My sense of having been born on a tiny island that has always been colonized—first by Spaniards, then by the Americans and the Soviets, and now by a conglomerate of foreign interests from Mexico, Canada, Italy, and Spain once again—became much more real, almost palpable. My mother had taken me away from this island. A sense of shame at my own privileged life in the U.S. came over me: I felt the guilt of the survivor.

Leaving Cuba in 1995 was not as hard as it had been in 1966, nor had I expected it to be. What I didn't anticipate, though, were the feelings of anxiety, fear, and almost desperation as I stood between the side of the airport where the crowds were so dense that you couldn't tell who was in line to get out or who was waiting for arriving relatives, and the other side, where one could buy coffee, rum, and cigars before flying away. As my documents were checked by a man from Seguridad del

Estado (State Security, the all-powerful agency that controls comings and goings), my hands began to shake and my breath grew short. I was terrified: What if I couldn't leave? It didn't help to know somewhere within my consciousness that my fear was irrational, since I also felt that the act of tearing oneself away from one's birthplace—no matter how high the degree of alienation—was also irrational. Once I crossed over into the duty-free area of the airport, I sat down and wept in pain, anger, and relief. Like I had as a child, I felt the agony of leaving behind a part of my life, of my self. But there was a crucial difference this time: even if it was fragmented, indefinable, and fluid, my identity was much more secure. I had a life in the U.S.: children, a loving husband, my mother, friends and relatives, my work, and other different parts of my self. I was going back to them.

The exile's return does not bring closure to the conflicts of identity, but it does heal the pain of fragmentation. For me, writing about leaving Cuba, assimilating to U.S. culture and forging my own place within it, and returning to Cuba, has been, and continues to be, a difficult process. "No es fácil," the Cubans from Cuba would say. Thomas Wolfe had it right: "You can't go home again." But perhaps trying to do so, even on the blank space of a computer screen, is good enough.

This essay was adapted from a longer work in progress.

Going Back

Tony Mendoza

Tony Mendoza was born in Havana in 1941; his family left the Island in 1960. He lives in Columbus, Ohio.

My family left Cuba during the first wave of immigration, during the summer of 1960, when Fidel Castro began the process of nationalizing all privately owned land, industries, and businesses, thus making it clear that he intended to create a socialist state. That prospect must have been an intolerable thought for the large Mendoza family; nearly everyone left that summer: grandparents, uncles, aunts, and cousins.

I left just a week before my nineteenth birthday, and I welcomed the move. That June, I had just graduated from Choate, a private school in Connecticut, and from my somewhat warped adolescent perspective, leaving Cuba seemed to be an excellent move. American girls appealed to me immeasurably more than Cuban girls, who not only didn't drink or neck on dates but also brought along a chaperone. I liked just about everything about American culture—American sports, the cult of cars, TV, movies. I was also very lucky. I had already been accepted at Yale and was looking forward to college life.

At Yale, it didn't take long to construct my new American identity. I progressively saw myself like I saw my peers: bright, ambitious, and privileged, focused on girls, fraternities, friends, studies, and the future. I was so busy with college life that there was little time to dwell on my Cuban past; I noticed, though, that it seemed to impress girls, who regarded me as someone different and exotic. But I don't recall missing Cuba or wanting to go back. Yale was an interesting place. My future in America looked promising. I spoke nearly perfect English, after five years in prep school. Discrimination, or being an outsider, didn't seem to be an issue.

While at Yale, I somehow managed to get interested in architecture, and in 1964 I enrolled at the Harvard Graduate School of Design. By the time I graduated in 1968, Cambridge had worked its magic. I now saw myself as an intellectual, seduced by the myth of Harvard and the exuberance and craziness of the times: the hippies, the antiwar movement, communal living, pot, acid, Rolfing, Primal Scream. Living became some sort of a grand experiment, where the only known fact was that how my parents (and their generation) had lived was not only outdated but downright harmful—witness the fact that the world was a total mess. The solution, I thought, was to start from scratch and try anything that fell under the rubric of an alternative lifestyle.

In 1970, I joined a commune in Sommerville, a working-class community next to Cambridge, with twelve men and women. Our minimal living expenses allowed us to drop regular jobs and pursue other interests, mostly in the arts. I lived in the commune throughout the '70s, and along the way I quit architecture and became an artist/photographer. During all this time, Cuba—and being Cuban—continued to fade from my consciousness.

All my friends in Boston were Americans, and I never spoke Spanish.

The Latinos and the few Cubans I met struck me as too traditional, too Old World, and unable—or unwilling—to consider and accept new ideas, just like my parents and the many relatives I had in Miami. Miami Cubans, it seemed to me, were determined to freeze time and live in the past; I was interested in the exact opposite—I saw myself as an avant-garde artist, interested in the new, in the future.

My almost total lack of interest in my Cuban background started to change when I moved to New York in 1980, hoping to give my art career a boost. New York was a much harsher place, and I started to experience an emotion I had never experienced in Boston: loneliness. I didn't have many acquaintances in New York and had trouble making new friends. After living in the commune for ten years, I realized that my social skills were rusty. I would go to openings with the intention of meeting people, and I would freeze.

Eventually, I did meet some Latino artists, who seemed a lot friendlier than the American art crowd. I also discovered some cheap Chinese-Cuban restaurants and started eating Cuban food. After many failed relationships with American women, I started seeing a Cuban woman with a background very similar to my own: Carmen had studied art history in Boston and was also a veteran of the '60s. Like me, she had lived with Americans in Boston and also felt that Cuban culture was too restrictive and traditional. She particularly didn't care for Cuban men, whom she considered to be too sexist. We started dating; it was the first time since leaving the Island that either of us had seriously dated another Cuban. We were both surprised to feel so comfortable and compatible, so we decided to move in together.

After speaking mostly English for twenty years, Carmen and I rediscovered the pleasures of our native language. We suspected that we got along so well because we shared a past and a culture, so we set out to explore it. We purchased an alarming quantity of cassettes and CDs of old Cuban music and danced in our living room to the rhythms of Cuban *boleros* and *danzones*. Black beans and fried plantains reappeared in our kitchen, and I started wearing *guayaberas*. After living in Brooklyn for a few years, we decided that New York winters were unbearable and wondered what it would be like to live in a Cuban community in the tropics; so we moved to Miami and liked it, with some reservations. We missed the museums, the art shows, and the endless choice of movies and concerts to which we had become accustomed in Boston and New York. We also were not used to living in the same city with a very large group of relatives, many of whom would start conversations by asking, "When are you two going to get married?"

Nevertheless, we enjoyed our relatives, the Cuban flavor of Miami, the restaurants on Calle Ocho. We loved the climate, the ocean, the wild parrots in our garden, and our late afternoon cheese and wine picnics in Key Biscayne—where we eventually got married in a ceremony by the sea. We would have stayed in Miami had it not been very difficult for an artist to earn a living there and, more to the point, we needed health insurance (Carmen had a boy from her first marriage, and we both wanted another child). In 1987 I was offered a job teaching photography at Ohio State University, and our family moved to Columbus—to the tundra.

At first, I thought living in the Midwest was an interesting novelty; that feeling, however, didn't last. People born on islands shouldn't move to the Midwest. It's too flat, and it takes twenty hours of nonstop driving to catch a glimpse of the Gulf of Mexico. Winters are too cold; summers are too hot. Midwesterners are decent, hard-working, solid people, but not very colorful or diverse. And in Ohio, they all seemed to vote Republican, which is not my favorite political party. All of these small gripes, though, are minor problems. My main problem with living in Ohio was that I was born on an island, and I missed the ocean.

The longer I lived in Columbus, the more I realized that I'm not cut out to live in the Midwest; and the more I felt nostalgia for everything Cuban. Carmen felt somewhat similar, but she's much more adaptable and flexible. As a result, we ate dinner at a restaurant in Columbus that serves Cuban dishes, and I bought every CD that featured a Cuban band. I also wrote a series of coming-of-age stories about a fourteen-year-old boy called Tony, who lived in Havana in 1954. Every time I saw pictures of Havana in photo books shot by European journalists, I strained to see if I recognized the streets, the parks, the buildings in the background. I remembered Havana as an exceptionally beautiful city, but in those days I was unconcerned with beauty, and I had no frame of reference. Now I know better. I wanted to see Havana again. I especially wanted to see the house in El Vedado where I lived and the huge mango trees in the garden, where I must have killed a thousand sparrows with my BB gun, which I now regret!

In 1996, I couldn't stand it any longer. I put aside my many misgivings about returning to the Island and flew to Havana for a three-week stay. I felt I had to step on Cuban soil again and straighten out my longings for a physical place I had increasingly remembered as some sort of paradise. I wanted to see all the places of my childhood and, especially, visit the sugar mill in Camagüey Province, where I grew up, and visit the islands we sailed to on fishing trips with my grandfather. But after a few days in Cuba, my focus shifted. I became very interested in how Cubans were adapting and reacting to life in post-Soviet socialist Cuba. What I saw and heard shocked me, and I spent most of my time recording conversations with Cubans about their daily lives. Support for the government and government policies seemed nonexistent. I can't predict the future, but when Castro dies, I can't imagine that any other figure in his government will be able to hold the socialist regime together.

On another level, however, this trip confirmed my intuition about how right the place feels to me. Even though it was August and hot, I still loved the climate, the vegetation, the architecture of Havana, and the beautiful undeveloped countryside, a curious benefit of communism. I kept thinking that I could live there again.

On the flight back to Miami, shortly after takeoff, I looked down from my window and watched as we crossed over the Cuban coastline. It was such a dramatic picture: the meeting of the blue ocean, the thin white line of the Santa María del Mar beach, and the green fields beyond. I pressed my face against the window and kept my eyes on that coastline as long as I could, wondering if I would ever see it again. I knew I would write a book or an article about the trip; and whatever I wrote was not going to please the Cuban government. So, for the immediate future I would probably be barred from returning to Cuba again, like other journalists who have written negative articles about socialist Cuba.

Nevertheless, as I write this, winter is almost here, and I'm reminded again of how much I dislike this climate. I'm hoping that in my lifetime I'll be faced with a decision between returning to Cuba or staying in the U.S. If I have to make the decision during the winter, I suspect what the answer is going to be.

See the photograph section for Tony Mendoza's pictures of Cuba.

Crossing the Generational Divide

An Afternoon with Ernesto F. Betancourt

Born in Havana, Cuba, in 1927, Ernesto Francisco Betancourt left the Island in 1953 after Fulgencio Batista overthrew the Constitution. Though he returned to Cuba following the 1959 revolution, he went into permanent exile with his family in February 1960. He is currently residing in Rockville, Maryland.

My wife, Raquel, and I came to Washington fifty years ago, right after we were married in Havana in 1948. We settled here in Washington, where I found a job at an automotive parts central wholesale firm. (Raquel had lived in Washington since 1939 and attended George Washington University.)

My initial experience in Washington was not favorable. Segregation was still prevalent; although being Latin was not as bad as being Black, you were made to feel out of place. In my office, the dominant person was a Republican lady from Alexandria, Virginia, who prided herself on being a "darling" (Daughter of the American Revolution). She hated Blacks, labor unions, and foreigners. My accent drove her bananas. (My wife said I spoke English like a Korean.) Other staff members—mostly young West Virginians—were friendly. But they openly acknowledged that they would talk more to me were it not for the fact that the lady from Virginia, who was the senior person in the office, nagged them for doing so. I also got along very well with the Blacks in the warehouse, mostly World War II veterans who had migrated to Washington from the South in search of a better future for their kids. The general manager was extremely supportive of me, but he had little influence on the social climate of the office. I finally got fed up and decided to return to Cuba in 1950.

Back in Cuba, I went to work for an advertising agency. Since I am also very politically oriented, it was with great relish that I joined the firm in preparing an advertising campaign for one of the presidential candidates, Dr. Roberto Agramonte of the Orthodox Party, in the 1952 election. Unfortunately, on March 10, the day before the presentation, Batista took power through a coup and canceled the elections, in which polls indicated that he was running third. This was a great disappointment for both my wife and me, as well as for our generation. We decided to come back to Washington and make a second try. By then we had two kids: Adela, who was born in Washington, and Ernesto, who was born in Havana.

We arrived back in Washington the day before Eisenhower's inauguration in January 1953. This time we made a commitment to a permanent stay. I registered at American University evening school with a major in advertising and marketing and returned to the automotive parts firm, where I was eventually promoted to office manager. Desegregation was progressing in Washington, and the Republican lady had mellowed. My English also improved as a result of my academic studies, thus melting my foreignness in her eyes.

In February 1957, Herbert Matthews's articles in the *New York Times* about his visit with Fidel Castro in the Sierra Maestra once again awakened my political hopes for Cuba. This was not traditional politics; rather, it was my generation resorting to arms in order to restore the Constitution of 1940 that Batista had abolished. My wife and I decided that there was something useful that we could do to help in Washington. We contacted groups in New York, Connecticut, and New Jersey that were already actively supporting the 26 of July Movement and, along with other sympathizers, started organizing representation for the movement in Washington. All of a sudden, I became the voice in Washington for those in the Sierra.

My employers were extremely supportive and never objected to my activities. I saw to it that my work was not affected by my extracurricular activities. My new activities were not well received in all quarters, however. After my first press conference, which was published in Cuba, I received an icy response from my mother: "In our family, our names do not appear in newspapers." The next two years were possibly the most fascinating and interesting period in my life. This period ended, however, when Batista fled Cuba on New Year's Eve, 1958.

After taking over the Cuban Embassy in Washington on January 1, 1959, I went back to Cuba and was present at Columbia's military base when Fidel arrived in Havana. Herbert Matthews (the *New York Times* reporter), his wife, and Jack Skelly, a Washington-based UPI reporter who had known Castro since his childhood days in Oriente, shared with me that historic and dramatic moment. Shortly thereafter, I was appointed to the Cuban Bank of Foreign Trade, and my wife and children joined me. Early in April, there was a call from Fidel's office asking me to accompany him as an advisor during his visit to Washington later that month.*

Following several tiring days in Washington—where we were overwhelmed by the adulation of hysterical admirers (though I must admit that as a former Washington resident, I personally enjoyed being able to go through red traffic lights without getting a ticket)—we went to Princeton, New York, Boston, and then on to Montreal. From Montreal, Fidel flew down to Buenos Aires with a stopover in Houston, where he met his brother, Raúl, in order to confer over an invasion attempt in Panama that had exploded in the news during our stay in Canada. The two brothers had quite an exchange of insults that evening at the Shamrock Hotel penthouse where we were staying. To this day, I am convinced that the invasion attempt was a deliberate effort on the part of Che and Raúl to derail any improvement in relations between Cuba and the U.S. that might have resulted from Fidel's visit.

Upon my return to Havana, I went back to my duties at the Cuban Bank of Foreign Trade, with the added responsibility of acting as the executive director of the Foreign Exchange Stabilization Fund (the national bank entrusted by law with the management of foreign exchange, a problem that was growing by leaps and bounds). At my suggestion, Fidel had started the practice of hosting weekly luncheons attended by the Economic Cabinet at the National Bank. It was at one of those luncheons, in mid-July of 1959, that I resigned, psychologically, from the Castro regime.

Castro informed us that he wanted feedback on the potential economic impact of a constitutional crisis: he was getting ready to depose Dr. Manuel Urrutia, the man he had installed in the presidency six months earlier. Castro explained to us how he makes decisions in those cases: in effect, he sees all the actors as moving on a chess table, and eventually his instincts tell him what to do. He concluded by telling us, "Man is a political animal, and some of us are more animal than others."

A few moments later in the discussion, Castro revealed those animal instincts after someone warned him that since we had already antagonized American business interests through the land reform law enacted in May, any political instability could provide an excuse for an intervention. Fidel did not hesitate for a second; he snapped back, "If they send the marines, I do not care. They will have to kill between 300,000 and 400,000 Cubans, and I will get a bigger monument than José Martí." The truth was out. The man did not care about the well-being of the

Cuban people; he only cared about the size of his monument. Right then and there, I decided this was not the kind of regime with which I wanted to be associated.

Although my wife and I decided not to stay in Cuba, we had to avoid giving the impression that we were defecting. As a result, we didn't tell anyone about our plans until shortly before all of the arrangements had been made for my departure. Finding a seat on a plane was one of the most difficult factors. A couple of days before my departure, we went around saying goodbye. However, on February 1, 1960, my wife started having labor pains while we were making the rounds, so we stopped at her obstetrician's at 5:00 P.M. He said no, the child would not come until the end of the month. The child, a boy we named Luis, was born at 10:00 that same evening. (He just wanted to meet his father before he left the Island.) I wanted to delay my departure, but my wife insisted that I take advantage of the opportunity and take the seat we had managed to secure on the plane. So the following day, I left for Washington.

Upon arriving in Washington, my first priority was to obtain a visa to get my family out of Cuba. The quickest way to do this was by getting a job at an international organization. The secretary-general of the OAS [Organization of American States], Dr. José A. Mora, was most helpful; and I consequently became the coordinator of the OAS Department of Economic Affairs. This sparked a career as an international bureaucrat that lasted almost sixteen years. My wife and three children arrived on April 4, 1960; and Raquel and I began setting up a house from scratch for the fifth time since our marriage. My mother and younger brother, Roger, came shortly thereafter. We were extremely fortunate to have left early and saved our children from being exposed to the hardships endured by those who left later.

Once my work and family situations were settled, I concentrated my attention once again on the issue of Cuba. In some sense, my life in exile has been devoted to promoting the cause of Cuban freedom. In 1960 I became the Washington-based representative for the Revolutionary Movement of the People (MRP). I had to act very discreetly, since Cuba was still a member of the OAS, my employer.[†]

I was one of the few Cuban Americans opposed to the Bay of Pigs and almost stopped it with the help of a good friend, the journalist

Charlie Bartlett, who was, in turn, a good friend of Jack Kennedy's. My efforts, however, earned me the accusation that I was procommunist from none other than the CIA director, Allen Dulles. After the Bay of Pigs disaster, I continued my activities on behalf of Cuban freedom; this time, however, I was associated with a group of Major Huber Matos's former officers. This also ended in a most unsatisfactory manner when U.S. officials refused to listen—despite the fact that we were dealing (through Charlie Bartlett) directly with Bobby Kennedy (who was the attorney general at the time)—when we told them about an internal revolt that was being planned shortly before the Missile Crisis. After the assassination of President Kennedy, I became convinced that we were wasting our time and decided to concentrate my extracurricular activities on professional development to enhance my career as an international bureaucrat. Our family had been enriched again by the birth of a child in 1961, Beatriz, and so I decided that I should devote more time to them, too.

As a result of my career efforts, Galo Plaza, the OAS secretary-general who had succeeded Dr. Mora, promoted me first to budget director and, after an academic leave to obtain my master's at the University of Pittsburgh, to director of budget and finance. I had reached the top level of my international service career. We could afford a very comfortable life. Our older children were entering college, and our younger ones, high school. Cuba had moved into the background in terms of my priorities, although I still followed events there and from time to time did some research.

It was also time to change my citizenship from Cuban to American. Although I was entitled to both by birth, it was not until sometime after the Missile Crisis that I had given up the hope of returning to Cuba and decided that no matter what, I would spend the rest of my life in the United States as an American citizen. However, when I suggested the possibility of changing my citizenship to my immediate superior at the OAS, he discouraged me from doing so. There were already too many high-ranking Americans on the staff, he argued, and since OAS had to maintain some geographic balance on the staff, it was preferable for me to maintain my Cuban citizenship.

When Galo Plaza's term came to an end, I decided that it would be best to move into a professional career as an organization and manage-

ment consultant. I resigned my job at the OAS and started my own practice as an independent consultant. I also went through the change of
citizenship process. It was Mother who accompanied me—the son who
had appeared in the newspapers from time to time—with great pride to
the ceremony. After participating in a joint consulting company, I established my own, which was very successful. This new phase in my life
took me all over the Americas on consulting assignments to assist governments that were undergoing reform.

In 1983, President Reagan proposed a law that resulted in the creation of Radio Martí. This led to my getting involved once again in
matters related to Cuba. Shortly before the law was passed, a journalist
friend of mine, Cord Meyer, who had been in charge of overseeing
Radio Free Europe and Radio Liberty for many years at the CIA, told
me that, in his opinion, somebody like me should be in charge of research, the key function for a surrogate station like Radio Martí. If I was
willing to accept the position, he told me, he would recommend me to
Charlie Wick, the director of USIA at the time. I talked this over with my
wife, and she told me, "Fine. They would be paying you to do what you
would do for free anyway."

Sometime in late 1983, Charlie Wick was on the phone offering me
the assignment. Although I would have to take a big pay cut, I accepted
the position anyway and started work in April 1984. Breaking the news
monopoly Castro had enjoyed was a great challenge. We went on the air
May 20, 1985; and after having successfully organized the research operation, I was asked to assume the directorship of the whole station.
Once again I was working on Cuban matters, but this time as a U.S.
government official.

My tenure at Radio Martí was the second most fascinating period of
my life. I had to learn about a new activity—radio broadcasting—while
putting to use all of my previous knowledge and experience in order to
create an effective instrument of public diplomacy. At the same time, I
was assisting the U.S. in promoting the cause of Cuban freedom. I worked
from 7:00 A.M. to 7:00 P.M. The station became a great success, and we
were able to overcome the skepticism of many.

After the collapse of the Berlin Wall in 1989, Jorge Más Canosa, the
man who deserves the most credit for getting the Radio Martí legislation through Congress, wanted us to use the station to boost his ambi-

tion to become the president of Cuba. Up to that time, he had not interfered in any way with my directorship. Realizing the damage this would do to the station's mission, I tried to resist. Eventually, political realities prevailed, and the director of USIA at the time, Bruce Gelb, offered to promote me to director of research for USIA. Instead of accepting the offer, I resigned my post at the station and returned to my consulting practice.

Despite the disappointment I felt over the failure of the Bush administration to take a principled stand, I did have some moments of satisfaction. One evening, a man called on my direct line as I was about to leave for the night. The caller said, "I have been in prison for so many years, months, and days. I came out of Cuba a few days ago and would have called you before but did not have your phone number. I just want to thank you. One day in prison, I was feeling demoralized. We had smuggled in a little radio and were able to listen to Radio Martí. All of a sudden, my name was mentioned. Somebody was denouncing my predicament in jail. At that moment I realized that I was neither forgotten nor alone. Hearing my name gave me the hope and strength to continue enduring my situation. At that time, I swore that if I ever got out of prison, I was going to call you to thank you." Nobody can ask for a better reward for his efforts.

As I go through my seventies, I am phasing out my consulting work in order to devote my time to promoting a civil society for the difficult transition period awaiting Cuba after Castro. As one of the people who helped Fidel Castro come to power, I feel that it is my duty to do anything possible to bring about a transition in Cuba. My unfulfilled wish is to have been able to make a contribution to better public sector management in Cuba, as I have done in many countries in Latin America. I blame Fidel Castro for depriving me of that opportunity. At my age, and because I am an American citizen, it is unlikely that I will be able make such a contribution as a government official by the time Castro is out of the way. It is younger people inside of Cuba who will have to take over. All that people from my generation can do is try to share with them whatever experience we have gained.

When we came to the conclusion that our initial plans to eventually return to Cuba were not feasible—that is, after the agreement to end the Missile Crisis froze Castro into power for as long as Mother Nature wishes—we decided that we were going to go out of our way not to impose on our children the emotional stresses of dual citizenship. This choice was not easy, since we both also continued to be very active and involved in the opposition to Castro. We also sought to instill in our children pride in their origins and cultural background. To our satisfaction, all of them have integrated themselves in the U.S. melting pot with ease, while at the same time not forgetting where they come from. (February 28, 1998)

(Interview conducted and translated by Andrea O'Reilly Herrera)

*There are many false stories and misinterpretations about that trip that, as a firsthand witness, I know are not true. One has to do with Fidel being offended by Eisenhower's not receiving him during that first visit. Quite on the contrary, Fidel tried to cancel his meeting with Vice President Nixon because he did not want to give the appearance that his Washington visit was official. In reality, we had deliberately come to the States at the invitation of the American Society of Newspaper Editors, despite the State Department's offer of an official visit. Only the esteemed ambassador Dr. Ernesto Dihigo's threat of resignation dissuaded Fidel from taking this step, for the former argued that canceling the meeting with Nixon would destroy his credibility.

† For more on this subject, see Ernesto F. Betancourt's essay "Kennedy, Khrushchev, and Castro: A Participant's View of the Cuban Missile Crisis" in *Society* (July/August 1998): 77–85.

Growing Up Cuban American

Adela Betancourt Jabine

Adela Betancourt Jabine was born in Washington, D.C., in 1949. She now lives in Silver Spring, Maryland, with her husband and daughter, near her parents, Ernesto and Raquel Betancourt.

DEPARTURE, APRIL 1960. AGE 10

I was excited as the plane taxied away from the airport. We were going home to Washington, D.C., where I had been born, where I knew the gossip and the history and what was okay to mention and what wasn't, and the landscape was as familiar as my face. Then I saw my mother, turned toward the window, tears streaming down her face as she said goodbye to Havana. A wave of pity swept over me. As long as I could remember, she and my father had worked for and dreamed of a free Cuba, and Fidel's victory a little more than a year before had been their victory as well. They had been so happy in January 1959, so eager to come back to Havana, to get down to the business of creating a new Cuba. Now it was goodbye to all that.

My grandmother had left Spain for Cuba, and my mother had left Havana for Washington, D.C. I was the third generation to be uprooted, though in my case, I have never figured out whether I was being uprooted from Havana or Washington.

WASHINGTON, D.C., 1953–1959

I started school in September 1954. My decidedly agnostic parents sent me to parochial school, my first exposure to religion. It wasn't just my lack of religion that made me feel different. Whenever we sang, "Land where my fathers died," I would sing, "Land where my fathers didn't die." Most of my classmates were Irish American, and I longed to have freckles and red hair and a normal "American" name like Maureen or Mary Margaret, instead of pale skin, dark hair, and the exotic name of Adela. When Cuba was mentioned in school, it was only in passing, as a place Columbus discovered. My fourth-grade classmates got the idea from the illustrations in our history book that Cubans still lived in thatched huts and wore very little. They were puzzled that I seemed to have adapted so well to shoes and houses. Their ignorance made me furious, though I soon learned that the way to get them on my side was to make them laugh.

At home my parents were fighting to keep us Cuban. "Just because Americans do that doesn't mean we do that. We're not Americans; we're Cubans." This was my father's mantra during my childhood. Cubans stayed close to their families, didn't talk back, and were always polite and respectful to their elders. Cubans didn't run through the neighborhood in gangs of screaming children, and they didn't go on sleepovers. And Cubans did not answer their parents' Spanish with English!

What Cubans <u>did</u> do, as near as I could tell, was talk. Despite the no-talking-back rule, my parents encouraged us to think independently, so that if I disagreed with them—and I often did—I felt free to speak up. Every night we would linger after dinner, and the whole family would talk about everything from politics to what went on at school and work to the adults' childhood reminiscences. My parents' parties also featured talk; I would sit at the top of the stairs, convinced I was invisible, and listen, enthralled by uninhibited adult conversation, mostly about politics, especially Cuban politics.

During that time, my father worked as an accountant for a local automotive firm, but his real job was Castro's representative in the U.S. I understood that the whole point of this activity was to get back to Cuba, to overthrow the dictator, Fulgencio Batista, and create a free, democratic Cuba. I understood with dread in my heart that life in Washington was temporary and our real life was in Havana. I didn't want to go back to Cuba, which I envisioned as the land of eternal propriety. I wanted to stay in Washington and be an American and go to dances unchaperoned. At the same time, I was curious about what it would be like to live someplace you knew you belonged, where you wouldn't be pulled between English at school and Spanish at home, where an inclination to exuberant chatter and political talk was seen as natural and not something to be forgiven the weird foreigner.

So it was with decidedly mixed feelings that I greeted the events of January 1959. All at once the television was full of live pictures of Havana, and I could only marvel at the euphoric crowds. My fellow fourth-graders were astonished to discover that I'd been telling the truth all along and Cubans now lived in houses and wore clothes, even drove cars—and American cars at that. (Little did any of us know how many decades they would be driving those same American cars!)

HAVANA, 1959–1960

My father left for Havana and a position in Cuba's central bank right away, and we followed him at the end of the month. My brother, Ernie, and I suffered our first culture shock within minutes of arrival: Abuela Luisa, my father's mother, offered us milk and cookies, and she heated the milk—children in Cuba didn't drink cold milk, she explained. "Oh, yuck," we thought to ourselves but did not say, always polite and respectful to our elders.

Life in Havana was very different. For one thing, there were these long-haired bearded guys in olive green uniforms everywhere. (No doubt this prepared me for my adolescence in the America of the sixties, when the guys were also bearded longhairs, though most were trying to avoid wearing olive green uniforms.) Also, we had household help: a cook named Fidelina, who fascinated me with her stories about Havana before the Revolution. Another big difference for me was that I no longer had to battle ignorance about Cuba. Instead, I had to stand up for the United States against postrevolutionary anti-American fourth-graders!

Public life was markedly different too, in a way I very much enjoyed. In Cuba people talked on the street, and not just to people they knew. Anything was fair game for comment, from your appearance to the news to sports. Singing and dancing might break out at any moment. Food was sold on the street—ices, roasted peanuts, *churros*, fried plantains, little sandwiches of roasted pork. And not just food: there were street vendors all over, selling everything from lottery tickets to clothes to furniture. Ernie's favorites were the scrapbooks of the Revolution. These were like baseball cards, only featuring the *comandantes* of the Revolution—not just the Castro brothers but Che Guevara and Camilo Cienfuegos and other heroes—as well as famous battles and episodes, such as the landing of the *Granma*.

While Ernie and I were preoccupied with school and fitting in, my parents were concerned with two things in particular: the way the Revolution was going and my mother's third pregnancy. By November of 1959, my father was concerned about the direction Fidel was taking; as a result, he resigned from the Banco Nacional. Even then it was clear that Fidel preferred to jail those who disagreed, rather than let them go free. So Dad began discreet preparations for our eventual departure, a little complicated by my brother Louie's early arrival February 1.

BACK IN THE USA (WITH APOLOGIES TO THE BEATLES)

On the way back to Washington we had to change planes in Miami, and Ernie and I went to the soda fountain. I ordered for us, and the woman behind the counter looked dumbfounded. "I didn't understand what you said," she told me. I realized that in spite of my joy at being back in the U.S., I had ordered in Spanish. I often wonder how that woman coped with the subsequent invasion.

Although we'd left Cuba, my father hadn't given up on the idea of a free and democratic island yet. Once again he had a day job, a top position at the Organization of American States, but his real interest was, as always, Cuba. Like many other Cubans at the time, he had great hopes of assistance from the Kennedy administration.

During those years, our house was always bursting at the seams with relatives who stayed with us for varying periods of time when they first arrived in the States. My friends were amazed by my extended family—not just that there were so many of us all in one house, but that everybody loved each other so much. "These people kiss each other good-bye just to go into another room," marveled my friend Nancy (then and now my best friend).

The Bay of Pigs in April 1961 effectively put an end to my parents' hopes for Cuba. I was horrified and depressed, only too able to imagine the parents of people I had known involved on both sides of the disaster. I was also worried about my father because I knew this was a serious setback. Fortunately, he is amazingly resilient, and there was much else to occupy him, especially the birth on September 1 of his fourth child, my sister, Beatriz. Many years later, my father told me that it was at about this time that he and my mother realized that they were unlikely ever to see a free and democratic Cuba and decided to focus instead on living in the U.S., though their devotion to and interest in Cuba has never flagged.

BETTY COED
I spent my freshman year of college at George Washington University, getting straight As and becoming involved in the antiwar movement. One day in that October of 1967 a Chilean girl I knew came up to me crying, "*Lo mataron, lo mataron!*" Che Guevara's death was neither the first nor the last time that I realized I had a different perspective than my cohorts. Although I was naïve enough in 1967 to admire him, I also knew he wasn't the Marxist saint my Chilean friend mourned, just as I knew Fidel wasn't the kindly, funny visionary other eighteen-year-olds of the time idolized. I had already noticed that whenever fellow antiwar activists learned I was Cuban, they discounted what I said about Fidel and Cuba precisely because they assumed my personal knowledge made me an unreliable witness. An anti-Castro perspective was automatically wrong. This infuriated me and made me skeptical of both Left and Right—a good thing in the evolution of one's thinking.

AND THEN THEY LIVED HAPPILY EVER AFTER
Flash forward to the present: we all live near each other. I talk to my

mother daily and to my father almost as often. My siblings, especially Beatriz, and I e-mail each other regularly. Although my parents had decided after the Bay of Pigs to focus their energies on living in the U.S. instead of trying to get back to Cuba, they certainly didn't lose interest in Cuba. Indeed, my father's encyclopedic knowledge regarding all aspects of the topic is legendary. So when Radio Martí was established, Dad found his dream job.

One thing that has always struck me as sad and ironic is that my younger brother and sister don't know Cuba, which has loomed so large in all our lives. As a little girl learning English, Bea naturally spoke with an accent—which her first-grade teacher thought was a speech impediment, to my mother's chagrin—and yet she's never seen the Island, since she was born after we left. Of the four of us, "*la americana*," as they called me at school in Havana, has the most memories of Cuba and of the Cuban Revolution. Growing up outside of a Little Havana or other broader Cuban communities has made it more difficult for us to distinguish between what's Cuban about us and what's Betancourt.

As for me, I never dated a Cuban, and I didn't marry one either. Because we only speak English at home, our daughter, Susanna María (María for her two great-grandmothers), doesn't speak Spanish. It's strange to have a child who doesn't speak your first language. Nevertheless, the lullaby I sang my daughter was the same one my mother sang to me, and when Susanna was little, English speaker though she is, she could sing the lullaby word for word with my same accent.

As I reflect upon my identity, I realize that, just as I couldn't deny the U.S. when I was in Havana, I can't deny Cuba now. Am I Cuban, I ask myself, because my comfort food is fried plantains? Am I Cuban because my extended family plays such a large role in my life? Am I Cuban because when I drop a hammer on my toe I shout Spanish slang for female private parts instead of an English swear word? Yet I married an American and am raising an American—in English. I count in English and think in Spanish only in moments of extreme emotion. My reference points are much more American and English than Spanish or Cuban. I truly am a Cuban American.

My Life in Exile

María Antonia Soto

María Antonia Soto, the mother of Francisco Soto, was born in Catalina de Güines, Havana Province, in 1926. She came to the United States in 1961 and currently resides in Miami, Florida.

In reality, when I left Cuba in 1960 I was very happy, since I was going to be reunited with my husband, who had left a year earlier for political reasons. Our family of five—my husband, my aunt, my two sons, and I—were reunited in Venezuela, and shortly thereafter we came to the United States, where our life in exile really began. Although at first we missed our family and friends, as well as our customs and our way of life, we thought, and sincerely believed at the time, that we were on a vacation that I, for one, wanted to last until my children learned English. Since I didn't have to work in Cuba (also, it wasn't customary for women with families to have jobs outside the home), my husband and I thought that we could continue that arrangement in the United States. Immediately upon our arrival in Miami, Florida, however, we realized that I could no longer stay at home; we now both needed to make money to support our family.

My husband, who had been a pharmacist back in Cuba, was now forced to take on whatever job came his way: a dishwasher in a Miami Beach hotel, a taxi driver, and other odd jobs. I thought that I could find employment rather easily, given my skills as a seamstress. However, since I didn't speak English, it was very difficult for me at first. This hurt me a great deal, since my family needed me to work. After I learned some elementary English, I began to find work as a seamstress. I remember one particular job in which I sewed uniforms for the United States Army. I was on "piece work"; that is, I would get paid not by the hour but for each piece of a uniform that I completed. My Cuban friend Magdalena, who had gotten me the job, and I were the fastest seamstresses in the factory. In our minds, the faster we worked, the more money we brought home to our families. I remember one day a group of American supervisors came to see us; apparently the word had gotten out that we were very fast and meticulous workers. They stood in front of our two sewing machines while we quickly moved from one piece to another. I remember that at that time Magdalena and I were earning around $150 a week, which back then was a considerable amount. It was with my salary that we paid for food and household needs. My husband's salary paid for the rent, the kids' education, and all other expenses. Now that I think back on that time, I realize how useful I was to my family.

Once we started working, my husband and I felt happy and secure in the idea that if we worked hard and pursued our goals, we would succeed in this country of opportunities. We also felt happy that our children would have the same opportunities; that is why we didn't care about making sacrifices or working hard to get ahead.

After a number of odd jobs, my husband was finally able to go back to school and study so that he could practice as a pharmacist in various states in the country. Around that same time, our economic situation began to improve a bit. I was still working as a seamstress, my husband was beginning to practice his career again, and my aunt was at home taking care of the house and the kids. Although things were improving, we also began to realize that the possibilities of returning to Cuba were diminishing. Our beloved Cuba was being destroyed and falling into an abyss. My husband, who from adolescence was interested in politics, struggled in whatever ways he could to help Cuba. He would spend all of his free time and whatever little money we did have on the Cuban cause, which for him was a sacred duty.

At home my husband, aunt, and I tried very hard to maintain Cuban customs, such as serving Cuban dishes and keeping the Spanish language alive for the kids. I felt, however, that by using Spanish at home I lost my best opportunity to learn better English. At home, the language of communication was Spanish; the Cuban way of saying things and expressing oneself was routine. Our food, stories, and comments were always related in some way to our Cuban customs. As far as politics go, we always tried to keep the kids abreast of events on the Island so that when we returned to Cuba—what we always expected and yearned for—the kids would be conscious and, therefore, could contribute to Cuban society. My husband, aunt, and I were happy that the kids felt comfortable and enjoyed interacting with other family members who began to arrive in the United States through the Freedom Flights starting in 1969. Overall, I feel that we did a pretty good job of teaching the kids to integrate their two cultures. As time went by, I saw my two boys grow and flourish. I felt that we were doing our best for them; that was our plan and our most profound desire—that our children would succeed in this country.

Now that I have time to reflect, I believe that in our struggle to succeed, we didn't realize that our children not only needed material support, which we worked hard to obtain for them, but also something much more important: our time. Today, I think that in our eagerness to get ahead, our hectic running around, we lost time that we could have devoted to our children.

I have lived in the United States for more than half of my life. These have been some of the happiest and most horrific years of my existence. I have had incredible adventures as well as catastrophic personal losses, such as the deaths of my husband and my eldest son. Yet, throughout it all, I have been grateful to, and respectful of, this nation that offers its citizens so many possibilities.

In conclusion, I would like to share one final thing: something quite special that I feel very proud of. On December 6, 1998, my husband's friends and colleagues gathered to hold a special ceremony in Miami to celebrate his accomplishments over the years in service to the Cuban community in exile. At that time, Southwest Second Street to Northwest Second Street was renamed Fernando Soto-Hernández. This recognition has been doubly significant to me, since my eldest son, a decent and fine human being, as well as a good Cuban like his father, was also called Fernando. In my heart, I felt that on that day both my husband and my son were honored. As I spoke to the crowd, I was not nervous; I did not hesitate. I spoke from my heart, and I know that I spoke well. *(Translated by Francisco Soto)*

Lost Memories and Nostalgic Obsessions

Francisco Soto

Born in Catalina de Güines, Cuba, in 1956, Francisco Soto left the Island in 1961. He lives in Westfield, New Jersey.

No te dejes arrastrar por el síndrome del cubano, de la jodida nostalgia. Tampoco la niegues, dosifícala, súfrela, pero sin obsesiones, que sea alimento espiritual y no veneno.

Don't let yourself be dragged down by the Cuban syndrome, the fucking nostalgia. But don't deny it; take it in doses; suffer with it, but without obsessing. Let it be spiritual food, not poison.

—*Zoé Valdés,* La nada cotidiana

I left Cuba when I was five years old. (I know that some people would say that a five-year-old boy did not make such a monumental decision on his own, that I did not choose to leave, but rather was forced to emigrate by my parents, who were fleeing Castro's revolution. The fact that I feel compelled to interrupt myself to comment on such a simple statement as "I left Cuba when I was five years old" indicates how complicated and tangled the Cuban diaspora, exile, emigration, flight from communism—call it what you wish—has been for those who left the Island. It's apparent that when Cubans talk about Cuba, very strong emotions prevail—the type of emotions that define you as a human being, that make up your very essence. On the other hand, when non-Cubans—be they North Americans, Europeans, Latin Americans, or whoever—talk about Cuba, while they indeed can appear emotional, these emotions are based more on political convictions and ideology, rather than actual life experiences. It is very hard, if not impossible, to simply talk about Cuba and being Cuban without being sucked into the politics of the matter. That is why my seemingly simple declarative sentence, "I left Cuba when I was five years old," will never be simple; it will always be politicized. I am quite aware that whatever I say or write about Cuba will be interpreted against the backdrop of Cuban politics. This is the Cuban reality. It has and will continue to be my reality as an individual who, fortunately or unfortunately, was born on an island destined to become the site of significant twentieth-century historic events. Yet, while I can intellectually accept how history has marked my existence as a Cuban, emotionally I want things to be different. I have yearned often to simply be able to talk about my Cuban experiences without provoking political interpretations in people's minds. Even now, when I would like to write freely and without anxiety, I am aware of the fact that what I articulate will be deconstructed to prove allegiance to one side or another of the Cuban political debate. I long to express myself, to tell my story, to write my testimony, my life history, my Cuban tale, without falling into a political vortex. Of course, I know I will fail.)

After leaving Cuba, my parents briefly made their way through Venezuela, then Miami, and finally ended up in Elizabeth, New Jersey. (I can't help but parenthetically reflect on how neatly I have just summed up the emotional traumas of my family's flight from Cuba and subsequent relocations in one sentence.) As it turned out, the number of Cubans living in Elizabeth grew over the years, and Elizabeth became a rather large Cuban ethnic enclave. Still, we were one of the first Cuban families to move to the area. I was sent to Catholic school, where my brother and I were the only Cubans in a predominantly Irish and Italian parish. Although accepted, I always felt that we were different: we never lived in a house (until he died in 1993, my father always rented, for he was always ready to move back to Cuba when things would "normalize"); we never ate typical American food like hamburgers and hot dogs; my mother's *tía* (aunt), Julia, a spiritual grandmother for my brother and me, lived with us (to this day I address my aunts and uncle by their Christian names and only use *tía* to refer to that special woman, whose love and devotion I will never forget); and we only spoke Spanish at home.

This last point—of only speaking Spanish at home—was further underscored by the fact that both my brother and I were sent to tutors for private Spanish classes. To avoid any misconception regarding privilege, let me say that during this time my family was lower middle class. Consequently, our tutors would often be elderly ladies who had been teachers back in Cuba and, therefore, charged very modest fees for work they performed out of a sense of dedication and commitment. Although I hated them at the time, it was because of these classes, after school and during the summers, that I learned to read and write in Spanish. My father, who was university educated, always stressed the importance of education. He would always say that my brother and I would never have any problems in life if we studied for a career and, in addition, were totally bilingual, without noticeable accents in either language. At the time, I though that he was foolish for saying this, but, indeed, the old man was right on target. I am eternally indebted to his foresight in this matter.

What has always been amazing to me is that I do not have one single clear or concrete memory of my life prior to leaving Cuba. Time and again I have asked people about their childhood, and it seems that most people can recall various events in their lives when they were as young as two or three years old. Most can recall a series of incidents, stories of themselves in their backyards or in their homes with friends and family members. I, on the other hand, do not have one single recollection of my life in Cuba. It is as if those first five years of my life never happened. Yet the black-and-white photographs in my mother's photo albums verify my existence in Cuba: little Paco at the beach with his aunt Martha; little Paco playing with his brother, Fernando, in Abuelo's house; the black-and-white passport photo of little Paco. I can recall my childhood fascination with that picture in the light blue Cuban passport. I would find it among my father's important papers; there I was, Francisco Soto, son of María Antonia Soto López and Fernando Francisco Soto Hernández, born on September 2, 1956, in Catalina de Güines, Havana Province. It is amazing: five years of life and not one single tangible memory. Old photographs and family stories are all I have to reclaim those lost years.

During my youth and adolescence my parents, along with Tía, dragged my brother and me to countless Cuban political and cultural events. My family was very patriotic, and my dad was a very active politician. The truth of the matter was he loved politics. (And to dispel the stereotype that all Cubans who are politically conscious are Republicans, my dad was a registered Democrat who campaigned vigorously for Bill Clinton.) In my mother's photo albums there are countless photos of me in front of different statues or posters of José Martí. This zealous patriotism knew no bounds. Often, our road trips would deviate in order to find a special Cuban landmark in the United States. One such example was our first trip to Niagara Falls, during which Dad did not rest until we found the plaque dedicated to the famous Cuban Romantic poet José María Heredia, about whom, at the time, I knew nothing. Years later, in graduate school, I would finally read Heredia's famous ode "*Niágara*," in which he evokes Cuba's impressive palm trees and his own exile condition. I was profoundly moved: "*Las palmas ¡ay! las palmas deliciosas, / que en las llanuras de mi ardiente patria / nacen del sol a la sonrisa ...*"

I could go on and on about the many (post-five-year-old) memories I have, which at times I recall fondly and at other times I recall with deep sadness. Why sadness? Because my soul cannot help but lament the anguish, losses, and separations that befell my father, mother, brother, and Tía Julia, the people whom I have loved most in my life. For it was the five of us who lived together and supported each other for well over a decade before other family members from Cuba began to arrive in the United States through the Freedom Flights in the late 1960s. During that decade, in our isolation from other family members, my father, mother, and Tía created a domestic space for my brother and me that kept Cuba alive. We ate, laughed, cried, celebrated, worried, feared, loved, and, to use Cristina García's turn of phrase, dreamt in Cuban.

I have spent the last thirty-six years of my life trying to understand what happened to me and my family once we left Cuba. For something did happen to us, something that marked us for life. Personally, it has marked me in such a way that as much as I have tried to escape from it, I indeed suffer from the "*jodida nostalgia*" that Zoé Valdés describes in her novel *La nada cotidiana*.

The negotiations I have conducted over the years with my name, Francisco, are quite telling in regard to the different cultural identities I have assumed and continue to assume in my life; in some sense, my names are in constant conflict, a conflict that represents my cultural fragmentation. Among my family, for example, everyone calls me Paco, the nickname common to all Franciscos. Instinctively, I respond and readily identify myself as Paco. The name triggers emotional as well as linguistic responses. As Paco, I am 100 percent *cubano* and communicate only in Spanish. Over the years, the few Americans who have tried to anglicize the pronunciation of Paco as a cute way of referring to me have been swiftly made to feel, in no uncertain terms through my demeanor, that I absolutely do not approve. Most of my longtime American friends call me Frank. This started back in high school when a teacher decided on the first day of classes that Francisco, the name I have always used to introduce myself, was just too long a name and that Frank better suited me. (During grammar school I had a series of aliases: Fran, which I loathed; Tubs, an awful nickname my brother christened me with during my fat stage; and Mr. Soto, the common form of address used by the nuns in parochial school.) Of course, high school peer pressure made it impossible for me to ever go back to Francisco after being baptized Frank. Anyway, Frank was a significant improvement over Fran or Tubs (which, at times, became Tubby when people wanted to be cute or mean). During college Frank stuck, for I saw it as a more virile name, thus assisting me in my sexual conquests. When I tried to introduce Francisco again during my first teaching job, for which I was hired to teach Spanish, the principal of the school again found the name too long and shortened it to Frank. It was not until graduate school, when I started to study Latin American literature, that I again introduced Francisco; and it was, of course, easily accepted. And it is Francisco that I insist people call me today when they first meet me.

Although I now readily use the term Cuban American to identify myself, I have had—and to a lesser degree still have—some difficulties with it. At first, I flatly rejected the term as a way of describing myself. I always felt Cuban, or at least wanted to feel that way. Despite the fact that I could not recall a single thing about Cuba, my allegiance was to that small island country. On the other hand, my American friends would always say that I was kidding myself—that I was more American than Cuban. I actually hated it when they would say this, for I feared losing even more of my "Cubanness," that unique manner of joking, laughing, celebrating, and perceiving life, than I had already lost. But I have learned to negotiate between the opposite sides of the hyphen. Indeed, I am a "one-and-a-halfer," as Rubén Rumbaut and Gustavo Pérez Firmat would say, neither totally Cuban nor totally American. I circulate within and through both cultures and, at times, reap the benefits of this intermediate location. Yet, at other times, I also despair from having to constantly accommodate myself within an American mind-set that I really do not share 100 percent. As much as Pérez Firmat would like to stress the positive side of those of us who live on the hyphen—how we feed on what we lack, how we are free to mix and match pieces from each culture, how we are excellent negotiators, and so forth—I believe that we pay a high price for this duality of being part Cuban, part American—a duality that at times can and does fragment the soul.

Let me just provide one anecdote that perhaps might shed some light on what I term my culturally fragmented weltanschauung, a worldview that over the years has left me in a rather unstable position, physically disconnected and emotionally disoriented. I will always remember one political event I witnessed as an early adolescent that at the time impressed me greatly; but only as an adult have I been able to understand the fullness of its charged symbolism. The event took place some thirty years ago on a Sunday afternoon in Union City, New Jersey, in an auditorium filled with Cuban families. Prior to the actual event, which was to commemorate either José Martí's birth (January 28, 1853) or death (May 19, 1895), we were ushered into a back room where a wooden raised map of the island of Cuba, with each of the six provinces (Pinar del Río, La Habana, Matanzas, Las Villas, Camagüey, and Oriente) all partitioned off, was on display. The model was curious in that it was raised a good foot in the air. Also curious was the presence of a large sheet of glass lying to one side of the room that was intended to fit over the raised wooden map in order to seal it off. Everyone's queries were soon answered when a large canvas bag was dragged into the room, the contents of which were poured onto the raised map of Cuba. What I saw was reddish soil neatly packed into each of the six provinces of the map and quickly sealed with the large sheet of glass. We were all informed that the soil, in fact, was from Cuba and had been procured through some clever means—given the strict travel restrictions to the Island at that time—once again proving how resourceful and inventive Cubans can be. Everyone just gazed through the glass, which in fact had been a brilliant stroke of genius—for the common dirt that was before my eyes had just miraculously been turned into a treasure that I coveted and wished to shove into my pockets like a common thief. As I sit here and finally write about this event, I am sure that the symbolism of the soil is rather obvious and apparent. Yet I am more interested in the symbolic value of the sheet of glass that prevented me from touching, holding, and ultimately taking home what I believed to be physical proof of the existence of Cuba. Certainly I am not the first to write about how my generation's idea of Cuba is largely based on the recollections and nostalgic reminiscences of our parents, who kept it alive for us. Thus, we have been influenced by our parents' Midas touch of nostalgia that turns every story into "But when we lived in Cuba...."The sheet of glass, however, signifies the other side of my yearning (for lack of a better word) for Cuba.

As a child, I suffered from a repeating dream that disturbed me greatly, so much so that I would wake up and seek refuge in either my parents' or my Tía Julia's bed. In this horrible dream, I was literally buried alive between my parents, but instead of the lid of the coffin above us, we were under glass as people walked over us and went about their business without noticing us. I guess you don't have to be Freud to figure this dream out, but as a kid I was clueless as to its significance. Apparently, but unbeknownst to me at the time, the flip side of yearning for Cuba and obsessing over my cultural allegiance was the fear of being swallowed up by Cuba and Cubanness and not living life or, as anthropologists would say, facing the forces of "acculturation" (acquisition of culture) and "transculturation" (the passage of one culture to another) that would allow me to "blend" or "assimilate" into the American mainstream. In *Life on the Hyphen: The Cuban-American Way*, Pérez Firmat challenges these notions and, in response, coins his own term, "biculturation," to designate a position in which Cuban Americans achieve a balance that makes it difficult to determine which is the dominant and which is the subordinate culture. Although I deeply respect Pérez Firmat's work and find his study uplifting in stressing the beneficial consequences of Cuban Americans' intermediate position, it fails to provide answers for the traumatic dreams of a young boy not equipped with the intellectual sophistication necessary to analyze his cultural dilemmas. And here I am not thinking just of myself—or of Cuban Americans, for that matter—but, rather, of the children of other ethnic groups who face similar cultural and social quandaries. Of course, now that I am an adult, I can appreciate the advantages of both cultures; but there is no denying that the past and its hardships have left emotional scars.

As I finish writing this, my mother is spending a few weeks visiting me at my home. She is helping me around the house by cooking Cuban food, sewing my clothes, and making me *un cafecito* in the afternoons. Between my running in and out to the university and doing my daily chores, we have time to sit and remember and retell stories from the past. Just this very night, she started telling me one about when I was a kid in Cuba, and she immediately interrupted herself by saying, "*¡Ay! pero es verdad, tú no te acuerdas de nada de Cuba.*" She's right; I don't remember anything. Yet I still wanted her to continue. And she did. And I felt that she was helping me remember.

Thirty-Two Years Later
(FOR MY SISTER, ALICIA)

Flora González Mandri

Flora González Mandri is the mother of Rachel Werner Baldwin. Born in Havana but raised in Camagüey, she left Cuba as an adolescent with her sister, Alicia, as part of Operation Peter Pan and was relocated to California. She now lives in Cambridge, Massachusetts.

When my sister, Alicia, and I landed at the Havana airport, thirty-two years after we had left in 1962, she insisted that I take a picture of her right after she stepped on Cuban soil:

"I can't believe we're in Cuba, together," my sister said. "Why don't you take a picture of me in front of the Cubana airplane?"

In 1980 I, alone, had returned to the Island after eighteen years of absence, looking for the little girl I had been back in the fifties and early sixties. I had also had my picture taken then, but I was so nervous that I managed to lose my camera before developing that memorable photograph.

On that first return, I was carrying with me all the carefully forgotten memories of having left with my sister, who had been eleven; I had been thirteen. My parents had said goodbye to us at the airport. "Just for a short while," they said. The separation would be temporary, they assured us, but my unspoken fears told me otherwise. We ended up waiting to leave at the airport for hours, inside the *pecera*, that memorable glass-enclosed waiting room. Our parents were on the other side of the glass, feeling the anguish of sending their daughters away for the first time in their lives, hoping against hope that they had made the right decision. They had to protect us from the threat of communism. We were so young and susceptible . . .

In order to protect myself from the mixed emotions of that goodbye, I had erased my parents' anguish from the map of my soul. So in 1980, when I felt I was an adult—like my parents had been—with a daughter of my own, I had returned to recover my lost past, my Cuban past. Was losing my camera in Havana a weak gesture representing my failed attempt to recover a memory? Because that first return failed to recapture those forgotten hours in the *pecera*, I persisted and persisted by returning. I kept boarding planes alone from Miami to Havana in 1985, 1987, and 1988. On each trip, I gradually recovered the streets and the houses of my childhood; I forgave my parents for letting us go so gently; and I began to reconstruct my ties to the red soil of my native Camagüey.

In 1994, while returning with my sister, I asked myself, "What memories and emotions would this trip bring?" With my Kodak camera, I did capture the image of my sister smiling. But what of my identity? Would I find it on the way to Camagüey with Alicia?

After several days in Havana, Alicia and I boarded a plane again, this time to accomplish the real purpose of our trip: to visit our cousin, Mario, and his daughter, Gloria, in Camagüey.

. . . Even though this was the fourth trip back to the land where I grew up, the mask of the knowledgeable traveler began to show gargantuan cracks. As a child, I was always guided around the streets of Camagüey by my mother, aunt, or grandmother; I seldom went out alone, other than the short walk to and from school. During previous trips, I assumed the persona of the family member who had returned after having made it big back in the United States. I often relied on the knowledge of the taxi drivers to get me around. This trip was different because I did not feel alone; I did not have to play the role of the provider. When we left Cuba, two sisters alone, I had stood as the parent to my younger sibling. Now, I thought, it was time to reverse the roles. So I began to rely on my sister, who had the advantage of a psychology degree and many years of practice reading my emotional well-being. This was not a casual trip to Cuba for me—if there is such a thing as that for me, or anyone who had left as a child, "never to return." Many of us who had left as children, the so-called *Pedro Pan* generation, did go back looking for their relatives and their roots. This time, however, I was returning with my sister, just as in '62 I had left with her. The circle now felt complete, even though on this trip she was the one in charge.

My fantasy had been that like that first exit, this reentry would put me, the older of the two, in the driver's seat. After all, Mami had told me, her thirteen-year-old daughter, "You take good care of your little sister now, you hear?" And I had taken that sentence as a command, as my destiny until "that wonderful moment when the family of four would again reunite." And like the "good" girl I had grown up to be, I had taken good care of my sister, always following the examples of my mother, grandmother, and aunts, who had given each of us the clear sense that we were a whole person, our limbs firmly secured to our torsos, our hair neatly combed, and our heads held high. A whole person definitely connected to a very large extended family.

But our goodbye at the Havana airport January 11, 1962, had shaken all that. And the feeling of taking one's own body for granted in all its integrity had disappeared. As if in fear that I might wake up one day with my arms and legs disjointed and dancing away from me to the sounds of some mysterious *New World Symphony*, I acquired the bad habit of unconsciously tensing my muscles to retain physical integrity. Only when I returned to the neighborhoods of my childhood did my body feel that it owned the space that surrounded it. Then the tension in my muscles melted and flowed through my toes into the cobblestones of the colonial streets in Havana, or into the rich, compressed dirt of the Casino Park in Camagüey. For the first time after my many returns, I could share these feelings with Alicia, who knew exactly what I was talking about.

"If we close our eyes and hold hands, we can pretend we never left, can't we?" she said, as if to bridge the chasm between Miami and Casino Park. As soon as she made the statement, we held hands so as to let the power of our shared past invade our present. But our pragmatic American selves knew better. I now know that remaining Cuban as a citizen of the United States means hard work. Hard work to retain my command of the Spanish language. For my sister, it is hard work to understand that being Cuban in Miami is not the same as being Cuban in Camagüey. Hard work to learn about the reality of Cubans who stayed. Hard work to imagine, "What if I had never left?"

My present intellectual work has me obsessed with the artistic production of Cuban women around my age who live and write their poetry, produce films, and paint canvases in a land with severe economic limitations, rather than in the "land of opportunity" where I reside. Their cultural expressions cross over to the mainland, terra firma, and become a lifeline for my sister and me, who left unexpectedly, unaware. During each trip to Havana, I collect more engraved images of the Cuban culture I experience, vicariously, as they stare down at me from the walls of my living room, adding color and warmth to the cold Boston winters.

Returning to Cuba in 1994 also meant dealing with our family's present. Those who had been enthusiastic about revolutionary changes early in the seventies now spoke about the different stages of hunger. The phrase "the Special Period," coined by Fidel Castro to help the population deal with extreme shortages, was pronounced in increasingly sarcastic tones. And as usual, Cubans dealt with it all by making jokes:

Q: How does Cuba resemble a Christmas tree?
A: When Havana is blacked out, Trinidad to the east lights up, and when Trinidad blacks out, Santiago at the tip shines brightly.

This reality and the manner in which my family deals with it was brought home to me during a cool night, as we sat around a table piled high with chicken and rice, plenty of fried plantains, and the sweetest of mangoes, when the lights went out. Our conversation didn't skip a beat as the younger cousins pulled candles of all sizes out of drawers around the house and restored our faces in the soft yellow hues of candlelight. I was certain that the abundant display at the table was possible because our visit came at the beginning of the month, when families received their food rations for the remaining four weeks. We were told that people could only manage with their rations for two weeks; after that, you had to *inventar* (improvise).

After a long exchange of news on either side of our experiences as a family forever split, two cousins in their early thirties walked us back several blocks to the house on San Pablo Street. They advised us that even though we could walk down the middle of the narrow streets, because there was no gas for the few cars in the city, we had to be careful because people speeding on bicycles would be unable to see us. In order to protect pedestrians, bicyclists whistled tropical birdcalls, and we opened up a path for them.

We walked as tourists, in a leisurely way. A soft breeze was blowing; people sat on their doorsteps; and up high, stars crowded the clear skies of a moonless night. I gazed up, overwhelmed by the serenity of a city without the luxuries of modern conveniences, and felt ashamed that I could find my peace at the expense of their hardship. That night, I was thankful for the young people in Cuba, who doggedly performed the daily chore of securing a meal by pedaling miles for a bag of corn, a handful of fruit, and, perhaps, some cheese. Even the most revolutionary admitted that without our financial "help," those bicycle trips to the farms, where a "dollars only" policy prevailed, would be out of the question.

At one point when Alicia and I were alone, she turned to me after a quiet moment and said, "Did you notice that we haven't once spoken about having to go on a diet?" Our work—as a professor and a psychologist in cities where cars seem to be the only means of transportation—makes it possible for my sister and me to help our cousins on the Island. Because our jobs are so sedentary, we "watch our weight," a preoccupation a Cuban would never have.

For many years, while living in Chicago, where whole communities of Mexicans and Poles worked to support their families who remained back in their countries of origin, I had felt proud that our family in Cuba was doing just fine without our help. It's ironic that my family, once divided over political issues, is now joined through the dollar economy in Cuba. We, on the northern side, live on the nostalgia of our childhood and with the hope that our contributions will ease our relatives' days; they, fully immersed in the culture we supposedly crave, survive the "Special Period" by making jokes and walking arm-in-arm with those of us who occasionally return. Having returned to Cuba with Alicia, who now lives in Miami, accomplished a long-unfulfilled desire for me: the desire to feel accompanied in the reconstruction of our shared memories. What remains to be done is for us to visit Camagüey with our respective children, Sean and Rachel. They must learn to experience Cuban reality without the nostalgic mediation that Alicia and I have provided for them. They, too, long to walk with their cousins arm-in-arm. We all look forward to the time when the U.S. embargo and electric blackouts cease to turn our island into a Christmas tree.

Island of Color

Rachel Werner Baldwin

Born in Hershey, Pennsylvania, Rachel Werner Baldwin is the daughter of Flora González Mandri. She currently resides in Watertown, Massachusetts, with her husband and daughter.

Feeling a little apprehensive, Tricia Torres and I walked to the meeting of the Carleton College Latin American Student Organization, which was mainly composed of Chicanos. The campus was writhing after a racial incident. Person after person turned to us to ask us how the Hispanic population was reacting.

Tricia is a red-haired woman born in the United States, but both her parents were raised in Puerto Rico. My name is Rachel Kathryn Werner Baldwin; I am half Cuban, with dark brown hair and eyes. Anyone who walked past us on campus, however—even someone who knew us— wouldn't recognize us as Latinas. Although I have dark hair and eyes, my name betrays me, just as Tricia's appearance betrays her.

When we walked into the small meeting room, we recognized that all the artwork on the walls was Mayan. It was not a room that would allow me to be Cuban. In my search for a sense of familiarity in the cool Minnesota landscape, I had found more uncharted terrain in this Chicano community. I had hoped for the colors and smells of my house, the colors and smells that I had so carefully hidden from at home.

Home had always been a transient thing for me and my mother. My parents had separated when I was five, and I stayed with Mom. She was a Spanish professor, who moved us from New Haven to Dartmouth, Chicago to Boston. The people and scenery around us changed, but inside our house, the colors and sounds of Cuba always remained. The walls beamed with the colorful paintings my mother had brought home from all over Latin America. The largest and the brightest consisted of two vibrant watermelon slices separated by a tree in a painting by the Cuban American artist Nereida García-Ferraz; inscribed in the painting is the refrain "*Para siempre volver a ti.*" The air was filled with Cuban *boleros* and the voices of my mother and her friends as they chatted in Spanish. I always responded to the voices in English, but I won't deny that I understood the words and belonged to the world of my living room. People came and went, but I always felt it was just the two of us clinging to our island of color in foreign surroundings.

The last home Mom and I had together was in Belmont, Massachusetts. When I used to bring friends home, it felt like I was bringing them to a new world. I would open the door, and the sweet smell of garlic danced around us. My friends would look around as if they had been transported without warning, like passengers getting off a plane, not knowing what to expect. The sudden change left them unsure as to whether they should be scared or excited at all the color in the paintings, rugs, and blankets. There were no illusions of things blending together in a pool of masterfully matched pastels and flower prints like I found in their homes. Colors in my house were shamelessly primary, clashing, and alive.

I would quickly shuffle newcomers into my room; I am not sure if I did it for their comfort or mine. It was a far more familiar place to them. It was a soft mix of stained wood and quiet colors, a carefully orchestrated world. My formerly yellow chest of drawers had been stripped to the wood and stained, and the brightly dressed dolls my mother gave me would be tucked behind a stuffed bear. James Taylor would play softly in the background. We would giggle like teenage girls from any country; and as they earned my trust and love, I would introduce my friends to the world of my Cuban living room, as if I were sharing the most intimate part of myself.

If I became too overwhelmed, I could always remind myself and everyone around me that I was half Swiss. My father is a tall, blond-haired, blue-eyed man who is awkward and introspective—the complete opposite of the loud laughter, food, and colors that characterize my mother and my Cuban family in Miami. As much as I held him up as an example, he had not been in my home since I was five. Our connection lived in music. He played his clarinet or piano, and I would accompany him singing or on my saxophone. The music we made was beautiful, but my home was located in the smells, colors, and food of my mother's island.

In going to Carleton College, I convinced myself I wanted to separate myself from all that was home. I hopped on a plane to the frozen world of Minnesota with only two suitcases, the bare minimum to survive. I was going to be an all-American college student in the Midwest, where the snow would wipe out any semblance of color I had left. I wouldn't have to face the difficulties of defining myself; I would let my surroundings define me.

I set up my dorm room with the desire to leave behind the chaos of color, but suddenly discovered I had lost the sense of comfort and belonging that came with the clashing of color. I quickly found ways to fill my room with hues of home. My roommate from northern Minnesota was overwhelmed by the glow of my side of the room, which faded softly into hers. I was building my own island, my own version of Cuba, with all the colors and things I had hidden away from my friends at home. My desire to define and explore myself was what had led me to the Latino meeting with Tricia.

When we arrived, Tricia and I looked around at the members of the club, all American-born Mexicans. A few minutes into the meeting, people began to ask us about ourselves. As we spoke, their faces remained cold and distant. Finally, one outspoken member questioned Tricia: "How could you possibly know what it is like to be a Latina with that red hair and fair skin of yours?" Tricia turned to me with a sigh and left the question unanswered. They demanded to know where we had learned Spanish because ours was much more rapid and inconsistent than theirs. Tricia spoke a brand of Spanish spoken among Puerto Ricans who live in Chicago; I had constructed a collage of the Spanish from the countries in which I had worked and studied during my summers abroad: Paraguay, Spain, and the Dominican Republic.

I felt like I was perched on the fence, where I often get stuck, somewhere between Cuban and American. My father had given me fair skin, Nordic features, height, and a sarcastic sense of humor. I was born and raised in the United States but am clearly a product of my mother's home and beliefs. The Cubans I have encountered are wary of a girl who has never stepped on the soil of Cuba or lived in Miami, and who is too fair-skinned and too tall. Americans are wary of my skin that is too olive, my laugh that is too loud, and my colors that are too bright. Neither world wants me, nor will they give me up completely to the other.

Tricia and I left the meeting early. "¡Qué barbaridad!" she muttered. "Since when do two Latinas have to look alike?" We reentered the *americana* world that had asked for our "Latina" reactions, a world that had pushed us into that Latino enclave from which we had just been rejected.

After leaving the meeting, I began to question what Tricia and I called "the mythical solidarity of Latinos." We had looked for a community in which to comfortably express ourselves but instead became aware of the diversity and complexities among Latinos. The fleeting thought that my experience would have been completely different if I had entered a room of Cuban Americans passed through my mind, but I knew then that I was once again oversimplifying and idealizing. After all, I am not fully Cuban.

My travels to Latin America have helped me restore the language of my childhood and foster my personal growth as a Latina. However, I cannot help but feel that my search is lacking as a result of my inability to travel to Cuba. I have explored half of my heritage by traveling to Switzerland to meet my paternal family, but the closest I have come to Cuba is standing at Key West and staring at a shadow on the horizon. I have seen my mother's photographs and listened to family members' voices in Miami, but in my heart, the true Cuba is the island of my mother's living room.

Life al revés

Alicia Serrano Machirán Granto

Alicia Serrano Machirán Granto was born in 1949 in Santiago de Cuba, Oriente Province. She left the Island in February 1963 and now lives in Buffalo, New York.

I left my childhood behind in Cuba at the age of fourteen. I still have a terribly vivid memory of my brother and me in the *pecera* [the fishbowl] at the Havana Airport, where they placed children leaving the country to keep them separated from their relatives as they waited to board the plane that would take them away from everything and everyone they had known since birth.

A couple of weeks after the disastrous Bay of Pigs Invasion, our family home was confiscated. My parents were given forty-eight hours to remove their belongings and go *"donde carajo pudieran,"* which turned out to be my grandmother's house. I, along with my brother and sister, was bewildered and in a daze; I was so full of pain that I could not even talk about it.

Together, my parents, Adela Machirán Ortiz and Diómedes Serrano Cala, came to the painful conclusion to send my brother and me out of Cuba when my father discovered that I was writing anti-Castro graffiti on the walls of a beach clubhouse that we frequented. After having overheard a *militario* say that if he caught the "bastard" who was writing things against *"El Comandante,"* he or she would regret it, my father became frantic with fear when my older cousin, who had already spent three months in jail for distributing pro-freedom-of-speech flyers, told him that I was the culprit. The deciding factor, however, came when my parents saw my name posted on a list at the Conservatory of Music of "promising piano students" who were chosen to be sent to Moscow on an art exchange scholarship.

In order to leave as a family, my father would have had to resign his job, which would have severed the means he needed to get us out of the country. With the same epidemic desperation caught by hundreds of parents, who were fearful that their children's brains would be "washed by communism," Papi and Mami sent my brother and me out of Cuba in January 1963; they remained behind with my sister, who was mentally retarded. We were sent to my maternal uncle and aunt, who lived in Miami; they had been exiled for a couple of months. I remember being in a daze for days. It was not culture shock yet—being surrounded by the family softened that blow somewhat—it was trauma, which thanks to my immaturity manifested itself in deep denial. In effect, I convinced myself that I was visiting the States as a tourist, and soon the vacation would be over and I'd go home to my parents.

In addition to the emotional stress, I went from lacking nothing in Cuba to living a provisional life in Florida. For example, because I had almost nothing to wear, other than the clothes on my back, each night I would wash the armpits of my dress with Ivory soap (I came to hate that soap) so I would have something clean to wear to school the next day. Despite the material poverty we faced, I still have some very fond memories, such as the occasional evenings spent with our Cuban neighbors playing bingo with pennies.

A few months after our arrival in the States, my uncle was relocated to Wilmington, North Carolina; and my brother and I went with him. (He was my mother's oldest brother, and he decided to take on the responsibility of caring for his sister's children.) This is when culture shock *really* hit me. Not only were there no Cubans around, but in the town where we lived, Blacks walked on one side of the street, and Whites walked on the opposite side. We were regarded with either curiosity or suspicion by both. I remember feeling completely displaced and not belonging; the possibility that I might not see Cuba again suddenly occurred to me, and it triggered a defensive reaction in me. As a result, I submerged myself in my studies so intensely that I became one of the top five students at the Catholic school I attended. Once in a while, I would wake up in the middle of the night with anxiety attacks. "Oh my God," I would ask myself, "am I ever going to see my parents again? Am I ever going back to Cuba?"

I skipped the tenth grade and moved up to the eleventh grade at a nearby public high school; and again, most of the unpleasant experiences that occurred stemmed from ignorance on the part of my classmates, or resentment and/or jealousy on the part of those who could not accept the fact that "a boat refugee" could excel academically. Things began to change, however, in January 1965, with the arrival of Papi and Mami.

After years of trying to gain passage out of Cuba, my parents were finally granted a visa, thanks to my cousin, who lived in Mexico and had Mexican citizenship. When they arrived in Mexico, they applied for entry into the U.S., certain that the worst of their trials were over and that we would soon be reunited as a family. To their great dismay, they were denied passage to the United States—a denial due, in part, to my sister's handicap. In desperation, my parents and my sister, along with several other Cuban refugees and Mexicans, crossed the Rio Grande in a canoe, were arrested upon their arrival in Brownsville, Texas, and were tried as illegal aliens. Although the judge at their trial announced that they were going to be deported—a pronouncement that caused my mother to faint right in the middle of the courtroom—my parents discovered soon afterwards that the trial had been a sham, staged in order to deport the Mexicans who had crossed into the States. As a result, all of the Cubans were granted entry, and my parents were flown to Miami, where my brother and I were waiting at the house of Adela Babún, who had generously offered to share her rented one-bedroom house with all of us until my parents could get back on their feet.

After only a few months in Miami, my parents announced that we would be moving, a decision based on the fact that most of the better jobs available to Cubans in south Florida had already been taken. At the Cuban Refugee Center, which was relocating Cuban professionals all over the United States, they learned that teaching positions were available in New York and New Jersey. (My father refused to allow my mother to work at any job other than teaching, the profession she had held in Cuba.) Although my parents had the option to go to New Orleans, they thought it best to move further away, in order to resist the temptation of returning to Miami. As a result, we moved to Niagara Falls in September of 1965; and my mother, at the age of forty-seven, went back to school to get her certification to teach in the States.

Despite our isolation (we were the only Cuban family in the area at the time), my parents worked very hard to preserve our Cuban culture. When I became engaged to a very old-fashioned Italian American, it was very important to us that the wedding ceremony reflect our heritage. As a result, I wore a *mantilla* as my wedding veil, and we insisted on paying for the reception meal so that we could serve the traditional Cuban *puerco asado* to our guests.

Soon after my wedding, however, my parents decided to move the family to New York City. Due in part to his inability to speak English, my father was unable to find work in Niagara Falls. In addition to feeling culturally isolated, he felt emasculated, for he was unable to fulfill his traditional role as provider and "man of the house." Knowing that there were teaching positions available to my mother in New Jersey, my father accepted a job in Merrill Lynch's Latin American division, a position that did not require him to speak English.

My family's departure, coupled with my father's sudden death in an automobile accident in 1969 and the reality of both marital and maternal responsibilities, brought my *cubanismo* to yet another stage. I remember one particular Saturday morning, while I was getting ready to do housework, I put on records of songs that were hot around the time I left Cuba, such as "*Sabor a mi*" and "*Imágenes*" (just writing about it now brings tears to my eyes); as I listened to the music, I succumbed to an enveloping cloud of nostalgia that would physically paralyze me for hours at a time. This would happen so very often that I started playing a little tune over and over in my head at night:

Espavílate muchacha, que no estás
haciendo na', te has quedado sin na' de allá, y
no estás creando na' por acá.

Wake up, girl; you're not
doing anything; you're left with nothing from there, and
you're not starting anything here.

Of course, the *allá* was Cuba, and the *acá* was my new life (which was supposed to be filled with marital bliss!) in Niagara Falls. Finally, I woke up one morning, gathered all my wonderful Cuban records together, and took them to Goodwill. No more Cuban music to listen to and get immobilized by! I also stopped trying to teach my (then) three babies

Spanish, and I joined and became very active in an Italian lodge, becoming the first non-Italian officer to serve in it.

In the meantime, my husband was unintentionally helping me define myself even more as a *cubana*. Soon after our marriage, I realized that we were separated by some very fundamental cultural differences. For instance, whereas he tended to be negative and shortsighted, I tended to be positive and always see a light at the end of the tunnel—whenever he focused on the dark side of things, my optimistic approach would cause him to accuse me of always wearing "rose-colored glasses." I was also misunderstood by others, such as my new extended family and my colleagues at the university, several of whom referred to me in a negative sense with terms such as indomitable, ambitious, nonconformist, cocky (more often than not), and the like. "Aren't you ever satisfied?" I would be asked. "Why don't you stay home where you belong?" Others still would ask, "Is the way you behave typically Cuban, or is it you alone, or, perhaps, the way that you were brought up?" In self-defense, I would always respond by saying, "I don't know. . . . I don't know how to be any other way. I don't think I would know how to behave differently." The fact that I didn't stay home raising my family and taking care of the housework, coupled with my professional success, defied their stereotypical notion of how a Latina should behave. In other words, I wasn't subdued and submissive and docile. Both personally and professionally, I have always felt driven to excel; I have tried to do my best and be as productive as possible, so as not to mar that prevalent image of my people as hard workers. In the same vein, I do not share *mis problemas y pesares* with the entire world (a typically Cuban trait!), and I grow weary of the manner in which many of my non-Cuban co-workers whine and moan and groan about their working conditions. I find myself thinking that rather than complaining, most of the Cubans I know would be moved to action, either by trying to change things or by looking for another alternative (perhaps even another job).

In addition to my own career and my work in the community, I wanted to pass on to my children the empowering legacy of their heritage. Oftentimes, I would wake up in the middle of the night and worry that my children were being deprived of the family warmth and caring that I witnessed during my own childhood. So surrounded were they by Italians while growing up, I feared no matter how hard I tried, I would fail. As a result, my most desperate effort throughout the last twenty years has been to instill in my children a positive frame of mind and an optimistic perspective (what they now refer to as "the Cuban mentality we got from our mom"). My interaction with my own children has always been guided by an attempt to replicate a collage of experiences from my early years growing up in Cuba—the caresses and hugging, the tolerance of everyone talking at the same time, the abundance of food (which I love to prepare), the warmth and company of family and friends. To have them feel that way is the greatest reward for my tenacity in adhering to teaching them by action and example and not by simply talking and preaching.

I can honestly say that every aspect of my life is impacted by my heritage, sometimes more than I would like. Externally, I have adjusted very well to American life. Internally, however, I often feel schizophrenic in my dealings outside of my Cuban "circle." In some sense, this other person inside of me sees and reacts to most things differently than my American twin. Whenever I am mistaken for something other than a *cubana*, or even called an American-Born Cuban, I have made it a point to explain that I am Cuban, born and raised. Why is this so? I'm not exactly sure if I can explain, but I suppose it reflects my tremendous pride in my Cuban heritage.

This testimonial, which is based upon several conversations, was co-written by Alicia Serrano Machirán Granto and Andrea O'Reilly Herrera.

On Being Cuban
Gina Granto-Penque

The eldest daughter of Alicia Serrano Machirán Granto, Gina Granto-Penque was born in 1968 in Niagara Falls, New York, where she still resides with her husband and two daughters.

How I feel: Growing up, I never had this instant revelation that I was the daughter of a Cuban-born mother. I have never not felt Cuban. Yes, there were the sure signs, such as the smell of Latin food always filling the air in our house, the rhythm of the Spanish language filling my ears;

and, of course, the music in our home had a slightly more Latin sound than any others in our neighborhood. However, the feeling of being different, of not belonging, was strong.

Now, I can't say that it was entirely the result of my Cuban heritage; but living in Niagara Falls, New York, in the early 1970s and having a Cuban heritage was nothing less than rare. I learned how to adapt to any situation and "fit in" at an early age. Now, mind you, I am a walking contradiction. I have golden blond hair (that was natural until age twenty-five, ha ha) and sky blue eyes; so it wasn't that I didn't belong physically—I certainly didn't look like your typical Cuban. Rather, it was a state of mind that characterized my behavior—a Cuban state of mind. In adulthood, that is how I can best explain the way I think, my contradictory features, and my love of the extraordinary.

Being Cuban is in my blood. I remember how I felt so alive, so a part of things, when we would go and see my cousins in New York City or Miami. Everything seemed to make sense; my cousins and I had this real connection that was instant and natural and was a result more of our shared Cuban heritage than of being cousins. I have found that Cubans are different from other Hispanics in many ways. I have met many Spaniards, Mexicans, and Puerto Ricans in my life. They are all wonderful, and their culture has so much to offer that I respect and love. But Cubans have this pride, this unique bravado, that is unmistakable. You would be hard pressed to find Cubans "down and out" for long. They have this uplifting quality that, if not examined carefully, can be mistaken for "cockiness."

My mother never had to explain Cuba to me. I knew it; I breathed it. I didn't have to be taught my heritage; it was all around me. I don't know why I identify so much with being Cuban. I was never embarrassed by it as some of my siblings may have been. I remember my sister being called a "half-breed" or "half-wit" (something like that) because of our heritage. That may have helped shape her need to "shed her Cuban skin." I don't blame them, nor do I fault them; I just accept that we have different experiences and feelings.

Being Cuban has contributed to me being a "staunch American," perhaps because, knowing what my mother went through as a Cuban exile, I appreciate this country so much. Clearly, the United States is not a perfect country, but the ideals and foundation, which promised freedom and liberty and made us once—and will make us again—the most envied and respected country in all the world, are there. As a result of my mother's experience, I now have what is almost a patriotic obsession with American politics—not so much from anything she did or said, but because of what and where my mother came from.

Mind you, my mother never told us some long sad story. She only spoke of fact and not feelings. I knew this because I read everything I could get my hands on and listened to every story that was told. (When the adults thought I was playing, I was listening and taking mental notes.) Mom dealt with the here and now. If I would inquire about Cuba or say, "Mom, how hard it must have been saying goodbye to Abuela and Abuelo. How did you do it?" Mom would say matter-of-factly, "Yes, it was difficult; but look at me now."

There were always a lot of unanswered questions and unexplained issues between Mom and us. It was almost as though if she dared to give Cuba her undivided attention, it might hurt too much. On a few occasions, I remember walking in on Mom crying. I knew she had been reminiscing about her childhood in Santiago. But tears and thoughts of the past vanished when anyone entered the room. At all costs, my Cuban-born mother made sure that her children never saw her hurting. And more than anything else, she made darn sure her kids were grateful for what they had and remained positive people in every sense.

Looking through my mother's eyes, bigger and better were always around the corner in our home. Nevertheless, I know that leaving your home, your country, your parents at thirteen years of age, for reasons that are impossible for anyone—let alone a child—to understand, is unnatural. It is extremely damaging to the mind and the heart. It creates a sense of distrust and anger that, even when buried and not brought up too often, can destroy the human spirit. But my mother and so many like her did bury these feelings and did press on and do what they thought needed to be done. Mom worked hard, first raising five children, then fulfilling a promise to her father to finish her education. Her sacrifices have definitely contributed to my drive and overall involvement in life; but I also temper it because I want to be home for my own children. As a young mother of five children, Mom had to work hard to prove herself, and, of course, it was difficult to "start over," something most of us don't have to deal with. After all, it isn't like starting a new job. It is leaving behind everything you love most in the world and, more importantly, everything you know. Like other Cubans whom I know, she never complained; she refused to be a victim, and she never expected a handout.

If I had been raised by second- or third-generation Cubans in America, I don't believe I would have seen or felt the pain of leaving Cuba. My grandmother speaks of Cuba with so much love, it consumes me. We have had many discussions in my family about going to Cuba, and we do fantasize about what it would be like to go and be there—perhaps we would find old friends and relatives and reclaim land and precious possessions. It is all romanticizing on our part, though. Nevertheless, my uncle (Mom's brother) insists that he is "going there to overthrow Castro and live on the Island in *his home.*" I have been hearing this all of my life; it is pathetic, in a way. This is what Mom never wanted: to be so absorbed in the *what ifs* that you forget to live. She always reminds us that we are living in the here and now; whereas poor Tío is still planning and scheming to get to Cuba. What he doesn't seem to realize is that despite the fact that Castro has robbed the Cuban people of their freedom and basic human rights and stolen the physical island of Cuba, he does not own the spirit of Cuba; it lives within its people and has survived and grown through the Cuban American generation. I feel it when I am with my cousins in Miami or on the Internet with other American-Born Cubans. There is an energy that is so sacred and so spiritual that it is overflowing into the new generation. I believe with all my heart that it is this spiritual energy that carries us and keeps Cuba alive in our hearts.

One Mother's Testimonial

An Interview with Ada Manero Alvaré

Born in Sagua la Grande, Ada Manero Alvaré left Cuba via Jamaica in August 1980. She lives in Miami, Florida.

Like many of our friends, we were initially sympathetic with Fidel and the revolution. We believed him when he assured us that the revolution was as green as the palm trees; but he betrayed the Cuban people. (Afterwards we joked that the revolution was actually more like a *guayaba*: green on the outside and red on the inside.) At the time, we thought that Batista's government had many problems; now, in retrospect, the corruption of his regime pales in comparison with what has been happening in Cuba for forty years.

By 1961 it became apparent that something was wrong. Not only was the government confiscating property, but they sent most of the nuns and the priests out of Cuba on a ship called the *Covadonga*. The government also took over the private schools and turned them into public institutions. All of the secondary students were told that they had to go to the *escuelas al campo* (the work camps in the country where student "volunteers" helped to meet agricultural quotas). The conditions at these schools were deplorable. Not only did the children have to sleep in hammocks, but they had to keep all of their personal belongings, including things such as toothpaste, at their sides, or they would be stolen. The children were also sent out into the country to do mandatory labor, such as cutting cane. I was particularly worried about my son, Carlos, mostly because he was asthmatic and could not endure the intense heat and the dust from the cane.

During those early years, we watched many people leave the Island. Knowing that Carlos would be sent to the military if he stayed, we decided that it would be best for him and his sister, Adita, to leave Cuba. When we began discussing the possibility of sending the children out of Cuba my husband, Cruz, suggested that regardless of my decision, he should stay behind. He was a surgeon who founded a well-known clinic in Sagua and worked for the government. He was fifty-seven when the revolution began. He felt that if he left Cuba, he would not be able to practice medicine in the States and that he would never find work on account of his age and his inability to speak English (my husband had absolutely no facility for language!). I didn't know what to do—I was emotionally torn between leaving the Island with my children or staying behind and caring for my husband, who was sixteen years older than I was. As a result, I consulted with a priest, who advised me to stay behind, a decision that Cruz also supported. The priest said that the children would adapt to the change much more readily than my husband would and that I shouldn't worry about them. Although it was a decision I would live to regret for the rest of my life, I decided to take the priest's advice. I never dreamed that I would be separated from my children for seventeen years.

Initially, our plan was to send the children out for a year or two until Fidel fell from power. We then began sending them money on a regular basis—that is, until Fidel seized the banks and proclaimed that the currency was no good. As a result, we could not change our money. In effect, we had to start all over again. For seventeen years, we worked to send money in *bolsas negras* [black bags] to the children, who were, by that time, reunited in the States and living with Cruz's sister, Yoyín. But the process was very slow because the exchange rate was one American dollar for fifteen Cuban dollars.

Soon it became clear that the sacrifice we had made for our children was in vain; by that time, we were not permitted to leave Cuba—they were detaining all medical professionals because the government desperately needed doctors. To no avail, Carlos and Adita tried to claim us several times. After the Missile Crisis, it was impossible to get visas to the United States. You had to gain entry through a third country, and we had no relatives or friends outside of the United States. We felt completely helpless and alone. We had no control over our lives.

This lack of freedom is epitomized for me in two events, both of which resulted in our being denied passage out of Cuba. The first took place shortly after we had finally been granted a visa to leave the Island. Once we knew that we were leaving, I offered to sell a piano that had once belonged to Adita to a neighbor who said he'd like to buy it—it was a way of raising a little money to take with us. When he refused to pay, I decided to give the piano to the nuns. Perhaps out of anger, the neighbor's wife denounced us by reporting the fact that we were giving away the piano to a friend of hers, who was on the Committee for the Defense of the Revolution. As a result, our exit visas were revoked. This happened a second time when I decided to give a neighbor, who was very poor, a couch for her son to sleep on—she had two young boys and only one bed. Once again, the same neighbor reported me to her friend, and our visas were suspended a second time! In effect, I realized that I didn't even have the right to give away the things that belonged to me.

Over all those years, I never gave up trying to leave the Island. I can't even begin to count the number of mornings I got up at 4:00 A.M. to catch the 5:00 bus, the first of several connecting buses to Santa Clara, where the immigration office was. As I sit here talking, I can still hear the sound of my heels tapping against the pavement and echoing in the deserted streets. Once you arrived in Santa Clara, you would have to wait in line just to get a ticket for an interview. (If you had to go to the bathroom, you were forced to use the facilities in a whorehouse that was across the street from the immigration office!) Sometimes you would wait in line for hours and never make it into the office.

In 1975 my husband, who was very ill, was finally granted permission to retire. We hoped that his retirement would make it easier for us to get an exit visa. One year before we left, however, Adita and Carlos came to Cuba as part of the Family Reunification Plan. Words cannot describe the emotions that I felt when I saw them. Adita arrived in June; she came with her son, whom I had never met. Carlos came for one week in August; when he got off the bus in Varadero, I didn't even know him. Do you know what it is for a mother not to recognize her son?

The following year, we finally received permission to leave Cuba. (We were only allowed to take one bag of clothing, weighing no more than forty-four pounds, between the two of us!) At the time, Adita was living in Venezuela (she's in Texas now), and Carlos was in Brooklyn; so we moved in with my sister, Melba, who had retired and moved to Miami. Although I was grateful for all of the help we received from the U.S. government and happy at the thought of being able to see my family once again, I cried the entire first year after our arrival. For the second time in my life, I was forced to make an impossible choice: for me, leaving Cuba meant leaving behind my memories of infancy and youth; it meant leaving behind my friends; it meant leaving behind my entire world. Can you imagine, at sixty years of age I had to start my life all over again (little did I know that within two years I would also lose Cruz, who came to the United States with lung cancer).

Although I still mourn the loss of my country, the ultimate exile for me was being separated from my children. In addition to being deprived of the joy of watching them grow up, I missed being present at their weddings, and I missed seeing the birth of my grandchildren. But we were not the only ones left alone; I had to close my old aunt's eyes because her children were in the United States and were not allowed to return to Cuba, even though she was ill and dying. There were so many of us left alone. Though I have many regrets, I want to close by saying that, despite all that is negative about communism, in some sense it taught me to be a better person, in that I learned to place all of my faith in my spiritual life and in human relationships, as opposed to material things. Nevertheless, if I were to live my life over again, I would never have sent my children out of Cuba alone—never. (March 16, 1999)

(Interview conducted and translated by Andrea O'Reilly Herrera)

Tía Ada's Arroz con leche

INGREDIENTS: 1 cup short-grain rice (*arroz valencia*); 5 cups whole milk; 1 quart water; 1²/₃ cups sugar; powdered cinnamon; cinnamon sticks; ¹/₄ tsp. salt.

Rinse rice well (3 or 4 times) in water. Then soak it for at least 4 hours (more if possible) in about a quart of water and ¹/₄ tsp. salt. Bring the rice to a boil and cook it for about 5 minutes on high heat; then lower heat and cook until the rice begins to get soft and most of the water is evaporated.

In the meantime, begin heating the milk; once it's warm, gradually add 3 cups to the rice, and then keep cooking on low heat. Once the milk is nearly absorbed, add the remaining 2 cups of warm milk and the sugar; continue cooking on low heat until the mixture begins to thicken and the rice is fully cooked. Then pour the mixture into a Pyrex dish, fold in cinnamon sticks, and sprinkle the top with powdered cinnamon. Allow mixture to cool; then cover and refrigerate.

Losing Eden

Carlos Alberto Alvaré

Carlos Alberto Alvaré was born in Sagua la Grande in 1948 to Ada Manero and Cruz Alvaré. He arrived in Miami at the age of fourteen in April 1962. He lives with his family in Upper Montclair, New Jersey.

My parents made the decision to send me out of Cuba when I was fourteen years old; my older sister, Ada, was sent by boat to family in

Venezuela three months ahead of me. At the time, I did not know what I was in for, and I really commend them for making such a difficult decision. I'm not sure I could have made this decision myself. There were rumors at the time about the government taking children from their families and indoctrinating them in the communist way of thinking; that prompted many Cubans, such as my parents, to send their children out of the country.

I must say, those were frightening times, as one did not know what one would encounter. Though on one hand I was excited about the new adventure that lay ahead of me, it was very difficult to leave my family behind. My father did not go to the airport to say goodbye; in retrospect, I think it was his way of avoiding a painful moment. Over the years, I have come to appreciate that nonact as being full of kindness; in some sense, he had spared both of us the pain of separation. My mother watched me depart from the edge of what was called "the fishbowl" (the *pecera*); there, you could see people leaving and being processed from behind the crystal wall until their flights were called. We were only allowed to take three pair of underwear, shirts, etc. (my sister had wanted to leave Cuba on a boat so that she could take more clothes!); we had to be frisked before leaving, and our suitcases were searched. My mother had insisted that I take my swimming trunks, which I was wearing underneath my pants. Rather than thinking about the fact that I was being separated from my family, I worried about that bathing suit all morning—though luckily I did not have to strip like most people. This goes to show you the silly things one worries about!

The trip to Miami went very quickly. The only thing that I remember is that the man next to me gave a sigh of relief about leaving Cuba; I, on the other hand, felt completely numb. I ended up staying with some distant relatives in Miami; and it felt like a very long, lonesome summer before my father's sister Yoyín (Cristina Villa) came and I was reunited with Ada and my cousin, René.

I spent my first two years of high school in Baton Rouge, Louisiana, with Tía Yoyín and René. René was studying at LSU at the time, having taken advantage of the special scholarships that they were offering to Cubans. My junior and senior years were spent in Lansdowne, Pennsylvania, near my aunt and uncle, Carmen and Nemesio Alvaré, who had settled outside of Philadelphia. I spent the summer in Avalon, New

Jersey, with my cousin Teté and her family. Throughout my years in high school, there was always a feeling of loss—something akin to the idea of losing Eden. It's a notion that many Cubans still hang on to, reflecting their impulse to idealize and functioning as a kind of defense mechanism that offsets reality. Though we were able to communicate with my parents through letters and an occasional phone call, we were very cautious about what we said and wrote because our letters and calls we censored, and we were afraid of saying something that would compromise them in some way.

After high school, I spent a year at Penn State studying engineering. The following summer I reunited (in Miami) with a former neighbor from la playa de Cayo Esquivel, who encouraged me to study in Salamanca, Spain. My plans to go abroad were complicated by the fact that I had a Selective Service number, which could require me to be sent to Vietnam. Thanks to the help of Teté and her husband, Hughie, I managed to file all the necessary paperwork, and in the fall of 1967 I left for the University of Salamanca, where I studied medicine. In part, I believe my impulse to go to Spain represented an attempt on my part to recreate my roots, for there we spoke the same language, and the temperament of the Spanish people and the way of life were similar to Cuba.

Despite the fact that those were very good years, I decided to return to the United States in 1973. Although I was still regarded as a refugee in the U.S., I felt as though I belonged more to the United States than to Spain; in Spain, I always felt like an outsider, perhaps because none of my family was there. Upon my return, I tried to assimilate and blend in.

In 1979, after seventeen years of separation, I returned to Cuba for a week. I remember the trip as taking only twenty minutes. It seemed so absurd to me that although we had been separated for so many years, my parents were actually only a short distance away. Seeing my parents was very emotional for me, for they were very different from how I remembered them. Of course they were older, but their personalities had also changed; I found them to be more mellow than I remembered, and more attentive. For one week I got to experience their lives; what struck me was their preoccupation with food, something they constantly talked about. For all that they had suffered, however, they retained their sense of humor, for they and their friends were always joking about the lack of food.

As I grow older, I am comforted more and more by the simple things I remember from my childhood, like the summers we spent together with friends at Cayo Esquivel. Although I believe that adapting to a new culture is more difficult for older people, since they are more set in their ways, I still struggle with the fear of losing my identity as a Cuban. This fear, I suppose, is part of my destiny as I grow older, for the second generation (which includes my own children) is not being raised, for the most part, with a Cuban sensibility.

In response to this fear, I have recently begun to listen to more Cuban music, as well as to read works by modern Cuban and Cuban American writers. Nevertheless, I have always felt as though I was on the outside looking in—a feeling I experienced in Cuba because I was regarded as a *gusano*, since I was preparing to leave and did not participate in the revolution; and, initially, in the United States, as a result of the differences in language and customs.

I must say that Cuba has always been a very special place for me; I think that as a child, everyone needs a place to which he or she can return (if only in memories) and be replenished. For me, the memories I have of Cuba are always accessible and provide me with a lot of comfort. In my view, Cuba was not just a place; it was also a happening, which is composed of music and food and the voices of people with which one is surrounded while growing up. I feel that I have come full circle in my appreciation of my Cuban heritage. When I left, I had to go through the stage of feeling numb and angry at the displacement and the chaos that characterized my years in the United States, followed by a period of mourning my loss. The sense of reconnection that I experienced by going to Spain consequently allowed me to return to the States and prompted my desire to assimilate and blend in. During the last few years, however, I have returned to my memories and look to my culture as something that brings me solace and comfort. I now see myself as having two countries—two cultures living side by side. Although I would like to return to Cuba again someday, I know it will not be the same as the way that I remember it, not that it should. For we have all changed, even though we continue to recreate the past. But the past changes, I suppose, just as we change.

Snapshots

La hora de los mameyes

FROM *Cuba: Poems*

Ricardo Pau-Llosa

Ricardo Pau-Llosa was born in Havana in 1954 and left the Island in 1960. He lives in Miami, Florida.

After the voyage from Spain,
during which the ship almost sank,
what most amazed my grandmother about Havana
were the *negros* and the *mameyes.*
At sixteen and fresh from steerage, with her ragged
world bundled tight as a proverb, she wandered
through the new city pausing only to stare
at the street vendor—Africa's teeth singing
about what must have been some kind of fruit,
elliptical, brown, covered with pubic strands.
Only later would *mameyes* become daily fruit.
Now they were a sign that her Asturian poverty
had been torn from her
by a hurricane in the mid-Atlantic.

My "*mameyes*" were the snows of Chicago
and the sounds that were not, could not be
words coming out of every mouth.
The first grade teacher suddenly uttered
a word I recognized: "idea."
It sparked in me the cognate's false hope
that worlds are all but one.
Only my grandmother standing in the sidewalk snow
waiting to walk me home
understood my dread of school
had nothing to do with winter.

Confusion stalks us, waited
for the decrepit French liner to stumble
onto a hurricane. The sailors, in life vests
and pistols, herded the immigrants

who had boarded at La Coruña to the deck.
Their prayful anthems did nothing.
Knuckles whitened on the railings
as the ship listed, and all they saw
on one side was ocean and on the other sky.
Was this *la hora de los mameyes*,
the moment of truth? How can one pass
the test of certain doom
when the outcome is determined by chance?
In the mind only, in the ideas that settle there
calmly amid the chaos of flesh and history.

Ideas have their own reasons.
I hear the accents of *asturianas* in Miami,
the seamstress or the woman
who makes Cuban coffee at *Versailles*,
and I am impelled to recall my grandmother
who never gave up her Celtic cadences
in seven decades among Cubans.
I recall her recalling Havana
and Asturias and how she went from immigrant to exile
during the Spanish Civil War.
She would scrounge to send monthly packages
of food, clothing, and medicine to her family.
Her neighbors in Havana loved to watch her
turn red with fury, so they would chant
"*Viva* Franco!" when she walked by.
She would tell me her stories over and over,
and, cornering everyone who came to visit,
she would discharge her rigorous memories
of unforgiven Spain. The stories were like a compass,
fixed recollections, like an actress
reciting her lines, her life desperate
to become an idea in someone else's mind.

"*Cada cabeza es un mundo*" was her refrain,
every mind is a world unto itself
aching to transmit itself, like the spoors

we leave in the snow. "In Asturias,
where your blood comes from, it snows like this.
The heat of Cuba has made you weak.
Close your mouth and breathe through your nose."
Let us hope, Abuela, that blood remembers.

Soon I will lose you, your ire-blushed face
and your stubborn sense of justice.
You will shake your Republican fist
in every story about you I will have to tell myself
when some accident of experience triggers it.
And I will shake my fist against Fidel
to taste a futile echo if nothing else.
The ship will regain its course
and the *mameyes* will welcome you to Havana.
Once an exile, now I am a native
limping through unbroken snow,
affirming in the silence of my head,
that worlds are different
even if rage and love
beg us to dream otherwise.

This poem was first published in *Manoa* 4:1 (Spring 1992).

Abui

María Cristina García

María Cristina García was born in Havana but left with her parents in 1961 when she was only seven months old. After spending a month in Miami, her family relocated to the Bahamas. In 1964 the Garcías returned to Miami; in 1976, when María Cristina was sixteen, they relocated to Guaynabo, Puerto Rico, where she completed high school. She now lives in Ithaca, New York.

During the 1960s, my grandmother was obsessed with hippies. "No, you can't walk to your friend's house by yourself because you'll get kidnapped by hippies and end up dead in the Florida Everglades with ants coming out of your mouth." This was her favorite admonition, and the way she tried to keep her Americanized granddaughters in line. "No, your parents can't let you be a Girl Scout because some hippie *marijuanero* will grab you as you sleep in your tent, and you'll end up dead in the Everglades with ants coming out of your mouth." "Don't walk off by yourself at the beach because . . ." Well, you get the picture. As far as I know, my grandmother never actually saw a real hippie, except on television. There weren't too many hippies in Miami, much less in Little Havana. Nor did she ever visit the Everglades. But they represented everything that was scary and threatening about life in exile. They were symbols of how long those ninety miles between Cuba and the United States actually were.

You could easily imagine that my grandmother—Abui, as we called her—was a timid little old lady who rarely left the house, afraid of getting mugged or lost in the crazy maze of Miami. There were so many Cuban grandmothers who did fit that profile in *el exilio* of the 1960s and 1970s, women who had suffered dislocation from homeland, friends, and family, and who now protected their hearts from further pain by refusing to venture outside the home for anything except church, the doctor's office, and grocery shopping, and then only accompanied by a younger relative who could act as bodyguard/interpreter. These women had left one society in transition to enter another, an American world that was very different from the one they had seen in the Hollywood films that had played in local movie theaters in Havana, Trinidad, and Santiago. This American world had mass murderers, hippies, and racist rednecks who screamed "stupid Cuban!" at you for just about any reason. So they stayed within the safety of their homes in Little Havana, Westchester, and Hialeah, baby-sitting their grandchildren so their daughters could work in factories and retail shops, and entertaining themselves by listening to call-in shows on La Cubanísima, watching *telenovelas* on Channel 23, and engaging in telephone therapy with friends. "*Oye, Cuca, que bueno lo tuvimos en Cuba, ¿verdad?*"

But Abui was just the opposite. She was fearless. The same woman who clipped articles about horrendous crimes from the *Miami Herald* to warn her granddaughters thought nothing of traveling alone on a Trailways bus to visit a cousin who had been resettled by the U.S. government on the other side of the country. Go figure. She learned enough

English to ask and understand directions, to call emergency services if needed, and to brag about her grandchildren to some poor unsuspecting *americana* who had the misfortune of sitting next to her on the bus. Yes, Abui not only knew the shortest itineraries between Miami and New York or Chicago, but she was an authority on the Miami city bus system. Refusing to be a burden to my father—who would have willingly and lovingly driven her anywhere—she learned how to get around the city on her own. She loved the independence of being able to take off whenever she wanted, restricted only by the bus driver's timetable. She was determined to embrace her *exilio*, to know Miami as well as she knew Havana, and she ultimately did.

So this same woman who protectively tried to clip her granddaughters' wings was probably the most adventurous person in the family. Widowed at the age of forty-nine, she moved in with her daughter and son-in-law, my parents, and quickly took her place as the matriarch of the family. For years, my mother never made a decision without consulting her, whether it be about dinner or disciplining her children. But unlike other Cuban matriarchs whose domain was limited to the household, my grandmother's domain extended to the streets. When cars broke down or rides were unreliable, friends and family called her to ask what bus lines they should take to get to work, Publix, or *el refugio*. "*Bueno, chica, tomas la número 32 y te bajas en LeJeune. Cruzas la calle y tomas la número 16, pero no te distraigas porque si te descuidas terminas en Hialeah. Oye, y no se te olvides pedir el 'transfer.'*"

Of all her grandchildren, my sister and I chose—or were chosen—to be her sidekicks on most of her adventures and explorations. After school we accompanied her to the Woolworth's on Miracle Mile for banana splits. On weekends we went to recitals and patriotic pageants at the Dade County Auditorium, or we went to see Spanish-language movies at the Trail or Tower theaters, stopping afterwards for a *pastelito* or *croquetica* at a nearby Cuban bakery before we headed on home. We went to Orange Bowl parades and the *parada de los reyes magos*, arriving hours beforehand with a picnic basket to ensure a good view along the route. We attended masses at the Ermita de la Vírgen de la Caridad del Cobre to pray for political prisoners and for Cuba's liberation from the despised Castro. We checked in on friends and relatives who had arrived recently on the Freedom Flights, exchanging food and clothing for stories. A few times we even attended political rallies sponsored by different exile groups at the Bay of Pigs monument on Calle Ocho, even though they bored my apolitical grandmother to exasperation. "*Estos cubanos hablan tanta bobería*," she'd mutter to herself. Believing in the regenerative powers of the ocean, she took her grandchildren to the beach to detoxify our systems of American carcinogens. "*¡Niñas, respiren! ¡Llenen sus pulmones de aire!*" As we swam, she taught us to sing the Cuban national anthem, as well as her favorite songs: "*He perdido una perla . . . la he perdido en el mar. . . .*"; "*Solamente una vez, amé en la vida . . .*"; and the perennially favorite "*Guantanamera.*" Every New Year's Eve, as our parents went to parties or stayed home and slept, Abui celebrated the new year with her grandchildren. At the stroke of midnight, as we drank our *cidra*, ate the traditional twelve grapes, and listened to the Cuban anthem on La Cubanísima, she offered the adamant toast, "*el próximo año en la Habana*," followed a few seconds later by a humble "*si Dios quiere.*"

So much of what we learned about Cuba and things Cuban was learned from my grandmother, not only on our adventures through Cuban Miami, but at home through her numerous stories, which she recounted as we did our homework, helped cook or clean the house, or prepared for bed. My parents were busy rebuilding their lives in exile, ensuring that we had clothes, food, and a roof over our heads; if they dreamt of returning to Cuba one day, they kept it to themselves. But Abui did dream about returning, and her constant talk of Cuba turned the Island into a tangible entity that sat down to dinner with us. But she never let her nostalgia paralyze her as it did so many of our elders; there were just too many things to do and see in *el exilio*, and she regarded her life as one fascinating, albeit painful, adventure. She never criticized her Cuban-born grandchildren for identifying more with the United States, perhaps because she was a Catalán by birth herself and knew that a homeland was more than just an accident of geography. Nevertheless, she was insistent that we appreciate Cuban culture, and this had more to do with her desire to relate to us and be part of our lives than with her dreams of relocating to Cuban soil. One day, while peeling potatoes for that night's dinner of *carne asada*—I must have been seven or eight—she asked me what I had learned at school. I replied in my awkward Spanish that I had learned about George Washington, the father of my country. She frowned, and after a few minutes' silence, she announced to me that it was time that I began Spanish and Cuban history lessons, neither of which were offered by the Irish nuns at my Catholic school. She made me agree to a pact: we would sit together for a few minutes every day after school. I would practice my Spanish by reading to her from the *Diario de las Américas*, and she would practice her English by reading to me from my school texts. We practiced this near daily ritual for years. Since we had no books on Cuban history, she told me stories about José Martí, the Cuban war of independence, and assorted Cuban scoundrel-politicians. Her accounts of family history were more accurate than her accounts of Cuban politics and society, the latter mediated by her race, class, and gender and a touch of creative license. But as a child I accepted her stories as gospel truth because I adored her and because she was my strongest link to this mythical island.

Among the few possessions Abui was allowed to take out of Cuba was a manila folder full of photographs, postcards, and even love letters written to her by my grandfather—each with a particular set of stories. My sister and I relished those afternoons when my grandmother would take out her photos and letters and go through each story again as if chanting a litany to the Virgin. We dropped everything we were doing to hear the stories again, laugh, and tear up. As we looked over the worn photographs of assorted relatives, yet one more time we reminded each other in hushed voices how lucky we were to have come out looking like one set of ancestors rather than another.

In 1991, after so many years of stories, I became the first member of my family to return to Cuba for a short visit: I was invited to participate at a conference at my parents' alma mater, the University of Havana. My parents reacted to the news of my trip with disapproval, concerned that my attendance in some way legitimated the Castro regime. My grandmother responded to the news by drawing me a map of Havana on a yellow legal pad. On this grid map with dozens of streets, she located all the places that were important to my family's history; the major landmarks were not government buildings, stores, or museums but, rather, the churches, schools, and homes where their lives had been nurtured. Most of the churches no longer stand, converted by the Cuban government into more utilitarian structures; and the schools and homes are in sad decay. But every Cuban to whom I showed that map was amazed by my eighty-year-old grandmother's memory of a city that she hadn't seen in almost thirty years. My mother's elementary school, the family business, my grandfather's tomb in the Cementerio Colón were all exactly where her map said they were. And as I walked through the streets that my grandmother loved and knew so intimately, I couldn't help but feel the presence of all those relatives whose faces I had stroked in the photographs of Abui's manila folder.

Abui died in 1997 in Texas, of all places. As fate would have it, over the years my entire nuclear family moved to different parts of this southwestern state for reasons of school or work. Abui reluctantly uprooted herself from Miami as well, wanting to be close to her family and believing that she could still be of use to my parents despite her increasingly frail health. She created a small Cuban world for herself in this Tex-Mex land, brewing her strong Cuban coffee every morning, watching Univisión because most of the shows originated in Miami, and tracking down any Cuban who lived within a twenty-mile radius for conversations on the telephone. Thankfully, she died in her sleep, surrounded by photographs of those living and those waiting for her. We arranged for her to be buried in her beloved Miami because it was the closest she could get to her beloved Cuba. The cemetery where we buried her in southwest Miami is full of *abuelitas* like her, who tried to instill a sense of *cubanidad* in their grandchildren, and who dreamt and prayed of returning to their homeland but never quite made it.

A few weeks before she died, on one of our regular road trips to visit Abui, my sister and I sat down with her for a familiar ritual. Abui pulled out her photographs one more time and recounted our origin stories. We laughed and cried and thanked God yet one more time that we didn't look like a particular great-great-grandmother. We told her about our lives: the baby my sister and her husband were expecting, the trips we had taken, the interesting people we had met. "Where did you learn to be so adventurous?" she asked us. We didn't bother to respond, since the answer was obvious. Later, as we got in our cars to drive to the different cities where we lived, Abui reminded us one more time not to pick up hippies along the way.

A Cuban American Memoir
AN EXCERPT FROM *La Habana*

Olga Mendell

Olga Mendell was born in Havana in 1940; she left the Island in 1960 at the age of twenty. She currently resides in Buffalo, New York.

A Double Exposure: Cuba and Buffalo. We're getting ready for Christmas in Buffalo. Yesterday, south on Route 219—boots, parka—to cut down a hemlock at Ellie's farm.

Tío Miguel had started a small forest when I was ten or twelve, and I was his helper, *cachanchán*, step-'n'-fetch-it. "What else are children for?" he'd ask, as if puzzled. Sometimes he'd follow up the question with "*Los niños hablan cuando las gallinas mean.*" [Children should speak only when hens pee.] And if I spoke out of turn, a cautionary aphorism: "*En boca cerrada no entran moscas.*" [Flies do not enter when one's mouth is shut.] We had our own small nursery: about one hundred mahoganies and cedars Tío Miguel had bought when they were about two feet tall. From quart-size oilcans to bigger and bigger cans, we transplanted them until they were ready for the big day. Rabiblanco and Amarillo, our gentle oxen, pulled the cart full of saplings out to the field for planting. Their breath was hot and fast, mysterious—as if it were coming out from the deep. As they lumbered on, they curled their tongues around blades of tall grass then gave them a tug, licked muzzles and nose rings to a shine. I trotted next to them in black high-top sneakers and pedal pushers, now and then offered a sweaty palm as a salt lick. "This is where my wedding will be ten years from now," I promised myself, "in this forest we've planted."

Tío Miguel and then Tía Consuelo died within days of each other at Jackson Memorial Hospital in Miami in the late '60s. In the hospital room, I brushed her hair back for the last time, massaged her puffed-up legs and feet with Jergens, her favorite lotion. Her skin, as far back as I can remember, had a faint almond scent. I thanked her for the years we had spent together on the farm—just us, our flowers, and our animals. She had trained an indigo blue morning glory vine so that it framed the bedroom window and made it look like something right out of a child's storybook. The blossoms were the color of her eyes. On my twelfth birthday, I'd almost bumped into a white horse all saddled up and bridled, tethered to a post behind the house. He had a pink bow and typed on a card over his white blaze, "My name is Sultán. I'm yours." Sultán ate crackers out of my hand and drank Coca-Cola right out of the bottle. One day we heard hooves on the cement floor of the house: he was in the kitchen. We avoided Maravilla, the goat, who inhaled our shoelaces and the clothes we had on before we realized what she was doing. Now and then a litter of piglets would be born, or a calf whose coat would feel as if God had sent it down to us dipped in wax. I loved the mice. Their minuscule droppings in cupboards and cutlery drawers always took me by surprise, their tiny teeth marks on unprotected guava paste, cheese, bars of soap. Those little mice who galloped across the wood beams late at night, over our sleep and into our dreams.

We hardly ever had visitors at Rinconcito—"Little Corner" was the name of the farm—except at New Year's, when my mother, Tía Consuelo's sister, and my father and brother arrived for the big feast. Pedro, the caretaker, butchered a pig behind the avocado trees—we could hear it squeal—washed it with boiling water, split it open, and marinated it overnight on the kitchen table under banana leaves. Herbs in pools of sour orange worked magic in the dark concavities. Next morning we helped Pedro place the pig on the filigreed wrought-iron headboard from a discarded bed, and out it went to swing from the trees over a pyre of firewood—first one side, then high drama when the adults (by noon, each would have had two or three rum *mojitos*) flipped it over, almost falling into the pit, and everyone yelled *¡Cuidado!* Careful! No matter where you walked on the farm that day you were inside a cloud of garlic and cumin, wood smoke, *olor a humo*. All of us, children too, took turns at basting and swinging *el animal* until the skin cracked loud as gunshot when Pedro cut into it. Black beans and rice, avocados, cassava—the kitchen was a busy place where even men wore aprons that day and children were not allowed, although we could watch through the open windows. Someone fried plantains slowly, squashed them flat between layers of paper bags, set them aside to fry again in hot oil at the last moment: *plátanos a puñetazos*, "fisticuffed" plantains. A big flannel colander on its tripod ready to filter Café Pilón. *Guayaba* pies I have never tasted since. Then we sat in our cowhide *taburetes* for the big meal. After dessert, when we had been excused, my brother and I raced each other to the Yucatán hammock for *siesta*. Heat, blasts of cicadas, Tío Miguel snoring, Tía Consuelo in her green-and-orange-striped canvas deck chair, reading—all was as it should be. And then Morning Glory herself closed her eyes.

A farm so small—twenty acres, if that—was a kingdom with its own vegetable garden under a mosquito-netting canopy to shelter it from sun and rain, two small fields (corn and sugar cane), a fall-down chicken house where they'd send me to feel for eggs under huge, aggressive hens. A bathtub with floating egg sacs and busy tadpoles was the watering hole for a milk cow and three horses. At dusk, peace descended on us when the sky turned crimson, orange, deep purple, gold. We took turns then watering the rows of lettuce, and it seemed farm and evening stretched far beyond what our eyes could see. My Sultán, no bigger than a tall pony, was Trigger and Silver and every stallion I had seen in a matinee Western at Teatro Miramar; our *bohío*—walled with boards and roofed with palm fronds—was my fortress. Inside the windowless hut where we kept grain and saddles, I'd bury my arms up to my elbows in burlap bags full of sweet feed, smell the scent of molasses and damp saddle pads, feel my knees give. Fidel should have taken me up on the invitation I sent him sometime after January that first year of the revolution. "Come to Rinconcito and rest with us. You look tired on TV."

I don't understand why there were no laments, why no one in the family complained about loss—as if all of us shared a tacit agreement not to look at the past that way, or as if we were missing the necessary words. Words like "Fidel took everything we had." Or "Look at us now. We've got nothing." Never the well-worn "We're getting every square meter back someday. Just you wait and see. *Tú vas a ver.*" They reminisced often, and I with them; then we'd fall silent. Easy for me: I had merely fed, grown, molted into adolescence, and then rested inside the cocoon they had spun. But *they* had worked for Rinconcito and for our house near the ocean in Miramar. Father, at his appliance store—La Casa Karman—in the old section of the city. Mother, at El Encanto, training employees and using her English and her French to welcome important visitors from abroad—Xavier Cugat, Errol Flynn, Edith Piaf—and help them shop. Our Sunday drive when we were small children included a stop at the post office so that father could pick up his P. O. Box #647 mail: payments and orders for batteries and radios he'd load into his two-tone station wagon and deliver to clients in Pinar del Río and in Matanzas, where he'd pick up *panqués de Jamaica*, corn, and molasses muffins for my brother and me. He had fallen asleep at the wheel one night on the highway and awakened in a ditch surrounded by *campesinos* gesticulating and pointing at the dent on the roof of his car.

I didn't want to hear from them the reasons why they didn't complain. In their very reticence, in the way they looked down or away when we talked of Cuba (Father would start a nervous hum), I saw their shame and shared it. It was akin to mine when I had to tell my children, "NO, put it back" and watch them surrender the box of expensive cereal they craved or that sugary fruit pie they'd wanted for their lunch boxes. Shame does not always come from something bad we have done. It may come from feeling naked before a world that seems fully clothed. Father showed off his high-mileage used Mercury he had bought on time; my mother, the list of wealthy Dallas clients for whom she sewed and, years later, the program from a musical they had gone to see in Solvang. These were their American trophies. But talk about home, and in their eyes you could see they were like trees that had dropped every leaf . . .

Song for the Royal Palms of Miami
(FOR GUSTAVO PÉREZ FIRMAT)

Virgil Suárez

Virgil Suárez was born in Havana, Cuba, in 1962. He left the Island with his family in 1970 and lived in Madrid until 1974, when they moved to Los Angeles, California. He lives in Tallahassee, Florida, with his family.

Everywhere they stand, slightly bent
against the nocturnal offshore breezes,

as if strained to hear the susurrus of wind:
free, free, free . . . Dear Gustavo, when

we spoke of this catatonia befallen
our fathers—this inertia of mind and spirit,

we might have second-guessed their wills,
the residue of hope left inside them; us.

Memories against the "*ventolera*"
as my old man calls the winds of change.

Here he is at Palm Springs Hospital
recovering once again from major surgery,

this time the offensive being against colon
cancer. (Little do I know he will not,

not make it out.) Listen, we too struggle
against the uncertainty, pulled by the roots,

remembrance of our lost childhoods.

I think of you on this clear
November day, when outside the hospital

window, the wind tussles the fronds
of a palm tree, not any palm tree, but a Royal

palm tree, like the ones all over *that* island.
My father knows its name: *palmera*.

So does yours. They know the *palmiche*,
fed to pigs to fatten them up, the leaves

of the fronds used to make good hats,
the earthworm-like trunks can be dug

out to make canoes.

They are everywhere
here in Miami: tall, proud, resolute

against the ravages of weather and time.
    I say they are built to survive everything.

    I say today they are mile markers of our
fathers' trip through exile, monuments

to their bravura of spirit—they've been planted
    here to remind all of us of the long trip home.

Photograph of My Parents
FROM *The Secret History of Water*

Silvia Curbelo

See Section I for the author's biographical sketch.

I like the way they look together
and how simply her smile floats towards him
out of the dim afterglow

of some memory, his hand
cupped deliberately
around the small flame

of a match. In this light
nothing begins or ends
and the camera's pale eye

is a question that answers itself
in the asking. *Are you there?*
And they are. Behind them

the wind tears down and blows
apart, angel of nonchalance.
The world belongs to the world.

For years he smoked down to the filters
sorting out the pieces of his life
with the insomniac's penchant

for detail. In the heart's
heavy forest, the tree of self-denial,
the bough, the single leaf

like the blade of a word held back
for a long time. The moment
she leans towards him the room

will become part of the story.
The light is still as a pond.
My mother's blue scarf

is the only wave.

FIRST SHIFT AT HERSHEY'S, 4 A.M.
FROM *The Secret History of Water*

My uncle climbed out of bed before
the alarm and shaved in the
half dark. He'd stand at
the bedroom sink and let the last
of the night roll off his shoulders,
what was left of the moon,
the mirror looking back.

I imagine him when he was a boy
lying in the tall grass in his
brother's farm and listening
to the first trains going past
like music playing in a distant
room. The rest of his life and
the rest of his life.

In bed his wife kicked
the thin covers to the floor.
I picture him walking towards her
with the straw hat over his heart.
The moon drifting across the
Caribbean. The cold place
where the blade touches the skin.

There are ships pushing off
distant harbors even now.
Cupping the water in his hands
a man knows the hard sleep of
rivers that keep moving and
turn over and wake without light.
Trees remember, stones hold
forth, fish lift the stars
on their backs. Light years before
the first coffee in his mouth

like the first breath, before
the whistle of the sugar
refineries and the hard bread
crumbling down the front of
his shirt, before he wipes
the lather from his face with
the white towel, before the water
in the narrow sink grows dark and
warm when the razor slips, the red
coming off his hands.

Inhabited Woman

Andrea O'Reilly Herrera

Andrea O'Reilly Herrera was born in January 1959 in Philadelphia, Pennsylvania, of a Cuban mother and a second-generation Irish American father. She currently resides in Colorado Springs, Colorado, with her husband and three children.

three women reside within me

grandmothergreatgrandmothermother

spooning and nesting
pushing and pressing
vying for my attention.
all three peer
with unwavering gaze,
as though from a single pair of almond eyes.
the third raises our brows in Pyrenees arches,
as she transforms us into a garden of powder and cologne.
then unannounced, the first appears in profile—
her lavender skirts spread out around her like a framboyán.
with small, child-like hands,
she pulls at the nylons that crease around our ankles and knees—
impatiently discards the modern, choosing instead
a circle of scarabs on linen,
a single cameo and pearls.
all the while, I sense the second,
present among the shadows
between two shores, riding
the dark waves of my hair,
across these endless seas
that unite us and divide us.

three women

reside
   within
      me.

Burialground
FROM *Lil' Havana Blues*

Nilda Cepero

Nilda Cepero was born in Havana, Cuba, in 1953. She left the Island in 1961 and was raised in Boston, Massachusetts. She currently resides in Miami, Florida.

To Zoila Collazo y Rubio

Backward, turn backward, O time in your flight,
make me a child again, just for to-night
                              —*Elizabeth Akers Allen*

They say I look
like my grandmother on my father's side

I saw a photograph they sent from Cuba
The likeness is remarkable
The only reminder, the last remains

We kept her image for a while
It traveled from place to place
and like all good Cubans
on their constant Diaspora
it settled in Miami
where humidity enveloped it without pity

Now there is only a name to remind me
of someone I never met
The stranger I learned to love
through a photograph
vanished into foreign soil

my unavoidable destiny

A Journal from the Bay of Mariel

Raquel Romeu

Raquel Romeu and her brother, Jorge Luis, were born in Havana. Raquel left the Island as an adult in 1969 as part of the Freedom Flights. She currently resides in Liverpool, New York.

SUNDAY, APRIL 27

It rains. The storm is over and there is nothing to do. I've decided to start this journal to kill time and so that I will never forget any of this.

. . . A. sits in the only chair on the *Fern Elinore*—the pilot's chair—and worries because the immigration authorities haven't been around to our boat to pick up our papers with the list of relatives we propose to claim. We have appointed her guardian of those precious sheets of paper. C. is the oldest person on board. She has come to claim her children and grandchildren. She's a very gutsy lady. I don't think she trusted any of us at first, but she is beginning to relax. E. is eating yogurt. We have each brought enough food for at least one week, plus enough to feed the people they will put on board. The captain says we have sufficient water, too. Both tanks are full and these trawlers usually stay at sea as many as twenty days at a time. Also, each of us brought two two-gallon containers of drinking water, and the shrimp storage compartment is full of ice.

We are eight plus the captain, and we are tied alongside the *Miss So Nicey* inside the Bay of Mariel, Cuba. I have never seen so many boats together. Last night I could see forty-eight shrimp trawlers and at least twice as many smaller craft, some less than nineteen feet long. I don't know how they were able to make it across the Straits with that strong Gulf current and the winds. A huge catamaran named *America*, said to hold three hundred and fifty people, came in last night. It's probably the largest boat in the bay next to the shrimp trawlers.

. . . All this started last Tuesday afternoon for me. A call from Miami alerted me that boats were leaving for Cuba from Key West because Fidel Castro had opened the port of Mariel to those who wished to go and fetch their relatives. My cousin in Key West wanted my consent to initiate negotiations with a boat to try and claim my brother in Cuba. My kid brother, Jorge Luis, who is thirty-four years old, had tried to get out of Cuba for years. He did his two years of military service in a labor camp cutting cane. Not being "integrated into the revolution," and having a passport that indicated his desire to leave the country, Jorge didn't qualify for military service as such, but he did qualify for the cane fields of Camagüey. Afterwards, he went back to school. He became a mathematician, got married, and had three children.

Four years ago I had doubled my efforts to get my family out of Cuba. My other brother was out of prison after serving nearly thirteen years for the political crime of being "against the powers of the state." A year ago last January he and my mother managed to leave Cuba. Jorge was still there. For the past year, he and his family had had visas to Colombia and Venezuela and resident visas to the United States, and their passage out of Cuba in U.S. dollars deposited at the Banco Nacional de Cuba. But the harassment, the waiting, the war of nerves had continued for them.

This past winter, I found out through a relative that Jorge had been imprisoned and interrogated for two days last summer at the Cuban Repression Bureau. His home had been searched thoroughly, with the excuse that he was thought to possess U.S. dollars, a crime punishable by imprisonment, even if just one miserable one-dollar bill was found. What they did find was a list of the titles of short stories he had written and sent to me, and a typed copy of the little book of short stories I had had printed years before for him under a pseudonym.

Jorge convinced his interrogators that he was just an unimportant person who wrote stories, but if they imprisoned him they would make him a hero, a writer forced into silence. They released him with a suspended sentence. He then instructed me to guard the stories with my life and not to publish anything more of his under his name or any other unless I heard he was imprisoned again.

When my cousin asked if I would give my consent to have someone go and get my brother, I felt this was *it*—our big chance. That night the *Syracuse Herald-Journal* had a brief account of the first boat from Cuba returning to Key West. It brought mainly people who had taken refuge in the Peruvian Embassy "and some other persons who had relatives in the United States."

I called Key West again. My cousin said it was chaos there. Cubans were pouring in from all parts of the United States with money to buy their passage to Cuba, or trailers dragging boats. Everyone seemed to want to go over. I decided to wait until Wednesday morning; and in the meantime, I spent all night trying to call Havana. I felt it was up to Jorge to decide whether he wanted to be part of this madness, and whether he was willing to risk the lives of his little ones crossing over in one of those boats.

At 6:45 A.M., I got a call from the Keys. A boat had just arrived with two hundred people, but three were wounded. They had been attacked in the streets of Havana as they left their homes to embark at the port of Mariel. It was dangerous—risky at least.

The telephone lines were closed between Cuba and the United States. I decided to try going through a third country. Within the hour someone had reached Jorge, and his reply was: "Come and get us, yes, by all means. I don't care if it is in a bathtub."

I began to make plans to leave. I knew that if I didn't go myself, nothing would be accomplished. Everyone at LeMoyne College was very cooperative and sympathetic. I made plane reservations. When I called Key West again, I was told, "Bring down $6,000."

Six thousand dollars! Where would I get that sum? I began making phone calls: my relatives, a friend who had offered to help weeks ago when all this was still a rumor.

On Thursday, April 24, I left Syracuse. I arrived in Miami with only twenty minutes to change planes. A friend and my uncle were waiting for me. Each handed me an envelope with money. It was like a gangster movie. I stuck the envelopes in my purse, which held all of the money I had pulled out of my savings account that same morning. Everyone contributed what he or she could. I had a total of $3,100—not anywhere near the $6,000 I was told I would need. As I would soon learn, many had even less, although some had considerably more.

. . . My cousin and I spent all evening until midnight trying to close a deal for a tugboat. We finally found one that would cost $2,100 per person. It would be leaving Key West the next day.

Early the next morning, someone went to look at the tugboat. He reported back to us that it would be dangerous to sail with the number of people they were planning to cram on board.

. . . Later that morning we were told that a shrimp trawler was available—for a $20,000 rental fee. I joined forces with seven others. Together, we hoped to claim forty-two relatives. The trawler could hold two hundred or more people, so even if the Cuban government added four people for each of our relatives, as it was rumored they might, we had a good chance of bringing everyone back. The $2,500 per person was paid gladly.

With throbbing hearts we boarded the *Fern Elinore*. We sailed at 6:00 P.M. that Friday. The sea looked calm and beautiful. It was still daylight. . . .

We were exhausted, mostly from tension, and each of us sought a spot in which to retire. It wasn't easy because the cabin was so small. . . . I climbed into one of the upper bunks. The window was open. Night began to fall. As we approached the Florida Straits, the winds became stronger and the waves grew higher and higher.

The sun went down. The sea got rougher. The chains and irons on board clanged frightfully. The captain ran from one side to the other, trying to keep the boat as steady as possible, and then to the rudder to adjust our course. I couldn't move. The waves kept increasing in size and force. Water began showering in through the open window. I was soaked. I reached for my raincoat and threw it over me. Spending a night all wet was the least of my worries.

I dozed off and was awakened by a terrible bang and the boat keeling over. W. [the captain] got N. out of bed and put him to work. He couldn't handle it alone. One stabilizer was tangled and had to be cut loose.

Later, things seemed to quiet down, and the next thing I knew it was daybreak and we were in Cuban waters. I stepped on deck. The sea was calm. N. greeted me. Rather than saying, "Good morning," he cried, "Land! Land!" I could see something on the horizon.

When we could orient ourselves, we saw we were indeed headed for the Bay of Mariel. We had made it in twelve hours in spite of the weather, and we had hit it right on the nose. Many others had ended up near Havana and further east! The number of boats waiting for permission to enter the bay was staggering. They were all sizes, all kinds, even some outboard motor craft. They all carried more people than they should and they were expecting to take even more back. Many were to be very disappointed.

. . . Once inside the port, we were ordered to moor side by side, tied to each other. At the end of the day our neighbors from the *Miss So Nicey* saw an immigration authority boat approaching. One of them shouted, "When are we leaving?" That triggered the acid reply: "We don't want you here and we are trying our best to get you out as soon as possible." The hatred in the official's voice was clear. Suddenly, I remembered all those years visiting one brother in political prison, the other brother in labor camp . . . and my own seven months on a farm doing hard labor just before I left Cuba. It frightened me more than the rough sea we had encountered the night before.

MONDAY, APRIL 28

The sun has disappeared. Black clouds have filled the sky, and heavy rain and furious high winds have begun to toss the hundreds of boats tied to one another. The shrimp trawlers are anchored in a separate area from the smaller craft, but last night they ordered new arrivals, no matter how small, to tie themselves to the shrimp boats. Many boats have lost their anchors, and they have to depend on other boats' anchors.

We can't see a thing, but we can hear the boats banging against each other. W. is running from side to side cursing, pulling levers, getting us away from all the other boats and trying to keep the *Fern Elinore* stable while avoiding a collision. He runs to the bow, then to the stern. "Everyone inside and out of the way," he yells. "We're leaving." Loaded down with many iron gadgets, it maneuvers slowly and painfully. Backing up a little, going forward a little, he gets us out of that confusion of ships.

A typical tropical storm, it all stops as suddenly as it had started. We make our way back to the *Miss So Nicey* from the far end of the bay where we had taken refuge. On the way we discover an incredible number of smaller craft anchored along the little islets.

I slept on deck last night. The captain made mattresses out of shrimp nets. E. and I slept near the bow; W. and N. slept in the stern. His bunk is being occupied by I. and M., the only couple on board. Life preservers are our pillows . . .

MONDAY AFTERNOON

We are facing the Naval Academy with its castle on a hill and its steep steps. Over the red-tiled Spanish roofs of the little town of Mariel, I recognize the old church with its old bell tower, and I remember a famous seafood restaurant that was nearby. When I was a child my father used to take us there for Sunday dinner. It was one of the most popular restaurants just half an hour from Havana. On our left, at the entrance to the harbor, is the cement factory. Next to it is the power plant. On our right, and further inland, are the two chimneys of the San Ramón sugar mill. They remind me of the smell of molasses, the soot, and my happy Easters spent in a sugar mill town. The palm trees are silhouetted against the blue sky. This morning I heard the roosters sing at dawn. How near and how far from Cuba we are; I have been thinking of José María Heredia, expatriated like us, sitting on a ship anchored along the Cuban shore, longing, but unable, to set foot on the land he loved so much. He wrote the beautiful "Song of the Expatriate," which I must read again when I go home.

TUESDAY, APRIL 29

I slept on deck as usual last night. It was cold and damp. To kill time we have washed the deck. . . . They have sent a flyer around saying that we will be here for more than a month, and that any boat that wants to leave now, without any Cubans, may do so. M. has gone into Havana. From the Hotel Triton he'll be able to call our relatives here and in the United States to let them know we have arrived safely. There have been many accidents. Our relatives here must remain in their homes. If immigration officials go for them and they are not home, they will miss their opportunity. There are all kinds of rumors about how long we'll have to wait and how many relatives, and whom, we shall be allowed to claim. . . .

THURSDAY, MAY 1

Rumors are driving us crazy. Some say you must go to Havana to hand in the lists of relatives to be claimed. Yesterday we heard over the CB radio that we should remain on our boats and wait for the immigration authorities; that there were some seven hundred persons left in the Peruvian Embassy in Havana; that any boats seized or damaged would be returned to their owners; and that gas, water, and food would be available for purchase.

Today is our sixth day waiting for the immigration authorities. We have decided to go ashore and call our relatives. I had vowed I wouldn't set foot on Cuban soil, but now I have made up my mind to go. I feel very moved, frightened, and, above all, very sad as we approach land. I had thought I would steal a handful of Cuban soil to take back with me. But when I step on it, it is dirty, trodden upon, hard, and barren.

The first thing that hits me is the odor from the improvised latrines. The dock is filled with people with different problems. Most of them have had boat trouble. In the sun, at an improvised table, two immigration officials write down claims of all sorts. People wait patiently in line. Later we were told that the two officials disappeared at 11:30 A.M., saying they were going to lunch, and never came back. The people waited until 5:00 or 6:00 P.M. to no avail.

We take a taxi to the cafeteria, which is only two minutes away. We are not allowed to walk around. The taxi costs $2 per person. The cafeteria is watched at all four corners by people in uniform or people with arm bands showing they belong to surveillance committees. One from our group recognized a neighbor who had gone outside to hang her clothes on the line. Discreetly he waved his hand a little; she put her hand in the middle of her chest, holding it very close, and answered him with the same gesture. A young boy recognized a boy from Mariel who apparently worked in the cafeteria. "There's my cousin!" he cried. The man accompanying the boy cautioned him not to talk to his cousin. "Don't. You'll bring trouble for him." The boy couldn't understand.

"Why? He's my cousin." And he moved toward him, excited. The boy from Mariel recognized them, opened his eyes wide, and kept shaking his head slightly, No, no! He dove into the first open door he saw to avoid meeting his cousin. Someone noticed. Immediately, two officials materialized. The elderly man said, "Leave him alone, son. You'll only bring him grief." They stood there, their eyes full of tears.

Everything is expensive. Fried chicken costs $12.50; steak, $15. I figure that if there are 2,000 boats here, with an average of ten people per boat who are spending $100 each, they have taken in $2 million at least. If one were to include the cost of water, gas, provisions, mechanical parts, and port taxes, I'd say they've harvested $4 million in one week.

When I talk to my brother over the phone, Jorge says, "Oh sister, to think you risked coming here just to get us out!" I felt terrible trying to explain to him that our lists hadn't been collected yet and that there was much confusion as to how many people each of us could claim. I told him my idea: I would claim all five if I were allowed to. If allowed four, I would leave the youngest child out; if three, the second; if two, I would leave all three children out; if one, I would only claim him. I told him: "You have your papers in order, you have your visas and the U.S. dollars for the plane tickets, and you're leaving a two-family house. Push from your end. I'm sure they'll let the whole family go." He told me that his papers were being retained by an immigration official, and that just today he had been in the immigration office. He was relieved to know that I was all right. Nobody knew anything on his end, either. All they heard were rumors. He agreed to all my suggestions.

When I returned to the boat and told M. about my conversation, he thought I had done the wrong thing. "You must let them decide," he said. "You can't assume they will all be able to leave. These people are not kidding. They will split up the family." I can't believe that could happen. God can't let it happen. I've asked M. to call and to tell Jorge to make the decision himself.

M. and two others have just returned from Havana. It was a useless trip. They have been given the number 1083 for their interview with the immigration authorities, but that afternoon only numbers in the 20s and 30s were being handled. I asked M. if he had called Jorge. "Yes," he said; my brother's instructions were that if I could claim only two, to claim him and his asthmatic son; if just one, my brother. I felt a chill. For the first time I admitted to myself that the family might have to be split up. But what really frightened me was his message that he was ready to leave his family behind. I knew things had to be very bad for him to make such a decision.

I'm not a pessimist. No one here is, thank God. M. and N. have left again for the shore to see if they can get the immigration interview. They say there is another office on the dock. . . . We have found a box of dehydrated mashed potatoes. We are making a tuna–potato pie when M. and N. return with the good news that they have seen the immigration people, have given them our boat's data, and that now we must wait for the authorities to visit us here.

It's raining, as it usually does at this time of year. It is the first rain of May and we've all gotten wet . . . for luck.

. . . M. decided to make a great big sign. He and N. have hoisted the sign high on the stern. It reads, "Nine days without a contract." The immigration authorities call the deal they make with the boats a contract: they give us a certain number of people they want to send out, and we take a certain number of relatives.

It has stopped raining and there is a beautiful double rainbow toward land. It encircles the lovely hills behind Mariel. That, too, is supposed to be lucky. Let's see if the immigration visits us tomorrow. The lists are ready on the table. Holding them down is a metal statuette of St. Anne of Beauprès. N. has a picture of Our Lady of Charity; E., of St. Martha. Beside the St. Anne I have placed a Sacred Heart of Jesus. Secretly we have all been praying every day. The longer we wait, the more we pray. Finally, today, when I brought out the St. Anne and put it on the papers, each one brought out his or her private saint and nailed it over the door or over the window.

The captain and the crew of the next two boats are friends of W. They have been drinking rum all day. W. is very drunk, and he's still drinking.

SATURDAY, MAY 3

It was about 1:00 A.M. when the nightmare began. We were all asleep. Suddenly W. appeared, screaming, "I'm going to kill him," and searching for a gun. Apparently the other two captains, who are brothers, had had a fight. They were all very drunk. M. tried to calm W. down. Very sternly M. said, "Look, if just one shot is fired, they will come and throw you in jail and you'll rot there forever. You don't know Fidel Castro." W. embraced M. and almost wept. Then he went back to his chant, "I'm going to kill him." He walked out on deck, and I followed him. Because he could communicate with me in English, we had had long talks, and he seemed to like me. I pleaded with him. "Please, W., I beg you. Leave it alone. Go to bed. Don't drink anymore." "All right, I'm going to throw the gun overboard. I won't do anything . . . but I want more rum."

We went back to bed pretty shaken. We were all sleeping inside. A while later, he stumbled into the kitchen looking for ice. In his hand was the Gatorade bottle he was using as a glass full of rum. He was beside himself and quite incoherent. His tone went from rage to meekness and back to rage. He loved us—he hated us. He left, but shortly afterward he was on deck pacing from bow to stern. We were all in the kitchen, and as he passed the window he would stick his head in and hurl insults at us. He kept repeating, "I love America. These Cubans don't love America." He put his head in the window, "Say you love America as much as I do." I said, "I am an American citizen, W., and I love America." That infuriated him even more. He slammed the window shut, then put his fist through it and put his head in it. He paced again, yelling obscenities.

Besides our fear of him, we were afraid the Cuban authorities might be there at any minute. Every night two or three searchlights scanned the sea, the boats, and the sky, and coast guard boats cruised the area constantly. W. said, "I'm leaving," and with that, he went to the captain's post and started the motors. M. and I followed him. "Don't, W., you are a good man," I said. Complete change in him. "You know it," he said, and shut the motors off. Then he went outside and yelled and paced for the next two hours. The obscenities were directed at us. It was like Dr. Jekyll and Mr. Hyde.

We sat in the kitchen, shaking. A. passed Valium around. As W. quieted down, we tried to sleep. . . . M. decides we need something more than just the sign to call the attention of the immigration authority's tiny boats. He cuts two strips from a red blanket—the only one we have on board—and now we wave them and make desperate gestures every time we spot an immigration boat.

SUNDAY, MAY 4

. . . At midnight M. and W. return from a visit to the *Comandante Pinares*. They have been informed that the reason no immigration authorities have visited us so far is that our first form, filled out outside the bay, has been lost. They can't process us.

TUESDAY, MAY 6

. . . E. has suggested that we call the "talking boat"—a large craft with a loudspeaker that cruises the area giving orders. There we go again, explaining how long we have been here and that our form seems to be lost. They suggest we fill out a new one and hand us one. So we do.

On the latest forms we have filled out, we have chosen contract A, according to which you wait for the relatives and take them back with you; B, you take part of the family and they send the rest in another boat; C, you take what they give you and the relatives will be sent afterwards on other boats. The boat that leaves empty breaks the contract, and there is no deal anymore. We knew choosing A would mean a longer wait, but we had heard of too many cases where they hadn't kept their end of the bargain. Each of us is able to claim five. How relieved I am. This is my brother's entire family.

We go ashore. I call Jorge's house, and my sister-in-law answers. My brother is not at home. I tell her happily that I am able to claim them all. She replies: "Now listen to me and don't get excited. This immigration official came by yesterday and returned our passports to us. He said he knew there was a boat waiting for us in Mariel Bay, but we could not leave by boat. 'Do you understand?' he said, 'not by way of Mariel. You have to leave by plane.'" They were told to buy their tickets from the Mexican airlines and that their seats would be confirmed Thursday. I don't trust the authorities. I tell my sister-in-law, "You listen to me now. You tell Jorge that I'm not leaving here until I bring you back with me. You tell him I don't care what that man said. If they come for you to go to the boats, you go. Whatever comes first. I came here for you, and I'm not leaving without you. I'm coming ashore Thursday again to find out if your seats on the plane have been confirmed."

FRIDAY, MAY 9

E. and M. and N. go ashore to call their relatives. . . . E. is the first one back. They haven't gone for her brother and sister yet. But she has good news for me. She called my sister-in-law and learned that their seats for Sunday are confirmed. They leave Sunday at 11:00 P.M. What irony! I have come here to get them out, and now they are being flown out and I am stuck, who knows until when.

MONDAY, MAY 12

I couldn't sleep again last night. All I could think of was: Have they left? Has my brother left? I even scanned the sky from 11:00 P.M. on in the hope of seeing a plane going northwest. Silly me, planes going to Mérida must take off from the Rancho Boyeros Airport and head straight out to sea.

I got up at daybreak and took the first boat that would take me ashore. I call Jorge's house. A woman answers the phone. "Nobody by that name lives here," she says. That's it. They are gone. Somebody else is already installed in the house my father built, but that is not important. What matters is that they have finally left Cuba. I have to be sure. I ask the operator to call another number: my old aunt's house. When she answers the phone I break down and cry. Dear aunt—to think I have been sitting on a boat twenty kilometers away and haven't been able to see them. She tells me they left at 10:00 the night before.

The rest happens as in a dream. My heart is not there anymore. I return to the boat only to find that W. has decided he must have more money if we want to stay longer. Everyone puts together whatever money he or she has left. Some of us have none. W. says he doesn't want our money. He wants the owner of the ship to pay him more. We strike a bargain. I want to go back, and E. and I. say they will come with me. W. will take the money as a guarantee. We will look up the owner and tell him what W. wants: half again of the money we originally paid for renting the boat. The others are sad that we are leaving, but they encourage us to go back. It is like breaking up a family.

We hail the first boat passing by. We land at Pier No. 3. They have just loaded two shrimp trawlers like ours. We ask about the procedure. Again, they give us a form to fill out and tell us to wait in line.

By 3:00 P.M. we are sailing to the entrance of the harbor. The coast guard holds us there. By sundown we are still there. They tell us the weather in the Gulf isn't good.

There are between one hundred and one hundred and fifty people on board. One can hardly walk on the deck.

TUESDAY, MAY 13

They let us go at noon. The coast of Cuba seems far in the distance already. I go back to look at it for the last time and begin to cry. It's sad to know you can never go home. An old Black man sitting quietly beside his daughter and grandson says, "It is very sad to leave one's homeland. All we want is a place to live and work in peace."

In mid-ocean, we spot the American Coast Guard: "U.S. COAST GUARD" in huge beautiful letters. The captain is hauling a line. I ask him if we are in American waters, pointing at the ship. He raises his head, nods, shakes my hand and we begin to jump like a couple of kids.

Excerpts from Raquel Romeu's journal were first published in *The Heights* (Summer/Fall 1980) under the title "A Journal from the Bay of Mariel." They are reprinted in this collection with the author's permission.

Political Exile

Jorge Luis Romeu

Jorge Luis Romeu was born in Havana, Cuba, in 1945. As a result of his sister Raquel's efforts, he left Cuba with his family in May 1980, during the period of the Mariel Boatlift. He lives in Syracuse, New York.

To all of those who remain in Cuba and suffer because they refuse to conform.

The Revolution of January 1959 seemed to represent a triumph for the liberal aspirations of the Cuban people. Its professed aim was to provide the material and spiritual renovation for which our nation had searched for a long time. The delivery of this revolutionary movement to Marxism-Leninism constituted, for many of Fidel Castro's original comrades-in-arms and supporters, a deliberate act of treason. It alienated a large section of the population that originally fought for the Revolution, many of whom had come from the ranks of the professional classes. As a result, the majority of the existing professional class was pushed into exile or incarcerated, due to their refusal to ally themselves with the unexpected detour that the new revolutionary philosophy had taken.

My experience as a student and professional in Cuba mirrors the experience of those who refused, or continue to refuse, to align themselves with the government. I have always been politically incorrect. I came from a family that supported the Revolution; when it became clear that Castro was procommunist, we actively combated his government. That was enough to brand me like a steer and to create great obstacles for my intellectual and professional advancement.

I arrived at the University of Havana in 1964 after graduating with a degree in arts and sciences from a public high school that had already become socialist. In some sense, I wanted to find out how far I could advance, how much I could achieve or accomplish, without being allied to the new government. I wanted to be judged for my potential and accomplishments, not my political affiliation. In 1963 and 1964, respectively, I obtained scholarships from the French government to study in Paris and Bordeaux; though hundreds of other students were being sent to socialist countries to pursue similar careers, the Cuban government denied me a student exit visa on both occasions because of my philosophical opposition to the regime. This prompted me to register at the School of Engineering of the University of Havana. After I had completed the program and successfully passed all of the exams, a "voluntary" labor session was organized, and students were compelled to register and participate. I refused to sign up and, as a result, was questioned at a public student meeting about my refusal. Consequently, I was expelled from the university with "a special motion to be sent to do military service."

During that same year, dozens of university students were expelled during public meetings, replicating the mass expulsions that had occurred in 1960 and 1961. Any student who appeared to be a natural leader and exerted any type of influence on his or her peers was given the opportunity to become a member of the pro-government group; a refusal was regarded as an antirevolutionary act, and they were promptly expelled. When the following semester started, hundreds more found their names on a blacklist when they reconvened to register. Those who were blacklisted were not regarded as leaders; however, since they were thought to have been influenced by undesirables at some point in time and were "contaminated," they were also expelled. Like me, they were prevented from pursuing their university careers any further.

These mass expulsions became so widely known that UNESCO compelled the Cuban government to revise their procedures. In response, the government granted the students who had been blacklisted a "second chance." Some received telegrams summoning them to the chancellor's office, where they were interviewed by a political committee. If they repented and confessed their guilt and their "ideological weakness," they were readmitted to the university.

Those, like myself, who had been expelled for their open opposition were not given a second chance. In 1966 I, along with more than thirty thousand other young Cubans, was sent to the UMAP (Unidades Militantes de Ayuda a la Producción) labor camps, which were concentrated in the province of Camagüey. In addition to political dissidents, the camps were filled with people from all over the Island representing all races, religious and sexual orientations, and classes. Special emphasis, however, was placed on the homosexuals; it was suggested by the government propaganda that the camps were quarantine wards for untouchables.

There, we learned to withstand and overcome long days of hard labor in the cane fields twelve hours a day, seven days a week. In addition to being underfed, we were constantly being reminded that we were the scum of the country and would be made to suffer our punishment until we demonstrated repentance and compliance—much like what occurred in China during the Cultural Revolution.

In the fall of 1966, the Cuban government was pressured into improving our conditions and, eventually, dismantling the UMAP camps after the U.S. delegation from the United Nations presented photographic evidence of the deplorable conditions in which we were living. Upon my release in the summer of 1968, I reapplied to the University of Havana, registering in mathematics. Though the mass expulsions had ceased by that time, students were required to fill out extensive questionnaires that required them to provide information such as their religious affiliation and whether or not any member of their family was out of the country or serving time in prison. The government used these forms to screen applicants, and career options were allocated according to the students' responses and records. Simply put, careers leading to managerial positions were reserved for the "politically pure." In order to obtain an education, I lied about my religious affiliation and other family and political circumstances. In effect I, like so many others, obtained a university degree in exchange for hypocrisy. In retrospect, it occurs to me that in addition to the disintegration of the family, one of Fidel Castro's most infamous accomplishments was to force so many of us to lie in order to survive. Integrity is, indeed, a high price to pay, but there were no other choices. The Cuban people's humiliation is the government's shame; a "new man," as a government slogan runs, was indeed created: the social hypocrite.

After completing my degree, I discovered that I had worked for very little, for there was also a double standard in the graduate placement services policy. Independent of proficiency or intellectual merit, political allegiance and orthodoxy were once again the main factors in determining placement and promotion. In consequence, I was one of the last nominated for promotion and, moreover, had to change my employment on several occasions. In addition, I was refused a student exit visa once again for a scholarship I had obtained in Spain; another government employee was sent in my place.

Perhaps one of the most painful experiences in my life was visiting my brother in *las tapiadas* of Boniato Prison, after not having seen or heard from him in over a year. He was a *plantado*, a "rooted one" in English. He was also a *tapiado*, a term that loosely means someone who is cloistered within. As a result of the Geneva Convention Agreement regarding prisoners of conscience, this particular group of political dissidents had refused to receive indoctrination, do chain gang work, or wear the blue uniforms assigned to "convicts." As a reprisal, they were first kept in their underwear in isolated wards and denied family visits or the right to correspond with relatives or friends. When this treatment failed to break them, they were transferred to Boniato Prison and cloistered (or *tapiado*) within dark cells in which the doors and barred windows were covered with steel planks. Completely cut off from the outside world, they were denied even the most basic human rights, such as the right to exercise or take the sun or even to communicate with one another.

After all that I had witnessed, I finally determined that the only way for me to effectively express my dissent and disagreement with the political regime and to spare my children the things that I had experienced was to leave the Island. Essentially, I had arrived at a dead end inside Cuba, for I had a dossier with the secret police and was, therefore, totally neutralized. Although the Revolution had already separated our family—my sister, Rachel, was already living in New York—in 1978 we made the painful decision to leave our dead and our childhood friends behind and go to a totally different country with a completely different language and, in our case, a completely different climate. Despite the fact that I had immigrant visas from the U.S., Venezuela, and Colombia, the government nevertheless denied my request to leave the country.

I was not allowed to leave until May of 1980, as a result of the fact that my sister had come to claim me in a fishing trawler as part of the Mariel Boatlift. During the two years that we had waited for an exit permit, I was demoted and my salary was greatly reduced; my wife, who was working as a school teacher, was fired; and our children were harassed at school. (Mercifully, our lifelong neighbors spared us the usual neighborhood harassment.) Finally, when the moment came to leave the country, all of our personal belongings were confiscated, something that every person leaving Cuba experienced; even my college diploma stayed behind.

Upon emigrating, we settled in Syracuse, New York, where my sister lived. When I first arrived, I wanted to prove that my lack of success in Cuba was a result of my refusal to align myself with the government, rather than a lack of proficiency or professional qualifications. In 1990 I completed a doctorate and secured a post at the university level, and my wife earned her master's degree and accepted a position as a Spanish teacher at the high school level; together, we have supported our three children without any allowance or intervention from any organization. Despite all of these things, however, we have also had hard times, each of us working two and three jobs at one point or another just to make ends meet. Leaving behind our beloved dead and discovering that friends and family members had passed away alone has been our main grief. However, we now have our own dead buried here in Syracuse, something that makes us real Syracusans. We still miss our extended family, which is now spread out all over the U.S. and other countries, so we often travel to see them. In addition to these hardships, we have also discovered how sometimes Hispanics have to work twice as hard to be considered half as good, even in politically correct circles; and oftentimes, we still remain outsiders. I particularly found this to be true in the academic world, where many of my accomplishments were minimized and devalued; as a result, I have taken to calling myself "the ugly duckling," an inside joke readily understood by those of us who have been discriminated against because of our ethnicity or nationality.

Although I have been disillusioned from time to time, I am still grateful for the many things this blessed democracy has given us. In addition to my desire to pay back the United States for the many opportunities it continues to offer me, I have devoted both my time and my efforts as a teacher and a freelance journalist to providing educational opportunities for students who otherwise might be overlooked, and to raising the consciousness of the public through my writing regarding human rights abuses both in Cuba and throughout the world. In addition to having the privilege to contribute to several newspapers, I have been able to produce a weekly short-wave radio program, which reaches my fellow Cubans who remain on the Island. Like a soldier fighting to deliver my country from oppression, the media has always been my trench. In addition to providing for my family, the opportunity to work for what I believe is true and just and sacred has been my greatest goal and achievement in my eighteen years of exile. This has been, and continues to be, my only justification for having left Cuba in the first place.

This testimonial was edited by Andrea O'Reilly Herrera, with the author's permission, from a compendium of Dr. Romeu's newspaper articles and scholarly papers: "Scientists, Universities, Professional Associations and Human Rights in Cuba After 1960" (an unpublished essay presented in New York City at the Workshop on Scientists and Human Rights of the 150th National Meeting of the American Association for the Advancement of Science on May 24, 1984); "Solitude of Political Exile" (*Syracuse Herald*, April 10, 1988); "The 'Last' Cuban Political Prisoners" (*Syracuse Herald*, Sunday Opinion Section, June 19, 1988); "Anniversary" (*Syracuse Post Standard*, July 6, 1997); "An Ugly Duckling Guards My Office Door" (*Hispanic Link Weekly Report*, April 13, 1998: 3).

The Culture Wars

The Facts of Life on the Hyphen

Gustavo Pérez Firmat

Born in Havana, Cuba, in 1949, Gustavo Pérez Firmat left the Island with his family in October 1960. He currently teaches in New York City and resides in Chapel Hill, North Carolina.

Some months ago I was translating into Spanish something I had written originally in English when I ran into the phrase "the facts of life." After scrolling my mental thesaurus for a while and not coming up with anything that sounded even remotely like Spanish, I turned to my reference shelf and, after ruffling around in several dictionaries, finally located the phrase in a book of idioms. It turns out that in Spanish, the facts of life are called *los misterios de la vida*, "the mysteries of life." Think about that: the same biological drives that for the English-speaking world are plain and simple facts, for us in Hispanic culture are nothing less than enigmas, conundrums, mysteries—as if the birds and the bees were creatures from another planet.

This curious cultural difference certainly helps to explain a few facts—and mysteries—of my upbringing (and perhaps of yours too), but I mention it here because it seems to me that for people who grow old straddling two cultures, for those of us whose good or bad luck it is to spend our lives on the hyphen, the world sometimes appears as an odd coupling of fact and mystery; of things that reassure us and things that rattle us; of events that make us settle and events that make us sink; of *destino*, which means "destiny," and *desatino*, which means "mistake." And nowhere is the merging of *destino* and *desatino*, of vocation and equivocation, more apparent than in the language we write and speak and live in.

The reason, of course, is that a language is much more than a passive, malleable instrument of communication. In Spanish, when one speaks a language well, one is said to "dominate" it. But I think that my mother tongue has it backwards—because we don't dominate languages, languages dominate us. It is the language that determines the domain, the dominion, and we as speakers cannot but submit to its territorial imperatives. A language shapes what we can and cannot say, think, or feel in ways of which we are not even aware. In this deep sense, who we are is what we speak.

This is truly a deep philosophical sense—the order of things that Michel Foucault and others have written about—but also in quite obvious ways. Take pronouns, for example. In a memorable line, the Spanish poet Pedro Salinas once celebrated the pleasure of pronouns: "*qué delicia vivir en los pronombres.*" This delight is particularly intense in Spanish, for as many of you know, Spanish has a great many more pronouns than English. In English, you are always *you*—singular or plural, male or female, subject or object. But in Spanish, you can be *tú* or *usted*, *te* or *ti*, *lo* or *la* or *le*, not to mention *vos* and *vosotros*. On the other hand, even if the Spanish language has a more diversified pronoun system than English, in some situations Spanish employs pronouns much less frequently than English. This is true particularly of subject pronouns, which in Spanish are often omitted because they are implied by the verb ending —as if the pronominal subject did not exist apart from the action of which he or she or it is the agent. For this reason, speakers of English say *I* much more often than speakers of Spanish say *yo*. Take the English version of Descartes's famous syllogism, "I think, therefore I am"—in Spanish, the phrase would be "*pienso luego soy*," where the personal pronouns are omitted because the verb ending designates the person and number of the subject.

Now, if it is true that language molds how we view our place in the world, the deletion of subject pronouns—which, according to linguistics, occurs in Spanish as often as 80 percent of the time—is by no means a trivial matter. A few years ago Esmeralda Santiago published a moving account of her childhood in Puerto Rico entitled *When I Was Puerto Rican*. When her memoir appeared in Spanish, translated by the author herself, the title became *Cuando era puertorriqueña*. Every word in the English title has an exact match in the Spanish title (when/*cuando*, was/*era*, Puerto Rican/*puertorriqueña*)—every word but one, that is: the first-person pronoun *I*. In fact, the Spanish title doesn't even make clear that the phrase should be read in the first person, for it could also be translated as "when she was Puerto Rican" or even "when you were Puerto Rican." And yet, whatever else one may lose when translating an autobiography, the one thing that shouldn't get lost in translation is the first-person pronoun; but this is precisely what happens here. While the English gives Esmeralda top billing, the Spanish erases her, turning the plain English title into something of an enigma, another of the "mysteries of life." (Interestingly, the Spanish does add something to the English: gender—"*puertorriqueña*.")

This is by no means a trivial matter. The piece of writing to which I referred at the beginning is a memoir entitled *Next Year in Cuba*, which I wrote first in English and then translated into Spanish. Many things about the translation gave me trouble, but the single most difficult part was figuring out what to do with my *I*s. Every time I translated a first-person sentence, my impulse was to begin the sentence with *yo*. But when I did so, the first-person pronoun became obtrusive, less an *I* than an *ego*, an advertisement for myself that my mother tongue seems to frown upon. To say *I* in English is a normal, nearly imperceptible form of self-expression, a convention of thought and syntax; but in Spanish, the iteration of *yo* quickly turns into an exercise in narcissism. It is a commonplace of Spanish and Spanish American literary history that autobiographies are relatively rare. Undoubtedly there are many and complex reasons for this, but one of them may be the inhospitableness of the Spanish language to subject pronouns. When the language itself makes the writer's *I* grammatically redundant, autobiography verges on barbarism, and self-disclosure risks becoming a slip of the tongue. Henry James once wrote that the two most beautiful words in the English language are *summer afternoon*. Sometimes when I am struggling with the facts and the mysteries of life on the hyphen, it has occurred to me that the *three* most beautiful words in the English language could well be *me, myself*, and *I*.

And yet—*sin embargo* (*y hasta con embargo*)—it's not as if I'm interested in or capable of renouncing Spanish altogether. Indeed, the more I live and write in English, the more I need and miss Spanish. In our psychology-obsessed times, we are always talking about self-esteem; it seems to me that one of the most disabling forms of low self-esteem arises from the conviction that one cannot speak one's native language well enough, the shattering sense of inferiority that arises, not when words fail you, but when you fail them. I have seen it again and again in students of Hispanic background. I have seen how they squirm and look away when they think you expect them to speak with native fluency. I have often squirmed and looked away myself, feeling that no matter how good my Spanish may be, it is just not good enough. I sometimes think that every single one of my English sentences takes the place of the Spanish sentence I wasn't able or willing to write. And if I handle English more or less capably, it is because I try to write such clean, clear English prose that no one will miss the Spanish that it replaces.

That it replaces, and that it can never replace, because my single solitary American *I* continues to long for a sense of community that for me exists only in Spanish. Let's compare another set of titles. The Spanish version of *Next Year in Cuba* is entitled *El año que viene estamos en Cuba*. When I began working on the translation, my title was simply *El año que viene en Cuba*, but at some point I added the verb because, with it, the phrase sounded more idiomatic. I didn't think about it again until a few days ago, when I was figuring out what to talk to you about, and then it struck me that there was a crucial though unintended difference between the Spanish and the English. The word that the Spanish title adds is *estamos*, "we are," which supposes that the speaker is a member of the community. The Spanish title not only places the speaker in space but also makes him part of a society of like-minded individuals, all of whom hope one day—next year—to return to Cuba: rootless individualism is superseded by collective dreams. *Estamos* is a verb of consensus. In Spanish, when you ask *¿estamos?*, you are asking whether your interlocutor agrees with you. Buried inside the verb is the first-person plural pronoun *nosotros*, which, perhaps fancifully, I break down to *nuestros otros*, "our others,"— that is to say, the others in our *I*. "Next year in Cuba" names a rootless hope; "*El año que viene estamos en Cuba*" expresses a community's sense of itself, its shared values and expectations.

As someone who was born a *yo* but will probably die an *I*, I find that my negotiations with the two languages often occur in those inner and outer spaces between *yo* and *you*, between *se* and *self*, between *tú* and *two*, between mystery and fact. If I'm grateful to English for making my displays of individuality seem a little less barbaric, I'm grateful to Spanish for not letting me forget the intense, intricate, and sometimes baffling web of human relations that constitutes me. English has given me many things, but nothing as fundamental as what Spanish has given me: the conviction that the highest form of self-expression is communal, that the only way to speak for yourself is to begin each of your sentences with *nosotros*.

¿Estamos?

Against the Grain
WRITING IN SPANISH IN THE USA
From *Inventing America*

Lourdes Gil

Born in Havana, Cuba, Lourdes Gil left the Island in 1961 as an adolescent as part of Operation Peter Pan. She currently resides in Tenafly, New Jersey, with her son, Gabriel.

Language is the main instrument of man's refusal to accept the world as it is. —*George Steiner,* After Babel

[T]he poet who lives and writes outside of Cuba . . . inhabits a political space that is, in fact, a Cuban space. Whether s/he likes it or not, accepts it or not, consciously or unconsciously the poet is a living testimonial.
—*Lourdes Gil, "Poesía y política, para otra visión del exilio"*

I rarely dwell upon the fact that I have lived in the U.S. for over thirty years. I don't think about it in numerical terms, but rather as a space I once entered, an exile space. The concept of exile, from its Latin root "*exsul*," identifies its inherent condition: "outside of." The expatriate is, then, the perpetual outsider, the individual ousted from the community. I entered this exile space involuntarily (I was a child and others made the decision for me), yet the transition from the old to the new occurred in painful awareness. Something was blunted in the process, and my perception of time was permanently altered. As I walked into the uncharted, timeless regions of exile, I felt as if I was receding into a state of suspension, frozen in time, waiting for a faceless Godot.

I have never pondered over the question too seriously—why I write in Spanish. It seemed natural to continue speaking the language I was born into, to proceed with the language I first learned to read and write in, the original vessel transporting me to the world of the imagination and wonder. I regarded it as an essential component of my biological makeup, like the tone of my voice or the color of my eyes. I suppose it belongs to the realm of what psychologists call personal identity, anthropologists perceive as cultural identity, and the more ancient science of philosophy describes as Being or consciousness of Being.

Why cling to one's native tongue over such an extensive period of time? Why the linguistic transgression? Holding on to one's identity in the face of the new can be an obstinate, fearsomely barren gesture of defiance. There is also an innate complicity in the act of choosing a language over another—a form of loyalty, perhaps, loyalty to the well-worn frame of reference where the self has been, up to that time, contextualized, an attachment to one's past, a devotion. We cannot forget that there are hidden meanings in speech: the subtle undercurrents carrying other ways of life, the solace of traditions, a world inhabited by people who left an imprint on our lives, the books we've read, even a more exact definition of ourselves. Is there a dominance of language over us, a level where it settles, and where our mode of communication with others is established? Is it the eccentric site where the "encoding" of our writing and our speech occurs?

Mine was an old Cuban family, steeped in the Cuban and Spanish traditions that appear to have been lost after the Revolution of 1959. It was through them that I acquired a sense of history, of continuity, as a child, a notion of our presence in the world. I had a special bond with my grandparents and their generation. They exposed me to anecdotes from the early years of the Cuban Republic, the student strikes of the thirties, the prominent figures in public life, the events of the Second World War. They sang outmoded couplets and recited classical poetry. They lent me old books with quaint Victorian drawings.

The half-dozen great-uncles on my mother's side were a fascinating lot who had traveled extensively and whose lives had been invariably linked to all ramifications of Cuban society. Some I knew and some had already died at the time I was growing up, but their stories were told over and over, so they, and the stories themselves, eventually acquired mythic proportions. My great-grandmother, a formidable woman who crossed the Atlantic six times, presided over a Commission of Teachers traveling to the U.S. during the American occupation of the Island in 1899. She always conveyed an unadorned vision of colonial Havana to the rest of us, something that we regarded as a rather uncommon feat.

So I grew up with a particularly loaded cargo—all of that which is transmitted in the bosom of an old family, a family with great respect for the life of the country. It was a very strong influence, a sort of initiation rite. It endowed me with a notion of who I was—or, at least, of where I came from—and this is something that stays with you for the rest of your life. The language we used was the glue holding everything and everyone together. Language was bound to my experience of life with others, bound to a sense of place, a sense of belonging. It never occurred to me that it could be any different.

Many Cuban American authors of my generation, also arriving as children to the U.S., have chosen English for their creative work. Their literary vision and aesthetic canon seem to conform to the Anglo-Saxon perspective, either from a Eurocentric focus or from an ethnicity within American society. Why have they chosen this course? Clearly, they do not see themselves, or their craft, within the predicaments and textures of the Spanish language and literatures. They, instead, see their inner selves better reflected in the more recently acquired sounds and inflections of the English tongue.

Their defining choice may be divergent from mine, yet both of these choices—theirs and mine—were made within the same given coordinates of time and space. Some had families as old and traditional as mine and were educated with as strong a sense of national pride as I was. Why, then, did they come to organize their literary discourse in the mainstream of American life? Why did their creativity and its written expression evolve as a part of the signs and abstractions of one language over another?

And yet, what inner dialectic dictates self-definition for an exile? There are no footprints on the snow and we have little to guide us through this path. Except, perhaps, for the internally exposed exile suggested by James Joyce in his *Portrait of the Artist*—the flight to a freedom from the social order and its entanglements, a process of dislocation, an erasure of the immediate surroundings, a subversion of codes, a liberation.

FROM "THE NECESSARY TREASONS"

Language and place can evoke fragments of ideas, shreds of images, visions, words—the cherished demarcations of our existence. A writer like myself, however—a Cuban living in the United States because of political reasons; an author who writes in Spanish in an English-speaking *milieu*—can only conceive of place and language as metaphors of anguish and loss, of strangeness and marginality, or as an intricate mesh of freedom and betrayal.

Place, for instance, is the here and now. Once I was uprooted, I lost what may be called a sense of place. This detachment may seem an extraliterary experience, but its incongruities are a part of my writing. I find myself where I never wanted to be (had I been given the choice, I would have lived in my own country). But there are situations where choice is not possible. I have learned that when you enter this world at the time of your birth, you also enter history. And history is a collective force that shapes your destiny, while individual lives are merely brittle twigs swept by its winds.

This humbling lesson did not restrain the deep, dark rage I felt against what I considered to be a violation of my space; and for many years I refused to accept my new habitat. Now that the old Furies are no longer with me, my deliberate retention of Spanish as a means of expression represents their legacy—the one gesture of defiance in an otherwise ordered, peaceful existence.

I have come to regard the transgressions of place and language as the necessary treasons; and when I call them treasons, I do so in reference to the words of Socrates, who declared that "there are necessary treasons to make the city freer and more open to man." Such a city or state would render the necessary freedoms for true creativity. Yet, as long as the orthodoxy of society, the conventions that establish who and how we are, stifle, deform and trivialize the identity of artists who are both "*de aquí y de allá*," we hold on to the necessary treasons.

What happens to those who choose the solitude of writing? How does the artist's individual vision dictate the form and language of his writing? There is always a moment when the writer's own Furies are released; his daemons set loose; his betrayals privately pursued. These are the places he inhabits—the presence of daemons in his work; the sanctuary of his words. For the act of writing springs from an internal history, an inward discourse, and it is consciousness that articulates and encodes the semantics of its own tongue.

Do we rewrite ourselves? Are we our own transcriptions? Do we develop a new self—become another—when we discard the old linguistic canon, a camouflage image, a disguise for our own true face? Or are we speaking of a parallel sensibility; a melody in a higher key; a marching "to a different drummer," as Emerson wrote? Do we gain a second life or lose the innocence of wholeness?

Thomas Mann, Czeslaw Milosz and Joseph Brodsky regarded themselves as amputated sensibilities—never free of the previous incarnation of their lives in Germany, Poland or Russia, respectively. They never left behind—for writers never can—the places where they truly lived: the verbal constructs of a verbal culture. For whatever and however I write—they write—the ancient Orphic rituals reenact their celebrations one more time . . . *

---

* This paper was originally presented in October 1996 as part of a lecture series at the New School for Social Research on a panel entitled "Language, Place and the Writer."

Understanding del Casal

Marta Elena Acosta Stone

Marta Elena Acosta Stone was born in Havana, Cuba, in 1953; in 1956 she relocated to the United States with her parents for what she believed was a temporary stay. She now lives in Gunnison, Colorado.

Unlike most Cubans now in the U.S., my parents and I came here shortly before the Revolution. At the time (December 1956) I was three and a half years old, and my parents were both in their early thirties. As recent graduates of the University of Havana School of Medicine, they intended to return to Cuba after completing their internship; but following Fidel's takeover of the Cuban government in 1959, they decided to stay in the U.S. until things settled down. As time went on, it became apparent from relatives' reports that conditions were getting worse in Cuba, and my parents realized that our stay in the U.S. was permanent.

We lived in New York for a number of years. At that time travel to and from Cuba was still possible, and my dad's parents, Mercedes Orihuela and Simeón Acosta y Robau, came to visit twice during those years.

My mom's dad suffered a heart attack during one of his stays with us in Middletown, New York, and it was with great reluctance and foreboding that my mom allowed him to return to Cuba after his recovery. As she had feared, a second heart attack soon took his life.

Devastated, she went to Havana in late 1960 to attend the funeral. I was seven years old at the time, and I remember seeing her off at Idlewild Airport and thinking what strange events were intruding into my life: my grandfather's death, my mother's incessant crying, and her trip away from us back to Cuba, back to the past.

Diplomatic ties between Cuba and the U.S. were severed shortly thereafter. For my mom, it seemed that her father's death marked the diplomatic break in a very personal way. She returned from the funeral prematurely aged, tearful, and overprotective. During the rest of her life, she never allowed any of her children to travel without her, fearing that they too might die far away. And although I was too young really to miss my grandfather, I came to associate his death with the mystery and the loss of Cuba, and with my mom's lifelong sadness. She clung tenaciously to Cuban ways, her world being too black and white to admit grayness, to appreciate cultural differences as only that and not issues of right and wrong.

My mother, Sara Artola y Carmenates, was a medical doctor, but her upbringing had prepared her primarily for motherhood. At home with small children (my sister was born in 1958 and my brothers in 1960 and 1964), she had little opportunity or need to evolve in a new culture. As her oldest child, I was affected by her inadaptability. I was not allowed to attend sleepovers or go on field trips, for example, since "perverts" might lurk on school buses or in friends' homes at night. Most of my mom's fears about her children seemed to revolve around sexual transgression and violence or death, and I understood early on that the restrictions placed on my young life had to do with being Cuban and living outside of Cuba. I lived in a Cuban household that had wound up, inexplicably and against all reason, in the U.S., just as Dorothy's farmhouse had suddenly appeared in the Land of Oz.

My father, Sergio Acosta y Orihuela, adapted comfortably to life in the U.S. He established a successful practice, interacted with many different people, and improved his English much more quickly than my mother. Arguments between my parents were a weekly, if not daily, event. They fought over everything: finances, children, jealousies, my dad's work, religion, even issues in the field of medicine. I understand now that at the root of their conflicts was the Cuban past and its irretrievability. It was a past that offered models of strict gender roles, extended family, and a more stratified society with clear values, all of which life in this new country had eliminated or placed under doubt. As a child, however, I integrated their anger and struggled hopelessly with my identity. No amount of retrospective intellectualizing can undo the childhood suffering that I experienced—unshared, I believed, by anyone else in my family. While my siblings were born here, I had come with my parents from Cuba; and my origin, my earliest memories, and my sense of self were woven into the very fabric of their troubled relationship with each other and with *el destierro*.

My mother's mother, Juana Carmenates, lived with us for portions of my growing-up years. She played the piano and tried to teach me piano, too, which of course became a source of strife; I understood nothing of her world, and she despised mine. She had been raised with eleven siblings on a cattle ranch in the province of Camagüey at a time when her father owned slaves, children obeyed unconditionally, and playing the piano was the hallmark of refinement in a young woman. She was strict and very cantankerous. Children were never supposed to have an opinion or laugh with their friends, and they were supposed to sit perfectly still while riding in the car.

Thus, the women in my line of descent were not a source of warmth or comfort for me. My dad was too busy with his practice to talk to me about issues of personal happiness or self-worth, and he was also uninformed, I imagine, about a young girl's emotional needs. Such a situation is no more typical of the Cuban American family than of any other, but in a Cuban American family, generational differences are compounded by cultural and psychological ones. Due to politics, there is no possibility of traveling freely to childhood homes on the Island and once-familiar landscapes. The past looms large; Cuba becomes the mythical, tropical, lush Garden that the Serpent conquered through deceit. Thus, Cubans of older generations idealize the homeland and its culture more than other immigrants, perhaps, and are more out of touch with their children and grandchildren who grow up in the U.S. Poor, misled innocents, never to know the true happiness of the Cuba of the

'40s and '50s! Not inclined to open rebellion, I married young to get out of the house where this attitude reigned, since of course, no "decent Cuban girl" would leave home before marrying; nor would any Cuban mother, especially mine, allow it, even when her daughter was admitted to Smith College. Instead, I commuted to Dominican University in suburban Chicago; and before I finished my master's degree in 1975, I'd already had the first two of my five children.

Growing up, I had always attended schools where I was the only Spanish-speaking child. Whether my parents purposely sought out communities that were well-to-do, away from concentrations of Hispanics, or whether it just happened that my father wound up on the staffs of hospitals in such communities, I don't know. My second cousins, on the other hand, grew up in Brooklyn and knew hordes of people who spoke Spanish, so that Spanish for them was both a private and a public language. For me, each language represented a separate universe, one that I inhabited by birth, and the other that I observed and interacted with marginally. Home (Spanish) was familiar, real, sincere, potentially boring, but rich in tears and laughter. Beautiful Spanish, heavy-laden with emotion, and the home environment to which it was intimately tied, were the color of my very soul; they formed the core of me. School (English) represented a reasonable, slightly covert world, perhaps even hypocritical, but intriguing because of its freedoms and ideas.

According to María Zambrano, Spanish writer and philosopher, the main ill of the French is avarice; of the Spanish, envy; and of the Anglo-Saxon world, hypocrisy. As a young child, I sensed this last observation to be true but did not find it too objectionable, since the absence of honesty meant a measure of equality and reason, two virtues not prized in my home. However, as a chubby, curly-haired, overprotected little Cuban girl who was not allowed to attend sleepovers, do tumbling, or ride my bike in the street, my part in the English-speaking world was mainly one of observing from the sidelines. Some affirm that the soul is rendered more sensitive by marginalization, and the large number of artists and writers who were misfits in their day bears witness to this truth. However, realizing this retrospectively and creatively reviewing one's childhood cannot erase the scars of the past. It was not until I was in high school that I became fully aware of two liberating truths: that the culture of the Spanish-speaking world is as vast, varied, and complex as that of the United States; and that I could participate as little or as much as I wanted in any culture in the world. Studying French, Italian, literature, and history allowed me to put my own cultural background in context, and travelling to Europe and Latin America presented me with a panorama of difference set against the movement of history. Intellectually, I understood my location on the graph of time and space. Spanish and English were reconciled, and the apparent dichotomy between home and the outside world was exposed as a false one. Obviously, all I had to do was leave home, and I would be rid of the troubling issues that boiled there as in a pot on the stove. But I did not realize that the pot boiled within *me*. And I never felt happy and easy with American boys like the American girls, who so casually joked with them. Hadn't those girls' mothers and grandmothers warned them about informal association with the opposite sex? The core—the live, deep part of me cast in Spanish and in Cuban tradition—was still hypersensitive to duality: male and female, winter and summer, land and sea, night and day, life and death, my intense, unbound inner life and the baffling reality beyond.

When I was about thirty, I moved to Miami with my first husband and children. I assumed it would provide an environment where the distinction between myself and the outside world would smooth out its jagged outline, but I was wrong. In Miami, I found I was too Americanized, too politically liberal, and too unconcerned with Fidel to feel comfortable in the Cuban community, just as in the North I had been too Cuban. Painfully, a new theory of identity emerged: I was out of place everywhere. In Miami, I hated the constant heat and sun, the roughness of the social fabric, the religion of materialism. I longed for the quiet introspection of a winter's day and developed an affinity for the poetry of Julián del Casal, who, though Cuban, preferred to withdraw into himself and shield his senses from the riotous, irrepressible reality of the tropics. The Cubanness I had hoped to re-encounter was elusive; many Cubans I met appeared cliquish, shallow, and unadaptable. Although my doctoral studies in Latin American and Spanish literature at the University of Miami offered some sanity, I underwent a personal crisis. Ultimately, the upheaval in me led to some positive changes, such as ending an unhappy marriage. But my emotions were unsettled; I felt victimized by their surprise assaults. My search for identity had ended in depression, unbearable anxiety, and the need to return north.

But being Cuban still defines my life. Cuba is where I was born. It is where my mother ate, drank, breathed, listened to music, and felt the mist of the Malecón, cool and salty as it blew off the ocean, while she was carrying me. Cuba is where my father was raised and learned about the world; and his views on science and philosophy, which he discussed with me when I was old enough to understand, were formed there. My research and teaching, however, are less affected by the fact that I was raised with a "Cuban sensibility" than is my poetry, in which I struggle with themes of exile, identity, and the human search for happiness after "The Fall." I usually write my poetry in Spanish. English, though I've spoken it perfectly for years, always seems a bit contrived, as though I were playing a part whenever I speak it, as if I were still trying to fit in as I did in grade school, and not being my original self. I have even written a novel (which remains unpublished) in English. But English only skims the surface of my soul.

All human beings are, in a sense, outcasts from a perfect place of which we have vague, ancestral memories but to which we cannot seem to return. My husband, who is from Kentucky and of Irish descent, has suggested that we go live in Cuba. I would willingly do so, with or without Fidel's presence, but I'm wary of such impulses since my move to Miami in 1984. That search for the idyllic homeland ended in failure. I have lived in New York, Chicago, Miami, and Utah; I returned to the Midwest to teach at Quincy University in Illinois; and I have recently relocated to Colorado. However, I do not feel that my geographical moves have either drawn me closer to, or further distanced me from, my origins. My moment-to-moment sensations exist on unclaimed terrain, unexplored and sometimes frightening, advancing without chronology or direction. But I've known love, I've brought children into the world, I've marveled at the beauty of the sun shining through the palms on Miami Beach, and I've skied through the blinding, white world of thickly-falling snow in the Rocky Mountains. These and other experiences of wonder are what elevate my soul closer to the mythical homeland.

A Cubana in New York

Mayling C. Blanco

Mayling Blanco was born in Havana, Cuba, in 1978; she left the Island with her family in 1982 at the age of four. After eleven months in Spain, her family was granted visas to come to the United States in July 1983. She now resides in New York City.

It was during the Mariel Boatlift of 1980 that my family took its first steps toward the United States. As a young man, my father had been optimistic about some of the changes that took place as a result of the Revolution, such as the literacy program and the promise to decrease racism. Nevertheless, he could not deal with the increasing infringements on his economic, political, and religious liberties. Eventually, my father realized that the only way to ensure a life for his family free from political and religious persecution was to leave Cuba; so in 1980, he left the Island on a boat heading north with nothing but the clothes on his back, his dreams of freedom, and the desire to reunite his family.

My mother opted not to leave on a boat headed to an unknown future with two small children, both of whom were under three years of age. Although I was not quite two years old at the time, one of the few memories I have of Cuba is the day my father left. I remember that two or three men, dressed in the customary military fatigues and riding loud motorcycles, came to give my father the news of his departure. He was given only a couple of hours to get dressed and say goodbye to us. I still remember, as if it were yesterday, going out on the stone balcony of my grandmother's second-floor apartment in Havana to wave goodbye to my father as he headed toward El Mariel. Little did any of us know then that we would not see him again for over three years.

What was supposed to be a short boat ride turned out to be one of the most horrific experiences of my father's life, for they embarked on very turbulent waters. My father later told us that he doubted he would make it to shore alive because the boat rocked back and forth and fell several feet every time it went over the crest of a wave. Men, women, and children surrounded him on that overcrowded boat; many were sick to their stomachs, vomiting everything and everywhere. Eventually, however, the weather got better, and the boat was met by a U.S. Coast

Guard ship, which escorted them to shore. Some Americans came aboard and greeted them with cigarettes and Coca-Cola. What better way to remind them that they were no longer in Cuba?

The long months that followed were not as welcoming, however. Rumors quickly reached the U.S. that Castro had let the prisons open and was "dumping" Cuban criminals and mentally ill people, along with the political refugees. As a result, upon my father's arrival, he was faced with a waiting period several days long and a series of interviews. The *Marielitos*, as they would soon be known, were then relocated to various military bases across the U.S. My father was flown to Wisconsin and taken to Fort McCoy, where he was interviewed a number of times once again. My maternal grandfather, who had immigrated in the '50s, claimed him. This made the resettlement process faster and easier. Eventually, my father was flown back to Miami. After a couple of months in Miami, he decided to visit a longtime family friend who lived in New York City. During his visit, he found a job and made New York his permanent home. (He later told us that one of the reasons he left Miami was that he was ready to move on. He often commented on how Miami Cubans "*tienen un pie aquí y el otro allá*" [have one foot here and the other one there]. That was one of the unusual things about my family—we had left Cuba for good and had little hope of returning anytime soon.)

During that time period, my father found himself performing a number of odd jobs, including waiting on tables and acting as a security guard. This was quite difficult for him because back in Cuba, he had been a professor at the University of Havana. But this was not the first time that he was forced to make an adjustment. As a child, he had grown up in a middle-class family and was sent to a private school with a number of upper-class kids, including the daughter of one of the Bacardis, who was chauffeured to school every day.

In the months that followed my father's departure, my mother applied for visas to a number of countries. Finally, after a two-year wait, Spain granted us a visa. Unlike my father, we left on a plane, making us more fortunate than most Cuban emigrants who were leaving the Island at the time. However, we were not allowed to take much more than what we were wearing. I think that is one of the main reasons why anything that came from Cuba is treated like pure gold in a Cuban home. For example, one of the few things my mother was able to salvage from Cuba was a baby doll she had played with as a child and had given to me. Once we left Cuba, I was rarely allowed to play with her, and she was always stored in places that I could not reach. Today the doll serves as a vivid reminder for my mother of her childhood in Cuba; for me, it recalls our departure, for I held onto the doll as we walked past Cuban authorities.

My mother, my brother, and I spent eleven months in Spain under residential status. Finally, in July of 1983, we came to the U.S. with the help of my grandfather. We arrived at JFK airport on a direct flight from Madrid. Even though the journey was long, my family was finally reunited, after three years and two months, in the city I would call home for the next seven years of my life.

By the time we arrived in the U.S., my father had already "assimilated." He had learned the language, he listened to disco, and he dressed "American," at least so he thought. The following year, when I was enrolled in school, I faced my first culture clash. Because our local elementary school was full, I, along with a handful of other children from my neighborhood, was sent to a school in Harlem that had no facilities for bilingual education. I remember that on parent-teacher night, my teacher told my mother that I was doing poorly. I think my teacher was a little oblivious to the fact that I didn't speak English. Though my father spoke some English, my mother had yet to learn the language, and besides, it was never spoken inside our home. That's how it was: English was viewed as a necessity—we used it at school, and my parents used it at work.

Fortunately, the following year I was able to attend the neighborhood school, which did offer a bilingual education program. The program eased my adjustment and learning process. On the other hand, my parents often complained that ESL (English as a Second Language) programs were not created to foster two languages but, rather, to have the students learn English and forget their native languages. After our first two years in school, my brother and I began to use English at home. This did not please my parents. There was even a period when I was growing up during which I refused to speak Spanish or admit that I was Cuban, mostly because the teachers at school didn't allow us to speak Spanish. I acted like I never knew the language; my parents blamed it on ESL. Regardless, my parents struggled to keep "our" language alive in me. It was not until I reached high school, when it was beneficial to know Spanish, that I began to speak it again on a regular basis.

Even though we did not live in Miami, Washington Heights is a largely Spanish-speaking community. Most of the businesses have Spanish-speaking employees, and the Spanish masses in our parish have higher attendance rates than the English ones. Reflecting the ethnic composition of my neighborhood, my elementary school was renamed Juan Pablo Duarte during my second year there; however, Dominicans, rather than Cubans, were the ethnic majority. As a result, the few Cubans my family knew in our neighborhood were treated as lifetime friends. This created yet another challenge for my parents because I would often come home and use words in Spanish that I had picked up at school. This did not please them either: they did not want me to simply speak Spanish; they wanted me to speak "Cuban" Spanish.

Oddly enough, we were one of the more "American" families in my neighborhood. We did not go shopping at the local grocery store, but, rather, we went to the supermarket in our car; my father read the *New York Times* rather than *El Diario*; and on the Fourth of July, my father's American flag was one of two flying high amid the loud *merengues* on my street. My father was proud of his Americanness. He pronounced every syllable when he spoke English, and the Fourth of July was always the most important celebration of the summer. Nevertheless, on Cuba's patron la Caridad del Cobre's feast day, a makeshift altar, with candles and flowers, would go up in her honor in our living room, while her statue was being paraded up and down the streets of my neighborhood by the small Cuban community. And while we flew the American flag high outside our apartment window and celebrated Christmas on December 25th with Santa Claus and Easter with a bunny, we also ate our *lechón* on *Nochebuena*, celebrated Three Kings' Day on January 6th, and ate Thanksgiving turkey with *sazón*.

In the same vein, though my parents always complained about the way Americans capitalize on holidays, my mother never forgot to wear green on Saint Patrick's Day, and my parents always gave me an Easter basket filled with candy and a bunny rabbit and bought me a whole new outfit for Easter Sunday. So, like so many immigrant families, my culture was a mixture of two. It was the Cuban and the American, sometimes separated by clear boundaries; but so many times these were mixed or blurred. Whether we were assimilated or not depended on whom you asked. My father, for example, would say "yes"; maybe he thought that huge American flag outside our window might hide the 101 cans of Goya black beans in our cupboard. Many of my childhood friends also believed that my family was American because we did not blast Spanish rhythms on our radios, and my mother had a job and my father tried to do his equal share of the housework. In my view, however, my parents never truly assimilated, because every time I asked them for permission to do something, they refused by giving me the excuse that I was a girl—and like a "good" Cuban girl, I was escorted everywhere by my mother.

Yet if you asked me what I am, I would respond that I am Cuban American. American because I value independence more than anything; because at the age of seventeen I left home to go to college; because *okay* is the most frequently used word in my vocabulary, regardless of whether I'm speaking English or Spanish; because if you ask me to sing my national anthem I begin with, "Oh say can you see." Yet I am Cuban because I was born on the Island; because I cannot overcome the overwhelming urge to go there; because I still feel that my roots lie there; and because Gloria Estefan's "*Mi Tierra*" is like my Cuban American national anthem.

For these reasons, naturalization was not a big issue for me. Becoming an American citizen was as exciting as turning eighteen because I was able to check off a different box on applications and participate in elections. Naturalization was not as simple for my parents. As a result of the incompetence of two administrations that failed to deal with the legal status of the Mariel immigrants, my father was on parole for seven years after his immigration to the States. Thus for him, receiving his green card was just as good as becoming a citizen. My mother, however, became a citizen in 1995. After my grandmother passed away in Cuba in 1991, I think my mother came to the realization that there was really nothing for her to return to. It was only at that point that Cuba became her past and the U.S. became her present and her future. For days after she received her citizenship she told me, "I am American" with a smile on her face; yet every morning my mother sits at the kitchen table repeatedly dipping her bread in her *café con leche*.

I know that if I ever go to Cuba, I will never be seen as a *cubana*, and if I go to the heartland of America, I will never be seen as an American; yet in New York City I feel at home, probably because everyone is so different in terms of their culture and race that no one feels out place. My Cubanness is something deep within me, yet I realize now that it is mostly something I have learned from my parents and the traditions they have instilled in me.

Arroz

Virgil Suárez

See Section IV for the author's biographical sketch.

comes to El Volcán, the corner *bodega*
run by El Chino Chan,
along with the food rations
the people of Arroyo Naranjo, Cuba,
line up and wait for, in the meantime
they listen as Chan
calls out "*alo, alo*" Spanish–Chinese
for *arroz*. Rice. I, six or seven, stand
in line, my mother next to me in the shade
of the *guayaba* trees, we watch as people
move in and out of the sun and heat.
Women fan their faces. Talk & gossip
buzz like the horse flies that fly up
from the ravine and brook. Chan tells
stories of when the great Poet jumped
into the river and the villagers, to keep
the fish from gobbling up the poet, tossed in
rice dumplings wrapped in bamboo leaves.
Arroz. The blessing at weddings. Constant
staple with its richness of spirit. Sustenance.
Slowly the rations are filled and the line
moves and my mother and I reach the counter.
Behind it hang *papalotes*, kites made

of colorful rice paper, next to them
the countless oriental prints of carp,
egrets, tigers and dragons. Chan talks
about the grain of rice kept in a glass
case at El Capitolio in the city, a love poem
etched on it in print so small one needs
more than a magnifying glass to read
what it says. Chan, rice, magic—the gift
of something different to pass the time.
Now, so many miles and years from this life,
in the new place called home, rice,
like potatoes, goes unnoticed when served.
Often, my daughters ignore it
and I won't permit it. Rice, I say to them,
needs respect, needs worship,
their full attention, for blessed is that
which carries so many so far.

What Kind of Cuban Are You?

Carolina Hospital

Carolina Hospital was born in Havana, Cuba, in 1957. She left the Island in 1962 via Jamaica and Puerto Rico, and in 1966 moved to Miami, Florida, where she currently resides.

I am off the hyphen. I have spent too many years trying to convince myself and others that I'm Cuban enough and American enough. As a student at the University of Florida, I diligently studied Cuban history, Cuban literature, Cuban politics, and even Cuban popular culture. To my parents' surprise, I learned to dance mambos and *guaguancós* there. I was a *cubana* in the sticks. Yet, in one seemingly insignificant encounter, in an elevator, I relapsed into my old feelings of inadequacy.

Alina, a college friend at the time, had abandoned Cuba at seventeen and was struggling to make a new life for herself in exile. We had left our Cuban literature class exhausted and hungry. In the elevator she told me, "I can't wait to get home to make myself an Elena Ruz."

I asked her what that was. She answered, "You don't know what an Elena Ruz is? What kind of Cuban are you?" Obviously not Cuban enough. I found out an Elena Ruz is a popular Cuban sandwich. Her question was seared in my brain. What kind of Cuban was I?

On the other hand, I considered myself as Anglo as apple pie. I read Hemingway and Gloria Steinem, wore T-shirts, jeans, and Topsiders, was a registered Democrat, and sang Carly Simon tunes. I tried hard to embrace both worlds. That was the problem: I tried too hard. I became a cultural schizophrenic, always second-guessing myself, always conscious of any cultural ramifications from my choices. Culture grounds you, but it can also drown you. Those of us caught between the tidal surges of two very different and often contradictory cultures are more vulnerable to going under than most.

Eventually, I realized my only chance to stay afloat was to declare myself a free agent: to stop feeling defined by either culture and seize the opportunity to pick what most appealed to me about both. It was OK to reject the patriarchal and arrogant *caudillista* tendencies of the Cuban culture while accepting its strong family values and its exuberant approach to life; reject America's cold utilitarian work ethic while accepting its democratic spirit and respect for fairness. These positive values I made my own, not because they were Cuban or American, but because they felt right. And so, I stopped asking myself where home is. Miami is home. In Miami, my native-born daughter and her Anglo friends at times have more Hispanic intonation than I; some of my non-Cuban colleagues regularly greet me with a friendly kiss and offer me *cortaditos*; everyone eats bagels; and at my daughter's school cafeteria, they serve black beans and rice with matzoh ball soup. No one takes notice. Just the other day, at a Publix in Coral Gables, an elderly Anglo gentleman asked the African American clerk at the deli for two "midnights." It took me a few seconds to realize what he wanted: two *medianoche* sandwiches.

I admit living in Miami can be confusing. Bewildered, confused, confounded is how I feel some mornings driving to Miami-Dade Community College, where I teach English. Yet, in the classroom, I see my students, and I am reminded that life in Miami is fluid. Take three of my students, who are not the exceptions: Gabriela is the daughter of a Costa Rican married to a Venezuelan, born in Colombia and raised in Miami;

Javier happens to be the son of an Italian married to a Peruvian, who was raised in New Jersey and recently moved to Miami; finally, Manama was born and raised in Japan, lives in Miami, and is married to a Cuban American. In their individual lives, indeed in their very genes, Miami is. I cannot deny that at times I'm fed up with Miami and all its troubles. However, I realize that conflicts may be transformations: though difficult, a way to truth. The truth can be enlightening; wisdom comes in fragments. In Miami, I have learned to loosen up about culture.

So, I named my new daughter Sonora: a state in Mexico, a desert in California, the name of an American horse diver from the 1930s, and Celia Cruz's first band La Sonora Matancera. My hope lies in my child's name. It allows for all sorts of cultural possibilities, like her mother and her town.

This article was first published in the *Miami Herald*, June 15, 1997, p. 10.

Tropical Flavor
FROM *Sugar Cane Blues*

Nilda Cepero

See Section IV for the author's biographical sketch.

To Hall Estrada, who loves Cuban *boleros*

I've developed a taste for escargot . . .
but sometimes I go to Cuban restaurants
to sense aromas from my past
the smell of black beans and fried plantains
that made me feel cheerful and safe

Sometimes I go to Cuban restaurants
and sit quietly in the back
Over calls for "*café, señora*"
boleros filter through the room
I relax and close my eyes
while enjoying Olga Guillot
pouring out melodies my mother loved

Sometimes I go to Cuban restaurants
and caramel and lemon peels
wake my senses, stir me inside
fragrances that reach my heart
bearing reflections of who I am

Sometimes I go to Cuban restaurants
to feel that other soul inside

Flags and Rags (On Golden Lake)
EXCERPTS FROM A BOOK OF MEMOIRS IN PROGRESS

Elías Miguel Muñoz

Elías Miguel Muñoz was born in Ciega de Avila in 1954. He immigrated to Spain in 1968 and arrived in Los Angeles in May 1969. He lives in Los Alamos, New Mexico, with his family.

The nation requires anthems, flags. The poet offers discord. Rags.
—*Salman Rushdie*

THE BONA FIDE AMERICAN

En route to Salt Spring Island, Canada, October 12, 1993. My wife, Karen, and I are here to visit her aunt. We're crossing from Vancouver on a ferry, watching autumn caress this cold-land vegetation. The islands appear imperceptibly, while in the background I hear Karen's conversation with a Canadian woman. Her name is Patricia, and she's a nurse, thirty-two, Ukrainian parents. Patricia is eager to share with us her views of this vast North American country. She talks about Canada's inefficient health care system, about the lack of multicultural awareness (as this is understood in the U.S.) that prevails here.

Patricia turns to me and asks, "Where are you from originally?" The word *originally* intrigues me. I mention that I'm Cuban and have been a United States citizen for twenty-five years. (I'm aware that those years won't count; that period of time has nothing to do with my "origin.") The Ukrainian reacts, "Oh, so you're a bona fide American." I nod in agreement. And I promise myself to ponder, later, the meaning of this other little word as well: *American.*

For all practical, legal purposes, I am indeed an American. Yet I've just presented—*defined*—myself as Cuban; not even Cuban American, but Cuban. How can I claim to be from a place I haven't seen since childhood? Because I still dream about my hometown, Ciego de Avila, perhaps. What better reason to assume a nationality?

But the leitmotif of my nights is a dream I wish to banish so I can sleep—*live*—in peace. The town's main street, Calle Independencia, is a labyrinth through which I run, trying to find a way out. (The symbolism of the street name, *independence*, doesn't escape me.) Sometimes the Calle leads to a stage, and I have to grab a microphone and sing an unknown song. The orchestra sounds as I hum the unfamiliar melody. But the lyrics don't come; they never do.

In some versions of the dream there are hotel corridors, interminable hallways where none of the doors will open. And there's yet another scenario: I'm waiting at the station of an underground train that I must board without knowing my destination. All I know for certain is that the stage, the hotel, and the station are located in Cuba.

CUBAN THREATS

I find in my 1992 journal an entry on "A Cuban Poetry Festival," an event that took place at Miami-Dade College. I gave a reading of my poems and participated in a panel discussion. The other panelists were the Mariel poet and scholar Roberto Valero; the renowned dissident poet Heberto Padilla; and Cuban American essayist Carolina Hospital, co-organizer of the festival. The topic: "Common Threads," a title that Valero and I interpreted, playfully, as "Common *Threats*" (because cultural monsters are among the most threatening).

I had decided to read a passage from *Desde esta orilla* (*From This Shore*), a book I published in 1988 on Cuban exile poetry. It was a sentimental piece that focused on the nostalgia that informs much of my writing: nostalgia that, presumably, characterizes many Cuban exiles. I shouldn't have hidden behind a book, basing my ideas on a depoliticized "memoir." I should've done what Heberto did: shout, bellow his opinions. But I've never been able to fight for the right to speak. This is without a doubt one of the lacunae of my Cubanness. In gatherings of Cubans, one must duel for the word. Cubans in groups holler their views, all at the same time. And somehow they manage to listen to one another, even understand one another!

Typically, I didn't say much during that debate, nothing beyond my reading. So Heberto felt free (true to his aging enfant terrible image) to zero in on my ridiculous nostalgias and ethnic romanticisms. And he was right on target! I should've been my own critic, instead of presenting the same old stuff: 1) my longing for a past that never existed; 2) my idealizing of childhood experiences so I can render them literary; 3) the aestheticizing of memory in order to express a position, an ideology.

That ideology, which had gone from a rejection of everything Cuban to a Marxist and pro-Revolution radicalization at the university, was nothing but the lack of an honest relationship with the Island. At the poetry festival, I didn't do what I hope to accomplish in the following pages: to interrogate the Cuban culture that runs in my blood.

Roberto Valero didn't escape Heberto's criticism, either. Apparently, Roberto had also created for himself a personal island, nourished by poetry, which had little to do with the realities of our diaspora or with life in Miami. It was in defense of that city and its culture that Carolina intervened. She didn't feel nostalgia because she'd lived since age two in Miami. She hadn't—couldn't have—brought from Cuba any memories to aestheticize. Even so, she said, her world had always been infused with Cuba and its process.

Instead of nostalgia, Carolina spoke of *presence.* The Island was present in her daily chores, her thoughts, her conversations. Living in Miami, for her, was like inhabiting a real, vibrant, tangible piece of the Island, an extension of Cuba.

The question I asked myself (and should've brought up) was: Which Cuba? I will admit that official Miami reality has much to do with the Island's ideological life: it feeds from and defines itself in opposition to Cuba's truths. But Miami, Little Havana, has nothing to do with the Cuban people's struggle for survival, with their hunger and their needs. Carolina's hometown isn't an extension of the Caribbean country but its photographic negative, a parallel dimension, an alternate universe.

My childhood in Ciego de Avila has as much right to exist as Carolina's "real" present. They both survive as myth, image, even simulacrum. Both are nourished more by nostalgia than by presence. Miami offers me a sweet yet deceitful caress: rich and abundant cuisine; an accent that sounds *cubano*; its identity, anchored in the vision of an idyllic island—the lost paradise. Except that many Cubans didn't lose a paradise, but an inferno: the hell of poverty and racism that prevailed in pre-Castro Cuba. A place that few dare to describe as what it was: Eden for a minority, whorehouse of North America.

I grew up in California, a world away from Little Havana's *patriotismo*. I don't share Miami's obsessions and idiosyncrasies, its superiority complex. That community insists on being unique, special, profoundly Cuban. Miami blows me away. It is somewhat comforting, like an image of home (a home in which you've never lived). Yet its beauty perturbs me. Because it was born—*invented*—from the ruins of a past that was never perfect. Miami demands a political posture and imposes its *tema*. Silence on this topic isn't an option here. If you don't scream out your anticommunist passions, then you're a suspect, an incomplete Cuban. Like me.

In spite of the loving, familial Cuban grandmas who serve *picadillo* at Versailles (and who always win me over), or of Willy Chirino's music (which makes me get down), I don't belong here. I'm not Cuban if that means living in this "present," marked by the absent presence of Cuba.

Yet I don't belong anywhere else. I've learned to accept this, finally: my home is not a specific place. Not Miami. Not California. Much less Cuba. In fact, if I were to return to the Island, I'd find myself in a foreign country. There's been a lifetime of change, too many years of distance and exile. Could I still connect? I admit I'd love to see my hometown again, the neighborhood where I grew up, revisit the ghosts of our old neighbors. But I suspect my motivation is more artistic than patriotic. I wish to feel—and, therefore, narrate—what I stopped feeling in 1968: the experiences of a chubby little boy living in a provincial Cuban town. But the tie that might exist between my life and Cuba has to be forged anew, from scratch. I should admit that fear is the reason I've never gone back—a fear that's real and specific, but also abstract, indefinable. Fear of not being able to continue inventing—idealizing—the Island on the basis of my memories. Fear of enduring again my family's 1968 exodus. The pain, my parents' tears, our farewell. When Gladys and Elías said goodbye to my brother and me; when they sent us to Spain, not knowing whether they'd ever see us again. To set foot on

Cuban soil: to walk on land that I tried so hard to leave behind. Returning to a painful past—what would be the point?

I am sure, at a rational level, that I wouldn't be at risk if I returned to Cuba. There would be no political repercussions and no dire consequences. But there exists an irrational realm where nightmares live, where the deepest feelings hide, and the most absurd personal truths lie buried. From within that place I see myself trapped on the Island, unable to return to this, my new and true *patria*, which is Karen and our daughters, Aidan and Annika—uprooted again from everything that gives meaning to my life.

MIRRORS AND PICADILLO

What is culture? In the words of Yale anthropologist Weston La Barre, "much of culture is hallucination." Cultural rituals, La Barre suggests, could be seen as a group wish to "hallucinate reality." For as long as I can remember, I've been reluctant to participate in collective hallucinations, in reality as others define it.

Indeed, it's been a challenge for me to fully incarnate Cuban culture. Yet there are people I've grown to love who got into my heart precisely because they were Cuban. But those friends don't write the "Official Cuban Story." On the contrary, they contest, each in his or her own way, the definitions imposed by the "Cuban Truth Patrol": on the Island, people who control the censorship machinery and decide what one can think and say, what can be termed a sin against the Revolution; here, in the United States, those enlisted in the conservative leagues, those who seek to project a sole image (of economic power, superiority, and right-wing rhetoric) to represent our entire diaspora.

Cuba has insisted on seeking me out, on welcoming me. Not as "the mark, the lost identity" I attempted to describe in *Desde esta orilla*: an inaccessible and mysterious land, the exile's cliché, a common place; but as a real and inviting land that awaits me. Cuba has summoned me through its messengers: my friends. Thanks to them, I've come to understand that my country of origin (where I haven't been in thirty years) is much more than a memory; more than a poetic image, theme of a novel, literary substance. The homeland I've finally discovered is a living idea, embodied by specific individuals.

The hip, musical, and fashion-crazy country, *La Cuba Pepilla* I've shared with Marisel Reyes: a Cuba sung by Los Memes in "*Otro amanecer*" and Marta Estrada in "*Abrázame fuerte.*" Or the one where Mercedes Limón lives: loud, given to excess, always in full Albita drag. I'm also thinking of the conflicting present-day Cuba that arrives through Senel Paz's friendship. (When first reading his work, I had the mind-blowing impression that I was reading myself.) Gustavo Pérez Firmat's Cuba, as well, elusively present at the Versailles restaurant, aleph of mirrors and *picadillo*; the Island inscribed in Ricky's "*Babalú*" and the Mambo Kings' "Beautiful Maria." Cuba calls us: calls Gustavo by way of *I Love Lucy* and Gloria Estefan; me, through a handful of people.

BEWARE THE WRITER

If I dared to speak of a Cuban "essence," I'd say that Cubans are prone to excess, to extremes, that they tend to impose their way of thinking. On the Island, the "essential" Cuban character is defined perhaps by its strength, its *choteo*, by an exuberant sexuality and an iron will to survive. In exile, this character defines itself through its quest for success (be it economic, political, or professional), its anti-Castro neurosis, and its ethnocentricity.

I'm generalizing, and I shouldn't. But, after all, I'm talking about what I've known and seen: *los cubanos* according to my experience. I haven't been able—nor have I wanted—to be one of the representative voices of our diaspora. Nor will I be, either, a spokesman for the future "free" Cuba. I understand much too well Rushdie's warning: "Beware the writer who sets himself or herself up as the voice of a nation." Which doesn't imply only a country, says Rushdie, but also "nations of race, gender, sexual orientation, elective affinity."

No, I can't hoist the Cuban flag because I know that flags are made of rags. Because my life tells stories that "Official Cuban History" cannot afford to recognize. Because my accent doesn't sound "authentically Cuban." Because I studied Marxism and tried—albeit ingenuously—to believe in its fantastic promises. Because I see the need for a dialogue, for solid bridges that aren't built on oppressive, obsolete ideologies. Because I seek the peace of a utopian future where no one is forced to hide his or her dreams, where no one is forced to accept official truths.

Within the tranquility and isolation of Salt Spring Island (so different from the other *Isla*), I turn to the pages of a diary. And there I take note of a golden lake that welcomes me. Back in time, lost in a fall day of 1993, from a present that still finds me writing and remembering. As I reread these pages, I'm amazed to discover that six years later, today, I'm still tormented by the same old quest. And it'll always be so, most likely. Until I die.

Here again, trying to understand who I am and what I feel beyond my Cubanness, beyond my skin and my voice and my exodus. Here, telling myself that Paradise doesn't exist, that there are no utopian islands. Still listening to a compelling message from a place called Exile: this other exile, which is more imposing, pervasive. There's no need here for the cloyingly sweet cup of *café criollo*, for black beans or *galletas cubanas*. No need for flags or revolutions.

Next Stop Ninety Miles
NOTES FROM A CUBAN V-29ER

Kenya Carmen Dworkin y Méndez

Kenya Carmen Dworkin y Méndez was born in Havana, Cuba, in 1955 and was brought to New York in early 1956. She lives in Pittsburgh, Pennsylvania.

To the memory of Professor Cleon W. Capsas, a true friend and scholar without whose inspiration I could never have written this essay. *Gracias, amigo, por tu risa fácil, tu mente astuta, y tu enorme corazón. Te quiero siempre.* February 13, 1998

This testimonial is born out of an anxiety that I have experienced personally, as a Cuban-born, American-raised professor of Hispanic literature, history, and culture. The anxiety is the result of a disquieting, persistent question that, implicitly if not explicitly, foreshadows the morning ablutions of not just me but every diasporic Cuban, every morning of every day, in the overwhelmingly monolingual-monocultural mainstream of the United States. Considering the Cuban/non-Cuban paradigm I face, it becomes clear that to some degree or another, depending on my geographic location and demographic circumstance, it is incumbent upon me to make this daily negotiation seem effortless, or risk the wrath of mainstream conservative backlash. This becomes even more complicated by the fact that I am, as a result of my upbringing, a secular Jew with highly developed Catholic sensibilities.

In thinking of just how much influence my Cuban heritage has had on my professional work, I realize that it has been overwhelming. I was hired by a language department, with adjunct positions in History and English, as a specialist in Latin American studies who teaches the literature, history, and culture of Cubans, Latinos, immigrant Hispanics, and Latin Americans. This has allowed me a privileged, although precarious, position from which to observe, analyze, and give a dissertation on the subject of my own ambiguous identity. (I recently remarked to the editor of this volume that I sometimes feel guilty about being paid to obsess about my obsession. She totally understood, saying she felt exactly the same way.)

Doing fieldwork and research in Tampa, which has taken me there over twenty times in the last four years, I discovered something incredible. When I am in Tampa, a place where I spend a lot of time, the city itself confirms my multiple identities through its people and their history and culture. All of my *tampeño* friends understand my "Cuban condition." When I am in Pittsburgh, where I live, celebrating my identity is more like a religious ritual, entailing sometimes simple and other times elaborate mysteries of my faith—my *cubanidad*. In Tampa, my morning *café con leche* and *sube y baja* take on eucharistic proportions; through them, I am redeemed and in communion with the community of Latinos there. In Pittsburgh, my morning shot of coffee and toast or oatmeal and milk pale by comparison. At home, even a daily splash of that holiest of holy waters, *Agua de Florida*, does not sufficiently prepare me for "crossing the border," for conscientiously reentering the world out there—a place that for me is really two places. When I am in my Cuban "place," I am an immigrant to the other. When in the other, I am in a permanent state of exile. I am a traveler without a country, a minority unto myself.

My mother brought me to this country when I was six months old, in early 1956, on a v-29 (twenty-nine-day) visa. Consequently, I do not consider myself to be in exile in the post-1959 sense of the word, although it seems I might have overstayed my welcome (the visit turned into a move). An accident of birth (a premature birth) gives me the right to claim "official" Cubanness. So does the fact that to this day, I have not become a citizen of this country (I am still a citizen of Cuba). However, if I had been born in New York, as was the plan, I would have been raised under the very same circumstances that have produced me, although the issue of nationality would be more ambiguous, perhaps causing me to feel an even greater need to justify my Cubanness. I was supposed to be born in the U.S., but instead made a very early debut, causing my father to leave for New York without us and my mother and me to stay in Havana until I was well enough to travel. This, to my way of thinking, establishes me as Cuban and not Cuban American. People have told me that those six months don't make a difference, that I should consider myself American, but I emphatically disagree. Recalling the lyrics of a song that was popular when I was a child, "What a difference a day makes," I feel that they couldn't have made more of a difference.

For this and other reasons, I have never become an American citizen. I also refuse to be categorized as a Cuban American and always identify myself as simply Cuban. Neither do I fit the "one-and-a-halfer" or "American-Born Cuban (ABC)" monikers used by Rubén Rumbaut or Gustavo Pérez Firmat, given the conditions of my birth (in Cuba), arrival in this country (at the age of six months), and later experiences (growing up in an intensely Cuban environment and with a highly developed Cuban sense of the world). Growing up, I found myself somewhere between being Cuban and an ABC, somewhere between Cuba and New York, between one island and another, exiled from the country of my birth to an island of estrangement. Not surprisingly, I sometimes feel I have a split personality.

Even my name evokes an identity crisis. Kenya (African) + Carmen (Hispanic) + Dworkin (Russian/Polish) + Méndez (Hispanic) is not only a mouthful, it is a challenge that defies national or cultural identification. I have been persistently called Carmen by an Africana studies professor at Berkeley, who couldn't bring himself to call me Kenya; I have responded to my name, Kenya, being called on the first day of class and had the teacher stare right through me and mark me absent; and Dworkin—well, I give up. Even the priest who baptized me in Havana (yes, I was baptized by my mother's family *por si acaso*—just in case) refused to consecrate me with only a "pagan" name. He added the

Carmen to appease a Christian god who might otherwise never let me into heaven for lack of a name St. Peter could recognize (as if that same Christian god wouldn't know that I'd probably never entertain such a lofty ambition anyway).

Getting back to my sometimes split personality, in Tampa I'm actually known by two names: Kenya Dworkin by the academics and most friends, and Carmen Méndez by a few of my older research informants for whom Kenya Dworkin was just too daunting. Perhaps that would be a neat separation of my two selves—the Cuban and the American—but it wouldn't work because the Carmen and Méndez half is much too intertwined with the Kenya and the Dworkin. Even the Catholicism and Judaism are mixed up, although I define myself as a secular Jew. One Christmas Eve, *Nochebuena* fell on the second night of Hanukkah, and what did I serve for dinner? *Pernil, arroz con frijoles negros, yuca y plátanos fritos.* And for dessert? Sephardic date cookies and almond honey cake. For me, this needed no explanation. Hanukkah had eight days; I thought at least one of them could be Cuban. Besides, there was time enough for latkes at breakfast. As I always tell my friends, "In the Caribbean—anything goes."

Yet, there are many places in this country where that is not true. I remember once, when I was about seven, my parents and I were driving to Miami from New York and stopped in South Carolina or Georgia. We had stopped to eat something at a roadside diner. Sitting down at the counter, my father ordered in perfect (accentless) English and then started to talk to my mother and me in Spanish. When the owner heard us, he got a funny look on his face, as did everyone else in the place. All of a sudden, a few men surrounded us, and the owner told us to leave. I wasn't sure what was going on, but I could sense that they were violent and my mother was frightened. Needless to say, we left. To this day, I am convinced that they were Klansmen.

The worst experience occurred, however, when I was about nine years old. We moved to River Edge (North Hackensack, New Jersey), to a house on a cul-de-sac in a totally "American" neighborhood. To my parents, this was a move up; to me, it was a move "out" because for the first time in my life, I was free to go out and ride a bike or play kickball. No more begging my mother to let me play stoopball or skullies back in the 'hood. No more riding my bike with training wheels in the basement of a six-story walk-up. Unfortunately, this street with no outlet, this dead-end street, would introduce me to the worst kind of discrimination: *despecho del prójimo*—rejection from your own kind. Miraculously, another family on the same cul-de-sac was Cuban, too. Although they had children my age, they were not permitted to play with me because my father and I were Jewish. Yet I played with the Irish-, Italian-, and Polish American kids (I guess their parents never quite figured me out). Cuban against Cuban was a concept I could not understand (although I did much later, much to my distress). This experience seemed to intensify both my Cubanness and my Jewishness because somehow I knew that being Cuban and Jewish was all about difference, and I'd always liked being different.

The experience of discovering you are the wrong kind of Cuban is particularly frustrating. I have relived this experience—a recurring daytime nightmare—many times, particularly in academic settings. Like in a string of *telenovelas*, the players are always different; the results, however, are always the same. More painful yet is the fact that I have experienced this attitude in Miami as well. I too often have had to defend my Cubanness to Cubans who think I'm either too white, too blue eyed, too Jewish, or too Americanized to have the authority to claim this sacred identity. If they find out that I have Eastern European blood, that's the final nail in my non-Cuban coffin. Many Miami Cubans have come to believe themselves to be the brokers of cultural and political Cuban identity, and that they alone have the power to acknowledge or deny the authenticity of the rest of us (even island Cubans!). I categorically deny them the authority to do that. According to Fernando Ortiz, "Mr. Cuba" himself (as Gustavo Pérez Firmat calls him), to be Cuban is entirely a matter of will—and I not only have the will to be Cuban; I *will* be Cuban, too, *coño*.

"The Bite of Exile"

The Bite of Exile

José Kozer

José Kozer was born in Havana, Cuba, in 1940; he left the Island at the age of twenty in 1960. Though he spent most of his life in exile in New York City, he recently relocated to Hallandale, Florida.

I

"Exile," that chic word, that lousy word. It means an expulsion. You leave the womb as you leave Eden, as you leave the Island. And live burdened by a vivid awareness that death has a hold on you; you meditate daily on death having a hold on you. That is exile. The bitch bites you in many different places. Sometimes she bites really hard, and sometimes she just scratches you. But that difference doesn't explain much. There is more. The bitch bites, and one of the bites takes you away from where you were born. What can you do? Get the hell out. It makes you richer; it makes you poorer. In the dialectic of profit and loss, a Cuban Jew (me?) looks at the balance sheet. After thirty-seven years of "exile" (OK, I'll use the lousy word), the balance is positive. I gained in freedom, in experience, in "modernity." And, to my definite advantage, the tongue I speak gained, too, becoming enriched by contact with English and with the different varieties of Spanish in Spain and Latin America. What more can a "poet" ask for? The poet *makes* poems, and to make them he dives deep into the mystery of "exile" (what a metaphor) and scratches the surface of episodes, passion, and language. Down there, devoid of language, he experiments. And like a deep-sea diver he ascends, breathing slowly, touching his diver's helmet (in fear that it may not be there), and he ascends naked and dead to the surface. He goes up, babbling. He has language, and he speaks languages and dialects, and he speaks in tongues, echolalic, has metonymies, breathes syllables that go on (Saint Augustine: "the syllables made their sound and went on"), leaving something in their wake. Poems, the string of poems, the row of a life. A life, moved. *Docere, delectare, movere*: teach, delight, move; the three foundations of the sermon, the three ideal functions of a poem and of a whole life devoted (in the religious sense) to the *making* of poems, the chore of a house-husband armed with a mop and with a "Zen" broom to sweep the threshold of a monastery. Exile? A community of poems sustains this exiled man and brings him joy: José Kozer, Havana, August 1960. Cubana airliner to Miami, Greyhound bus to New York City. And thirty-seven years later, out again. An old man moves to Spain, to a mountain village called Torrox, where dirt will one day fill those astral voids called the body.

2

I left Cuba because I was twenty and was restless. The place was becoming too narrow.

I never felt discriminated against as a Jew in Cuba or in the U.S.

If Castro falls and Cuba turns into a real democracy, I will visit for long periods of time. But to settle there after so many years, to settle there—I don't know what that means.

I adjusted fabulously to life in the USA. I lived New York intensely. I made a career. I earned a living. I contributed to maintaining my family. I was happy. Everything was in order, thanks. I always paid my taxes.

It is essential that there be a continuous dialogue among Cubans, among those abroad and those on the Island—a dialogue that allows for a real reunion, a single thickness for that singular island called Cuba. (April 20, 1997, New York)

AUTOBIOGRAPHY

Here is a Jew who doesn't live in Israel, never sets foot in a synagogue, doesn't care whether he is buried or cremated, wants God to exist even though it may be the God thought up by Christians or by Moslems—a Jew who feels deeply Jewish but will never be able to represent Judaism.

Here is a Cuban who has not lived in Cuba for the past forty years, has no sense of rhythm, is totally incapable of moving his feet to music, doesn't know Cuban history (*mea culpa, mea ugly culpa*) or its geography or its literature, doesn't look like a Cuban or sound like one, his Havana speech having deteriorated from incorporating so many elements from so many other varieties of Spanish.

Here is a guy who lives in Spain dreaming of Italy, then goes to Italy, stays a while, enjoys it, gets to know it, but soon wants to go to Vermont. Vermont in summer.

Here is a reader who reads Kafka but soon starts thinking of Hawthorne, then recovers the transcendentalists while remembering that he knows next to nothing about the American Civil War. Must read Ballagas, must reread *The Idiot* and *Anna Karenina*. Must read Julián del Casal, reread the whole of Sterne and the whole of Büchner. Say, who are you?

You don't have to answer that dumb question. Nothing is dumber; nothing shows more clearly both the arrogance and the shortcomings of a people than the famous "I know who I am" of the Knight of the Sad Countenance. How sad is that figure that stands for something, whose essence is defined, has a single meaning, is an excluding singularity, which is evil, or at least makes it easy for evil to invade the lives of people—it is the evil that shows itself as pogroms, genocide, subjection. The subjection of a people, of a nation, an ethnic group, a race; the subjection at home of a wife, a child, an ill person. The subjection of the healthy by the unhealthy, of the mother by the child, of the husband by his wife, and the other way around in every case. Ferocious, ferocious. Ferocious is he who practices subjection: ferocious and banal, banal and trivial. The nothingness that is the hole. (April 20, 1997, New York)

(Both works translated by Jorge Guitart)

Culture and Exile

An Interview with Heberto Padilla

See Section II for the author's biographical sketch.

When I arrived in New York March 17, 1980, I knew that I would be separated from Cuba forever. I no longer had hope that there would be substantial or immediate change. I flew out through Canada and was met at La Guardia Airport by members of my family and several of the people who had interceded in my behalf and organized my departure: Senator Edward Kennedy, the writer Bernard Malamud (who was at that time the president of the PEN Club), and Bob Silver, the director of the New York Review of Books.

After spending a few days in a hotel in New York City, I received a phone call from Mario Vargas Llosa, who was in Washington. Mario had a fellowship at the Woodrow Wilson International Center for Scholars, and he informed me that the Center offered me another grant. I had stayed at Richard Sennet's house on the campus of New York University in the Village. It was a beautiful house. While I was there, I spoke to Susan Sontag, an old friend from Havana, and Derek Walcott, and asked their advice regarding whether or not I should accept the offer from the Wilson Center. Susan didn't think that I should go to Washington; rather, the place for a writer, in her opinion, was New York. Perhaps she had a point. But the advice of those who surrounded me was quite diverse, if not contradictory, and only served to disorient me more. The grant from the Wilson Center seemed to me to be something concrete.

I proposed my unfinished novel manuscript *Heroes Are Grazing In My Garden* [*En mi jardín pastan los héroes*] as a possible project for the fellowship, and they accepted it right away. I finished my novel in Washington; and when Plaza y Janes published it in 1981, I traveled to Madrid for its presentation. The publisher wanted to hold it at the Instituto de Cooperación Iberoamericana, but the Cuban ambassador protested. Finally, it was held in a huge club in Madrid; thousands of people were in attendance. I received payment for the novel, and the publisher gave me an advance to write *La mala memoria*.

After receiving that money, coupled with the royalties from the novel, I thought that that was the moment to remain in Spain. I wanted to live in Spain, where I had (and still have) many friends, most of whom are writers. Spanish was my native language, and Spain was where my literary work had had major repercussions. But my family, like most exiled Cuban families, preferred living in the United States.

During my time in Washington, both Vargas Llosa and Angel Rama recommended Princeton as the best place for us to live. In truth, I had not attended the Latin American Program at the Wilson Center very frequently. I felt more comfortable with the Russian, Polish, and Rumanian scholars—the defectors of the communist world—who gathered at the Kennan Institute. I lived in that world in Washington more than in the Latin American world.

In 1982, I was offered and accepted a lectureship at New York University and a fellowship from the Institute of the Humanities, which was affiliated with the university. I moved to Princeton but did not feel comfortable there. There were no libraries or bookstores that carried books in Spanish. I also did not have access to any works written in

Spanish that focused on Latin culture, probably because they were not used in the classroom. Unlike the United States, Europe preserves a more open posture when it comes to anything dealing with international culture; and the publishers in Spain immediately translate and publish everything. The world is represented on the best-seller list in Madrid; in the United States, it's almost exclusively North American writers. Nearly all of the latter could be translated in Madrid; yet the reverse would never happen. North American publishers are selective in regard to what concerns them—in other words, they tend to publish what interests them or what the public wants. Nevertheless, my admiration of North American literature has grown over the years. It is a literature that has permanently enriched me.

In the same vein, the foreign writer living in the United States has no other option but to become an academic. The North American writer, however, encounters too many limitations in the academy and, as a result, dedicates himself to journalism or publishing. Yet writers like Nabakov, Hannah Arendt, Brodsky, Derek Walcott, or Antonio Benítez-Rojo have become incorporated into North American universities. It's a type of bomb shelter. Spanish departments in the United States were started as a result of the collaboration of Spanish writers immigrating during the Spanish Civil War, such as Jorge Guillen, Pedro Salinas, Damaso Alonso, Navarro Tomas, Francisco García Lorca, and Julian Marias. They were not best-sellers, but they had experienced success and prestige for their literary work. All of these individuals were responsible for creating Hispanic culture here. It is lamentable, however, that this level of excellence has not been maintained; as a result, Spanish departments are cold and gray.

In my opinion, exile is one of the biggest catastrophes of any age; however, it is worse for writers. You are disconnected from your natural environment or milieu and from your native tongue, and thus you are never the same again. However, I don't believe—because history has demonstrated this—that tyrants are eternal: Pinochet, Franco, Stalin. I believe that one day we will reunite once again in our country, like the artists and intellectuals who returned to Spain after the arrival of democracy. (April 1999)

(Interview conducted by Lourdes Gil;
translated by Andrea O'Reilly Herrera)

The Wages of Exile

Ricardo Pau-Llosa

See Section IV for the author's biographical sketch.

To console themselves over setbacks large and small, Spaniards can still be heard to say, "*Más se perdió en Cuba*" (More was lost in Cuba). Sadly, Cubans themselves often fail to see the theft of their homeland and way of life as a standard by which losses are measured. One would imagine that the ongoing totalitarian nightmare, forty years and counting, would have triggered serious reflection on Cuban civilization on the part of its children, and not just acrimonious debate on Cuba as a political and economic battleground.

Cuba was anomalous by all standards of size and wealth that we regularly and unquestioningly apply to judge a nation's cultural importance and its influence in the world. Small, seemingly overshadowed and controlled by powerful neighbors or distant centers of power, apparently underdeveloped, newly independent (hence presumably immature), politically unstable, tropical (hence presumably frivolous), primarily agricultural (hence presumably simple in its technology and worldview), Cuba is easy to misjudge and stereotype, although it is difficult to ignore. Cuba's history and current image in the foreign media are shamelessly distorted to suit the biases of reporters and editors. Regrettably, Cubans have also distorted or neglected the image and history of their nation. Hardly anybody—native or foreign—understands that Cuba was a unique civilization, one of the four pillars of Hispanic culture in this century (along with Spain, Mexico, and Argentina), and the loss of this civilization to totalitarianism in 1959 has had horrible consequences for the Hispanic world and for other cultures in this hemisphere and beyond.

Cuban civilization reached its maturity in the blaze of cultural activity of the 1950s, and the globally recognized emblem of this ascendancy was the nation's multifaceted and completely distinctive popular music. Although what most foreigners knew about Cuba was its music (and perhaps its cigars), what made this particular art form truly glorious were the aspects of the Cuban worldview and civilization that are reflected in the music.

Cuba was a crucible where genres and traditions and art forms interacted to produce a dazzling array of new forms of expression, beliefs, and lifestyles. By the mid-1920s, Cuba had become the first modern nation to obliterate the distinction between "high" and "popular" culture; all points on the spectrum of its national culture influenced and nurtured every other point on that spectrum. Popular musical genres like the *danzón* and the *son* absorbed complex European and West African musical ideas and popularized them. And while these vernacular genres influenced "high" musical compositions (e.g., Julián Orbón, George Gershwin), as well as Cuban poetry (e.g., the work of Nicolás Guillén and other *negrista* poets), what is important to remember is that popular music was Cuba's "high" art form. From the *rumba* and the *punto guajiro* to the *bolero* and the *charanga*, popular music and lyrics reflected the life, wisdom, and character of the Cuban people with greater wit, depth, and diversity than any other cultural expression, "high" or "low." Indeed, popular Cuban music provided themes for and, more importantly, influenced notions of rhythm and complexity in painting (e.g., Amelia Peláez and others in the Havana School, 1920s and 1930s) and fiction (e.g., Enrique Labrador Ruíz, Carlos Montenegro, Alejo Carpentier, Virgilio Piñera, Guillermo Cabrera Infante, Reinaldo Arenas, Severo Sarduy, et al.). The sounds of Cuba of the first half of the twentieth century constitute the most recognizable yet varied, the most alluring yet complex popular music of the world.

One of the basic premises of modern musical innovation—the creation of a vibrant synthesis that ostensibly preserves its constituent elements but that actually alters them solely by how they interact in specific pieces—would achieve its first and still most original and varied elaboration in the music of Cuba. This, for example, is one of the glories of the *danzón* and of later genres like the *charanga*. What the Island's musicians exported to North American jazz and the Argentine tango—to name two of the better-known foreign traditions impacted by Cuban music—was not only rhythms and idioms, but a manner of thinking about music and its osmotic relationship to every other aspect of life. This was the essence of what Cubans meant by the word *sabor*, or "flavor." It had to do with the power of an art form—not just music, but exemplified by music—to take ideas and inspiration from everyday life experience and, in return, energize that everyday public existence with a rhythm as powerful and pervasive as any belief, faith, or "meaning."

This was the spirit of Cuban civilization—the mutual nurturing of culture and life at all levels at the same time. The replacement of *sabor* with "salsa" and the transformation of Afro-Cuban music into "Latin jazz"—both recent developments in the U.S.—have obscured the essential originality of the Cuban worldview as exemplified and forged, in part, by its music.

Afro-Cuban religious beliefs and rituals—not to mention rhythms, stories, and languages—did not just "survive" slavery; they shaped the Cuban national soul in an open, everyday, and pervasive manner. Every Cuban, regardless of racial heritage, was deeply influenced by the life-affirming, transformative, and "magical" nature of the Island's exuberant West African legacies—brilliantly studied by Fernando Ortiz and Lydia Cabrera. The unique kind of syncretism that produced *santería*, among other belief systems, and that is manifested in the music, art, slang, and customs of Cuba, rests on the principle that genuine synthesis preserves the identity of its constituent elements. In that way, the synthesis that results can keep evolving by nurturing itself from the original elements. It is a synthesis of constant recombination, which contrasts sharply with the homogenization that characterizes North American "assimilation."

To illustrate the working of this synthesis outside the realm of Afro-Cuban religions, one need look no further than to the work of Cuba's premier modernist painter, Amelia Peláez. In her paintings, Peláez synthesized Parisian Cubism and Havana's colonial stained-glass windows, or *vitrales*, to generate designs where intricate, undulating lines are set against hard-edged planes of color—images, that is, where the aesthetic concerns of twentieth-century modernism interact with the aesthetic and existential concerns embodied in baroque and neoclassical architecture of the colonial era. Cuban synthesis bridges continents, eras, races, and beliefs and keeps the sources of these fusions alive in the national soul. "Cuban time" should mean a sense of the present as a congress or forum of pasts, a prism of poetic causalities and interactions between ideas, images, and sentiments that have been freed from the chains of chronology and rationality.

The heart of Cuba as a civilization, and as the setting of one of the major renaissances of the modern world, was the dialogue between order and pleasure. The articulation of this dialogue drives all aspects of the Cuban psyche and the culture it produced. Cuban time and Cuban synthesis are simply the instruments by which this dialogue became manifested. From syncretistic beliefs and rhythms to the ubiquitous *choteo*—a satirical joking aimed at undermining anyone and anything that is remotely serious or high toned (it was studied by Jorge Mañach and others)—Cubans oriented their lives toward reconciling gratification and its seeming opposites—order, law, reason, pattern, custom. *Choteo* functions as a kind of policeman, an anti-superego that imposes the rule of pleasure and anarchy on the tendency of individuals and societies to become complacent, smug, status-conscious, and yoked to routine. *Choteo* plays a role in the legendary sexual extroversion of the Cuban, a citizen of Eros who revels in the pleasures he parodies, and vice versa.

It is revealing of the Cuban national character that *choteo* is complemented by the insistence on *lo cómodo* (comfort), a pursuit that imbues all aspects of daily life and style (art, décor, family relationships, architecture, romance, financial planning, politics). While comfort is the hallmark of the Cuban concept of fulfillment for all classes and groups, *choteo* ensures that comfort as an experience and as a goal remains immediate and alive. *Choteo* makes certain that comfort does not become a sign of status or power. The balance implicit in *lo cómodo* keeps *choteo* from going overboard and becoming *relajo* (dissipation). Curiously, this orientation toward comfort earned precatastrophe Cuba the scorn of Puritan North America, given its obsession with austerity. Cuba was Cleopatra. It is no small irony that the defunct spirit of 1950s Cuba turned out to be a prototype of the ethos of 1990s North America, complete with cigars, sexual flamboyance, and Cuban music. Prophesy is the best revenge. There is no Actium that the common sense of pleasure, with time, cannot reverse.

The dread of becoming the object of the *choteo* of others and of being damned as *pesado* (heavy, i.e., pedantic, unpleasant, and/or irascible) makes success-driven Cubans expert reconcilers of opposing motivators in themselves and in the society at large. This fear and its resulting mental abilities have had a deep impact on Cuban views of success, power, achievement, and status. It merits pointing out that the same people who inexplicably elevated the Western Hemisphere's sole totalitarian system have psychologically survived its miseries and persecutions through an irrepressible, if internalized or discreet, *choteo*. To function as the sole law of the land, the communist regime had to replace *choteo* with ideology, leader worship, and jingoism. Likewise, the regime replaced the attainment of comfort with demonstrations of obedience as the prime indicator of personal fulfillment. Little wonder that not a single caricature of the *máximo líder*, his policies, or his henchmen has been published in Cuba for four decades. But the attempt at uprooting *choteo*, while failing to eradicate it, has succeeded in displacing it from its original role as anti-superego. In this, and in so many other aspects of the Cuban national psyche, the communist regime's effect has been fatal. The one civilization that placed leveling ridicule in the role of cultural superego must now engage parody as every other culture does, as a common mechanism for coping with frustration.

For all of its irrecoverable uniqueness, precatastrophe Cuba was, at the same time, the most intensely modern and cosmopolitan nation in Latin America, the rival in this regard to Argentina. But Cuba's cosmopolitanism was both up-to-date and totally original. Unlike Argentina, Cuba entertained no silly fantasies about being a European nation. Unlike Mexico and Spain, Cuba practiced a nationalism that was open to the world and, above all, to modernity. Never prone to zealotry, Cuba's Catholicism was more like that of France than that of Spain or Mexico. Above all, Cuba was confident that it could shape the modern to its spirit and necessity (and it did so, repeatedly and brilliantly), and Cubans believed, as a matter of course, that *lo cubano* would manifest itself within *lo moderno*. While Cuba was not—and still is not—free of racism, the nation did generate a culture in which the contributions of all races and their legacies were felt by all sectors and classes. If ever there was a melting pot—of races, religions, rituals, languages, cultures, and styles—Cuba, between 1902 and 1959, was it.

This distinct cosmopolitanism and modernity nurtured Cuba's culture, art, and attitude toward life, and it pervaded the nation's vibrant cultural and media institutions. Yet precatastrophe Cuba is often misrepresented as a backward nation. According to the Bureau of Inter-American Affairs's 1998 study *Zenith and Eclipse: A Comparative Look at Socio-Economic Conditions in Pre-Castro and Present Day Cuba* (from which the rankings below are taken), in the late 1950s Cuba was one of Latin America's most advanced countries, in some categories among the most advanced in the world. Cuba's six million inhabitants boasted fifty-eight daily newspapers; numerous weekly magazines (some of which, like *Bohemia* and *Vanidades*, would become Latin America's most preponderant continental publications); one of the finest literary magazines in Latin America (*Orígenes*); pervasive radio stations (ranked eighth in the world); excellent art schools, museums, symphony orchestras, and a renowned National Ballet; island-wide color television broadcasting before it became pervasive in the United States (ranked first in Latin America and fifth in the world in television sets per capita); a bold, cutting-edge advertising industry; and some of the best and most varied architecture (colonial, art nouveau, art deco, modernist) in the Western Hemisphere.

Cuba in the 1950s had one of the best literacy and food consumption rates in Latin America, a higher standard of living than Spain, and a burgeoning multiracial middle class. Cuba had generous social programs, excellent medical and educational facilities freely available to the poor (lowest infant mortality rate in Latin America and thirteenth lowest in the world), a progressive legislation protecting women and workers, active independent unions, and a panoply of political parties the likes of which we have yet to see dawn in these tolerant, democratic, and advanced United States. Despite notoriously corrupt post–World War II governments, the national treasury the communists inherited in 1959 was very much in the black, and the peso was traded on par with the U.S. dollar. These factors, combined with the Island's legendary agricultural fertility, its insularity, its many excellent harbors, its strategic position in the middle of the Western Hemisphere, and its proximity to North America and Europe, made Cuba the most international and progressive country in the hemisphere.

Contrast the picture in 1958 with present-day conditions. In every macroeconomic indicator, Cuba rates at or below the level of Haiti. It is the only Latin American nation where the number of automobiles has fallen since the 1950s. The number of phone lines has remained the same for four decades. Literacy and educational rates, high in 1958, have remained so; but censorship is absolute. And Cuba suffers under one of the most repressive governments on the planet today.

For all its uniqueness and vibrancy, Cuban civilization had its flaws: flagrant, deadly flaws. *Choteo* often gave free rein to envy and severely undermined a desperately needed meritocracy, the absence of which reinforced cronyism (*amiguismo*) and poisoned the social fabric with distrust and disillusionment. Ultimately, the balance between order and pleasure can only be struck within individuals, not an entire society; so while this tension produced dazzling personalities and creative brilliance, it provided little social cohesion or even a sense that social cohesion was a necessity. No national myth could take hold with sufficient strength to imbue the Cubans with a clear sense of collective ethics. When the circumstances were propitious for it, as they were in 1959, armed chaos in the guise of nationalism took over, annihilating the fluid, magical, dazzling civilization that had once flourished and slandering it ever since.

The loss of Cuba was indeed a catastrophe, not only for Cubans, but for the Hispanic world and for the modern world in general. Pre-debacle Cuba was a beacon for Latin America. In 1959, Cuba's plunge into medieval terror, squalor, and intolerance severed the region's umbilical cord to the forces of modernization. Yes, industry and other manifestations of modernity have proliferated in Latin America, but no other unique society has emerged there, as it had in Cuba, in which the modern was so quickly transformed into the national, and the national quickly projected onto international expressions of the modern. For all its factories and skyscrapers and expressways, Latin America in spirit continues to be premodern. Cuba was the only nation in the region that had turned its modernization into a definition and projection of its national identity, and its continued development along these lines would have served as an enormously beneficial and instructive example to the rest of the continent. Instead, since 1959 Cuba has become a totalitarian siren, drawing the region's shaky republics away from modernization, free enterprise, and democracy through deception, terrorism, and the fanning of anti–North American sentiments.

Above all, the unique intersection of cultural, geographic, historical, and religious elements that had converged in Cuba had naturally produced a style of life that could resist any and all political and economic calamities, provided these remained mostly within their own domains. But totalitarianism by its very definition establishes control over all aspects of life in the nations it victimizes. The spirit of the place, the genius of Cuba's ethos, and the vitality of its culture of synthesis have not survived forty years of communism on one front, exile frivolity and amnesia on another, and on a third front the manipulation and distortion of the facts by foreigners with their own agendas and neuroses. Assailed from within by lies, envy, and terror, and from without by oblivion and distortion of facts, Cuba as a continuity, as a civilization, has perished.

This is not to say that there has been no interesting art or culture over the last four decades in Cuba or in the 15 percent of its population currently in exile. Far from it. But in Cuba a vital link has been lost—the link between a nation's original impulse to be itself and the evolution of this impulse into original expressions in all aspects of life, including the arts. Cuban civilization did not have to die; it could have survived in the passion and memory of its exiles, and in some cherished secret form of the everyday life of its population within the Island. But that has not been the case.

Nowhere is the death of this once great nation more painfully evident than when talking to young Cuban Americans in Miami, the so-called *capital del exilio*. These children of exile seemed to have received little or no information about Cuba from their parents. Typically, Cuban Americans have no idea who key figures in Cuban history and culture were—including such overwhelmingly popular musicians as Ernesto Lecuona, Beny Moré, Rita Montaner, or La Orquesta Aragón; never mind the poets, painters, filmmakers, or political figures. Cuban American ignorance of Cuba mirrors that of North Americans, for whom Cuban history began with the communist takeover in 1959 and its key dates are the 1961 Bay of Pigs Invasion, the 1962 Missile Crisis, and the 1980 Mariel Boatlift. Like their North American counterparts, Cuban Americans latch on to talk about the embargo—regardless of the position they take on the issue—as an unconscious way of announcing that they know nothing (else) about Cuba.

In reality, the Bay of Pigs, the embargo, etc. are hardly defining events in the history of Cuba's terminated civilization; yet Cuban Americans seem, by and large, unaware that their minuscule vision of Cuba is pathetically inadequate to support their reiterated claim that they are "Cuban." Such embarrassingly uninformed pledges of allegiance help explain why so many Cuban Americans can only conceive of the catastrophe that befell their homeland, or that of their parents, in terms of lost family properties or personal references (e.g., an imprisoned relative). When there is no overall vision of the historical, the historical can only be registered as personal grievance.

The failure of exiles and their children to articulate a coherent account of the catastrophe of Cuba that goes beyond the personal and the familial aspects of that loss explains in part why it is that foreigners (the press, celebrities, politicians, human rights activists) who readily embrace the plight of other enslaved peoples (e.g., South Africa, Tibet) see the Cuban disaster as a bizarre family quarrel that does not concern them. To borrow the words of W. H. Auden in his poem about the drowned Icarus, for Cuba to become an "important failure" to others, it must first be felt and expressed as such by Cubans themselves.

Perhaps the death of Cuba is too great a loss to be heartfully assumed by Cubans, in exile and within the Island. Perhaps for that reason, the personal focus of these testimonials of pain and nostalgia is made to eclipse the Minoan fate of Cuba. The wages of exile are the death of collective memory. The overthrow of Cuba as a civilization, as a destiny, may find no room in the sane heart and can only be accommodated in a numbing silence masked as personal regret. When a new Cuba eventually emerges, it will have the same disconnection to precatastrophe Cuba as contemporary Greece and Egypt have to the ancient civilizations that happen to share their names. The difference is that it took the Greeks and the Egyptians the endurance of myriad foreign occupations over millennia to achieve the totality of cultural severance that Cubans have been able to pull off entirely by and onto themselves in less than two generations.

There is always the imagination—the only landscape, the only extension—where sufficient fragments of a once great project might gather into a possible remembrance. The imagination leaves no room for graves. While Cuba can no longer evolve as it should have, in the imagination its past may yet clarify into lessons and reflections.

Foreigner's Notebook

FROM *Foreigner's Notebook*

Jorge Guitart

Jorge Guitart was born in Havana, Cuba, in 1937 and emigrated to the U.S. in 1962.
He lives in Buffalo, New York.

For Howard Wolf

1
There's art
in the American backyard.
Note the rustling
on the bushes
by the fence. It is the word
rustling that pleases
and the birds hesitating—
an American hesitation.
They fly, but they're real.
So many birds today.
American, and real.

2
Insects and annelids
in the American dirt.
Bugs and worms!
They, too, are American
but they're more
of the mind.
They strain
credibility.

3
Jazz from the house:
an argument
about freedom
or an argument
about the lack
of propositions

or it is
what it is
carelessly
convincing.

4

An American song:
a white man
singing like a black man
who wanted to be white
and a black man
singing like a black man
who wanted to be
darker.
A white man
and a black man
singing together
without suspicion.

5

Sexual and pure
the American flowers.
Names so far
unknown.

6

Night. Un-American
shadows,
Old Country shadows,
aunt and uncle
dumb cousin shadows
motley, vulgar
fat, and plain.
But they will pass.
Look up the names
of the flowers
in the American dawn.

IN THE WILDERNESS
FROM *Foreigner's Notebook*

Lieutenant, said the apeman
I wish there were more maps
to tell me where we are
and who I am.
What makes this jungle green
become yellow canary.
To this there must be a corollary
but I don't understand!

Am I to man the apes or ape the men
make my wine from wild grapes
or leave them hanging from the vines?

You shall tell me, my friend
what tongue to use
what language to abuse
and where to start
and how to end.

Living on Borrowed Ground

Connie Lloveras

> *Connie Lloveras was born in Havana, Cuba, in 1958; she left the Island with her family in 1960. She lives in Miami, Florida.*

I left Cuba at the age of two with my parents and my six-month-old brother. We moved into a large two-story house with twenty-two other family members for what they thought would be a temporary stay but would eventually turn into permanent exile. What I know of Cuba is what I have been told, for I have no recollection. My mother died shortly after we arrived in the United States. I was six years old. Maybe it was her loss, or my having to encounter that harsh a reality at such an early age, that created a sensitivity to life as it went on around me and awakened in me a need to express these sensitivities through an art form.

I have drawn since I was a small child. I received a degree in fine arts with a major in painting but began experimenting with clay shortly before I graduated. Since then, I have worked consistently, developing a language of symbols and expressing them in an art form that is unique and personal (FIGURE 5). My work is not bound by materials, but rather by ideas. I work just as readily in paint as I do in clay and use both mediums interchangeably. There is an immediacy and freshness that I have with paint that I try to instill in my clay works. And there is a richness and texture to the clay body that I try to incorporate in my paintings.

Through the use of unrecognizable yet familiar images, my work draws on the viewer's personal experience. My works speak of the universality of the human condition. They explore the complexity of human emotions, particularly as experienced by women. My work often depicts themes of loss and separation, as well as human pain and suffering. And although my work does not consciously make reference to a lost homeland, there may transpire in it a sense that my roots are somewhere else—that, in fact, we are living on borrowed ground.

Clotheslines

Virgil Suárez

See Section IV for the author's biographical sketch.

The day my mother stood in the kitchen
 & cooked all the turtle meat from the turtles
  I helped my father kill & she screamed
when the sizzling chunks started to jump
 & we rushed in to check on what was up
  & my father told her that it was okay,
that turtle meat always did that when fried
 & then we got back to the slaughter of the pig
  my father had bartered a dozen rabbits for
& when we finally cornered it at the end
 of the walkway by the side of the house,

next to the chicken coop, it squealed & set
all the chickens aflutter & a cloud of dust
    rose in the air, a combination of dirt & dung
        & my father got something in his eyes
& he laughed & I sneezed & sneezed
    & when the chickens settled down the pig
        snuck by us & ran back to the patio
knocking on its way the stick holding up
    my mother's clothesline & all the laundry
        drying fell on the dirt & the pig trampled
it & it made my father so angry he took
    the wire from the clothesline, looped it over
        the pig's neck & when the pig stood still
my father reeled it in & with a broom handle
    he applied a tourniquet to the pig
        & with a final squeal it dropped on its front
knees, choked by the wire which cut so deep
    blood spurted out onto everything, mainly
        my mother's washed clothes & the pig stood
still long enough for my father to plunge
    a knife into its heart. There we stood, my
        father & I, out of breath, he with bloodied
arms & myself with the pangs of excitement
    in my chest. Amazed by the slaughter
        of so many animals in one afternoon, I stood
there quiet, caught in the splendor of my mother's
    whitest laundry. My father put the clothesline
        back up & one by one I picked up all
the garments from the ground & carried them
    to my mother. My father leaned against
        the door frame with a satisfied look on his face,
a smile on his lips. This was in Havana in 1968
    & I have never seen my father more content.
        Now when I travel on the open roads of the US,
I look out across the expanse of peoples' yards
    & when I see clotheslines, heavy with laundry,
        swaying in the breeze & the fact that someone

worked so hard at putting it up & out, I think
about how much debris time & distance
have kicked up into my own eyes.

Letter to His Niece

Carlos J. Alvaré

*Born in Havana, Cuba, in 1924, Carlos J. Alvaré moved to the United States when he
was nine years old in 1933. He lives in Valley Forge, Pennsylvania.*

28 February, 1997

Andy:

My father moved the family to the U.S. because his future here seemed
more promising than it did in Cuba. I was nine years old at the time and
had no say in the matter. That was 1933.

When we first moved here, I liked this country much better than I
do now. Nevertheless, Philadelphia seemed very gray and frumpy compared to Havana. I was used to marble and terrazzo floors, so the wooden
floors here seemed very rural.

We spoke both English and Spanish at home. My mother's grandmother was an American, so we had relatives in Philadelphia, some of
whom are buried at St. Mary's Church. My father had gone to college in
this country at Harvard and MIT. Both my mother and father had been
in this country before we moved here. When we were children, we always went back to Cuba in the summer; later we went on our own.

As I look over the questions you sent me, it occurs to me that I feel
more at home in Latin countries than I do here. As I grow older, I feel
people in the U.S. look down on all of Central and South America and
on Spanish culture in general. Naturally, they know very little about any
other cultures besides the Anglo-Saxon. Everybody south of the border
or who speaks Spanish is a Hispanic or Latino—this includes Blacks,
Indians, Mestizos, Whites, etc. Now Hispanic has become a race. . . .
Mexican Indians are considered Hispanics, while American Indians in
New Mexico are called Native Americans. Schools in this country are
also very provincial in that respect. . . . I was once asked by the wife of an
English professor at Yale if Spanish literature had any other writers be-

sides Cervantes. My sister was once asked by one of her high school teachers if the women in Havana wore grass skirts. . . .

I really do not see where the situation will improve as long as the only thing that matters in this country is wealth. The U.S. is polluting the entire world with our Coca-Cola, Walt Disney, and McDonald's— with that also comes their imbecilic Hollywood movies, television shows, and crass materialism. A demoralizing influence everywhere.

Oh, well, that's enough griping.

ps: As far as my identity in my art is concerned, it's a mixed bag of Latin and Anglo-Saxon thoughts. I learned my art here, not in Cuba.

EDITOR'S NOTE: Although Carlos Alvaré's family settled in the Philadelphia area, his mother fully expected that one day they would move back to Cuba. For years, she and her children spent summers with their grandmother in Havana, and she returned to her mother's home to give birth to her youngest daughter, Lourdes. The events of 1959, however, permanently shattered her hopes of a return to her homeland. Because they were already established in the United States, their home became a kind of safe haven where family members stayed (and in some cases settled) for varying periods of time once they were able to leave the Island.

In a series of letters, my uncle explained to me that his formative years were partly spent in the U.S. and, as a result, his artistic vision was shaped by an Anglo perspective. Over the years, however, my uncle and I have had what seems to be the same conversation over and over again about his sense of inner exile. He tells me that even as a child, he felt as though his life had been divided into severed halves, and that spiritually he belongs neither here nor there. In a seemingly endless act of repetition, we pick up the frayed end of this single thread of conversation each time we are together. Just recently, however, he told me that he has finally come to the realization that this is the shape of his life—in effect, this sense of division and fragmentation, with which he has struggled since childhood, "is the thing" in and of itself, and he has finally come to accept this after almost seventy years.

Both his more recent personal projects and his artwork, however, continue to represent these schisms and his sense of rootlessness (FIGURE 6). In addition to compiling a family tree that reaches back to the sixth century, he has completed a series of watercolor paintings, partly based on old photographs and stories, that depict not only the places where Carlos has lived in Havana, Philadelphia, Paris, and Valley Forge, but our ancestral homes in the south of France, Cantabria, and Asturias. In effect, they represent, if unconsciously, his attempt to recuperate, reconstruct, and ultimately make sense of a cultural archeology that is deeply personal, yet at the same time speaks for generations of Cuban émigrés who can never return to the world they left behind.

(Andrea O'Reilly Herrera)

exilio
FROM *Entre el agua y el pan*

Emilio M. Mozo

Emilio M. Mozo was born in Camagüey, Cuba, in 1941. He left the Island for Canada in 1958 and eventually relocated to the United States in 1984. He lives in Andover, Massachusetts.

congelado en precipios
está mi triste exilio
no de un país
ni es la lejanía de una isla
es ese otro
profundo en su verdad
de estrellas olorosas
donde la esperanza es peor que el amor

sombras de espíritu flotante
de noches calurosas y vibrantes
donde el cuerpo duerme
buscando la mano que no llega

consuélame tierra
abrázame de llanto
bésame de agonía
imprégname de soledad
floto en la monotonía de las cosas

EXILE

frozen in a fragment
is my sad exile
not being from a country
nor the distance from an island
it is the other
profound in its truth
of fragrant stars
where hope is worse than love

shadows of a floating spirit
of hot and vibrant nights
where the body sleeps
seeking that hand that does not arrive

console me earth
embrace me crying
kiss me in agony
impregnate me with solitude
I float in the nothingness of things
(Translated by Margarita Curtis and Mark Schorr)

SOMBRAS
FROM *Entre el agua y el pan*

sombras de ayer
somos caminos sigilosos
fantasmas finos y brillantes
músicos sordos
amantes del agua insípida del miedo
somos
el cero que roba de un común denominador
victoria de lombrices
triunfo de retornos
pabellón de recuerdos
sombras de ayer
somos

SHADOWS

shadows of yesterday
we are
silent roads
fine and brilliant ghosts
deaf musicians
lovers of water insipid with fear
we are
the zero that steals from a common denominator
a victory of worms
a triumph of returns
a pavilion of memories
shadows of yesterday
we are

(Translated by Martín Herrera)

Paradox
FROM *Lil' Havana Blues*

Nilda Cepero

See Section IV for the author's biographical sketch.

Ah me, Postumus, Postumus
the fleeting years are slipping by   —*Horace*

In Miami I never feel
my Cubanness like I did in Boston
In the sunshine I live Cuba
in the cold I dreamt it
Nostalgia is a peculiar thing

No time to spare
Lotta continua!

Where Are You From? A Cuban Dilemma

Pablo Medina

Born in Havana, Cuba, in 1948, Pablo Medina left the Island with his family in 1960. He lives in Montclair, New Jersey.

> . . . And he suffered
> Much also, in war, till he should build his town
> And bring his gods to Latium . . .
>
> —*Virgil,* The Aeneid

Ask the question, ask me, and you will hear me hesitate before answering. In the awkward silence I will try to determine why you are asking. Is it a social affair and you are merely trying to spark some conversation? Is it a professional inquiry? Have you heard my name? Are you genuinely curious about my origins? Once I gain a perspective, I will refer to one of four places that have a claim on me: New Jersey, where I have lived on and off for the last twenty-three years; Washington, D.C., where I went to school, where I married, where my son was born, and where I taught for two years; New York City and environs, where my family landed when we finally settled in this country; or, deep in the fog of the past, Cuba itself, that dim country where I was born and where I lived the first twelve years of my life. Notable for its absence from my list is that city that is as closely associated with Cubans as the Island itself—Miami. But more on that later.

The real answer to the question, and one that is never far from my consciousness, is, simply, "I don't know."

To say that I am from New Jersey would be as inaccurate as saying that I am going to stay here for the rest of my life. I am here out of convenience, and I expect that convenience will take me out. To say Washington or New York, much as those places left their marks on me, would be a falsehood I would use for my benefit or defense. To speak of Cuba as my place of origin would imply, to me if to no one else, that I intend to return there at an indeterminate future time. The fact is that the Cuba for which I long is a figment of memory, a shadow of a shadow of a country that no longer exists.

If you are legitimately interested in me and I, in turn, trust you, I will

---

say, "I am from nowhere," and to calm your surprise, I will add, "Such is the fate of the exile." This last comment may sound overblown and melodramatic, but it is true. Ask a Jew, a Palestinian, a Native American; ask anyone who was uprooted from his homeland. Chances are that he or she will answer likewise. For the exile, the doors to the past—and to the geography of origins—have been shut, never to be opened again. If he has a model, a prototype, in Western civilization, it is Aeneas, the Trojan who escaped his city as it was being pillaged and burned by the victorious Greeks. I like to believe that the word *exile* comes from the Latin *ex Ilium*, "out of Ilium," the last being another name for Troy. Aeneas, at least in the story told by the Roman poet Virgil, was to be the patriarch of the Roman people, the man from whose blood would spring the greatest empire of the Mediterranean basin, and some may argue, of all of Europe: greatness born from loss.

After the fall of Troy, however, Aeneas was a most unhappy man. Once he left the ruins of his city, he led a life of privation, sacrifice, and unsatisfied love. It was not he but his son who was to found the first Trojan settlement in the Italian peninsula. Aeneas died on some lonely shore, a forlorn man who abandoned the great love of his life (Dido, queen of Carthage) for the sake of posterity and the future good of his people.

Imagine yourself facing this sad fellow at a cocktail party in a Lavinian shore mansion. His face is drawn and shadowed, his lips stained by the thick Etruscan wine he favors; his shoulders are stooped from carrying about all that historical weight. He is, perhaps, a little drunk. You can tell he would much rather be in another part of the *Mare Nostrum*. No harm in a little cocktail party friendliness, you say to yourself. You approach him, nod your head, blurt out a quick greeting, exchange names, and get to the overwhelming question: "So, where are you from, Aeneas?"

What on earth would he answer? Would he say, "I am from Troy, but that doesn't exist any longer, not for me, not for my descendants. I can't turn back. The gods have told me so. I am merely wandering about until I find the Tiber River. I was in the underworld briefly, but I didn't quite fit in. I spent time in North Africa, but I'd rather not talk about that"? And would he then break out into tears and lamentations, or would he shuffle himself away, leaving you with a sour taste in your mouth?

Ask me the question once again, and I will answer this time (with apologies to Gertrude Stein), "I'm in the process of being from some-where, but there's no *there* there yet." Miami was once a possibility, but during the time I spent living there, I felt more a foreigner than any-where else. It did not help that I arrived one week before Hurricane Andrew. For weeks, I moved about in a strange, uprooted landscape—streets without signs, houses without roofs, neighborhoods without lights, a place, at last, where exiles could truly feel at home. I moved to Miami under the mistaken impression that my Cubanness had been corrupted by the Northeast and needed to be restored in the subtropical climate, nourished by Cuban food and the Cuban language. The reality was that my Cuban self was purer, more closely guarded, and, therefore, less con-taminated than what I found in Miami; but that is another story. After two years, I moved back north.

The most pertinent answer I know was given years ago by José Ortega y Gasset: "*Yo soy yo y mis circunstancias.*" There is, after all, Western civili-zation, from which I dangle like a spider suspended over the void, and books to write, and people to love. Aeneas did not have an easy life, but a meaningful one. That is good enough for me. *Ciao.**

THE CHOSEN
FROM *The Floating Island*

They stand on the shore
with faces set, eyes to the horizon.

I cannot hear their voices
for the waves.
I cannot feel their breath
or touch their lips.
Some unexplainable distance
spreads between us, like a beach
widening or a snow field
that can only be crossed on fire.

Who are these ghosts,
all with the same slow motion,

their seven-fingered hands,
their eyelids strung with wire?

They stare out and they look in,
the horizon goes to mist.
What are those veins,
crossing and recrossing the sky,
centered on a grain of salt,
a plangent hope, a culture of water?[†]

[*] An earlier version of this essay was published in *Cuban Heritage* 3.1 (1990).
[†] Originally published in *Pivot* 40 (1992) and reprinted in *The Floating Island* (Buffalo, NY: White Pine Press), 1999.

Even Names Have Their Exile
COLLAGE OF MEMORIES

Carlota Caulfield

Carlota Caulfield was born in Havana, Cuba, in 1953; she left the Island with her husband and son in 1981. She lives in Oakland, California.

A traveler is motivated by a thirst for adventure and knowledge. I am one. Some of my most memorable recollections of Havana are my visits to the port to watch ships enter the bay. I grew up obsessed with Dominic Behan's verse: "The sea. Oh the sea is a *gradh geal no chroi*" (bright love of my heart). Diaspora, the Cuban experience.

There are also other memories that take me back to my adolescence of the late 1960s. Then, I was longing for personal freedom; and I keep longing for it. Here, I am writing my testimony about my Cubanness and my Cuban exile, trying to write my way home—not like the poet Ovid, who wanted to return to Rome, but as a poet for whom memory and imagination were always her home. When I was seventeen years old, I began having recurrent dreams. I would see myself walking on unknown streets. I remember waking up in the middle of the night, my heart beating very fast, and saying to myself, "I want to be there." "There" became my obsession. "There" became a mind game, a territory where I became the wanderer that I am today.

I first became aware of the changes my family faced when one night my father, my mother, and my cousins gathered around a table late at night to listen to Radio Rebelde. This memory takes me back to 1957. Then, I developed a fear of radio news that I was able to conquer only recently. My cousins and my best friends left the country, but my parents decided to stay. They opposed the Batista dictatorship and for many years supported the Revolution.

I remember when the Cuban authorities confiscated my mother's perfumery. It was 1968. Some of our best neighbors, now changed into Castro's inspectors, harassed her. They took possession of the place and made my mother sign surrender papers in the name of a New Society. She became an exile in her own home, and the following years were very hard for us. But my mother decided that her place was in Cuba; and she is still there.

During that same time, I was the target of many of my classmates, who would point their fingers at me, saying, "She is not like us." Yes, during many years I experienced social and spiritual persecution. I censored myself many times. I found myself in danger for speaking, for staying quiet, and for not belonging in the Cuban mainstream.

Some years later, my life's "security" was put to test once again. In 1980, I witnessed many violent outbreaks in Havana. Trouble was everywhere. People who tried to leave the country were persecuted, humiliated, and sometimes killed. We (my husband and I) decided it was time to leave Cuba. After innumerable false starts, one day we found the way to leave behind the desperate situation we were experiencing, now that we were without jobs and the target of neighbors and other people. Among the more than fifteen thousand books at the Library of the Jewish Patronato in Vedado, we discovered Jerzy Kosinski's *Blind Date*, a book that became the key to designing a map for our definitive journey out of the country. I left Cuba for ethical and moral reasons.

In January 1981, I, along with my husband and my five-year-old son, embarked on an Aeroflot flight to Moscow with fake documents. We abandoned the plane in Frankfurt. From there, we traveled to Zürich and were granted political asylum. Living in Zürich was an enormous relief. I felt like, and in many ways was, a new human being. For the first time in my life, I learned the meaning of poverty and being foreign. Escaping out of exile to be in physical exile was an insignificant difficulty.

The most important thing was to be away from the nightmare. In Zürich, I began trying to self-induce amnesia but could not forget anything. Memories persisted for many years; and I often dreamt that I was traveling, against my will, back to Havana.

Like Samuel Beckett's Molloy, I tried to isolate myself in a fictional space:

> But I could not, stay in the forest I mean, I was not free to. That is to say I could have, physically nothing could have been easier, but I was not purely physical, I lacked something, and I would have had the feeling, if I had stayed in the forest, of going against an imperative, at least I had the impression.

The Argentinean José Isaac wrote in one of the poems of his *Cuaderno Spinoza*, "*Hasta los nombres / tienen su exilio*" (Even names / have their exile), an aphorism that reflects the ambiguity surrounding my name and my person. Not only did I carry multiple identities in Cuba, thanks to my Irish name, but I also carried the face of a "foreigner." In many of my poems, I talk about that "otherness" that motivated my writing and my continual transformation.

THE PHOTO THAT WATCHES

I, who have been so many angels

In the square people gather.
The piercing hiss
tinges the pen
when the word stone insults.

During the ascent I open my arms
and catch your inevitable reflections.
I do not weep.
Peace comes toward us,
locks herself in our house.

Soldiers push me.
I emerge from the dream.
I confess that I know you.
Exiled, I die.

Your shadow enters my body.
In the square people gather.
The piercing hiss
tinges the pen.

Branded a heretic, I change form.
Branded an angel, you are taken.

I intuit the embrace.
Self's present is passed.

You, who have been so many angels.

(Translated by Carol Maier)

Those years in Havana left me insecure and exhausted. The word *future* lost all meaning. But life's unpredictability led me on an educational journey. It is possible that I have never lived more fully than I did when I left Havana. I wanted to go to the center of things: sometimes by train; other times, by parachute. I always landed somewhere: Zürich, New York, San Francisco, Dublin, New Orleans, Barcelona, Oakland. Many places are my home and my places of rebirth. I will probably not return to Cuba. Why? I don't know. I am not sure now, and I probably still won't be sure later. But maybe my life will end in slow circles there, in Havana, returning to the town that I left without regret, and that I am missing now. Cubans everywhere argue over the idea of going back. What are these words anyway?

From the same etymological root of the word *exile* (*ex* = "out of"; *salire* = "to leap") comes the word *exult*. In Zürich, I was exultant, merry, jolly and cheerful, rejoicing, looking at the river Limmat, enjoying the Joycean metamorphosis of the Gaelic word *lindemaga*, or "big snake." Using Joseph Conrad as my model (he called his exile a "jump," and he began seeing himself as a "*homo duplex*"), I found that one of the many advantages of being in exile was to be constantly "jumping" and transformed into a hyphenated woman.

"Where are you from?" is the question I am most frequently asked. "I am Irish Cuban and more," I reply.

Since 1981, I have been "jumpy" and suffer through continual metamorphosis. Years later, in the late 1980s and 1990s in California, people didn't know how to pigeonhole me, due to my "complex" origins; thus, I created confusion for the lovers of order. I am labeled Cuban American, Hispanic, Latina, Cuban Irish American, Caribbean American, Cuban Irish Catalán Jewish American, and a woman of color. I remember somebody saying that my combination of blood made me a Molotov cocktail. But I remained without nationality. Like the sephardic song "*Morena me llaman*" (They call me the darkness / But white I was born), I keep changing colors like a chameleon. I will be forever foreign in Cuba and in the United States. Should I go on? I wonder. I mean, go on drawing up an inventory of experiences and feelings. In any case, I think I'll stop here: about to be or not to be foreign. More foreign feelings will follow.

My mixed identity has created many problems for me. For some people, I am "too White and European" to really represent a minority group. I don't suit the taste of people who regard me as having the wrong ethnic origin. I don't suit the taste of people who ignore or deny that hybridity is one of the main features of Latin Americans. Many times I have been questioned about my Cubanness. Some people want to reduce me to my "native land" and to a national identity to which I do and do not belong. But what is the meaning of belonging, anyway? What is the meaning of being Cuban? There is something universal about the Cuban spirit that I admire. Probably the right word to use here is *invention*. Live and invent. Be a Cuban and keep inventing as a way of survival.

Many people were/are surprised when they encounter my linguistic and cultural otherness. "You don't look like a Cuban" or "Because of your accent, I knew you were not a real Californian." Yes, my accent as my self (we) are a mixture of bloods and languages, many of which probably don't even have a name.

Besides keeping away my weariness about identities and catching up with life around me, I spent my first five years in the United States adjusting and somehow happy. New York and San Francisco offered me a haven for art and poetry. I developed my style as a writer and as a person. But in the last ten years, I developed a new awareness of my fast-changing surroundings. I find life in the United States oppressive, both physically and ideologically. The ramifications of this are both immense and disquieting. Even though I earned two of my three university degrees in the United States and I became an American citizen out of choice, many times I see myself as "a stranger in paradise."

In my view, exile can take various forms: physical or cultural imprisonment, or economic repression. But what about language repression? In exile, what would you give up? What would you save from your past? Saving my language added substance to my art. My "fuller, more meaningful status" (as Edward Said puts it) was choosing to write poetry in Spanish. I couldn't escape my orphanhood, my difference.

From my past, I saved my childhood memories. I reclaimed my Irish Catalán Jewish ancestors as a way to escape from muddy solitudes. My permanent bridge to Cuba is my mother. We can call this (not always golden) bridge an epistolary anxiety, or phone complexities, or, above all, frustration and despair. My son is my second bridge to Cuba. This bridge has a different kind of construction. It's made of his parents' memories and his own discoveries. My son didn't grow up as part of any Cuban or Hispanic/Latino community. He grew up with the Swiss, Greeks, Irish, Jews, Italians, Spaniards, Latin Americans, Asian Americans, African Americans, and many so-called Anglo Americans. He became American. He discovered his Cubanness through Cuban music three years ago; and he takes me back to the Island through sounds.

The most striking feature of exile is its very complicated spaces. For many years, I didn't try to preserve many connections to the Island. But they were always there. In exile, I became an avid reader of Cuban literature. In exile, I became another Cuban writer in exile. Yes, it's always an easy-difficult task to talk about exile, and in particular about our exile. You always take risks (many emotional ones) with Cuban matters. Between a Cuban and his/her Island, there are many bridges (silences, dialogues, and quarrels), with his/her self and with others. As circumstances change, we deal with them. Having entered the twenty-first century, Cubans everywhere continue to argue over which direction things will take. Let's see how many more years we keep playing with pebbles on the seashore. Let's see how many more years we keep singing the same song.

"Grace under Pressure"

Cubans in the U.S.

AN EXAMPLE OF ETHNIC IDENTITY IN THE MAKING

Leandro Soto

See Section I for the author's biographical sketch.

EXILE AS A POETIC CONDITION

A lot has been said about exile as an existential condition, but little has been said, in my opinion, about exile as a poetic condition for artists. We Cubans acknowledge the fact that we go around the world with the Island on our shoulders. We have a long history of intellectuals and artists in exile, such as the Duchess of Merlin, José María Heredia, Gertrudis Gómez de Avellaneda, José Martí, and Felix Varela, to mention just a few nineteenth-century writers. Though they yearn to return, Cuban intellectuals and artists leave the Island behind; but they take with them an archetypal island that contains our collective memories. As time goes by, Cuban exiles have been forced by reality to give up the idea of recovering the Island, which has been replaced in their memories by a mythical land, a poetic paradise. As hard as it is to believe, this particular attitude encourages Cubans to integrate into the American way of life and, at the same time, allows the historic memory of the Island to remain intact, thus helping them to preserve their cultural identity. As an artist, I rely on this poetic condition. It is true for any artist that a certain degree of solitude is desirable. But to be an artist in exile contributes, in my opinion, to the creative process and promotes what Ernest Hemingway called "grace under pressure."*

It is not uncommon for the Cuban artist on the Island to feel a certain loneliness or disconnection from the mainland and to be isolated from the rest of the world. When that same artist leaves the Island, that loneliness becomes a yearning for the Island itself. Dreams, forgotten feelings, and memories with nostalgic overtones become the material for creativity; they nurture and feed the artist's "inner land" or *patria*, where identity is reconstructed, re-adapted, and revitalized. The need for self-expression becomes the need to recover that mythic Island, the lost paradise. For me as an artist, exile is a poetic condition per se because in addition to any particular artistic talents and achievements I might have accomplished, I also now have a context that shapes my feelings, thus creating a unique frame of mind.

The exile is now over forty years old. Within that period, the diaspora has had several waves; each, in turn, has helped to keep the culture alive without interfering with the assimilation process. As an artist who has recently arrived in the United States, I already share the responsibility of contributing to the renovation of Cuban culture in exile and of making Cuban art known in the U.S. This concern for the preservation of high culture has also permeated the newest generation of Cuban Americans born in the U.S. (the ABC, or American-Born Cuban, generation).

In order to understand the cultural presence of Cubans in the U.S. and their particular contribution to mainstream culture, it is important to use the terms *cultural appropriation* and *cultural translations*. Cultural appropriation is associated with the inward behavior mentioned above: the preservation of the Island's historic memory. To rename new territories according to our memories—which, by the way, is nothing new in history—preserves the culture through the Cubanization of every possible object, event, situation, or space. A humorous example is the decision to rename a building in Miami UNEAC (which stands for the National Union of Cuban Artists and Writers) because so many artists and intellectuals live there, or the fact that a neighborhood in Toronto is called Guanabo, the name of a Cuban beach.

More complex is the process of cultural translation, a creative and experimental process that always involves the presence and awareness of the artist. This process works by transferring values from one culture to another, thereby creating a new set of possibilities that can refer to both the original and the new orders.

A GLANCE OVER THE GARDEN

A series of installations that I call *A Glance over the Garden* (FIGURES 7 and 8) is based on the concepts of cultural appropriation and cultural translation. Installation art is a very popular form of artistic expression in the U.S. Upon my arrival in the U.S., I decided to pursue this particular form of artistic expression in order to be in closer contact with the observer. I realized that, in general, installation art is more appealing because everyone creates installations in their homes.

A Glance over the Garden is an itinerary show that is based on the real-life experience of a Cuban family recently exiled in Buffalo, New York. This middle-aged couple carry with them their cultural memories and beliefs. Both are initiated as priest and priestess of two different Afro-Cuban religions. Our encounter was a pleasant and emotional experience. We met during a Buffalo winter, very far from our land of origin. Every conversation was held against the snowy winter background that covered every garden. For me as an artist, it was extremely important to observe how their practices and beliefs were challenged, adapted, and transformed by their new environment. Their experience was also a mirror in which I could see myself.

The collection of works that together constitute *A Glance over the Garden* fundamentally encapsulates, as well as elevates and transforms, the experience of a forced exile. New places offer new opportunities, new places to rename, but at the same time they suppress part of our cultural selves. The same thing happened four hundred years ago when Africans arrived in Cuba during the colonial period; they also suffered an exile from the native lands from which they proceeded. (The Africans were not the only ones flung into exile; many other ethnic and religious groups, such as the Jews, the Arabs, and the Asians, were as well.) Elevating the cultural presence of my African ancestors in this collection, as well as the experience of my friends in Buffalo, restores them within the Anglo context of this experience. In effect, I plant "a garden," a garden that functions as a metaphor of living together, of order, and of the appropriation and integration of this new land.

This testimonial is based on a paper that Leandro Soto presented at a conference sponsored by the State University of New York, Buffalo, on October 24, 1998, entitled "Ethnic Identity, Culture, and Group Rights: A Discussion across the Disciplines on the Situation of Hispanics/Latinos in the U.S."

*"Grace under pressure" is a concept Ernest Hemingway developed. It refers to the manner in which his literary characters become heroes under extreme pressure or circumstances.

Exile

REALITY OR IMAGINATION

Grisel Pujalá-Soto

Grisel Pujalá-Soto was born in Camagüey in 1951; she left the Island with her family at the age of seventeen in 1968 and settled in New York City. She currently resides in South Hadley, Massachusetts, with her husband, Leandro Soto.

The idea of writing about exile and the Cuban American experience came to me while teaching a course on Latino writers in the U.S. The special topic for the class was Cuban and Cuban American exile literature. Since I teach at a women's college, my class was like a microcosm of the Latina community, for it was composed of Chicanas, Puerto Ricans, and one Cuban American. During the course of the semester, the Chicana students expressed their rejection both of their Spanish heritage and of Anglo culture; they also expressed their sense of having what they characterized as a "rootless identity." On the other hand, the Puerto Rican students seemed to share the Chicanas' attitude toward Anglo culture, yet they did not reject their Hispanic heritage. Unlike her peers, the Cuban American had a very strong sense of identity—something, she told us, that she owed to her Cuban grandmother in Miami. Born in the U.S. to parents from the "one-and-a-half generation," this twenty-one-year-old explained that before coming to college here in New England, she had never questioned her identity as a Latina and/or Hispanic in the U.S. In effect, she was a member of a generation that, in Gustavo Pérez Firmat's words, has no choice but to be American; in her mind, she was simply Cuban American, a state of being that implies that she is both Cuban and American.

Upon being asked to talk about her experience, my Cuban American student claimed, to her peers' amusement, that the United States was the land of opportunities. The other students in the class argued that, on the contrary, Chicanos are voiceless in the U.S. and Latinos in general feel colonized and left out of history. This caused me to ask myself, Why is the Cuban American predicament so different from that of other Latino groups in the United States?

In general, we are the least preoccupied with identity construction in the U.S., and, in general, we do not feel so "out of place." In the words of my good friend Mario Ernesto Sánchez (director of the International Theater Festival), "we seem to be less bitter than other major Latino minority groups." Perhaps the reason is that when we measure our alternatives, we always come out feeling very happy to be here, rather than in Castro's Cuba.

The condition of being in exile is not new to Cubans; strange as it seems, some of our best literary works have been written in exile. We have continued the tradition of exile not by choice but forced by conditions such as political instability, revolution, dictatorship, persecution, and censorship. The feeling of *insularidad*, which is a longing for or desire to be always *allende al mar* (near the sea), has forced Cubans to reach out and become aware of the entire world, while traveling in that imaginary inner space that Lezama Lima calls *insilio*, a place in the imagination or fictional space that prompts a kind of creative license caused by a feeling of being left out.

Here in the U.S., the process is reversed. Cuban American intellectuals talk about carrying a mythic island within them. The longing is the same for all of us, but now we long for the Island itself. Faced with this feeling, the translational process of giving space to a new culture, although acceptable and practical, does not help. In spite of it all, Cubans have made room for American culture without becoming less Cuban. We can still go to Europe and miss the United States and go to Mexico and have a good fight on behalf of U.S. democracy. Yet exile makes us dwell in an imaginary space so deep that poets are endlessly referring to it. As long as we carry the mythic island within, we can adapt to any circumstance, and, in some sense, we are stronger and more able to deal, as Latinos, with life in the United States.

Entre el gato y la casa
FROM *A Fountain, A House of Stone*

Heberto Padilla

See Section II for the author's biographical sketch.

I

Entre el gato y la casa
hay un plano inclinado lleno de gentes
con pinta de arlequines,

que se quieren mover en un campo de acción
muy lejos de mi alcance,
además, como ya no hace sol,
se desdibujan y enredan
en las ramas de arce.
Se han pasado todo el otoño ahí,
apoyados algunos en la cerca de piedra,
otros en la cumbrera de garaje,
alertas como gallos.
Yo permanezco inmóvil.
Yo llamo a estos los actores
extrapolados de mis escenarios
o, si prefieren oir, de mis ficciones.

2

Escribo en Princeton
desde una casa en Markham Road.
El gato que menciono es un siamés
que cada día sube la escalera
de la puerta del patio; husmea y come,
pero no entra jamás.
Cuando hace mucho frío se cobija
en las yerbas más altas,
esperando que se abra la puerta.

3

Entre el gato y la puerta
Entre el abrigo y la orfandad
Entre los ojos de un animal cualquiera
Entre los sueños y la desesperanza
Entre un idioma y otro
Entre un país perdido y otro que no aparece
Yo permanezco inmóvil, al acecho.
Después abro los ojos
Y afuera lo que veo
son los ojos del gato.

1

Between the cat and my house
there is a diagonal plane full of people
painted as harlequins
who want to move in a field of action
well out of my reach;
besides, since there is no longer any sun,
they become blurred and tangled
in the branches of the maple tree.
They have spent all autumn there,
some leaning on the stone wall,
others on top of the garage,
like roosters on the watch.
I stay still.
I see them as actors
projected from my inner stage
or, if you prefer, from my fictions.

2

I am writing in Princeton
in a house on Markham Road.
The cat I have mentioned is Siamese;
every day it comes up the stairs
from the yard to the door,
sniffs and nibbles
but it never enters the house.
When the cold comes it finds shelter
in the high brush,
waiting for the door to open.

3

Between the cat and the door
Between shelter and abandonment
Between the eyes of any animal
Between dreams and despair
Between one language and another

Between one lost country and another still to appear
I stay still, waiting.
Then I open my eyes and what I see outside
are the eyes of the cat.

(Translated by Alistair Reid and John A. Coleman)

Musicians in Motion

Raúl Fernández

Raúl Fernández was born in Santiago de Cuba in 1945. He arrived in the United States in 1962 and currently resides in Los Angeles, California.

The power of Cuban music is such that the musicians in most of the surrounding countries usually play Cuban music, instead of exploring their own musical traditions.   —*Paquito D'Rivera**

More than any other cultural form, Cuban *musicalía* has been constructed as a synonym for Cuban national and cultural identity, for it reflects a fundamental aspect of Cuban reality. As Carlos "Patato" Valdés once observed, "*sin ritmo no hay ná*" (*Sworn to the Drum*, a documentary by Les Blank). Over the decades, music has been the Island's superior export commodity, providing to outsiders more *sabor* and a different flavor than contrapuntal sugar and tobacco.

The aesthetic of *sabor* is central to the Cuban musician's ability to constantly mix formerly separate Cuban genres and to readily incorporate musical elements from other cultures to produce newer forms. The most characteristically "Cuban" musical expressions have been, in part, the result of *criollo* "versioning" and reinvention, for Cuban musicians are constantly reaching into ancestral roots (such as classical European music, Spanish melodies, and the sounds of African instruments), borrowing from modern musical forms of all kinds (such as jazz, soul, and rock 'n' roll), and utilizing the already rich heritage of Cuban music to refashion new ideas and fuse together and reflavor old offerings.

It is often said that Cuban popular music traveled everywhere. Indeed, the Cuban musical heritage is everywhere evident in the Caribbean, Latin America, Mexico, and the United States. As Cuban musicians traveled and sometimes settled outside the Island, they established "bases" of Cuban music and even "colonized" extensive territories. Consejo Valiente (a.k.a. Acerina), for example, helped establish *danzón* in Veracruz and Ciudad México; Isaac Oviedo visited Puerto Rico and trained the first Puerto Rican *treseros*; Machito and Machín carried their sound to New York and Spain, respectively; Humberto Cané transplanted the *son* to Mexico City; Julio Cueva took it to Paris; and Armand Oréfiche and Don Aspiazu spread Cuban music around the world. Following the 1959 revolution, however, scores of Cuban musicians and vocalists left the Island, migrating in order to negotiate a variety of political, economic, and social situations. Though their musical productions are a result of what Leandro Soto, borrowing from Ernest Hemingway, refers to as "grace under pressure," the following excerpts (which are partly based on interviews that I conducted for the Smithsonian Institution) reveal the beneficial results of Cuban exile artists such as Celia Cruz and Cachao, both of whom have established careers outside the Island and whose music continues to transcend geographical borders and cultural frontiers and influence musicians all over the world.

FROM "CELIA CRUZ"†

I have thirty-seven or thirty-eight years outside my country, and the longing for it is precisely what allows me to conserve that feeling and never lose it. . . . I'll continue with my Cuban music until the last day. You can call it "salsa" or "sulso" or whatever you want to call it; it's still Cuban music. I will always have it present within me. I can be here in Mexico or in Venezuela or in Spain or Argentina, and my accent is still a Cuban accent.

(Interview with Alberto Nacif, 1997)‡

. . . The revolution of 1959 radically changed not only the social structure in Cuba, but the musical world as well. The consequent cessation of the flow of tourists and the eventual rupture of relations with the United States rapidly broke down the scaffolding that sustained the tourist industry and prompted the quick decline of the music industry.

Many independent musicians stayed in Cuba; many others left. The renowned Cuban singer Celia Cruz left the Island with the Sonora

Matancera to work in Mexico in July 1960 and has never returned to Cuba.... [Following her departure] she stayed in Mexico for a year and a half, a period during which she toured the country with the company Toña La Negra and appeared in the film *Amorcito Corazón*, in which she sang the celebrated *bolero* "*Tu voz*." Feeling limited by the market in Mexico, she decided against renewing her contract with the Sonora Matancera in 1962 and traveled to the United States to test her fortune.

... In his book on Cuban music, Cristóbal Díaz Ayala points out the importance of salsa as the rhythm that served as a bridge among various groups of Latins (of diverse origins) residing in the United States.... [S]alsa provided a sense of communal cultural identity not only for Latins residing in the States, but for audiences throughout Latin America. During the '60s salsa was one of the musical forms developing in Latin America for Latin Americans, independent of a birthplace. Upon that base lies the importance of Celia Cruz's artistic work.

...There is no doubt that Celia Cruz is a central figure for understanding the phenomenal popularity of Cuban, Latin American, and Caribbean music in general. Her artistic career, which spans six decades, has much to do with the success of salsa and the development of Latin jazz. But luck alone cannot account for the impact of her music; not only does Celia have a great voice and an even greater presence on the ... stage, but her involvement in artistic decisions, her direct interventions in every detail of her recordings, and her choice of musicians (many of whom she has made famous) have made her an important intellectual artist whose music has had a worldwide impact.

Her musical labors have directly contributed to the gradual spread and transformation of what has become a hybridized Cuban music ... by means of a constant process of amalgamation and synthesis. This transculturation has given Latin Americans from a host of countries, as well as those who live in Latin diasporic communities in North America and Europe, a sense of pride, solidarity, and collective pleasure, for they recognize in the music of Celia Cruz an aspect of their inheritance that is genuine, modern, and continuous.... Her voice, her music, and her songs have come to represent an important chapter in the history and the presence of Latin American culture in the world, distinct from, yet sometimes responding to, the music produced in northern Anglophone countries.

...As a result of her own personal initiative, Celia Cruz attempted to modify the potential and character of music to the point of making it part of the folklore of Latin America. The queen of salsa and rumba, the *guarachera* of Oriente and of Cuba is the musical guardian of all Latin America.... *(Translated by Andrea O'Reilly Herrera)*

FROM "LA MAGIA MUSICAL DE CACHAO"§

At the beginning of 1995, a CD recorded by Israel López "Cachao" won the Grammy Award in the category of Latin Tropical. In June of the same year this Cuban bassist won the National Heritage Fellowship from the National Endowment for the Arts. Later that same month, he was a featured artist in the Playboy Jazz Festival in the Hollywood Bowl in California.... Shortly before this notoriety, however, the name of Cachao was virtually unknown outside of a small circle of Cuban expatriate musicians residing in the United States. Up until the '80s, he had worked in relative obscurity in south Florida. Of course, some may argue that his unexpected popularity as a bassist is a passing fad for the new and his recent success is little more than a combination of luck and an astute agent who promoted him at the moment when the market for Latin music in the United States was growing. On the contrary, I would suggest that the growth of Cachao's audience goes beyond being contingent upon the market or the affinity for ephemeral novelty;...rather, it is an essential aspect of the separate, parallel, and intersecting histories of Cuba's and its neighboring countries' hybrid music.

Over the decades, music that originated in Cuba has gone through successive periods of popularity on the American scene. In the 1990s Linda Rondstadt's and Gloria Estefan's acclaimed Latin Tropical records reached the top of the pop charts. In the early '80s salsa underwent a boom that brought recognition to New York–based musicians such as Rubén Blades. And in the late 1940s, the craze for mambo led by Pérez Prado and others left an important mark on the jazz world and on popular dance music in the U.S.

Born in Havana in 1918 into a family of musicians, Cachao grew up in the town of Guanabacoa, the birthplace of Ernesto Lecuona (the composer of "Siboney") and the center of Afro-Cuban musical traditions. During a long professional musical career, the work of Cachao has been identified with various musical genres, such as *danzón*, mambo, salsa, and other more recent varieties of rhythm of Cuban origin. In the late '50s . . . the innovations and realizations of Israel López Cachao not only played a significant, though largely unknown, part in the development of popular music in Cuba and of pan–Latin American music, but they influenced the style of music in neighboring countries, including the United States.

. . . In 1962 Cachao left Cuba for Spain, and in 1963 he established himself in New York. . . . This was an important period, for the Latin youth in the United States had difficulty identifying with contemporary idols of popular music, such as The Beatles; they were looking for their roots in the realm of Afro-Caribbean sound. More than anything else, the '60s were a period of cultural transformation, social rebellion, and new ideas. Cachao was one of the musicians who inspired many younger musicians, who regarded him as being experienced. . . . [T]he recordings that Cachao made during his residency in New York are regarded as being legendary, due to the impact they had on contemporary salsa musicians.

In the early 1970s Cachao relocated to Las Vegas, a place that offered him steady work and decent wages. There, he played every kind of music imaginable at Caesar's Palace, MGM, the Sahara, and the Tropicana. . . . He retired to Miami in the early 1980s. In a Cuban community, with little interest in Afro-Cuban music except for the perfunctory homage paid to the singer Celia Cruz, he lived for almost ten years in absolute obscurity, playing at weddings and family parties. . . . [T]hings started to improve, however, in 1989. During that year, Cachao traveled to San Francisco to participate in the Conga Summit. At that event, he was contacted by his old fan Andy García about staging a special concert in Miami. This marked the beginning of a new period in Cachao's career, and for the first time, he received the notoriety that was long overdue.

. . . The music of Cachao represents a mixture of classical, popular, and folkloric, European and African, dance and sound. He took the already existent, stimulating hybrid of the Cuban musical tradition, which had developed its particular instruments, nomenclature, and languages, added new elements, and expanded its vision and took it beyond the

Caribbean. If music is, in the words of José Martí, "the soul of the people," to return to the music of Cachao is to listen to the soul of Cuba, the Caribbean, and the United States.

(Translated by Andrea O'Reilly Herrera)

* Quotation taken from Luis Tamargo's interview with Paquito D'Rivera, *Latin Beat Magazine* 2:3 (April 1992): 20–22.

† The following excerpts are taken from Raúl Fernández's article "Celia Cruz," which is based upon an interview Fernández conducted on September 25 and 26, 1996, and which originally appeared in *Deslinde* 21 (July–September 1997): 103–21.

‡ This quotation is taken from Frances R. Aparicio's article "The Blackness of Sugar: Celia Cruz and the Performance of (Trans)Nationalism," *Cultural Studies* 13:2 (April 1999): 223–36. See especially pages 227–30, where she discusses Celia Cruz's attitude toward exile and its relationship to her work.

§ The following excerpts are taken from Fernández's article "La magia musical de Cachao," which is based on an interview Fernández conducted on January 24 and 25, 1995, and which originally appeared in *Huellas* 44 (August 1995): 3–13.

Yesterday/Ayer
FROM *Outside Cuba/Fuera de Cuba*

Carmen Herrera

Born in Havana in 1915, Carmen Herrera left Cuba via Texas in 1939. She now lives in Manhattan.

The Sepulveda School in Havana provided a very good basic education for me and many women of my generation. Art in my family was almost hereditary; I attended art school and also studied architecture at the University, but a lot of time was wasted due to political turmoil. Under President Machado, schools were often shut down; in the midst of that unrest, meeting with a group of women at the Lyceum to paint and sculpt was truly an oasis. Conditions were perfectly chaotic, and getting an education was a task that demanded great willpower. I am not sorry I didn't finish architecture, for I feel that it would have interfered with my development as a painter. The hard-edged style of my work emerged in Paris during the forties. I was able to free myself from the influence of academic painting and started to conceive spaces differently. In Europe there were always less prejudices against women;

there were many in New York. The difficulties for me were aggravated by my being Latin American. It took a long time before anybody took me seriously. Between scholarships and exhibits, I often traveled to Cuba; I never broke ties with my family or with the Cuban artists I knew. All the Cuban artists of my generation—Lozano, Bermúdez, Mariano—remained my friends. The last time I went to Cuba was when my mother died in 1963; I have not been back. I like to think that my work is a continuation of that of Amelia Peláez, especially where color is concerned. Although I have lived outside of Cuba for so many years, I regard myself as a Cuban painter. (FIGURE 9)

Yesterday/Ayer is part of the artist's private collection.

El descanso del héroe
FROM *Outside Cuba/Fuera de Cuba*

Rafael Soriano

Rafael Soriano was born in Cidra, Matanzas, in 1920. He left the Island in 1962 and currently resides in Miami, Florida.

There was no reference to art in Cidra, except what could be found in library books; even this was quite basic. As a boy, I used to paint with watercolor on slabs of marble. My father encouraged me, and there is great merit in that because in those days the logical thing was not to be an artist, but to study a profession that would provide a living. I began to study art when we moved to the city of Matanzas; there were several of us young students, hopeful to make it to San Alejandro in Havana. And we did. Upon graduation, the entire group returned to Matanzas, enthused with the idea of creating the first School of Fine Arts in the province. The dream came true between 1943 and 1944, with the sponsorship of the provincial government. We worked without salary for three years for the pure love of the arts and so that other young people could study without having to move to Havana. I was school director for thirteen years; although not many students graduated each year, we accomplished plenty. The revolution shattered the nineteen years of my life I gave to that school. I came into exile with my wife and my daughter in 1962; my uprooting was such that for two years I couldn't paint. It was an exhibit organized by the Lowe Museum at the University of Miami that gave me new hope. It was encouraging that I, a Cuban exile who had just arrived, was given the chance to participate without needing anyone's influence. My work began to change; it was something spiritual that cannot be measured in material terms. I believe that art is a means through which the spiritual side of our being evolves. My work also reflects Cuba; perhaps my palette reflects my recollections of how the water changed colors six or seven times a day in the Bay of Matanzas (FIGURE 10). Exile for me is like a journey that hasn't ended.

Head and Vessel
FROM *Breaking Barriers*

Rocío Rodríguez

Rocío Rodríguez was born in Caibarien, Las Villas, in 1952. She left Cuba in 1961 and now lives in Atlanta, Georgia.

The painting *Head and Vessel* (FIGURE 11) belongs to a series of works I did during 1990–1995. During that time I had been making paintings that involved issues of identity, loss and transformation. My childhood in Cuba and subsequent exile to the United States created a duality at the core of my being. The displacement borne of exile is at the heart of this work. I used the human body as a metaphorical terrain to express psychological and emotional loss. This metaphor yielded symbolic associations that paralleled the sense of emotional amputation from one's birthplace. In these paintings, the human figure was in some state of disintegration. Heads became absent or severed, arms disappeared, until in the later works there remained on the canvas a singular shape much like a wound. *Head and Vessel* speaks to the physical and psychic separation experienced within the condition of exile. The head is on one side, the body is on the other. The body is halved much like one's soul when one cannot return to one's homeland. (July 1997)

From *Outside Cuba/Fuera de Cuba*

Luis Cruz Azaceta

See Section I for the author's biographical sketch.

The first few years in exile I spent in New Jersey with relatives who had gotten me a job at a trophy factory. Working conditions were so bad that I tried to organize a union. I was fired in the midst of winter. I knew very little English then, and so for several weeks all I did was look for work in the morning and in the evening go to the movies. One day I asked myself, what am I going to do with the rest of my life. I decided to start painting. I shall never forget the first time I shopped for art materials because while I was at the store, I heard the news of President Kennedy's assassination. It was November 22, 1963. In 1966, I registered at the School of Visual Arts in New York. Upon graduation, I went to Spain where I discovered Goya, Velázquez, Bosch. Among those masters I found inspiration to paint the human condition (FIGURE 1). Back in New York, everybody would tell me that expressionism was outmoded, but I kept hearing an inner voice telling me to go ahead. One has to listen to one's own voice. Being an exile and not belonging are essential factors in my work. . . . For many years I painted my self-portraits where I appeared both as aggressor and victim. The subject of violence in my work relates to the urban conditions under which we are living, but also those in Cuba. I believe that here, violence is psychological, while there, it is political. My recollections of Cuba are filled with tragedies and fears, with superstitions and taboos. It also includes good and loving memories.

Historia rota (Broken History)

María Martínez-Cañas

María Martínez-Cañas was born in Havana in 1960 and left the Island for Key West as an infant during that same year. In 1964, she relocated to Puerto Rico with her family and didn't return to the U.S. until 1978. Though she spent several years each in Philadelphia, Chicago, and Spain, she currently resides in Miami, Florida.

For more than fifteen years I have been making art about issues of displacement. Having been born in Cuba and raised first in Puerto Rico and then in the United States (since 1978), I have encountered many people throughout the years who have asked me if I feel connected or divided by these three cultures. I have experienced and have been influenced by many things in this country, which have helped shape me as a person and as an artist.

Since I was not born here, I have always felt a great sense of loss for a country of which I have no memories. I have many feelings of displacement, which are quite natural for people who are born in one country and raised in another. I always ask myself why I feel Cuban, even though I have never lived on the Island. Puerto Rico taught me many things about my language and Spanish culture; the United States has taught me a tremendous amount about who I am; and Cuba has taught me many things about where I come from. I don't feel divided by three places—I feel very fortunate to have learned different things from each one.

Growing up in the Caribbean with Spanish and Anglo American cultures, I found myself developing a consciousness of "place" that was infused with social meanings and values. My concern is to transcend the mere recording of a particular locale; my work, therefore, becomes a personal interpretation. My photographs are a combination of two things: a fascination with the medium and a necessity to express myself (FIGURE 12). I have never accepted the idea that the camera's function is only to record.

Through photographs, I constantly confront myself with personal issues like belonging, alienation, and my position in the outside world. I hunt for images to achieve a new vocabulary. A map, for instance, is not only a representation of a territory. To me, it is a visual source for a unique language and, at the same time, a painful tool for understanding where I came from and who I am.

During 1986, I spent six months in Spain on a Fulbright-Hays grant collecting and researching visual material for the development of my work. I felt the need to utilize the old maps and letters pertaining to Cuba's discovery by Christopher Columbus, and to be exposed to the form and content of these objects. The work developed as a personal interpretation of what a map is literally used for: to find a specific location, or as a means for us to "find" ourselves. I wanted to utilize the maps as a way to find my roots. The time that I spent in Spain marked the beginning of a body of work, which would take me ten years to complete, devoted entirely to cartography.

I have spent a great deal of time trying to understand what "memories of Cuba" are, since I do not have literal ones. The memories I have are all "created fragments" of facts handed down through family stories, books, maps, and documents. My work attempts to create new memories that have to do with who I am and the influence that growing up in Puerto Rico has had on my life. My work attempts to tackle the complex issues of identity, which forces me to look at Cuba and its heritage and relate it to my life.

My work is actively and visually exploring the image and world as mediated by the symbols, icons, and indexes, which mediate our knowledge of this world. This is a personal odyssey; the images are "events" that transcend one another as a never-ending chain from the past to the present.

Exilio
FROM *Los espacios llenos*

Orlando Rodríguez Sardiñas (Rossardi)

Orlando Rodríguez Sardiñas (Rossardi) was born in Havana in 1938. He left Cuba in 1960, first settling in Spain and then relocating to Austin, Texas. He currently resides in Miami, Florida.

Se va haciendo camino al andar   *—Antonio Machado*

Irse. ¿Es eso todo? Y regresar
por los discernimientos, ¿no es más suceso? ¿No es mucho más
volver con cada cosa no vivida a lo vivido en el poema?
¿No es algo así como andar de limpio y fresco en los amparos?
Es que duelen, por no dichos, los secretos:
Ellas, las cosas que han podido ser, ¿dónde van quedando?
¿Dónde ya habrán brotado? ¿Por dónde han florecido
los besos y las manos por brindarse, los ojos y los gestos por abrirse,
los cariños por ser? ¡Qué son hoy día si ya fueron?
¿No es que es eso la alegría que mantiene el tiempo en su por siempre?

Pero aquello fue la infancia desgajada;
aquello, lo dejado en lo posible, lo por ser metiéndose quizás dichoso
    por la historia,
por la ruta de aprender, desatropelladamente,
a cruzar las plazas y las almas llenas; aquel aquello es ya lo nunca olido,
lo jamás visto, lo antes nunca palpitado;
    el "quizás" parado en su "de lejos", guardando sus secretos entre letras
        carcomidas,
adornadas con tapias y rejas floreciendo, con parques y altas, blancas
    lunas;
guardado en un *yo quise* que pudo haberlo sido mucho más dulce
y suspirado que aquella estrella que no sé si pudo ser por aquel cielo.
Aquello, a lo mejor, fue la vez de los Transcursos
en que dieron a rodar las penas más feroces de la más sencillas penas,
o fue el momento aquel—quizás—de llevar armas por robar la algarabía.
Pudo ser. Podrá haber sido todo eso mucho más que los acuerdos
en que suman su destino *amar, comer, partir* . . . ¡y luego
arder, furiosamente, en el "nunca haberlo sido",
como si de echarse hacia Lo Eterno se tratara!
¿No es eso mucho más la primavera? ¿No es eso más jardín
con sus acequias, sus flores, sus fuentes,
sus veredas convergiendo en el camino? Llegar.
¡Es eso todo! Lo atado en el deseo al transitar por los asuntos.
Lo que fluye en las mareas a la playa
y queda caracol por las arenas. ¿No es eso entrar por el principio?
¡Es eso! ¡No saber y haber armado la estructura, piedra a piedra,
en las Ideas, con sus puertas siempre abiertas, sus escalas enfiladas,
sus patios floreciendo, y mucho de por dentro en lo de afuera!

EXILE

One creates a path by journeying.   —*Antonio Machado*

To go away. That's all? And to return
through the meanderings of the mind, isn't that a greater event?
Much more,

to come back bringing every thing unlived to that which (we have
lived) within a poem?
Isn't that much like coming as a waif, yet clean and new?
It is the ache of secrets never told:
The things that could have been, where do they stay?
Where might they sprout? Where bloom
the kisses and the hands yet to unfold, eyes, gestures to outpour,
the loves to be? If they once were, what are they on this day?
Are they not of the joy that keepsakes Evermore for Time?
But that was childhood torn;
that was what it was left behind which could be possible as well;
and yet to be, forcing itself, gladly perhaps, upon the past,
upon the road to learning how—with ease—
to walk across town squares and plenished souls. That over there is now
the never
    smelled,
the never seen, the never, ever felt to beat,
the "maybe" standing still at "from afar," keeping its secrets among
letters worn away, adorned with walls and flowering ironworks, with
parks and high, white moons;
within "I wanted" kept, which could have been much sweeter,
better sighed, than the one star which I'm not sure could be (which
I'm not sure belongs) about that sky.
That was, perchance, the time of Passages
when the most feral woes from the most simple woes were set adrift,
or that one time—perchance—of taking arms (just to steal the roar).
It could have been, could all of it have been
much more than the agreements where
to love, to feed, to leave, sum up their fate . . . later
fiercely to burn, in "Never Having Been,"
as if the purpose were to lay oneself for the Eternal!
Isn't that more like Spring? Isn't that more like a garden
with its grooves, its flowers and ponds,
its paths converging on the way? To arrive.
That is all! That which we carry tied in our desire as we transit
the business of the day.
That which flows on the sea-tides to the beach

---

and stays shelled in the sands. Isn't that quite like entering from
the start?
It is! Not knowing, yet having built the structure, stone by stone,
on thoughts with ever open doors, their scales all in a row,
their courtyards all in bloom, and much of the inside on the outside!
(*Translated by Orlando Rodríguez Sardiñas [Rossardi]*)

Abode

Roberto G. Fernández

*Roberto G. Fernández was born in Sagua la Grande, Cuba, and came to the U.S. in
1964. He lives in Tallahassee, Florida.*

Dawn in the tropics and thirty-three pallbearers carried the agonizing
cricket deep into the anthill. As usual, I had already escaped the apartment. I was jogging in the same direction as I did every morning, but
inside myself I plodded aimlessly. I was going to cut across the empty lot
but came to a standstill, astonished at seeing the coral house blocking
my way. I thought I had taken the wrong turn, but the Royal Palm with
the bleeding heart of a forsaken lover carved in its trunk was where it
had always been, except it now formed part of the front yard of this
house.

I cautiously neared the house, opened the iron gate, and entered. A
strange sensation of calmness came upon me. I pushed the door open
and slowly took a few steps inside. The house had a series of stairs
leading to different levels. I was so engrossed that at first I failed to
notice a monk with a black Byzantine beard, who was burning incense
in front of a triptych which portrayed three men with their hands in
prayer in a capsizing canoe. When I looked at him, I saw the birth of a
smile that never was. He pointed to the incense sticks jutting out from
an ebony urn. I reached and gave one to him. He lit it, and with the
smoke he outlined the contours of my face while directing me to one
of the chambers. I began to climb the stairs, and with each step a pleasant sensation enveloped me. I reached the threshold and slid open a
bagesse door.

Once inside, I sat in a hammock that wanted me to divulge the burdens of my life. It seemed to ask me to empty my sorrows where nobody else could hear them. I realized I was in a timeless place where one could view the world, but the world could not intervene. It was there that I listened to the deepest of silences, the sorrows of the wounded eagle, the emotions trapped in photos of last good-byes, the sighing of walls that kept many secrets—and smelled the scents of flowers captive on canvases.

My morning escapades ceased to be an idle exercise, and I happily came each morning to see the bearded monk, who would point me to the right chamber: the sisters of augury, the going under, the bilingual blues, the brand-new memory, the angel dust.

It was the day of the upside-down rainbow when I noticed a number of tiny scarlet violets growing in the cracks of the tiles. I clipped one and showed it to the monk. He was taken aback. I offered him an incense stick to distract him, but he put his hand up and looked away. The flower had absorbed his thoughts. He nestled it in his palms. Then he turned around and closed the triptych. I became anxious and began to hear the deafening sounds of the outside world: rapping voices, radios blaring, tires screeching.

Confused, I started to hurry back to my apartment, but halfway up the road, I turned back. I returned to the house exhausted, and I saw the monk. His beard had fallen off, and in its place there were tiny scarlet violets. He moaned with pain, gestured for me to remove the flowers, and pointed to the Royal Palm. I dashed to the front yard and gathered its berries, and as I rushed inside to give them to him so that he could wipe his face, the tiles rained hard on the archway, and loosened coral stones rolled down in a great avalanche. As hinges twisted away from their frames, nails tumbled through the air and huge gaps appeared in the crumbling walls. Time hurled itself against the timeless house, shrinking it until nothing was left but an empty lot with a frondless tree.

Years have gone by, and I ask myself if there ever was a bearded monk and a coral house. I walk where my home once stood, searching for the solace of yesterday, hoping that one day the monk will reappear. I can still smell the scent of incense in my hands.

Lluvia y primaveras

FROM *Sin decir el mar*

Jesús J. Barquet

Jesús J. Barquet was born in Havana in 1953 and came to the U.S. in 1980 as part of the Mariel Boatlift. He lives in Las Cruces, New Mexico.

Es de este amor de fondo de pozo
del que dependen mis lluvias:
de este ser tierra y mar y fuego y cielo
siendo sencillamente hombre.
¡Si los peces pusieran sus huevas en las nubes
y no en lo profundo de su limitación. . . !
Si caminaran los árboles, ¡cuántos ejércitos leñosos
a defender la Primavera!

———————

El hombre es un roble, pero su robledal es el sueño.

———————

A veces me siento como un árbol que anda buscando su terruño.
No todas son tierras de vivir, por eso mi casa es ese emigrar
    constantemente de cuerpo en cuerpo, ese
hincar y deshincar luego tenuemente las raíces, ese batir siempre
    tan ligero de mis ramas,
ese dormir siempre tan despierto.
Pues uno nunca sabe dónde se harán voces los ecos, hombres las
    sombras,
sol todo astro que pase.
Y reímos, hasta el fondo tristísimos;
y salimos a conversar con la noche en este reducto que suele ser
    la ciudad,
de noche,
sin testigos que nos obliguen después a comparecer ante el fuego.

———————

RAIN AND SPRINGS

It's about this love from the bottom of a well
on which my rains depend:
about my being land, sea, fire and sky
being merely man.
If fish were to spawn in the clouds
and not in the depths of their limitations. . . !
If trees were to walk, what a lot of timber armies
to defend Spring!

———————

Man is an oak tree, but dreaming is his oak grove.

———————

At times I feel like a wandering tree looking for its home ground.
Not all lands are for living, that's why my house is that
    migrating constantly from body to body, that
plunging my roots and afterwards pulling them out tenuously, that
    endlessly airy beating of my branches,
that sleep always so alert.
Since one never knows when echoes will become voices, shadows
men,
    a sun every passing asteroid.
And we laugh, from our sad depths,
and go out to talk with the night in this haven
    the city usually is,
at night,
without witnesses summoning us afterward to appear
    before the fire.

            (Translated by Kristine Lee, Beth Pollack, and Jesús J. Barquet)

Autobiography, Historiography, and Mythography in Matías Montes Huidobro's *Desterrados al fuego*

Yara González-Montes

Born in Havana in 1939, Yara González-Montes left the Island with her husband, Matías Montes Huidobro, and their daughter, Ana María, in 1961. After spending many years in Honolulu, Hawaii, the couple recently relocated to Miami, Florida.

When I think about Matías Montes Huidobro's *Desterrados al fuego*, I find myself in the peculiar position of contemplating a novel in which I myself am one of the principal characters. Reflecting upon *Desterrados*, the first thing that comes to my mind is the complexity of the creative process, which has converted into a work of art moments in which our personal histories (mine and Matías's) have intertwined with official history. What I want to analyze in this essay is the creative process whereby simple biographical facts are transformed into fiction. Having been a part of both the real-life and, in a slightly different sense, the fictional experiences that comprise the novel, I find myself in a somewhat privileged position from which to carry out my proposed analysis.

MATÍAS MONTES HUIDOBRO (interpolation in the voice of the author): Although I can't exactly define the goal I had in mind when I set out to write the novel, I am sure that I didn't intend to write a documentary of our external, objective experiences. In my opinion, the novel is indeed a documentary of the process of exile, but internalized in such a way as to treat the inner history of this process. I take as my point of departure three specific details—the typewriter, the wedding gown, and the overcoat—but immediately I abandon exterior reality, which is what has dominated Cuban narrative dealing with similar historical situations, and I move to the internal process that this reality represents. It is not a story about the physical trauma of exile but, rather, a novel about the psychological and metaphysical experiences of exile, which are those that leave permanent scars. Though narrated in the first person, it is not an autobiographical novel, albeit it does utilize elements of our experience in the creation of the narrative voice and in the characterization of Amanda.

In the novel, not only does our situation interconnect with the point of departure of the initial exile, but our lived experiences are integrated into the overall context, without regard to the chronological order normally associated with autobiography. I've always been fascinated by the lengths to which critics will go to determine what is and what isn't a genuine autobiographical novel. In this case, unless I (or we) enter into specific details, it is very difficult to pigeonhole a narration that is simultaneously fiction and the representation of a given personal and historical experience. The position of Yara, distancing herself as she does to see both the novel and herself within the novel, creates a very privileged interpretive focus.

The action that takes place in *Desterrados al fuego* is geographically located in four cities: Havana, Miami, New York, and Honolulu. It was written in Zelinople, a small town just outside Pittsburgh, Pennsylvania, during the foggy, Siberian winter we spent there while I was completing my doctoral exams. The tale presents us with an autobiographical and internal narrative, laced with black humor, about the conflict of two people who are fully aware of the destructive intensity of the moment in which they are living. The significance of what our own exile was going to mean for us began to be apparent even before we left Cuban soil: "The departure from our country took place under such alarming conditions that one had less the sense of a voyage than of a pathological persecution" (27).

The impact of our exile on our lives determines the style used and the issues treated in the novel, thus affecting Matías's writing in a critical manner. The multiplicity of situations that the different levels of language address, the use of interconnecting myths, and the rituals and allegories developed within the text all contribute to the creation of a novel of great complexity and literary richness. *Desterrados al fuego* is a constant search for authenticity and identity at various levels. The theme of the novel really isn't exile per se but, rather, the anguish endured by the protagonists throughout the trying process of a forced abandonment of their homeland and subsequent efforts to adapt to their new lives as strangers in a foreign land. As Gemma Roberts observes,

The central element in *Desterrados al fuego* is not its political content. The historical, economic, and social factors implicit in the circumstances of the narrator-protagonist are transcended by psychological, ontological, and ultimately religious-mystical dimensions that universalize the theme of exile, in spite of the specifically Cuban context and the writer's use of local and popular expressions. Reading it we are reminded of some of the great masters of the alienated psyche: Dostoyevsky's *The Double*, Gogol's *The Nose*, and even, at times, of Kafka. (96–97)

The preamble to the road to exile in Castro's Cuba was one of the most complex and difficult existentialist rituals anyone headed for exile can endure: to choose three changes of clothes and take the minimum additional baggage possible so that your entire world of possessions is reduced to the bare minimum. "Among them," the narrator tells us, "there were two things we couldn't bear to leave behind: Amanda's wedding gown and my typewriter" (9). The sentimental character of the first and the intellectual nature of the second point to what would become determining factors in our existence. I want to make clear that the previous quotation comes from our real-life experience. We wound up sending the wedding gown and the typewriter to Matías's mother, who at that time was living in Sagua la Grande, with the intention of saving them; but when the package arrived, someone informed the authorities and it was confiscated (see photograph section). I should also mention that the clothing, which is a fundamental theme of the novel, comes to play an important role in the history of the protagonists' exile and the subsequent process of adaptation to life in the United States, to which I referred above.

Upon arriving in Miami, a Catholic relief agency provides the couple with two overcoats that they very much need in order to continue their journey to the north. The acquisition of these coats is also based on a real event. In the novel, these coats function as a point of departure and suspense, from which the author describes, reifying and mythologizing, his real-life experiences—the existential period in which the characters of the novel, especially the author, establish a personal connection with the coats, thus turning them into symbolic expressions of their own psyches.

The internal wound the reader witnesses in the text is the product of the shock inflicted on our lives on the 27th of November, 1961, the date on which we left Cuba and were forced to deal with a culture enormously foreign to us in many respects. Nevertheless, and almost in spite of ourselves, we carried on, driven by the realization that we would never be the same people again and could never return to the lives we had in Cuba. There was simply no alternative but to press on. Matías took refuge in his writing. To write this novel was, for him, an act of exorcism that liberated him, at least in part, from the profound sense of separation and dislocation it was our lot to endure. The autobiographical aspects are of central importance in the novel. There exists, however, a certain distortion of the autobiographical components, due to the creative conversion of these to fiction and to the subjective nature of the author's selection process, in which he chooses his most essential experiences.

By way of example, the following paragraph from the novel demonstrates how this creative process develops and how lived reality relates to the literary work:

> Concerning Amanda, I will only add (regarding these aspects I am planning to treat) that she was typical in the extreme in matters of personal hygiene and that one of the great crises prior to our exile took place when, fearful that the lack of soap would be a certainty and frightened at the force of her own logic, she began hiding cakes of bath soap inside the plaster lamps we had in the living and dining rooms. The obsession (very similar to that of Ray Milland in *The Last Weekend*, a title I think I have wrong) seemed to point toward a no less traumatic conclusion, especially the day we discovered that the bars, thanks to a shadow created by the light bulb, caused pantomime shapes to appear on the ceiling. The decline of filth is a matter of history, and its national rejection gave rise among counterrevolutionaries to the nickname "*bola de churre*," or ball of filth. For reasons of public and private hygiene our departure from the homeland was imminent. (15)

Not too long after the arrival of Castro's forces in Havana, shortages of certain foodstuffs and other basic items began to occur. In a televised speech, Che Guevara reminded us all of the need to make sacrifices for the revolution, and he encouraged us to suffer these shortages stoically.

I have to confess that I began to buy bath soap as soon as I realized it was beginning to disappear from the shelves, and in so doing, committed what the revolutionary government qualified as a counterrevolutionary act. It's true that I did hide them in the lamps; and it's also true that the shadows the bars of soap projected over the ceiling one night when I turned the lights on were enough to send me away.

When I tell this story today, it sounds almost silly, but when you consider how serious it really was back then in Cuba, you begin to realize the degree of terror and paranoia that was beginning to take hold, not only of the national psyche, but also of the intimate details of our personal lives. Facts such as these, taken from our actual experiences, form the basis for the narration, a basis from which the author interpolates a series of elements that radically transform the real-life facts. Amanda, for example, is presented as a national feminine archetype of cleanliness, a move that places her on an idealized level. The reference to Ray Milland's film contributes to the creation of a certain distortion and, at the same time, a distancing from reality, to which the author adds expressionist elements, like the projection effects. Black humor and irony contribute to intensifying the sense of unreality. The counterpoint of cleanliness and filth also offers a way to introduce hyperboles that serve to increase the level of distortion. The phrase "dirtball," an epithet given to Castro during that period, allows the author to refer to him indirectly, without mentioning his name. Framing everything we've mentioned so far is the concept of hygiene, which, in the final analysis, functions as a metaphor for the concepts of purity and ethics.

The various manifestations of the cleanliness-filth binary, exemplified in the paragraph cited above, travel with the protagonists as they journey into exile. In spite of the fact that the omniscient narrator recognizes that "the reasons for the mass exodus had overtones in the personal hygiene, which formed one of the dominant routines on our island, including a marked rejection of the filth and dirtiness of the regime in power" (16), he is going to cling to that same filth on his voyage to the depths of his being, as if by holding onto this he could remain attached to the very roots of his previous life. It follows, then, that the male protagonist is a complex, contradictory, tormented, and multivalent being.

On the other hand, although at the beginning of the narrative Amanda is an active participant in the dialogue and her reasoning is logically irrefutable, little by little she is silenced, even though she/I rebel against our creator, much as Augusto Pérez did against Unamuno in *Niebla*. Both authors, however, are resolute in their intent. In my case, the author justifies himself from a literary standpoint, something Matías and I have debated many times, thus insinuating a possible amorous relationship between Amanda and the man who offers her a job because "naturally," as the protagonist would say, she finds a job and he doesn't. Be that as it may, what is certain is that during the course of the novel Amanda passes through a crisis that the narrator describes as "the painful period of the overcoat," losing in the process all vestiges of her previous elegance and finally reaching, in the end, a state of reification. Nevertheless, her process of adaptation to the new environment is not presented as being traumatic. It is possible that the author unconsciously avoids presenting it as being traumatic because in the deepest recesses of his heart, he knows that she possesses the secret of his resurrection. Amanda, in contrast to the process of decomposition that the protagonist is undergoing, throws herself into her work in the mask factory as if this were her bulwark of resistance. Possessor of the secret hidden below the deceiving surface of the epidermis, she will be, in the final analysis, the only one who restores the narrator to the wholeness of being.

MATÍAS MONTES HUIDOBRO (in the "silenced" voice of the author): I compose Amanda's portrait with elements that belong to Yara, but I also add elements not pertaining to her, which distort the image. In the final analysis, you can't say which is which. This occurs in other texts, but on a somewhat reduced scale, though at times with larger alterations because everything would be okay if I simply were to write about Amanda and me, me and Amanda. The difficulty in writing a novel in the first person is that the reader identifies the author with the protagonist, when such is not necessarily the case. I am not the protagonist, nor is Yara completely Amanda, but, rather, only partially so. And there are certain events in the novel that I definitely don't want attributed to my personal life. Finally, I want to indicate that the novel is also political. Destined to perish, the characters survive and reaffirm themselves. The Cuban revolution sought to take from us two things that represent us as human beings, one profes-

sional in nature—namely the act of writing—and the other personal—the wedding gown as a metaphor of our personal union
through love. Both are intransigently personal vis-à-vis the collective
order. The novel itself is a confirmation of the act of writing, and the
re-encounter represents a reaffirmation of conjugal love. Consequently,
the revolution wound up taking nothing from us: it only took from
itself. I don't deny that there have been much suffering and grave
difficulties, but this text is for me an act of recuperation and a reaffirmation of my identity (our identity, as Amanda would say) as a writer
and as a human being. In this sense, it is a political novel, a recuperation of the things Castro couldn't take from us: the freedom to write
and the triumph of Eros.

(Translated by Jerry Hoeg)

In 1975 *Desterrados al fuego* was awarded one of Mexico's most prestigious literary
awards in the Fondo de Cultura Económica's Primera Novela competition. It was
translated into English and published as *QWERT and the Wedding Gown* by Plover
Press in 1992.

WORKS CITED
Montes Huidobro, Matías. *Desterrados al fuego.* Mexico: Fondo de Cultura Económica,
1975.
Roberts, Gemma. "*Desterrados al fuego* de Matías Montes Huidobro." *Revista
Iberoamericana* 96–97 (1976): 642–644.

"Inheriting Exile"

On Being an American-Born Cuban from Miami

Gisele M. Requena

Gisele M. Requena was born in 1972 and raised in Miami, Florida. She now resides in San Francisco, California.

When I introduced myself at the Hispanic Faculty and Staff Association meeting at the University of Texas, where I worked, I stated my name and my hometown, saying, "I come from Miami, which means I am Cuban." At first I was surprised at what came out of my mouth, but the further I travel away from Miami, the more I identify myself as Cuban and locate myself geographically as being from Miami. I do this not because I am finding my roots away from home, but because when I am home I don't have to search for them.

I was born in Miami—well, at Hialeah Hospital—in 1972 to Cuban parents and grandparents. My mother had been in the United States for eleven years, my grandparents for merely four. Since the day of my birth to the last time I spoke to my mother on the phone, I have had Spanish spoken to me. Likewise, when my mother worked and my grandparents took care of me all day, it was Spanish and only Spanish, except for the children's programming on television. I have no idea what it is like to live in a nonbilingual household. I grew up drinking *café con leche*, celebrating birthdays with cake frosted with that oh-too-sweet Cuban-style *merengue* and *piñatas* you do not hit but pull at with ribbons. I spent time sitting with my Abuela Mercedes after we came back from the *peluquería* to watch astrologer Walter Mercado, or turning on the evening *telenovela* after we had *ropa vieja* or *bistec de palomilla* or *arroz con pollo*. My grandfather would walk me to the bakery, singing traditional Cuban songs and buying me *pan cubano* before we went home to play dominoes. In elementary school, where the administration, teachers, and students were mostly all Cuban, I learned the basic subjects, but they also tried to teach me sewing. And while the girls were being instructed on how to knit, crochet, and hem skirts, the boys got free time to do their homework or play—an arrangement no one questioned. My teachers drank *cafecitos*, and the lunch line featured black beans and rice instead of burgers and fries. Even now, with my mother and grandfather still in Miami, my grandfather listens to the Cuban radio stations, reads the Cuban newspaper, and still speaks to me in the only language he knows. And when Hurricane Andrew was coming our way, wouldn't you know it—my mother and I had both stocked up on the essentials: the hurricane could come; we had *pastelitos!* When I return to Miami, there is no doubt that I am Cuban American. When I am far away, I keep reiterating that fact, pushing it in people's faces, reminding myself of who I am and where I come from, and making it clear that being Cuban American is one of the main ways I identify who I am.

Having been in academia and having studied works of Cuban American literature, I am familiar with the different terms used for all of us, the question of whether Cubans are exiles or immigrants, of whether I am an "American-Born Cuban" or, as Gustavo Peréz firmat puts it, a "Cuban-Bred American." For us Cuban Americans who grew up in two cultures and who were raised with Cuban traditions while living in the United States and participating in American society, there are always questions about how ethnicity and identity intertwine. Therefore, I must explain that I see myself as Cuban American, in that hyphenated place between the two cultures—not stuck on the border of both, but fully participating in each. I like to say that I am updating my Cuban self and adding *sabor* to my American half. I could not be the same Cuban girl my mother was back in Cuba, having her *quinceañera* and wearing her lace and bows. Yet it is no surprise to me that many of my family members don't understand why I am not "home" in Miami "where I belong," and why I insist on moving throughout the country, instead of settling down in Miami. My grandfather told me to just get a simple job and come back to Miami. In fact, having or not having a career is fine with my family, and news of my getting a new job is not as welcome or as important as news of an engagement would be. For example, as I was graduating magna cum laude from college, my extended family was paying more attention to my cousin's wedding in New Jersey than to my commencement exercises. Even though I was graduating in Miami, I got a few cards, while hordes of family members made travel arrangements for *la boda* up north.

There are certain gender expectations placed upon me as a young Cuban American woman that are at odds with my feminism. I can see that in moments when my great aunt looks at me—and the freedom and choices I have in my life—and recalls her youth in Cuba, where she and her sisters got married and had kids as was expected of them. Every time I visit with Tía, she still asks me if I am "seeing anyone," and then when I am dating someone, I am always asked if he is Cuban. My family members are proud of my accomplishments, but I know they also wonder when I am going to find a good husband. While the *cubana* in me respects family and values her grandparents' traditions, the American teenager I was has produced an adult who is intent on following her own way and exerting her independence. At the same time, I pepper my English with Cuban sayings, and my friends who have been in the car with me during rush-hour traffic have learned some choice Spanish words! I also add Latin steps to my moves on the dance floor, and I prefer Gloria Estefan's Spanish songs to her CDs in English. Somewhere along the way, I find the balance that makes me who I am.

How did I come to feel so Cuban, though? I see many others in my twenty-something age group who, while being aware of their ethnicity, do not stress it as much as I. My friends will tell me that centuries ago their families came from Germany or Scotland or Ireland, but they do not insist on holding on to these heritages or commit to passing them on. They think of their ancestry and leave it in the past; they are simply Americans. Yet for me, the Cuban flag is as much a part of the present as seeing fireworks on the Fourth of July. My family members didn't choose to immigrate to the United States. They loved their Cuban lives and thought they would get to go back, so assimilation was never fully considered. They already had a flag and an anthem and a way of life; and settling in Miami, they did not have to give these up. They chose to pass it all on to me; and it is a gift I have accepted. And so, I go back to explaining: I am from Miami. And that means I am Cuban.

Miami is a strange, wonderful place—an international city more Cuban than anything else—and a place where I have been able to grow up with a Cuban sensibility. I think it's all because *el exilio* pushes its ideology onto you; and whether you believe it or not, you accept it. For example, take the "myths" that we are all told about Cuba. From a young age, we twenty-somethings, who grew up surrounded by Cuban *abuelos* and *tíos*, heard not just family stories, but stories about how things were in Cuba. On the hottest and most humid day in Miami, we were told that in Cuba it was never that hot. During trips to Miami Beach, we were told that the water was a far cry from the glorious beaches of Cuba. And so it was with the food we ate, the experiences we had—everything was just better in Cuba, the land of perfection. And when the *Miami Herald* or, more often, *Diario de Las Américas* or Univisión told stories about horrible crimes, well, of course, such things did not happen in Cuba. Not one of us grew up without hearing those famous words, "*eso no pasaba en Cuba.*" And while at twenty-six I am aware that these were exaggerations born out of love and homesickness, in a way I believe them, even though I know they are not true, because at the same time, these stories *are* partly true—perhaps because I want to believe them, perhaps because believing them makes me feel more Cuban, or perhaps because I realize that this magical Cuba exists only in the imagination, where anything is possible and anything can be true. When my mother sees Cuba on television, she doesn't recognize it because the now run-down buildings were in their full architectural splendor when she was last in Havana. The images we see tell us that the rich and colorful Cuba of my mother's childhood no longer exists physically. So then why not make its "memory" all the more beautiful and better? For that is how the country is held in the hearts of the Cubans among whom I was raised. Therefore, it exists in the same way somewhere deep in my own heart; and it was growing up where I did and when I did that placed it there.

I would not know how to even tell anyone about myself, about my life, without saying I come from Miami and I am Cuban. Because while I am an American at the same time, with a master's degree in English from the University of South Carolina, who reads books and newspapers in English and eats pizza more often than plantains—when I look at the Cuban flag, it is my flag. When people speak of the Island, it is my country. And even when people talk of the great fall of fidel that will someday come, when they will be able to "go home," I understand. While I do not plan on being on the first boats back with them, I—who have never set foot in Cuba—also want to return to see my town of Bayamo for the first time and to see the house my family had to leave. Granted, I know that after so many years of deterioration and disrepair, the house I will someday look upon may barely resemble the one in which my mother lived. I realize things change. Nevertheless, I will still be setting foot in my house, on the soil of my homeland. (Actually, if I could get any souvenir from Cuba right now, that would be it—a small handful of dirt, a part of the land, to always remind me of home.)

This schizophrenic state may seem strange, but this is what it means to me to be an American-Born Cuban. To deny that Cuba is my homeland is to deny a part of myself, just as rejecting anything American would be crazy. And instead of becoming more Americanized, the part of me that is Cuban gets stronger every day. It's as though you can take me out of Miami, but you can't take Miami out of me. In fact, I had never been regarded as a minority until the fall of 1994, when I began my graduate work in South Carolina. For the first time in my life, Cubans did not surround me. There I was—a Latina all my life—and for the first time an ethnic minority, part of the smaller percentage, different. So what did I do? When I called my mother, I spoke to her in Spanish (OK, Spanglish). When I went to the grocery store, I bought *frijoles negros* and *guayaba* from the "international" food aisle. At school, I found myself discovering a new body of work; and while I took my exams in British literature, I wrote my thesis on Cuban American poetry. And after graduate school, when I was looking for a new city in which to live, part of the reason I moved to Austin was because I knew that in Texas I would hear my other native tongue.

And so, I continue to introduce myself as a Cuban, to explain to people why my family left, to tell outrageous stories about fiery Miami and the Cuban exiles, whose dreams of Cuba affect their reality. I consider myself very lucky to have been raised in Miami, where *el exilio* reigns and where Cuban culture continues. There, I have been raised as a Cuban and am part of a group that can truly claim to be as much Cuban as American. Being Cuban American means a great deal to me personally, but I believe it is also important on the grander scale of life in *el exilio*. As time elapses and the older generation passes away, it becomes increasingly difficult to keep Cuban traditions alive. It becomes important to hold on. And so, the fact that of my grandfather's four grandchildren only I, the Miami-bred one, see myself as Cuban becomes a triumph. For all Cubans it is one less loss in a situation where so much has been forfeited already.

From "Stories My Mother Never Told Me"

María de los Angeles Lemus

María de los Angeles Lemus was born in Puerto Rico in 1967 of Cuban parents. Her family relocated to Miami, where she still resides, when María was a year old.

I. PALIMPSEST

My mother is a storyteller. She only tells one story, and she tells it again and again, so that she will not forget, so that I will not forget, about a past I only know because of her story. She tells me about the house where she could see the bay down the sloping hill. There, the old men gathered at night. Jasmine and tobacco swirled with ocean breezes. Sometimes fishermen would bring a fresh catch to my grandfather's doorstep. The Jamaican servant, whose name she can't remember, would prepare it immediately. My uncles, boys then, would laugh when my grandmother put an olive in a broiled snapper's eye. Garlic and sweet peppers, starched linen, misted ferns, polished, gleaming tile floors, and imported lace from Spain: everything in order, vestiges of an old regime.

My mother could not bear to play Chopin *barcaroles* at twilight because an odd, clinging melancholy would overwhelm her. She'd cry before she'd even lived, just as she cries, years later, now that she has lived, every time she hears Chopin.

Later, she'd stop playing the piano. She was more interested in afternoon strolls, in passing warships on the docks, in recognizing the scent of American cigarettes that followed the exotic, Anglophone words of soldiers. Somewhere, beyond the sea, a war. Here, only a schoolgirl trying to understand the Voice of America on short-wave radio, a schoolgirl who couldn't bear to play the piano, a schoolgirl who didn't know she'd be married and pregnant by age sixteen.

Now: a daughter who knows English and the house on a hill somewhere in Cuba. A house I know because of memory; a house whose image I can't repress. Perhaps it still stands; perhaps old men still gather at its doorstep. The last time I heard the story, I realized I did not know its address. Would I recognize it if I stood before it? No photograph exists of my mother's childhood house.

My mother—she'd never marry an American man. She married a man who became a Marxist before she married my father years later, when the scent of American cigarettes had disappeared from the ports. History prepared her body for me, who arrived in San Juan, Puerto Rico, not far from Cuba—three children, three exiles, and three decades later.

I'm also a storyteller. This Cuba, this past, this testimony itself is a lie. My mother's childhood house—that's also a lie. I've spent my life attempting to comprehend why Cuban exiles thrive on this lie, why fact never loses its grasp from fiction, as in Michelangelo's creation: two fingers just barely touching each other, at the end of two hands, and all I see is the space in between, as if my entire life depended on the gesture of these two hands, just holding, or perhaps releasing.

This interstitial site—the space in between two hands, two lives, two generations, and above all, between the words "Cuban" and "American"—represents a stage of conflicts for both my mother, who tells the story not only of the house itself but of the nostalgia she feels for this unrecoverable place, and me, who must hear the story and imagine the presence of this missing, invisible house. A conflict germane to exile, where truths always echo like fiction. When I hear my mother's stories, I peer into a narcissistic mirror that distorts my mother's memories, as well as my own sense of Cuban history. These memory-waters reflect only what her eyes want to see or remember; this vision evolves into a process of storytelling, of turning historical events into an urgent, nostalgic repetition.

I know my mother's story well; and her manifest nostalgia—her storytelling—is the only textual map where I can locate her house. I am perhaps still nowhere, between the house my mother knew and a house somewhere, from where I will tell my own story. In Cuba? No. Her Cuba no longer exists. That is why my mother always tells the same story—to keep it alive, to keep it from dying again.

If Cuba exists at all for me, it's in the movement of words and sounds of words on the vast, open territories of unexplored, uninvented texts—a world of invisible houses, of photographs that have never come to life. My mother's childhood house lives trapped in a memory that has not yet seen the light of day. *Dar a luz,* to give birth: when you soak a printed negative in a chemical solution, the image begins to appear, painfully, slowly, out of its invisible emulsion. To find myself written into my family's exile history is to undergo a similar, laborious process. I live in between two worlds, like a photograph that is always developing, never finishing, always in transition or perhaps translation, between past and present, English and Spanish, Cuba and the United States, the invisible and the visible, truths and lies.

This testimonial represents every effort on my part to resist writing about Cuba, perhaps because my mother's stories have saturated my store of ancestral longings, or perhaps because my sense of Cuba is, and always has been, fictional. I can only add layers of imagined stories and photographs of invisible houses to my mother's palimpsest. Eventually, you might not know where my mother's history ends and my fiction begins. The scrawling of a thousand words over time will appear more like a grotesque, indecipherable baroque structure: curves turn into one another; edges become blurred; every beginning is an end and every end a beginning. When I write about Cuba, I encounter distortions, variations, contradictions at every turn, as in a hall of mirrors. . . . Cuba in Miami: a shipwreck ninety miles off the florida Straits and miracle of a syncretic history—so much a part of me and yet, like the appendix, a vestigial organ without which I might easily survive in a physiological sense, but also like an amputation. Occasionally, I still feel a twitch, a slight pain in my ghost limb.

II. POLITICS AND GEOGRAPHY

I'm not interested in exile politics. I'm a monster, really, insensitive to the Cuban cause. Even though I can easily satisfy any craving I might have for the savory, soul-fulfilling dishes that I ate as a child, I can't taste the longing, the anger, the frustration of Cuban exiles and even of some of their children, who are willing to risk their lives for the sake of Cuba's liberation. . . . I knew my teenage years of rebellion against all things Cuban came to an end when I had a vision of my family leaving Cuba: my father, mother, two sisters, and brother hand in hand, crossing the airport gate, possessing nothing more than the clothes on their backs, each other, and a future. I didn't see my mother's face; I saw my own. I also saw the face of a man I haven't yet met, and the faces of children I haven't yet had. So I can understand now, but I can't taste.

I have asked myself why I rebelled against all things Cuban, and why, even after my revelation, I couldn't bear to write about Cuba. . . . Even though I couldn't possibly have known it then, as a teenager I resented not having what my American friends had: freedom. Freedom from history and from exile. Freedom from choice, from the need to choose

between one culture and another, one language and another, one help-
lessly overdetermined past and needlessly overdetermined future. . . .
Nevertheless I'm grateful. I've got something I wouldn't have had if I
hadn't lived most of my life in Miami: an appreciation for any stability,
for the sound of a root grasping the hot ground.

If I think of Miami as a product of the old world, as an extension of
its far-reaching roots, I'm able to add more nationalities between the
hyphen that joins the words "Cuban" and "American" and realize I'm
not alone. Sometimes Cubans mistake me for a *gringa*, and that jostles
the leaves of this hybrid I've become. But I've seen other trees like me,
even with roots beyond Cuba, on other islands. I appreciate the warm,
familiar recognition of a Cuban, or the acknowledgment by an American that I'm Cuban, even if I have blue eyes and a pale complexion. To
hear a Haitian speaking Creole or meet a Dominican whose accent I
can't quite place offers comfort. . . .

Miami is, therefore, more than Cuba—a Cuba that can vanish when
I put on my *gringa* face—or a Cuba that might, if I ever longed for it,
overwhelm me with its pathos. Miami is an extension of Cuba, but
Cuba is not the only island in the Caribbean, albeit the largest. If you
look at a map, Cuba seems to be an arm carved off Florida's lime-
stone—a strong, fleshy arm stretching west toward the Yucatán. Miami
falls somewhere around the heart of this maimed creature, who has lost
her other arm, the one that would reach east to Europe; and is it any
wonder? Instead, her hair dangles south in a fragmented braid, to touch
the shores of Guyana. Her legs might stretch north toward the rest of
the North America, but clearly she yearns to let go of this continent.
She latches on because so many of her children live there; because she's
afraid she might drift aimlessly into the Atlantic; or she might wash up
on the shores of West Africa, where so many of her children were born,
where eyes may fail to recognize her now. . . . I live in the heart of this
woman; Miami is, without a doubt, a part of the twisted and amputated
limb of an archipelago known as the Caribbean. Anything else is a geographical accident.

III. GHOSTS IN OLD SAN JUAN
When I was thirty I went back to Puerto Rico, my birthplace, a transi-
tional home between Cuba, Spain, and Miami, where my family would

eventually settle. I always thought I was Cuban American, more American than Cuban, and certainly not Puerto Rican. My mother always emphasized how my bloodlines go back to Spain; how I'm nothing more than a colonial, third-generation Spanish girl. . . .

I greeted San Juan on a journalist's assignment. San Juan greeted me like a polite, disinterested relative. Neither she nor I cared for long, harrowing sentimental journeys into the past. Taking notes, taking photographs—the sort of photographs my would-be daughters might see to clearly witness their mother's past; photographs not nearly as meaningful as the one no one ever took of my mother's childhood house.

As I passed the cathedral of El Convento, my camera's lens noticed the image of a Virgin painted on ceramic tiles; the woman's body was split perfectly in six squares, twelve tiles tall. Architectural details distracted me. Looking at everything, seeing nothing, I let the lens hush voices from the cathedral's dark recesses that had summoned me even before I'd seen light, while my mother carried me in her womb, for I was and still am and always will be an image in the process of developing.

Once inside the cathedral, I made the sign of the cross and sat on a pew close to the altar. Slowly, slowly, I closed my eyes and could feel the Virgin's on mine. Cloaked in white lace, she held a dove in her hands. She looked like me: a Celtic Puerto Rican, gaunt face, blue eyes, black hair, and pale face. Only it wasn't the Virgin: it was my grandmother, whom I barely met, who held me in her arms shortly before I left my birthplace, before she died thirty years ago. She said, "welcome home, child." I knew home wasn't San Juan or Cuba or Miami, but everywhere and anywhere. . . . I live the life my grandmother, my mother, and my sisters never had. Women connected by an invisible umbilical cord through blood, flesh, time, and the indifference of centuries; separated by boundaries of clocks, exiles, tribes, and the differences among days.

I understand now why I couldn't find Cuba until I met my grandmother. I understand now why I couldn't find Cuba until I could see the Caribbean as a whole—as a living, breathing woman who gave birth to me. I understand now my need to write and my mother's compulsive storytelling. . . . Little does it matter that I've found Cuba and that it still doesn't exist for me, that I still don't care about politics, that letters from relatives I've never met sit unopened on my desk. . . . I've learned to be a product of exile in exile from exile. I've managed to find my way in the hall of mirrors, living comfortably with contradictions and ghosts in houses I've never seen.

ABCs in South Florida Suburbia
Victor Andres Triay

Victor Andres Triay was born in Miami, Florida, in 1966. He lives in Middletown, Connecticut.

My family went into exile in the fall of 1960, when it became apparent that the Castro regime was intent on creating a totalitarian communist dictatorship in Cuba. Having been part of what began being painted as the Old Regime, as well as finding the prospect of life under a Marxist regime intolerable, the family found itself in a vulnerable position.

I was born in Miami in 1966, part of the first generation of children born in the United States to Castro-era exiles who had left during the early 1960s. By the time many of us were old enough to be aware of our surroundings, the dislocation and trauma of exile experienced by our families were somewhat moderated. It was simply not part of my generation's experience; we could only live it vicariously through the stories of our parents and grandparents. Most of us admired and re-spected the older generation for having endured such an experience—especially since so many of them were strong enough to begin anew in a foreign land.

For American-born and American-bred Cubans (or, as some have called them of late, ABCs) living in Miami, such as myself, the issue of cultural identification and assimilation was dominant during childhood. Being Cuban in one sense and American in another was a paradox that was at once interesting and troubling. For purposes of cultural orienta-tion, alternative connotations arose for the term "American," all of which depended upon the context within which it was used.

One use of "American" was to describe someone whose home lan-guage was English and who was not Hispanic (which, in Miami at the time, meant Cuban). Whether the person was from an Italian American,

Jewish American, Irish American, Polish American, or Anglo American background was irrelevant—he or she was *americano* to us, and the characteristics usually attributed exclusively to Anglos were indiscriminately placed on all *americanos*.

There was, of course, some justification for this distorted view of Americans. In the first place, except for African Americans, the *americanos* were not organized into separate ethnic communities, since before 1960, Miami had little history of being home to large, first-generation immigrant groups. Most Americans in Miami had left their roots in other parts of the country, and even the White, non–Anglo, nontraditional groups were, by then, highly assimilated to Anglo American culture. In order to officially distinguish them from Cubans, who were mostly white, these Americans in Miami would eventually be placed into such official categories as "non-Hispanic White" or, as simple as it was inaccurate, "Anglo."

The Miami of our childhoods was thus divided between "Cubans" and "Americans." Nevertheless, those of us born and raised in the United States with Cuban parents had another context within which "American" was used: to define our national identity. Although falling on the "Cuban" side in the everyday social world of Cubans and Americans in Miami, Cuba itself was not part of our experience. Because of the political situation, the Island may as well have been ten thousand miles away. Even if hatred for communism and fidel Castro helped mold our political outlook, to foster any genuine nationalistic sentiment for Cuba— that is, the Cuba that was and the noncommunist Cuba of the future— would have been a hopeless crusade. Moreover, exposure to Anglo American culture in school, the popular media, and other influential entities fostered high levels of American patriotism among ABCs. This patriotism was accompanied by a tacit, and sometimes blatant, recognition that our generation was rapidly becoming assimilated to United States culture—or at least what we were told being "American" was and what we imagined it to be.

Other factors, however, were also at work in this simultaneous process of cultural assimilation and patriotic nurturing. Besides the detachment from Cuba and the American influence mentioned above, there was the natural inclination of first-generation Americans to show their loyalty to their nation. Moreover, there were no major waves of immigration from Cuba during the most formative years of our childhoods in the 1970s, as the Freedom Flights had ended early in the decade and were even then greatly reduced from their levels in the 1960s. This lack of Cuban cultural infusion seemed to set the stage for a relatively conventional pattern of assimilation to some form of Anglo-Americanism. In fact, any attempt by the older generation to impede this process was met with resistance from the young.

The older generation's outward loyalty to the United States was likewise important in this process; for, constituting the anticommunist side in the conflict over Cuba, they found themselves on the American side of the more global Cold War struggle. Because of this, even though they were Cuban nationalists at heart, no contradiction was seen between being a Cuban and an American patriot. Finally, the cultural influence our parents and their ancestors experienced in prerevolutionary Cuba was of great significance. Like many middle- to upper-class groups in Latin America, the older generation was definitely more Western and Iberian in their outlook than other segments of their society. Also, because prerevolutionary Cuba was more a part of the United States's economic system than that of Latin America, our parents' generation was exposed to an especially high level of American culture during their own youths, which complemented their Western/Iberian orientation. For many, this cultural exposure could have included close ties to Spain, business dealings with Americans, working for American companies, studying in the United States, or attendance at an American- or Spanish-run school in Cuba. That prerevolutionary Cuba had such a relatively large middle class meant that a sizable portion of the population—although by no means a majority—was part of this social milieu. This worldliness made them, as well as their children, a great deal more adaptable than one would expect from a first-generation, non-traditional immigrant group.

On the other hand, our parents' backgrounds may have, in another manner, prevented full-fledged assimilation. In no way was a university education, a career, or a home in the suburbs an alien or uniquely American concept to them—in fact, it was what they had known, valued, and were taught to strive for in their own country before the communist takeover. Moreover, they were never informed that some people considered a work ethic something inherently Protestant. In the end, abandoning the native culture in a deliberate fashion—or, even worse, steering the children away from it as other groups had done in the past—was not seen as a prerequisite for achieving success and status in the United States. That so many Cubans instinctively flocked to the suburbs when presented with the opportunity, while not hindering the rise of Cuban neighborhoods, prevented a ghetto situation from developing.

This phenomenon of cultural retention had a number of implications. Whereas it was recognized by the older generation that assimilating to some extent was necessary to be successful, many parents were clearly scared that their children were becoming so assimilated they would lose touch with their own heritage and be swallowed up completely by Anglo-Americanism. Perhaps this was one reason why, even in homes in which the parents knew how to speak English fluently, some level of Spanish was maintained. An even more important vehicle for retaining Spanish was grandparents, who frequently lived in the home (or nearby) and who would never accept their grandchildren not speaking Spanish. Although sometimes the result for ABCs was what some have termed a "bastardization" of Spanish, or "Spanglish" (a mixture of "home" Spanish and English), most ABCs in Miami, however poorly, could understand and communicate in their parents' tongue. Even if in some homes the children spoke Spanish better than in others, those who spoke it badly could (and often did) refine it years later. My own parents, to this day, rarely if ever speak English to me or my brother, even though they are both fluent. To have spoken to my grandparents in English, even to my grandfather, who had spent his youth in New York and New Jersey boarding schools, would have seemed preposterous. This tendency to foster Spanish in the home paid huge dividends in the future, though it was often mistakenly interpreted as hindering assimilation and thus hurtful to the children (an argument many Anglos used to justify their anger at people speaking Spanish). Not only did my generation speak English as fluently and flawlessly (and unaccented) as our middle-class American counterparts, but, as genuinely bilingual and bicultural Americans, we developed a distinct advantage that not only contributed to our success but was a major contribution to our community.

The ABCs' Americanization in school and the world in general also produced a number of accommodations, many reached unconsciously, between the two cultures in everyday life. For instance, in my home at

Christmas time, a fairly traditional *Nochebuena* was celebrated—yet, it was Santa Claus and not the Three Wise Men (*los reyes magos*) who brought the gifts. Birthdays became more important than saints' days. In our social world the rite of passage for a teenage girl remained her fifteenth birthday, or *quinces*, and not a Sweet Sixteen—however, English-language music was played at the party, and the young people used a bastardized translation of the word *quinces*: "fifteens." Most Miami ABCs would have been at a loss if asked to describe the procedure for a non-Cuban funeral yet would probably be likewise unable to recite the Lord's Prayer or the Hail Mary in Spanish, in spite of having had to endure many Spanish masses during their youths.

CUBAN AMERICANS' COMING-OF-AGE IN THE WESTERN SUBURBS
I grew up, until my senior year of high school when my parents moved to Coral Gables, in a suburb called Westchester. My parents (along with the rest of my relatives and their families) settled there at a time when many young Cuban families began moving to what I will call, for lack of a better term, the western suburbs. Besides the less pretentious areas, such as Westchester and West Miami, there were also wealthier western suburbs such as eastern Kendall, Coral Gables, and certain parts of South Miami and the areas southeast of it. Later, as Dade County expanded further west, new neighborhoods like Village Green, International Gardens, and the various developments of western Kendall began to emerge and were added to the network of western suburbs. It is important that these suburbs were not detached from Miami proper; they were in fact directly connected to the city and to one another. This prevented the sense of suburban isolation experienced in other parts of the country.

Many Cuban families among whom we found ourselves and with whom we shared our lives during those years in the western suburbs held in common a number of characteristics. As in our case, the households were headed by people who left Cuba in their late teens to late twenties a decade earlier and, by the late 1960s and mid-1970s, had finished their education and had begun their careers in earnest or had established their businesses. Many had young families that included children born in the United States and, quite often, elderly relatives. A number had known one another as youths in Cuba or, connected to similar social circles, had mutual friends and acquaintances. A large percentage were from prerevolutionary Cuba's middle and upper-middle classes (and some were even from the upper class)—herein referred to simply as "middle class." Of course, families of similar backgrounds who found themselves in the same types of groupings were developing in other parts and were not restricted to the western suburbs. Also, there were families not from the aforementioned areas who were connected to those from the western suburbs through family relations, friendships, or institutional associations.

In any case, it was a strange world—perhaps because, as children, it seemed so normal to us. At first glance, a community was merely going through the conventional stages of development. Yet between their own adolescence and the time they had settled down, started a family, bought a home, and become reacquainted through their children, our parents' generation had experienced a revolution, a communist takeover of their country, and political exile, and had been on the center stage of the Cold War. Some had spent time in political prisons, and a handful had served in the anti-Castro underground or the Bay of Pigs invasion—in Miami a distinction greater than money or success. Plus, they were spending their adulthood and raising their children in what was to them still a foreign country.

The western suburbs were also populated by all sorts of Americans during those years. Again, not possessing the knowledge or sophistication to distinguish between Americans of different regions or ethnic backgrounds, Cubans saw them all as simply "*americanos.*" However, the class and educational differences among them were easily discerned. There were those of more middle-class, educated backgrounds, and those of more humble, blue-collar roots. Likewise, although less prevalent in the more upscale suburbs, there did exist a "redneck" element (which does not necessarily mean they were Southern): what someone in the older generation might have referred to as an *americano chusma* and what an English-speaker might have labeled "white trash."

Whatever bigotry we experienced during those years was usually from, although definitely not limited to, Americans of the *chusma* variety. Employing phrases such as "f—ing Cubans," "God-damned Spics," or "Go back to Cuba," this group was seriously intimidated. They were surrounded by what they regarded as a bunch of foreign, pushy, ambitious, Spanish-speaking families who were shoving past them on the economic ladder, despite the fact that they had been desperate refugees only a decade earlier. Many people today remember the bumper stickers that read: "Would the last American leaving Miami please bring the flag?" This slogan seemed ironic to us because, as mentioned earlier, our sense of American patriotism was quite high. In fact, some Cubans responded with bumper stickers that read: "Don't worry, the flag will still be flying when you return." Yet, what we were ignorant of was the phenomenon of nativism and its proponents' blending of patriotism and national identity with ethno-cultural orientation. In other words, for them, possessing any foreign characteristics—and, worse, not being ashamed of them—was fundamentally antipatriotic and un-American.

This is not to say that Cubans in the western suburbs—or anywhere else, for that matter—were somehow impacted or intimidated by the resentment some Americans felt. Although it certainly was not pleasant, especially if someone you loved was involved in an incident in which he or she was treated with disrespect, there was really little of which to be afraid. Despite the views of bigoted neighbors, they were in no position—economically or otherwise—to do us any harm. Needless to say, a derogatory comment would rarely go unanswered.

In spite of those cruder elements we encountered, most Americans with whom we shared our schools and neighborhoods were kind and decent people, regardless of their social backgrounds and political views. In general, we were never made to feel like second-class citizens—or our parents like unwanted intruders—by most Americans. Then, again, we probably would not have let them.

By the time our generation reached adolescence, a definite social network of Cuban American youths had developed in the western suburbs. The network was really an endless chain of interconnected cliques, further divided into individual peer groups, which evolved and changed throughout high school and college. As more ABCs in Miami reached adolescence throughout the period during and after the mid- to late 1970s, the network expanded. Although rivalries existed among the various cliques and peer groups—as well as great differences in income, the types of social functions in which one participated, and other differences that usually divide young people—there were certain consistencies that provided the basis for a genuine network. Those consistencies, which paralleled the characteristics that tied their families together, gave rise to a unique youth culture among middle-class Cuban American youths in the western suburbs.

A number of institutions also tied the network together. Certain clubs, neighborhoods, and family familiarity were certainly important in bringing together some cliques. Yet one's school, especially high school, was even more important. The vast majority of these cliques were centered in the area's parochial schools and Catholic high schools, as well as other private academies in the area. A few in the network attended local public schools. However, the greatest distinction was the possession of certain attributes and characteristics that not only made the group different from non-Cuban Americans but that, in fact, made it different from many other Cuban American youths. It was also important that there were many middle-class American youths who were part of the general social scene.

Although in the present project it is impossible to offer a detailed summary of the cultural norms and social life of the particular branch of Cuban American youth culture around which I was brought up, suffice it to say it was a peculiar realm. Made up of a mixture containing one part middle-class Cuban mores inherited from parents and one part middle-class Americanism as introduced in school and elsewhere, it was a world with its own idiosyncrasies, dialects, styles, and varieties too complex to describe in the present context. It began when the first generation of ABCs came of age in the mid-1970s and continues to this day—although it is more likely that today's youths have parents who spent a good part of their own childhoods in the United States.

THE IMPACT OF POST-1980 HISPANIC MIAMI AND ADULTHOOD
It wasn't until I began community college in the fall of 1984 that I noticed how immeasurably Miami had changed since my childhood. Perhaps twelve years in Catholic school had secluded me a bit, or perhaps I had just been too busy to notice. Whatever the case, the Mariel Boatlift of 1980 (the first major wave of immigration from Cuba since the end of the Freedom flights) had brought in 125,000 new Cubans to the United States, most of whom settled in Miami. Subsequent waves of Cuban refugees followed over the next two decades. Also, the Sandinista Revolution brought thousands of Nicaraguan families to Miami. Beyond that, people from all parts of Latin America began de-

scending on the area in a massive wave of immigration that continues to the present day. In the blink of an eye, Miami had gone from being essentially an Anglo city containing several hundred thousand Cubans who had immigrated during the 1960s, to a largely Hispanic city in which the 1960s Cubans—who had been such oddballs only a few years earlier—were suddenly, in many areas, among the most "American" families on the block.

This was also a time when many Cuban professionals came into their own. Although there were always successful Cubans, the group who had come during the 1960s as young adults with the youth and energy to continue their studies for the professions or to establish successful business enterprises was truly breaking through. Hot on their heels—and in time even more successful—was the generation who had come from Cuba as children during the 1960s (sometimes referred to as "YUCAS", in response to the American "yuppie"; the letters stood for Young Urban Cuban Americans, but when pronounced, the name sounds the same as a popular root-grown vegetable common in the Cuban diet). Thanks to these groups' business penetration of Latin America, their business savvy, and their own Latin roots, they rose to the highest levels in banking, trade, commerce, academia, and politics in the area. As their status and wealth grew, an increasing number of Cubans (by no means representing a majority) began populating the more exclusive areas in the western suburbs and the more upscale parts of Miami. When one ponders that this was accomplished by the generation who came as immigrants (many already adults) and did not have to labor in factories while pinning their hopes on the second generation, it is truly astounding.

The impact of all these changes on my generation was profound. The new immigration from Cuba and the rest of Latin America diverted our quick march toward Anglo American assimilation. For the first time in our lives, many of us came face-to-face with people our own age who primarily spoke Spanish and struggled with English. For me, as well as many others, this was strange, since Spanish, until then, was something spoken exclusively to older people upon whom one could count to understand "Spanglish."

Strange as this was, these developments were a great benefit to us, for they exposed us to a level of Hispanicism we would probably not have experienced otherwise. Many ABCs have discovered that being bicultural provides a distinct economic advantage; as a result, many have gradually reclaimed their roots. While feeling no less American, we suddenly became interested, in one form or another, in who we were and from whence we came.

As a result of all this, the Spanish of many ABCs in Miami struggled past "Spanglish." Speaking Spanish as adults in board rooms with clients and, as in the case of my brother and me, to those we interviewed as journalists or scholars, we became conscious of the enormous favor our parents had done for us. That we are coming of age as middle-class, bilingual, bicultural, college-educated Americans at a time when the United States is becoming increasingly Hispanic seems like impossibly good timing. As a result, many of us today are in a desperate struggle to teach Spanish to our own children.

Besides language, many ABCs have rediscovered things like Cuban food and music as adults. That Latin food and culture have become chic as of late caught many by surprise. I find it interesting that people from other parts of the country regard a night at a Cuban restaurant—whether it is a trendy place on South Beach or a mom 'n' pop joint in Hialeah—as an exotic experience. I also get a kick out of seeing German tourists cut a rug to Latin music. In Miami, as well as other parts of the United States, these things have gone from local ethnic peculiarities to high culture.

A few ABCs have even directly involved themselves in their parents' anti-Castro political crusade. I have a few friends who, although American-born, have joined certain exile political groups and have become regulars at anti-Castro rallies. Some are actually even quite militant. Also, following the example set by some YUCAs, a handful of ABCs have moved into the older neighborhoods near Little Havana, which their parents left when they went to the western suburbs—the result of this gentrification has been a revitalization of those areas and skyrocketing real estate values.

At any rate, the social network has expanded. No longer limited to particular geographic areas or institutions, many of us identify more readily with the broader world of Cuban Americans who came of age between the mid-1970s and the 1990s. American-Bred Cubans from different parts of Miami and, in fact, the country, have connected socially and are bound more by shared notions of being Cuban American than the peculiarities that marked certain neighborhoods or schools, regardless of age or background.

Since early adulthood, I have spent most of my time away from Miami and have been immersed in other cultures—ranging from central Italy to the deep South, and currently southern New England. If I have learned anything, it is that the familiarity one feels among people of one's own community is a powerful thing, especially when one is an adult raising children. True community, moreover, is something that could be neither imposed nor invented at will. Geography, culture, and ties to a similar past are the ingredients of community—and community is the stuff of life. A prolonged detachment from the community at a certain age is necessary when one seeks to discover new worlds. For a time, this is even desirable, since the world is indeed an exciting place. However, one's soul remains with one's community; and that soul ultimately draws the individual home.

Perhaps this is why the older generation of Cubans—especially those who came during middle age or as elderly people—tend not to romanticize their experience as immigrants or exiles. To them, a tragedy had occurred from which neither romance nor the warm glow of nostalgia could be extracted. They idealize the Cuba of old, and their souls inevitably continue to dwell there, even though it has been irretrievably lost. I am lucky—my soul is in the community the older generation created in the United States. I could answer its beck and call at will.

Appropriated Memories
A Conversation with Alberto Rey

Although his family is from Agramonte, Cuba, Alberto Rey was born in Havana in 1960. He left the Island in 1963, first traveling to Mexico and then on to the U.S. in 1965. He lives in Fredonia, New York, with his wife and daughter.

The artwork of Alberto Rey functions for him as a way to investigate, interpret, and preserve his own personal cultural identity. What is distinct about his exploration is the fact that up until his recent trip to

Cuba in July of 1998, his memories of Cuba were vicarious or, in his words, "appropriated."

From the very outset of the revolution, Rey's father (Enrique) actively worked against fidel Castro. As a result he, along with most of the other men in his town, was imprisoned for a week after the Bay of Pigs. "There were regular raids in our town," Alberto tells me, "individuals were gathered together at night and either imprisoned or shot." As a result, Mr. Rey left the Island in 1962 ahead of his family and sought political asylum in Mexico; he arrived with nothing more than the clothes on his back. After a year, he saved enough money to send for his family. "When the time came for her to leave Cuba," Rey adds, "my mother didn't want to leave her homeland and her family. My grandmother was the one who convinced her that she had to follow her husband."

In 1963, the Rey family immigrated to the United States. "My earliest memory," Alberto recalls, "was being on the bus between Brownsville, Texas, and Miami and watching my mother cry for most of the trip. She had just found out that her younger brother, who was a political prisoner, had died in prison." In Miami, his mother (Olga Guerra) worked at home as a seamstress doing piece work for a factory, and at one point she spun thread over the ferrules on fishing rods. Though his father had a doctorate in mathematics and was a school superintendent in Havana, his degree and work experience were not recognized in the U.S.; as a result, he worked at a sugar refinery in the Everglades, then took a job as a mechanic for an airline, and later ended up building fiberglass boats.

A year after their arrival in Miami, Rey's father was selected for a special program in North Jersey to certify teachers who had taught in Cuba. Separated from his family once again, Mr. Rey completed the program and took the first job that he could find. As a result, in 1965 the Reys relocated to Barnesboro, Pennsylvania, where Alberto spent the remainder of his childhood and young adulthood. Though they spoke little English and were culturally isolated from other Cubans, in Barnesboro the Reys became part of a majority of people struggling to survive. Nevertheless, once they saved enough money to get a car (after five years of living in Barnesboro), they would regularly drive over fifty miles to visit the only other Cuban family in the area. "In exile," Rey comments, "all Cubans are family; these people were like relatives to us."

Prompted, in part, by the death of his grandmother and several conversations with his parents, Rey's exploration into his own cultural identity began while he was in graduate school. Rey recalls one particular evening several years later when he listened to his parents talk for the first time about their experiences as exiles living in the United States. Following that conversation, Rey experienced what he describes as an intense feeling of alienation. These combined events sparked a personal aesthetic exploration of an "inaccessible" past and culture, which he had previously rejected as a teenager, through images that are at once personal and universal.

Though he, like scores of Cuban Americans, had no first-hand memories of Cuba, Rey gradually became aware of the fact that his identity was shaped not only by his cultural heritage and by the events of the revolution, but by his life in the United States. Though he was acutely aware of his temporal and spatial "alienation" from Cuba, and his role as an inside/outside observer, his works are "autobiographical statements," which function as vehicles through which he can research and define his ties to his family and his culture and, ultimately, establish some "perspective" on his life. In his attempt to negotiate this ambiguous cultural space and identity, Rey creates his work within what I call the vacuum left in the wake of an inherited or vicarious diasporic condition.

Rey's exploration, which to date culminates in his return visit to Cuba, follows a trajectory that traces specific stages of the artist's attempt to balance his current life with his cultural past. Providing a kind of bird's-eye view of his various and sometimes competing cultural perspectives, his early paintings possess a "map-like" quality that represents the "aerial view" or "vantage point" from which he attempted to assimilate his own and his family's various responses to the experience of exile. For example, in an abstract painting entitled *Looking for Home* Rey collapses the distance between Cuba, Mexico, Miami, and his home in western Pennsylvania by depicting all of these places on a single canvas. Gradually, however, Rey sought to create compositions other than those that were flat and two-dimensional in order to include more symbolism or "narrative" in his paintings; his *Binary Forms* series, therefore, began as a way to incorporate several themes together in a single composition through the representation of more abstract, or "less identifiable" and spatially ambiguous, objects. In essence, abstraction allowed him to combine multiple symbols, while still portraying a minimalist aesthetic.

For Rey, the movement from realistic layering to abstract images more directly represents the elusive nature of memory and, more fundamentally, the difficulty of translating into realistic objective form emotion and experience. As he himself has observed, the overlapping images, which appear in diffused layers, attempt to portray the layering of thoughts in our memories. Moreover, these abstract images function as metaphors that contain multiple and conflicting meanings that express his feelings toward Hispanic/Latino culture, specifically in relation to religion and spirituality. In more general terms, however, they represent the romance, innocence, and sense of the unobtainable that is an aspect of vicarious and actual memory.*

From 1992 to 1995, Rey simultaneously worked on several series, including the *Icon Series* and the *Madonnas in Time*. The works in the *Icon Series* depict everyday objects that would be familiar to most Cubans but unfamiliar or abstract in their connotations to an outside audience. In effect, these paintings create two very distinct sets of aesthetics, for they suggest the difficult task presented to the artist, who is at once an insider and an outsider, of portraying his personal exploration to an audience that is outside of his culture. Like writers such as Laura Esquivel (Mexico), Rey began depicting familiar culinary dishes and typical Cuban foods, such as the painting *Ancel Guava* (FIGURE 13), suggesting his recognition of the integral function of food in preserving and transmitting culture, memory, and tradition.† Cultures, he claims, are best defined by everyday objects; paradoxically, however, these objects simultaneously highlight the differences and the common ground between the artist and his audience (all people have the experience of eating, for example; however, they do not all eat the same foods).

The *Madonnas in Time* series expresses what Rey believed at the time to be the apolitical nature of his artwork. Rather than attempting to position himself within any political arena or location, he insists that his work simply represents his attempt to reconnect with his cultural past in order to make sense of his present reality. Furthermore, these paintings reflect his attempt to fill a kind of inner void or vacuum; in his own words, politics tend to "contaminate the purity of the quest." In this series Rey juxtaposes images derived from archival photographs of Cuba taken between the 1890s and the 1920s with scenes from western New York, where he currently resides. He states,

The significance of the images dating from the turn of the century through the 1920s is important to me because they seem to lose a great deal of their political baggage. . . . Due to my departure from the Island at an early age, I have experienced Cuba almost entirely second-hand and only then in a very turbulent political atmosphere. It has always been difficult for me to discover the importance of this country, due to the political complexities that have always seemed to cloud any image or story that has occurred in my lifetime. I wanted to find a connection to this country in the purest manner, without people or politics. I wanted to get immersed in the country's land-scape. I needed to find images of Cuba that were politically neutral to me in order to feel more connected, more educated, more fulfilled.

The tropical landscapes that he renders in the *Madonnas in Time* series, such as *Niagara Falls/Isla de Pinos* (FIGURE 14), are set in abstract contexts and painted in black and white in order to suggest their separateness from his current life; whereas the scenes from his immediate environ-ment, despite their quasi-iconographic connotations, are painted in color and set in religious-like inserts, which reference Mexican folk art, in order to bring the unattainable or irretrievable past into relation with his present-day experience.[‡] In addition to being endowed with per-sonal meaning, *Niagara Falls/Isla de Pinos* is embedded with multiple meanings that link it to a long history of exile. On one hand, this paint-ing represents the timeless landscape of the Island, replete with Royal Palms; although this is not what Rey had envisioned when he created the work, this particular setting is a painful reminder of the contempo-rary Cuban's exilic condition, for the Isla de los Pinos housed one of Castro's most notorious prisons. In the same vein, the image of Niagara Falls functions as a kind of iconographic emblem of the pristine and sublime beauty of the United States and, at the same time, is linked to the classic ode written in exile by the Cuban Romantic poet José María Heredia, "*Niágara*" (1824), a poem that protests Spanish colonial rule.

The final series of works painted prior to Rey's return to the Island are entitled *Las Balsas* and the *Appropriated Memories* series, respectively. Inspired by Rey's 1996 trip to the Cuban Refugee Center in Key West, which currently serves as a temporary housing location for Cuban immigrants and contains a small collection of rafts and materials used by the *balseros* (rafters), the paintings in the *Las Balsas* series function as visual metaphors. Mounted in austere black, coffin-like boxes, which Rey describes as minimal altar pieces that are suggestive of "silence" and "isolation," they are moving testimonies not only to the thousands of Cubans who have fled the Island, but to Rey's own grandmother, who was also lost during one of these passages. Like the rafts housed in the refugee center, they are silent monuments to an ongoing human tragedy. The paintings in the *Appropriated Memories* series are, on the other hand, mimetic representations of familiar landscapes and scenes in Cuba. Rey realistically reproduces loosely parallel images, such as the Morro Castle, in order to "connect" with places that he recognizes but had not, until recently, seen. As he painted these large black-and-white landscapes, which seemed to capture his previous interest in minimal aesthetics, he felt as though he were walking through Cuba with each brushstroke. (March 1997)

In July of 1998, Alberto Rey made the decision to return to Cuba after a thirty-six-year absence. In his own words, the experience was completely different from what he had envisioned—"it was like traveling to a place caught in time, a place that didn't even seem to belong to the people living there." More shocking, however, was the realization that there was a much different connection between the physical island and the place he had vicariously envisioned through photographs and stories. In addition to feeling somewhat infantilized (a result, perhaps, of the fact that his family members only remembered him as a toddler), his sense of alienation and difference was increased by the fact that his grandmother was embarrassed by their poverty and the conditions in which they were living. Moreover, though Rey had previously claimed that his work was apolitical, he returned to the States convinced of the impossibility of ever again creating politically neutral work when it came to representing anything connected to the Island.

During the course of our conversation, it was visibly difficult for Rey to express what he had seen; the trauma of witnessing the suffering of his own family members who remained on the Island, coupled with the oppressive atmosphere and what he described as an almost irrational fear of being detained in Cuba and permanently separated from his wife and newborn daughter, were almost overwhelming. Though the differences between himself and those who remained on the Island were put into relief during the course of his visit, ultimately, he admits, he felt at ease and comforted in the presence of his family. In his own words, he has already begun to "sink back into the state of nostalgia" that characterizes his earlier work—a nostalgia, he adds, that many Cubans living on the Island continue to nurture and preserve. "At the very least," he tells me, "this trip has opened my eyes and matured my vision. It has enabled me to better appreciate the choices my parents had to make and the consequent losses and separations that they endured." Ultimately, Rey tells me, he feels more whole, though he was humbled by the realization of the intensity of others' suffering.

Although the long-term effects of Rey's trip to Cuba have yet to be seen in his artwork, his immediate response has already begun to manifest itself in the new additions to the ongoing series of portraits that he has begun to paint of people, including his own family members, whom he met in Cuba, and of exiles living in the United States. In effect, these portraits, which aim to represent actual people, visually bridge the gap between the imagined Cuba that he attempted to recuperate and reconstruct prior to his return journey and the actual place that he has finally seen with his own eyes. One can see at a glance that these human faces, like the pristine landscape of his earlier work, capture a kind of fundamental and timeless aspect of Cuban identity—of the Cuban spirit—that no regime can efface.

Like many of his contemporaries, Rey's art represents his ongoing effort to fuse together both the past and the present, albeit in a precarious balance, with the complexities and paradoxes of contemporary life. Although his work is largely autobiographical, ultimately it transcends the personal by portraying the experience of a generation of spiritual and emotional exiles—people who are caught between cultures and, as a result, are struggling to reconcile their present lives in the United States with a haunting past and an untenable present that simultaneously contain both ephemeral and enduring aspects that continue to shape their cultural identities. (March 1997, September 1998)

(Interviews conducted by Andrea O'Reilly Herrera)

All quotations and paraphrasing are taken either from personal interviews or from "Artist's Statements" that Alberto Rey composed to accompany exhibitions of his paintings.

★ The "Incongruence of Memory" (the title of Rey's 1995 exhibit at the Castellani Art Museum at Niagara University) is, perhaps, best represented in the artist's painting *Miami, Florida, 1965* (not shown), in which he layers a "corrected" image of his childhood home in Miami (based on a photograph) with his recollected image of the house.

† Perhaps alluding to the much-debated relationship between art and life, Rey often displays the actual objects or "icons" on a shelf that hangs next to the paintings. *Ancel Guava* is in the permanent collection of the Museum of Art in Fort Lauderdale, Florida.

‡ Much like the Mexican artist Frida Kahlo, Rey was inspired by Mexican retablo painting—devotional paintings offered in thanks for individuals who were assisted through the intercession of some saint or Virgin—during a trip to Mexico in 1988.

Inheriting Exile

Margarita Engle

Born in 1951 and raised in Los Angeles, Margarita Engle is the daughter of a Cuban mother and an American father. She currently resides in Clovis, California.

My mother was born in the central Cuban town of Trinidad, a picturesque anachronism of cobblestone streets and exquisite colonial architecture. My father, an artist from Los Angeles, traveled to Trinidad after seeing pictures of Cuba in the January 1947 issue of *National Geographic*.

My parents did not speak the same language when they met and fell in love. In fact, in a sense they did not even occupy the same century. My father had just survived several years as a merchant seaman during World War II. My mother was still cloistered in a romantic eighteenth-century realm, where *pregoneros* sold fruit by singing its praises; old men took their caged songbirds out for walks on quiet evenings; and single women could not be courted unless a vigilant maiden aunt or widowed *viejita* served as a chaperone. Nevertheless, love at first sight prevailed. My mother married my father and moved to Los Angeles. Deeply in love, but also homesick and wistful, she re-created her childhood world by listening to Cuban music and telling stories.

I was born in Pasadena in 1951 and grew up listening to romantic *boleros* and hearing family legends. I absorbed the rhythms of *son montuno* and, simultaneously, the frightening tales of sharks in the Río Manatí and moray eels lurking in coral reefs of enchanting beaches. Terrified, I braced myself against hurricane winds that could, according to my mother, turn palm fronds into flying swords. Molded by images of the Island, I gradually learned the long, mellifluous Spanish names of relatives I'd met during a visit to Cuba in 1953, while I was still too young to understand and remember. Fragments of the intriguing secrets of each branch of my mother's enormous extended family eventually became indistinguishable from daily reality. Cuba became just as real as any other childhood fairy tale, a safe place to hide and dream.

My mother's nostalgia had brought marvelous Cuban music into our house, via records sent as gifts by the relatives left behind, my grandfather and my uncle. Then, during the late 1950s, the lovely *sones* and romantic *boleros* were abruptly replaced by revolutionary marches and martial chants of "*¡Cuba sí, Yanqui no!*" Within a few months, my perceptions of the Island as a magical kingdom would be confirmed. My mother had decided to visit her relatives "before it was too late."

During the summer of 1960, I finally met all the relatives my mother had told me about. I received a hearty welcome from a population that seemed to consist entirely of grandmothers, aunts, uncles, and uniformed *barbudo* cousins, handsome young members of Castro's triumphant army. I understood that in a sense I was the dreaded *Yanqui*, northerner, enemy; but I was also half Cuban, and as such, I was made to feel at home. In fact, I felt more at home in Cuba than I ever had in Los Angeles. In Cuba, I had the chance to spend several months in the semirural outskirts of Havana, and in the placid, slow-moving town of Trinidad, and on my great-uncle's lush, green tropical farm at the foot of the Escambray Mountains.

I learned a great deal about myself that summer. I learned that I was more of a *guajira* than a city-dweller and discovered that I had an innate passion for farm life. Riding horses, climbing fruit trees, chopping weeds, rounding up cattle, and harvesting sugar cane made more sense to me than the urban lifestyle I'd experienced in Los Angeles—a dull, gray, smoggy place where I'd always felt alienated and isolated. I left Cuba determined to come back and determined to live the way my great-uncle did, surrounded by wilderness and family.

The rest, of course, is history. After the Bay of Pigs invasion and the

Missile Crisis, Cuba became a floating island. It disappeared from the maps of North American travelers, and my mother's extended family vanished in its wake. Walking on the moon became a more realistic goal than visiting my grandmother. My passport prohibited journeys to the only place where I'd ever felt a sense of belonging.

At school, people asked if I was Mexican. When I answered, "No, half Cuban," they looked at me with horrified grimaces, pitying me because Cuba was now regarded as the devil's territory. It was as if the paradise of tropical pastures and flamboyant blue skies I remembered so clearly had been dreamed instead of experienced. Once again, I became an emotional exile. I now felt incapable of ever belonging anywhere.

My next visit to the Island came three decades later, after a series of absurd and futile attempts to obtain permission from both the U.S. and Cuba. Trained as an agronomist and botanist, as well as a writer, I had finally been granted a journalist's permit from the U.S. Treasury Department. It was, in effect, an exemption from the Trading with the Enemy Act. Suddenly, I was free to travel to Cuba. I planned to write objective editorial columns about agricultural projects. At that point, I regarded myself as being open minded. I truly did not know what to expect. Would I find the relatives I hadn't seen for more than thirty years contented and satisfied? Had they adjusted to life under the communist regime? Was Cuba still, as I'd always imagined when I was little, some sort of utopia?

Between 1991 and 1997 I visited the Island five times. Instead of utopia, I discovered anguish. Over and over, I was confronted by the appalling loss of personal liberties that had been endured by disillusioned revolutionaries, who now dreamed of nothing but escape. Everyone I met wanted to leave. My mother's relatives welcomed me with open arms and whispered horror stories. I found myself writing about spiritual dilemmas and human rights issues instead of crop production.

In Cuba, such dramatic events had occurred that I couldn't ignore them. Objectivity became impossible. I felt compelled to write fiction instead of journalism, in order to protect the identities of all the desperate people who had confided in me. After learning that my great-uncle, the farmer, had been unjustly arrested as a counterrevolutionary sympathizer shortly after my childhood visit in 1960 and had spent his remaining years suffering in political prisons and forced labor camps, I wrote *Singing to Cuba*, a lyrical, hopeful novel about central Cuba's brutally "relocated" peasants, known on the Island as *el pueblo cautivo*, the "captive towns." Later, after a heartbreaking yet inspiring firsthand encounter with my cousins, who tried to leave Cuba on a raft while I was in their home, I wrote *Skywriting*.

Once again, Cuba had become home; in an odd sense, it was the place where I belonged. I no longer wanted to live there, but I had, inadvertently, become a witness. I felt obliged to try to speak, no matter how humbly, for those who had no voice. And yet, at the same time, the fictional characters and fictionalized family histories I was creating were profoundly apolitical. I was exploring my own emotional landscape, my own childhood yearnings; it was my own highly personal discovery of the contrast between the idealized homelands of exiles and the imperfect ones offered by reality. I was, in other words, returning to the enchanted realm I'd inherited along with my mother's nostalgia.

Un testimonio
FROM "NO ACCENTS ALLOWED"

Cecilia Rodríguez Milanés

The daughter of Cuban parents, Cecilia Rodríguez Milanés was born in Jersey City, New Jersey, in 1960. She currently resides in Orlando, Florida.

. . . Back in blue-collar Bayonne, New Jersey, in the 1960s and '70s, everyone was ethnic. Next door and around the block, people still spoke Italian or Polish at home; many spoke Spanish—dominicanos, puertorriqueños, cubanos, and españoles. Storytelling by elders, my parents, neighbors, and parientes framed my existence. . . .

My parents' Cuba was an island I could not see for myself, a place that never belonged to me, though visions of untamed jungle (manigua), fine powder beaches (Varadero), lush mountains (Sierra Maestra), and endless fields of caña plagued me. I could not confirm any of it, though I could look at some black-and-white photographs that my mother had brought with her to the U.S. in the '50s as a single woman—but I'm getting ahead of myself. No, I had to rely on stories. . . .

In Bayonne, there wasn't any satisfactory term for my kind; North

Americans simply referred to us *all* as "Spanish"—more often it was "Spics". Defined as Spanish, my emerging self had to find some connection to España, but it just wasn't important in my home. Habana, Luyanó, Taguayabon, Formento, these I had heard about. San Juan, Buenos Aires, Santiago, Maricaibo, these were cities that had stories related about them. The problem was exacerbated in that I didn't see anything familiar among the traditionally black-garbed Galician widows and españoles that haunted my neighborhood. My mother dressed in modern clothes and had a shoe fetish, which I inherited. My father did not go to the Spanish American club to drink and play dominoes, though now he plays quite a bit with his compadres in Miami Beach.

Well, I was not Spanish, but was I a Spic? From what I could see, americanos referred to anyone who spoke Spanish and annoyed them as a Spic. Well, I probably was a Spic, but I sure didn't like the way it sounded. This name-calling did not affect me too much because I was used to hearing the dozens, jump rope cadences, the snappy reply or get left in the gutter street talk. . . .

And then my family moved to Florida in 1974. Up until then ethnicity and class were just not prominent in my life. I was enrolled in a predominantly white and upper-middle-class public high school in a Miami suburb. All of a sudden I was a different version of "Spanish"—actually, my Cubanness (this was important in Miami) became noticeable to all, especially me. I began to see, more fully, what the "others" saw when they saw me. My individuality was gone, and suddenly I was invisible. Painfully, I learned much about the differences between Miami Cubans and other Cubans. At one point in my life I made a decision to call myself a woman of color, a Latina.

Latina is the correct Spanish, appropriate signifier for who I am. Calling myself a Latina is an act of rebellion from the mother country, from imperialism in general. Hispanic, for me and many others, connotes colonialism. Saying I'm Hispanic doesn't speak of my experience; it doesn't say I'm exiled; it doesn't tell anyone where I'm from. It does say that somewhere in my genealogy, my people were colonized and colonizers. My connection to the mother country is one other imperialists have forced on me: "You're Spanish, aren't you?" And "Yes" would have been forthcoming and unquestioned from a younger, more innocent self. . . . No one has ever asked me if I was from the Dominican

Republic or a Chicana. I am too light-skinned; many North Americans would allow me to "pass" for Italian, especially when I lived in a small western Pennsylvania town with no Latino natives. When I speak to my daughter, I use the mother tongue, not the Spanglish in which my partner and I are most comfortable, because I want her to hear "correct" Spanish; and as I write these words I cringe. Am I colonizing her? In Miami, where she was born and where all of her large extended family lives, I didn't need to make this effort; bilingualism is the norm. There are several Spanish-language television channels, numerous choices for Spanish or Creole or English radio programming. Her grandparents can sing her the songs I'm only learning now—acculturation requires immense concentration on English, and my parents had no time to teach me décimas or lullabies. . . .

But when I was little, I memorized all the names my parents could remember and reclaim. Cecilia Rodríguez Gaston Coto Ostolaza Chávez Hernández. But there was no way I could own all those names, never mind having accents over letters in one name; so my parents never told me there was an accent in Rodríguez. I found out through a Costa Rican friend, who assured me he was right because he, too, had a Rodríguez in his name.

Stories of exile and dispossession are routine for my people. For a while I was sick of them, sick of diaspora and the familylessness I had in my cells. Over there, across an ocean more tangible than any border, was mi familia. No abuela, no primos, no tías here—what could I do but invent them? I became a liar first and later a writer. I lied about my parents' friends, making them instant relatives, uncles and aunts and their children cousins! Anytime we spent more than a day with anyone, they were candidates for family. All the gaps in my life I filled with stories that could be probable—not fabulous, though I was capable of inventing some incredible stuff. . . . I just wanted to know who my family was, what they were like, who I looked like.

I lied about myself, my home, my name. Stuck with Rodriguez (no accent), I had to spice it up somehow. If I couldn't have any other last names, I could take a middle name—many of my friends had them. I took one at the time of my confirmation in the Roman Catholic Church—I chose a name that sounded elegant, French, sophisticated—Yvonne. When I thought about being a writer, I considered using my mother's maiden name along with Yvonne to have a fancier nom de plume—Yvonne Gaston, definitely not Latina.

I lied to fill in the gaps of the stories I didn't hear, wasn't privy to, stories I'm only hearing lately, due to the arrival of a few blood relatives from Cuba since 1979–1980 and my recent trip to Cuba. My history, personal and political, has been greatly enhanced. Now I hear more stories about Cuba, a different place than that of which my parents spoke; my family names are taking on new meaning, but I still haven't given up my old habit of lying. . . .

The Grand finale

Gabriel Rodríguez

Born in Secaucus, New Jersey, in 1984, "Don Gabe" (the nom de plume of Gabriel Rodríguez) now lives in Tenafly, New Jersey, with his mother, Lourdes Gil.

Alone she floats, surrounded by water and fully isolated from the rest of the world. From the Cabo de San Antonio to la Punta de Maisi, she has been stripped of everything she fought for. As a result, I have been born and raised here. I'm as American as the next kid and show no signs of being Hispanic, except for my name. I myself have never experienced any prejudice, and the whole issue is really no skin off my nose. But every time I hear about the raft problem in Cuba, about ethnic jokes meant for Boricuas but directed towards all Hispanics, I feel a sense of pride that I thought was lost.

And so this testimonial is for all the land that Castro has taken from us; for all the dignity that Americans have taken from us because they are too ignorant—too ignorant to be able to tell the difference between the Boricuas, who were displaced in the '40s and '50s for economic reasons; the Cubans who migrated here in the '60s for political reasons; and the Mexicans who have been here forever. We're all the same to them.

I can see myself winning an Oscar and giving my acceptance speech thanking Martí and only seeing blank faces of no recognition in the audience. And so, Sr. Martí, I pray to you and the Cuba you brought forth from the Cabo de San Antonio to la Punta de Maisi, a space between which I have never known. I pray to you, José, for *Cuba libre*. I am now in America typing this at the computer next to a beautiful lady whom I could never find in Cuba; but if Castro hadn't come to power, I could be in Cuba right now typing at a computer next to a beautiful lady whom I could never find here.

Like I said, it's really no skin off my nose, but for Martí, I pray. For my mother and all the kids who came during Operation Peter Pan, I pray. And for my cousin Humbertico, who's still in Cuba now, I pray.

Memoirs of a Tampeña

Maura Barrios

> *Born in 1949, Maura Barrios is a native of Tampa, Florida, where she currently resides with her son. She is the granddaughter of Cuban cigar makers.*

My family has been leaving Cuba for more than one hundred years. According to my grandmother, our exile began in the 1870s when my great-great-grandfather, José Alvarez, encountered a Spaniard who said, "All of the women of Cuba are whores." José responded by hitting the Spaniard on the head with a kerosene lamp. He and his wife and nine children had to leave Cuba that night in a rowboat that landed in Cayo Hueso. This was at the height of the Ten Years War, the Cubans' failed attempt to gain independence from Spain. He left Cuba in order to live on.

My grandmother was a very patriotic *cubana*, so she may have invented this story. I've heard other versions from the Alvarez clan. Some of them insist that José was a Spaniard! But I like her version. I have had a constant desire to get my own history straight. This may be particularly difficult for exiles. Our histories are rewritten or forgotten to adjust to new worlds.

My great-grandmother, Juana Alvarez, was married to a cigar maker and moved between Key West and Cuba. The cigar industry later moved to Tampa in 1886. Juana's generation shaped and defined the *tabaquero-cubano* communities of Key West and Tampa. They transplanted their Cuban culture to the Florida swampland of the nineteenth century. They built cigar-maker cottages around the *fábricas de tabaco* (factories) and exquisite buildings to house their social clubs, like Céspedes Hall in West Tampa and Círculo Cubano in Ybor City. They organized several mutual aid societies and the first union in florida (La Resistencia). They spoke Spanish and rarely changed their citizenship. They paid *lectores* to read newspapers and novels to them each day while they rolled the "famous" Havana cigars. They invited José Martí to Tampa, where he established the Cuban Revolutionary Party. They financed the Cuban independence movement by sacrificing one day of pay each week for the cause of *Cuba libre*. The Vanguard of José Martí! We *tampeños* have a particular pride in our ancestors' role in Cuban history. However, our Tampa history also includes Teddy Roosevelt and the Rough Riders camping here before departing for Cuba in 1898. I had to search beyond the high-school history books to discover my pride in the ancestors. The cultural-historical conflict is present right from the beginning.

By the early 1920s, all of my Cuban grandparents had settled in West Tampa, a cigar factory town in the Deep South. The cigar industry boomed during the roaring era. And the city's whole economy depended on cigars. The "Cigar City." West Tampa was very Cuban. The unincorporated town elected five Cubans as mayors in the early years. The streets are named Habana, Gomez, Matanzas, Martí.

Abuelo Francisco (*el asturiano*) died of TB in 1929; his job was to move tobacco in and out of the cold storage freezer. We romanticize now the golden era of cigar making in Tampa. But the truth is, the *tabaqueros* lived poor lives, and many Cubans died in Tampa, filling the cemeteries. The one in West Tampa is named Colón, of course.

My *habanera* Abuela Pepilla was a stripper (*despalidora*) at the Morgan Cigar Factory. Widowed, she worked all of her life. My memories of her defined Cubanness for me in my childhood: a dignified presence; a clean style (coiffed, powdered, and perfumed); an attitude (proud and self-assured and opinionated).

There is a Cuban *vanidad*—*cubvanidad*. I learn that *we* are the sharpest, wittiest, most generous, most cultured people in the Americas. Did I learn this from my grandmother? Or more from my parents? A shield of self-protection, a defense for the conflicting cultural worlds in which we reside?

My parents were born in Tampa and lived in West Tampa all of their lives. Their generation marked the *tampeño/cubano* transition from immigrant to *americano*: a confused process. They called themselves *cubanos*, though they had never lived in Cuba. At other times they asserted their *americano* birth. They grew up poor during the Depression era. That experience formed their social-democratic ideals, which are consistent with the cigar-maker/José Martí ideals of their parents. After World War II, the cigar industry declined. My parents' world expanded beyond the Cuban/Latin enclave. The encounters with that other southern Anglo world were complex and often filled with conflict. They tell of racism and discrimination toward *cubanos*. They recall a sign that read "No Dogs and No Cubans" at a public park, or was it a beach? They recall that young Cuban American women could not be cheerleaders or majorettes at Hillsborough High School; and they could not hope to get a job at Maas Brothers, the downtown department store. They tried to fit into the American pie-puzzle, negotiating here and there. Did they give up their Cubanness? I don't think so. Did they become *americanisado* or *encracado*? Absolutely yes. They spoke two languages—and mixed them up. "¡Ay, que cute!" They went to see Hollywood movies, and they went to the Casino for Spanish movies. My mother sang on the radio, popular songs from Latin America and popular songs from the U.S. They went to the Círculo Cubano for New Year's Eve, where they played Cuban music on the patio and Big Band *americano* music in the ballroom.

I was born in 1949, following the births of a brother and sister. We lived in a house that my father built—a Cape Cod cottage facing a park in West Tampa. I attended public schools, where most of the students and many of the teachers were Latinos. Television taught us how to behave like *americanos*, and we tried. But the images did not fit with our Cuban bodies, our Cuban souls. Our grandparents lived nearby, so that we would always be reminded—*nosotros somos cubanos!*

I wanted to be pure *americana*. My adolescent rebellion involved rejecting my family's values and culture and making fun of my grandparents' bad English. I did not want to be dark-Cuban-poor. I wanted to be blonde-English-rich. I drove with friends to the wealthy, ordered, quiet Anglo neighborhoods and wished that I could be there, in *that* family. Wouldn't life be easier? No pride in the old *la lucha* (struggle) for me. After four generations in this country, I thought it time to take our rightful place. But I didn't get any invitations.

I learned to work to buy independence from my family/culture during those years. I got a car and went to the university, expanding those Latino-bordered horizons. A shock to learn that most people were not Latino or Cuban, and that they were mostly "middle class." I had to adjust my definition of that term. I had to adjust lots of definitions. I was a rare tropical exotic in a middle-class Anglo university landscape in my own hometown, which I did not really know. And it was 1968. The year of the Great Society and Vietnam and antiwar demonstrations and Black Power.

At age twenty I married the perfect Anglo, Richard Carpenter. A sophisticated New Yorker, he was fascinated by my family and culture in those radical-liberal-hippie days. I lost my identity and my soul in that marriage, which lasted five years. I had to get divorced to find myself—that included my Cubanness again. And to find my Cubanness, I had to reconcile with my family on *their* terms, a process that takes forever and never really works.

I recovered my (Cuban) identity in a gradual process. But first I had to study history in order to feel pride. All of my education had *not* ever mentioned *cubanos* or Latinos in our collective, proud, culturally superior, national *americano* heritage. We/I was invisible in that history—or marginally present: that young woman staring at the comfortable home in that other neighborhood wishing to be someone else. I had to recover the lost memories of my great-grandmother.

During those liberal-radical-hippie times, the Cuban Revolution sparked a sense of pride, especially among Latin Americans with idealist tendencies. The Anti-U.S. Cuban Revolution! What a conflict. My anger for all injustices could conveniently be blamed on the racist-capitalist system of the U.S. I could join the whole Third World and the Chicanos and the Blacks in an angry revolt—a different kind of cry for help, acceptance. A demand to be included! To have voice! Didn't I, the child of the Vanguard of José Martí, have something meaningful to say?

I spent many years wandering, sometimes lost; I even exiled myself to Europe for a time. I traveled around the world and then landed back home in West Tampa. It was the only place where I could raise my child—the place that is family and acceptance and warmth and generosity and lively and humorous and proud and intelligent—¡viva cuvanidad!—I wanted my son to have that too.

Una cubanita pasada por agua

Andrea O'Reilly Herrera

See Section IV for the author's biographical sketch.

> For double the vision my Eyes do see,
> And a double vision is always with me.
> —*William Blake,* Letter to Thomas Butts

> To be sure, the Cuban presence on the North American conti-
> nent is at least as old as the Florida city of St. Augustine, which
> was founded in 1565. But it is one thing to be Cuban in America
> and another to be Cuban American.
> —*Gustavo Pérez Firmat,* Life on the Hyphen

Having been born in Philadelphia [the proverbial *cradle of liberty* as they say] only a skip and a heartbeat after Fulgencio Batista fled a New Year's Eve party in Havana and my mother [who was carrying me at the time and had nearly reached full term] threw herself down upon a Victorian love seat in tears [promptly causing the front right leg of the sofa to give out and, consequently, sending her to the floor] upon learning that the *cidra* that my grandparents had brought from Cuba and my father had saved for a special occasion turned out to be as flat and bitter as vinegar, my earliest childhood experiences are inscribed by the Cuban diaspora and the painful realities of exile. So immersed was I in these realities that I grew up identifying myself first as a Spaniard [my grandmother insisted upon aligning herself with her Iberian ancestors, though she never actu-ally traveled to Spain], and then as a Cuban [calling myself an American never entered my mind]. (After overhearing me tell a Puerto Rican shop-keeper, in Spanish, that I was Cuban, my mother affectionately began referring to me as *una cubanita pasada por agua*—a little Cuban girl "passed" through water.) It wasn't until adulthood that I came to the realization that my social and political consciousness was displaced, as it were, for it had been shaped not nearly as much by the Civil Rights Movement as by the historical events in Cuba, which were discussed every Sunday at my grandparents' house in counterpoint with the stories my relatives recounted (with variations) about a place—a world—none of them would ever re-visit again, except in memory and imagination.

Despite the fact that my mother self-identifies as an American, has no trace of an accent, and rarely spoke directly to us in Spanish, I, unlike most of my siblings and cousins, grew up longing for and dreaming about a world that no longer exists and a physical place I have never seen, except in photographs, but somehow know. As a result, I am confronted with a sense of deep personal loss, which is at once ephemeral and haunting. Over the years, I've tried to locate the source of my longing and discontent. Have I unconsciously acquired what Herbert Gans calls a "symbolic ethnic identity?" I ask myself. Would a day, or even an hour that happened to mark the passage from one year to another, have really made a difference? But where, then, do I begin to explain the fact that even though my mother tongue is English and I was partly weaned on cheese steaks, soft pretzels, TastyKakes, and scrapple, the soft, sing-songy rhythm of Spanish pulses within me like a kind of inner cadence, and I can somehow find continuity between the past and the present in the ritual preparation of a "pie" *de guayaba* or a Catalán *paella* (al Avi)? Perhaps, I tell myself, my response represents some distant ancestral call or echo that manifests itself, as my poem in this volume suggests, in the three generations of Cuban women inhabiting my name and my person (Carmen for my grandmother, Andrea for my great-grandmother, and Teresa for my mother). At the same time, however, the competing and sometimes combative aspects of my cultural identity reveal themselves in my vastly different responses to Irish and Cuban music ("Am I depressed or do I want to dance around the butcher block in the kitchen?" I ask myself, as I select a CD) and the curious juxtaposition of my Christian names with my surname, O'Reilly. Further complicating my life, as one of my contributors has pointed out, is the fact that one of the main thoroughfares in Havana is O'Reilly Street. Alluding, perhaps, to my paternal family's checkered history on the Island, it bears a plaque (which was placed there by the Irish sometime during the eighteenth century) "commemorating" the relationship between the Irish and the Cubans. As a result, when I'm in Miami many of the people whom I meet assume that O'Reilly is a Cuban name, despite the fact that my Philadelphia twang and my physical appearance partially belie this association.

All I know is that the last time I was in Miami Beach sharing a pastrami sandwich with my *tía-abuela* Ada, I felt as though I was in the presence of my grandmother once again. And when in Spain, I am certain that I saw my grandfather walking down a path in the Botanical Gardens across from the Prado—with his pants belted at chest level—leading my grandmother by the elbow. In both places, I was surrounded by tastes and sounds and smells and shadows that confirmed a way of life, a past, that is for me at once cherished and familiar.

Perhaps because I grew up in cultural isolation—in an extended Cuban "family" (consisting of relatives and friends who collectively formed a kind of "Island unto themselves")—the revelation that there were others who shared my nostalgic, vicarious desire for Cuba, coupled with the discovery that not all of us are called into this ambiguous and oftentimes troubling space, crystallized for me a lifetime of "unbelonging" and dislocation. In a word, it prompted in me a kind of creative and intellectual self-exploration (which has culminated in this collection and in a recently published novel) regarding my own relationship, if not to the Island itself, to the idea of Cuba that my mother and my grandparents so lovingly nurtured in me and cultivated over all the years, and regarding a worldview that informed my unconscious life and has nourished my imagination since earliest childhood.

Now, as I think back upon the countless number of conversations I have had with others who have grown up in the margins of this diaspora and pore over the words of those who, as Pablo Medina so aptly puts it, are "exiled by association," I realize that despite the fact that this second-hand exile condition has been for some of us a spur to creativity and creative possibility (and several among us seem to enjoy the freedoms that our gypsy status allows—for like tricksters we can easily cross cultural borders)—for others it is also an endless journey, an unquenchable thirst. In spite of our differences, however, we all seem to be suffering in varying degrees from having been deprived of the opportunity to recall or physically know a world, a civilization that has all but been erased. As a result, we are bound together in the search for a cultural home. In this sense, we are all nomadic wanderers, undergoing a journey that has no final destination—for we are caught up in what Stuart Hall once called in an interview "the enigma of an always postponed 'arrival.'"* The journey, I suppose, *is* the thing in itself.

---

* "The formation of a diasporic intellectual: An interview with Stuart Hall by Kuan-Hsing Chen." In *Critical Dialogues in Cultural Studies*, by Stuart Hall, 490.

Cata's "pie" de guayaba

Hand-mix the following ingredients together: 1 cup flour; 4 tablespoons sugar; 1 stick softened butter; 2 egg yolks; a pinch baking soda; 1 teaspoon vanilla.

Once the ingredients are blended, spread out the dough in a pie pan; knead ¹/₂ of a (large) bar of Ancel Guava paste (see FIGURE 13); and then fill the crust by gently spreading the guava paste with your fingertips. Bake at 325 degrees for approximately 20–25 minutes, or until crust is golden brown.

SELECT BIBLIOGRAPHY

Alegría, Fernando, and Jorge Ruffinelli, eds. *Paradise Lost or Gained? The Literature of Hispanic Exile.* Houston: Arte Público, 1990.

Alvarez-Borland, Isabel. *Cuban-American Literature of Exile: From Person to Persona.* Charlottesville: University of Virginia Press, 1998.

———. "Displacements and Autobiography in Cuban American Fiction." *World Literature Today* 68:1 (1994): 43–49.

Armengol Acierno, María. *The Children of Peter Pan.* Needham, Mass.: Silver Burdett Ginn, 1996.

Azaceta, Luis Cruz. "Dead Rafter II." In *Breaking Barriers: Selections from the Museum of Art's Permanent Contemporary Cuban Collection,* curated by Jorge H. Santis. Ft. Lauderdale, Fla.: Museum of Art of Ft. Lauderdale, 1997.

Barquet, Jesus. *Sin decir el mar.* Madrid: Playor, 1981.

Behar, Ruth. *Bridges To Cuba/Puentes a Cuba.* Ann Arbor: University of Michigan Press, 1995

Bertot, Lillian D. *The Literary Imagination of the Mariel Generation.* Miami: Cuban American National Foundation, 1994.

Bosch, Lynette. "Maria Brito: Metonymy and Metaphor." *Latin American Art* 5:3 (1993): 20–23.

Boswell, Thomas D., and James R. Curtis. *The Cuban-American Experience: Culture, Images and Perspectives.* Totowa, N.J.: Rowman and Allanheld, 1983.

Boza, María del Carmen. *Scattering the Ashes.* Tempe, Ariz.: The Bilingual/Review Press, 1998.

Burunat, Silvia. "A Comparative Study of Contemporary Cuban-American and Cuban Literature." *International Journal of the Sociology of Language* 84 (1990): 101–23.

Cepero, Nilda. *Sugar Cane Blues.* Miami: LS Press, 1997.

———. *Lil' Havana Blues*. Miami: LS Press, 1998.

Clark, Juan M. *The Cuban Exodus: Background, Evaluation, Impact*. Miami: Union of Cubans in Exile, 1977.

Conde, Yvonne. *Operation Peter Pan: The Untold Exodus of 14,000 Cuban Children*. New York: Routledge, 1999.

Cortés, Carlos E., ed. *Cuban Exiles in the United States*. New York: Arno Press, 1980.

———, ed. *The Cuban Experience in the United States*. New York: Arno Press, 1980.

Croucher, Sheila L. *Imagining Miami: Ethnic Politics in a Postmodern World*. Charlottesville: University Press of Virginia, 1997.

Curbelo, Silvia. *The Secret History of Water*. Tallahassee, Fla.: Anhinga Press, 1997.

Didion, Joan. *Miami*. New York: Simon & Schuster, 1987.

Dixon, Heriberto. "The Cuban-American Counterpoint: Black Cubans in the United States." *Dialectical Anthropology* 13 (1988): 227–39.

Dominguez, Jorge. "Cooperating With the Enemy? US Immigration Policies Toward Cuba." In *Western Hemisphere Immigration and United States Foreign Policy*, edited by Mary Anne Johnson and Christopher Mitchell. University Park, Penn.: Penn State University, 1992.

Fernández, Raúl. "Celia Cruz." *Deslinde* 21 (July–September 1997): 103–21.

———. "La magia musical de Cachao." *Huellas* 44 (August 1995): 3–13.

Fuentes-Pérez, Ileana, Graciella Cruz-Taura, and Ricardo Pau-Llosa, eds. *Outside Cuba/Fuera de Cuba: Contemporary Cuban Visual Artists*. New Brunswick: Office of Hispanic Arts, Rutgers University, 1988.

García, María Cristina. *Havana USA*. Berkeley: University of California Press, 1996.

Gil, Lourdes. "Against the Grain: Writing in Spanish in the USA." Pp. 371–375 in *Inventing America: Readings in Identity and Culture*, edited by Gabriella Ibieta and Miles Orvell. New York: Saint Martin's Press, 1996.

Greenbaum, Susan D. "Afro-Cubans in Exile: Tampa, Florida, 1886–1984." *Cuban Studies/Estudios Cubanos* 15 (Winter 1985): 59–72.

Grenier, Guillermo J., and Alex Stepick III *Miami Now! Immigration, Ethnicity, and Social Change*. Gainsville: University Press of Florida, 1992.

Guerra, Felicia, and Tamara Álvarez-Detrell, eds. *Balseros: Oral Histry of the Cuban Exodus of '94*. Miami: Ediciones Universal, 1997.

Guitart, Jorge. *Foreigner's Notebook*. Buffalo, N.Y.: Shuffaloff Books, 1993.

Hall, Stuart. *Critical Dialogues in Cultural Studies*. New York: Routledge, 1996.

———. "Cultural Identity and Diaspora." In *Colonial Discourse and Post-Colonial Theory*, edited by Patrick Williams and Laura Chrisman. New York: Columbia University Press, 1994. Originally published in J. Rutherford,

Ed. *Identity, Community, Culture, Difference* (London: Lawrence and Wishart, 1990): 222–37.

Heyck, Daly Denis, ed. *Barrios and Borderlands: Cultures of Latinos and Latinas in the United States*. New York: Routledge, 1994.

Hoobler, Dorothy and Thomas. *The Cuban American Family Album*. New York: Oxford University Press, 1996.

Hospital, Carolina. "Los hijos del exilio cubano y su literatura." *Explicación de Textos Literarios* 16:2 (1987): 103–14.

———. "What kind of Cuban are you?" *Miami Herald*, 15 June 1997, 10.

Ibieta, Gabriella. "Transcending the Culture of Exile." In *Literature and Exile*, edited by David Bevan, 67–76. Amsterdam: Rodopi, 1990.

Levine, Robert M. *Tropical Diaspora: The Jewish Experience in Cuba*. Gainesville: University Press of Florida, 1993.

Llanes, José. *Cuban Americans: Masters of Survival*. Cambridge, Mass.: Abt Books, 1982.

Masud-Piloto, Felix R. *From Welcomed Exiles to Illegal Immigrants: Cuban Migration to the US, 1959–1995*. Lanham, Md.: Rowman & Littlefield, 1996.

———. *With Open Arms: Cuban Migration to the United States*. Totawa, N.J.: Rowman & Littlefield, 1988.

Medina, Pablo. *Exiled Memories: A Cuban Childhood*. Austin: University of Texas Press, 1990.

———. *The Floating Island*. Buffalo, N.Y.: White Pine Press, 1999.

Menocal, Narisco G. "An Overriding Passion: The Quest for National Identity in Painting." *The Journal of Decorative and Propaganda Arts* 22 (1996): 187–219.

Mozo, Emilio M. *Entre el agua y el pan*. Salamanca, Spain: Universidad Pontificia, 1996.

Olsen, James. *Exiles From the American Dream: First-Person Accounts of Our Disenchanted Youth*. New York: Walker, 1974.

Padilla, Heberto. *El hombre junto al mar*. Barcelona: Seix Barral, 1981.

———. *A Fountain, A House of Stone*. New York: Farrar, Straus, & Giroux, 1991.

Pau-Llosa, Ricardo. *Cuba: Poems*. Pittsburgh: Carnegie Mellon University Press, 1993.

Pedraza-Bailey, Silvia. *Political and Economic Migrants in America: Cubans and Mexicans*. Austin: University of Texas Press, 1985.

Pérez, Lisandro. "Cubans in the United States." *Annals of the American Academy of Political and Social Science* 487 (September 1986): 126–37.

———. "Immigrant Economic Adjustment and Family Organization: The Cuban Success Story Reexamined." *International Migration Review* 20 (Spring 1986): 4–20.

————. "Unique But Not Marginal: Cubans in Exile." In *Cuban Studies Since the Revolution*, edited by Damian Fernández, 258–71. Gainesville: University Press of Florida, 1992.

Pérez, Louis A. "Cubans in Tampa: From Exiles to Immigrants, 1892–1901." *Florida Historical Quarterly* 57 (October 1978): 129–40.

Pérez Firmat, Gustavo. *Life on the Hyphen: The Cuban-American Way*. Austin: University of Texas Press, 1994.

————. *Next Year in Cuba: A Cubano's Coming-of-age in America*. New York: Doubleday, 1995.

Portes, Alejandro, and Alex Stepick. *City on the Edge: The Transformation of Miami*. Berkeley: University of California Press, 1993.

———— and Robert L. Bach. *Latin Journey: Cuban and Mexican Immigrants in the United States*. Berkeley: University of California Press, 1985.

———— and Rubén G. Rumbaut. *Immigrant America: A Portrait*. Berkeley: University of California Press, 1990.

Poyo, Gerald E. *"With All, and For the Good of All": The Emergence of Popular Nationalism in the Cuban Communities of the United States, 1848–1898*. Durham, N.C.: Duke University Press, 1989.

Rieff, David. *The Exile: Cuba in the Heart of Miami*. New York: Simon & Schuster, 1993.

————. *Going to Miami: Exiles, Tourists and Refugees in New America*. Boston: Little, Brown and Company, 1987.

Ripoll, Carlos. *Cubans in the United States*. New York: Eliseo Torres, 1987.

Rivero, Eliana. "Cuban American Writing." In *The Oxford Companion to Women's Writing in the United States*, edited by Cathy Davidson and Linda Wagner, 228–30. New York: Oxford University Press, 1995.

————. "Cubanos y Cubano-Americanos: Perfil y presencia en los Estados Unidos." *Discurso Literario* 7 (1989): 81–01.

————. "From Immigrants to Ethnics: Cuban Women Writers in the US." In *Breaking Boundaries,* edited by Asunción Horno-Delgado, 189–200. Amherst: University of Massachusetts Press, 1989.

Rodríguez, Rocío. "Head and Vessel." In *Breaking Barriers: Selections from the Museum of Art's Permanent Contemporary Cuban Collection*, curated by Jorge H. Santis. Ft. Lauderdale, Fla.: Museum of Art of Ft. Lauderdale, 1997.

Rodríguez Milanés, Cecilia. "No Accents Allowed." *Women's Review of Books* IX (July 1992): 10-11.

Rodríguez Sardiñas (Rossardi), Orlando. *Los espacios llenos*. Madrid: Editorial Verbum, 1991.

Sandoval, Mercedes Cros. *Mariel and Cuban National Identity.* Miami: Editorial SIBI, 1985.

Souza, Raymond D. "Exile in the Cuban Literary Experience." In *Escritores de la Diáspora Cubana*, edited by Julio A. Martínez, 1–5. Metuchen, N.J.: Scarecrow Press, 1986.

Suárez, Virgil. *Spared Angola: Memories From a Cuban-American Childhood.* Houston: Arte Público Press, 1997.

Torres, María de los Angeles. "From Exiles to Minorities: The Politics of Cuban Americans." In *Latinos and the Political System*, edited by F. Chris García. Notre Dame, Ind.: University of Notre Dame Press, 1988.

Triay, Victor Andres. *Fleeing Castro: Operation Pedro Pan and the Cuban Children's Program.* Gainesville: University Press of Florida, 1998.

Tweed, Thomas A. *Our Lady of the Exile: Diasporic Religion at a Catholic Shrine in Miami.* New York: Oxford University Press, 1997.

Weyr, Thomas. *Hispanic U.S.A.* New York: Harper & Row, 1988.